A HISTORY OF
THE SCOTTISH MINERS

BOTTOM OF PIT SHAFT, 1860

A HISTORY
OF
THE SCOTTISH
MINERS

FROM THE EARLIEST TIMES

R. PAGE ARNOT

GEORGE ALLEN & UNWIN LTD
RUSKIN HOUSE MUSEUM STREET LONDON

First published in 1955

*Printed in Great Britain
in 12 point Baskerville type
by R. & R. Clark, Ltd., Edinburgh*

FOREWORD

I AM truly proud, on behalf of the Executive of the Scottish Area of the National Union of Mineworkers, to commend this book to miners and all other workers.

It is a great history of a great industry and of the men who, through long years of bitter struggle, of hardship and suffering, laid the foundation of the powerful organisation which now embraces in one unified body the miners of Scotland, England and Wales.

Is it any wonder that in the fight for a life far advanced from that of a serf, and through the long period of striving for trade union organisation, it was the miners who first raised as an organised body the demand for the common ownership of their own industry?

What a record of suffering and of heroic struggle against the soulless mine-owners this book puts before you.

From the very lowest depths of living standards we have risen, proud to be able to claim that for the past fifty years we have been in the vanguard of the working-class movement. Never in the history of the Scottish miners has the union been so powerful, efficient or so democratic as it is at the present time. In the days when they were linked in a federation (The Miners' Federation of Great Britain), and even before then, the Scottish miners in time of crisis stood shoulder to shoulder with their brethren in other parts of the British coal-field. Now that we are organised as one body in the National Union of Mineworkers, we in the Scottish Area have been able in these past ten years to play our part within the larger organisation. At the same time there remains a Scottish industry, a series of purely Scottish questions on which the Scottish Executive and the Scottish delegate conference have to decide. With these matters, to which the last portion of the book is devoted, the general reader can become acquainted and so be enabled to form his own opinion of trade union activity.

We have ourselves seen something of the coal-fields not only in Europe but in America, in the Soviet Union, in China and other Asian countries, and we have found that miners throughout the world, though they speak with different tongues and work under very diverse conditions, have a common language based on their experience underground and the hazards of their industry.

I hope that the story of our fight for safety, as well as our efforts for the continuous improvement of the miners' lot, will become known not only to the miners but also to the workers of other industries who have, in many respects, problems similar to our own. Therefore the more we know of each other, the stronger will be the bonds between us until that great day dawns when the dream of our pioneers will be realised.

In conclusion, may I quote our National Bard, Robert Burns, whose vision was of an international character:

> Man to man, the world o'er,
> Shall brithers be for a' that.

Peter Mees

Fife District Secretary,
NATIONAL UNION OF MINEWORKERS.

Dunfermline,
January 1, 1955

PREFACE

Six years ago in a preface to the first volume of the British miners' history I said that each trade union of the coal-fields had its own history. That same year I was asked to write the history of the Scottish miners from the earliest times. I willingly agreed. Some of my earliest memories had been of Fife colliers coming off shift with candles in their caps: and though I was born at the whinstone end of Renfrewshire, there barren of coal measures, I knew in the upper ward of my county there was a coal-field around Paisley: within a few miles of its venerable abbey, pits were still being sunk a hundred years ago with names such as Inkerman attesting their origin during the Crimean war. From boyhood, too, I had known that the early conditions of mining in Scotland were distinctive: for I had often heard my father tell how in his youth he had met an old man who had been 'born a serf' in a Scottish colliery. The task was congenial and it seemed it would not take over long to do it.

But the task proved greater than was expected. The difficulties were first in the poverty of materials in the earlier trade union period, second the multiplicity of materials in the latest period. For the earliest years the difficulty lay partly in the relative backwardness of historical studies in Scotland and the consequent poverty of standard works. Anyone who has to deal with feudal times is thus hampered, though progress has been made in recent years. In the nineteenth century for the most part records of the trade unions are lacking—some lost, some destroyed. To overcome this obstacle took many months of search in the often imperfect files of local newspapers in the hope that mention might be made of the miners and their trade union activities. Only for the last sixty years of the story have I been able to rely on union records. These, handwritten up to 1914 and thereafter printed, made clear the sequence of events so far as they were minuted. But they were bare and meagre up to the beginning of the war. Since then, and especially in the last dozen years, they have been all that could be desired, fully documented, containing debates, decisions and appendices, and supplemented by masses of other printed and duplicated material. The difficulty in these last dozen years has been transformed into the task of selection from so much important material.

It could be argued that to do full justice to the centuries-long story of the Scottish miners more than one volume would be necessary. But it appeared that the needs of the general reader as well of the mineworkers would be best served by presentation of the record in one volume. Accordingly the book has been condensed from the original manuscript, which gave much more detail and was very fully documented, while the last chapters on the more outstanding union actiivties in recent years have been entirely rewritten.

To the very many friends who have given their help I am indeed grateful. Some helped to gather material from dusty files in the British Museum and other libraries. Some copied official publications. Others typed drafts and redrafts of the work in progress. On one fell the arduous labour of cutting down the manuscript to nearly a quarter of the original size. Others gave their advice, criticism and suggestions at each successive stage from manuscript, through typescripts to galley proofs and page proofs. To all of them I give my thanks.

Finally I must thank the Scottish miners themselves: the president, vice-president and general secretary; the members of the Executive Committee; the agents and pit delegates; the staffs of the head office and district offices; the many members of the union I was privileged to meet. It was their courtesy and helpfulness and indeed companionship which made it possible to complete the undertaking. I was given every facility to do the job, at pits and pit meetings, at miners' schools and at rest homes, in tours round coal-fields and detailed discussions at collieries. I was present on occasions both grim and gay. I was invited to the fortnight's enquiry into the Knockshinnoch disaster: I saw the closing celebrations of the miners' school. There at Dunoon men who spend their working day in the pits could look while they listened, look down the Firth of Clyde and see the ships powered by their underground effort steaming toward Ailsa Craig and the ports of all the seven seas.

R. PAGE ARNOT.

45 Fitzroy Road, London, N.W.1,
January 15, 1955

CONTENTS

FOREWORD   *page* v

PREFACE   vii

CHAPTER
I.   BONDSMEN   I
     1. The Coal-Heughs
     2. Slavery by Act of Parliament
     3. The Colliers and their Families
     4. The Emancipation

II: CHILD LABOUR AND CHARTISM   14
     1. Early Combination
     2. The Children's Employment Commission
     3. Women and Children Underground
     4. 'Poortith Cauld'
     5. The Act of 1842
     6. Unions in the 'Forties

III. THE COUNTY UNIONS   38
     1. An Outstanding Leader
     2. The Coal and Iron Miners' Association
     3. The Free Colliers
     4. Fife and Other County Unions
     5. Strife in the Scottish Coal-fields
     6. The Fife and Clackmannan Lock-out of 1877
     7. The Blantyre Calamity
     8. McDonald's Work in Parliament

IV. THE GREAT STRIKE OF 1894   66
     1. Keir Hardie and the Federation of 1887
     2. The Scottish Miners' Federation
     3. Wages
     4. The Strike begins
     5. New Signals from England
     6. The M.F.G.B. meets at Edinburgh
     7. The Strike ends

V.   CONCILIATION ON TRIAL   89
     1. Aftermath of the Great Strike
     2. Lanarkshire organises
     3. The Scots and Socialism
     4. A New Era
     5. A Conciliation Board
     6. The M.F.G.B. are warned
     7. A Crisis builds up
     8. The Miners' Federation intervenes
     9. Winston Churchill intervenes

CHAPTER
VI. THE GREAT STRIKE OF 1912   *page* 112
   1. The Political Background
   2. Abnormal Places
   3. The Scottish Conciliation Board
   4. The Minimum Wage Claims
   5. Government Intervention
   6. The Wheels stop
   7. When Scot meets Scot
   8. Growth of the Scottish Miners' Federation
   9. The Scottish Miners' Houses

VII. WAR AND ITS SEQUEL   139
   1. The War of 1914–18
   2. The Sankey Commission and After
   3. The Year 1920
   4. The Great Lock-out of 1921

VIII. THE LOCK-OUT OF 1926 AND ITS
      AFTERMATH   161
   1. A Troubled Period
   2. The Situation in Scotland
   3. General Strike and Lock-out
   4. Lock-out Scenes in Scotland
   5. In Fife and Lanarkshire
   6. Strife and Schism
   7. Adamson's Breakaway
   8. Rival Unions

IX. THE WORLD ECONOMIC CRISIS   197
   1. The Second Labour Government
   2. The National Government
   3. Effects of the Slump
   4. The Slump and the County Unions
   5. The United Mineworkers of Scotland

X. THE MINERS AGAINST FASCISM
   AND WAR   223
   1. The Coming of Fascism
   2. Help to the Spaniards
   3. Help for the Czechoslovak Miners
   4. An Upward Swing
   5. Reunited

XI. THE WAR YEARS 1939–45   238
   1. Man-power and the War
   2. Valleyfield Disaster
   3. Wages and Working Conditions
   4. Dual Control and Output Problems
   5. Political Standpoint on War Issues
   6. One Union for Scotland

CHAPTER
XII. NATIONALISATION   *page* 267
      1. The Labour Government
      2. The Miners' Charter
      3. The Nationalisation Act
      4. Confiscation or Compensation?
      5. The End of Private Ownership
      6. Control and Democracy
      7. Price Policy
      8. Technical Development
      9. Concentration, De-watering, Distillation
      APPENDIX: *Power-loading Agreement*

XIII. WAGES AND HOURS UNDER STATE
      OWNERSHIP   295
      1. Early Gains
      2. Cold War and Wage-freeze
      3. The Scots fight the Wage-freeze
      4. Sir William Lawther in Scotland
      5. The Wage-freeze and the T.U.C.
      6. The Claim for the Lower-paid Workers
      7. The Extension of Hours continues
      8. Wages and Rearmament
      9. N.C.B. says 'No!'
     10. A New Wages-structure
     11. Compulsory Arbitration
      APPENDIX: *The Wages Advance of January 1954*

XIV. INTERNATIONAL RELATIONS   339
      1. War or Peace?
      2. The War in Korea
      3. Miners in the U.S.A. and in France
      4. Delegations Abroad: Poland, Soviet Union,
           Czechoslovakia, Germany
      5. Peace Delegations
      6. The Chinese People's Republic
      APPENDIX: *Address by William Pearson*

XV.   KNOCKSHINNOCH   369
      1. Earlier Moss Disasters
      2. Knockshinnoch
      3. The Inquiry
      4. Moffat on behalf of the N.U.M.
      5. Sir Andrew Bryan's Report
      6. Justice for the Dependents
      7. The Prosecution and its Sequel
      8. Newcraighall Colliery

XVI. THE UNION TODAY   402
      1. Trade Union Democracy
      2. The Disputes Committee

3. Education
4. Youth
5. Health and Welfare
6. The Union in the Labour Movement and
   in Politics
7. Conclusion

BIBLIOGRAPHY   *page* 428

INDEX OF NAMES   431

GENERAL INDEX   435

ACKNOWLEDGEMENTS

To the trustees and staff of the British Museum for their
courtesy and help in the matter of books and prints (notably
facing pages 60, 61).

To the National Coal Board for their courtesy and help in
supplying illustrations facing pages 26, 27, 120, 121, 136, 137,
176, 177, 208, 224, 401 and frontispiece.

To *Picture Post* library for their courtesy in supplying repro-
ductions of the illustrations facing pages 240, 241, 256, 368,
369, 384.

To Scott Brothers of Edinburgh for permission to use the
illustrations facing pages 352, 353.

ILLUSTRATIONS

Drawn and compiled by Reginald T. F. Turner

Bottom of pit shaft; from *History of the Coalfields*, by W.
Fordyce, 1860   *frontispiece*

facing page

Bearers of coal in Scotland; from *Mines and Miners*, by
L. Simonin, 1869   26

Women coal bearers in Scotland; from *The Mine*, by
I. Taylor   27

The Blantyre Colliery Explosion, 1877. Calling for volunteers for the exploring parties. (Contemporary print)   60

The Blantyre Colliery Explosion, 1877. Scene of the disaster. (Contemporary print)   61

Blantyre No. 2 Pit, Lanarkshire, 1953   80

Newcraighall Colliery, Lothians, 1953   81

Demonstration for 8-hour day   96

Veterans of the Industry. Andrew Connor   97

Scottish Miners' Federation : Graph of Prices and Wages   110

New pit construction, Kirkcaldy, Fife, 1953   120

New pit construction, Kirkcaldy, Fife, 1953   121

Old style miners' houses, Lumphinnans, Fife   136

New housing, Crosshill-Meadows Estate, Argyll   136

Pithead, old style: Barony Colliery, Ayrshire   137

Pithead, new style: Comrie Colliery, Fife   137

Kingshill No. 3 Pit, Lanarkshire, 1953   160

Bothwell Castle Colliery, Lanarkshire, 1953   161

Pithead baths, Michael Colliery, Fife   176

Tillicoultry drift mine, Clackmannan   177

View towards Bowhill Colliery, Fife, 1953   192

Nellie Pit, Lochgelly, Fife, 1953   193

Miner working in a narrow wet seam, Canderigg Colliery, Lanarkshire   208

Miner at work, Priory Pit, Lanarkshire, 1953. Sketched at the coal face   209

Miners at work in a new pit, Comrie, Fife, 1953   224

Miners at work in old-type pit, Priory Pit, Lanarkshire, 1953. Sketched at the coal face   225 *facing page*

Valleyfield Colliery Disaster, Fife, October 1939. Wives
and children waiting for news   240

Valleyfield Colliery Disaster, October 1939. Rescue squad
bringing in one of the victims   241

Valleyfield Colliery Disaster, October 1939. Waiting at
the pithead for news   256

West Fife M.P. with veteran miners, Lumphinnans, 1950   257

First Scottish Mining School at Dunoon in May 1947   272

Andrew McAnulty at the 1947 Gala   273

Scottish Miners' Gala Day, 1950   288

Scottish Miners' Gala Day, 1950   289

Miners' rows, Cowdenbeath, Fife, 1953   304

Old Scottish houses, Shotts, 1953   305

Scottish Miners' Gala Day, 1953. Aneurin Bevan with
miners' leaders at the head of the procession   320

Scottish Miners' Gala Day, 1953. Section of the huge
assembly   321

Veterans of the Industry. William Easton   336

Miners' dwellings, Cowdenbeath, Fife, 1953   337

Scottish Miners' Gala Day, 1953   352

Scottish Miners' Gala Day, 1953   353

Knockshinnoch Castle Colliery Disaster, Ayrshire, September 1950. Two views of the cave-in   368

Knockshinnoch Disaster, September 1950. Rescue squad
with breathing apparatus going into the pit   369

Knockshinnoch Disaster, September 1950. Rescuer overcome in attempt to reach entombed miners   384

Veterans of the Industry. George McTurk   385

Arthur Pit, Fife, 1953   400

Site of a new sinking, Glen Ochil, Clackmannan, 1952   401

Veterans of the Industry. James Cook   416

Devon Pit, from Tillicoultry, Clackmannan, 1953   417

CHAPTER I

BONDSMEN

I. THE COAL-HEUGHS

COAL, the main source of heat and light and power in nearly every country, has been dug in Scotland for years beyond reckoning. Eighteen hundred years ago the Roman army of occupation between Forth and Clyde were using coal. Thereafter for 1000 years, though we may guess its use in the dim but long-lasting kingdom of the Picts, there is no sure evidence. Half-way back in time to the Romans stands the lurid figure of Macbeth, the end of whose reign as King of Scots marks the threshold of feudalism. Not till after the feudalisation of Scotland set in strongly in the twelfth century do we get on durable parchment the record of *carbonaria*, or as they are called in Acts of Parliament, the coal-heughs. Thereafter, working of coal on a considerable scale developed, mining by the monks at Newbattle being the earliest recorded.

By the time of Mary Queen of Scots in the mid-sixteenth century the annual output of coal in Scotland was no less than 40,000 tons, about a fifth of the whole production of the British Isles; and in no country in the world did coal then play as big a part in the national economy as it did in Scotland. Coal, used up to that time mainly for salt-making and lime-burning and only to a less extent for household fuel or export (except in the case of the 'great Coal'), was soon to give an impetus to the growth of glass-blowing, soap-boiling, sugar-refining, tile-making and the manufacture of alum, saltpetre and gunpowder. Small wonder then that James VI, shortly to become also James I of England, as he saw from the Lomonds hard by his palace of Falkland the puffs of smoke rising from the shore of the Forth, described his kingdom as 'a beggar's mantle with a fringe of gold'.

Where were the coal-heughs, this golden fringe soon about to broaden into a source of wealth for the owners but with almost unspeakable exploitation for the toilers? Most of them lay on the shores of that eastern firth in whose praise Robert Fergusson wrote:

> There's nane sae spacious and sae noble
> As Frith o' Forth.

To the west there were few pits as yet, mainly because of carriage. Only vessels of the lightest draught could sail the shallow Clyde at or above Glasgow, then the fairest and greenest little place a bishop could wish for his cathedral town. The Scottish coal-fields in their location present a lesson in geology. All Scotland is divided into three parts, highlands, lowlands and southern uplands. The northern Scottish mountains have among them the most ancient rocks, far older than the coal measures. In early days these mountains and glens maintained a hardy population, more numerous and in their own way more independent within their clan than the hewers of coal. Now the position is reversed. The glens are depopulated but the mining areas have extended; the miners have come into the forefront of the organised workers. The ranges of the southern uplands from the Pentland Hills to the Cheviot are similarly barren of coal. In the relative plain of the lowlands, with the valleys of Forth and Clyde and other streams, lie the main coal measures, though outlying fields were known then and have been opened up since. Within these limits came the rapid growth of the coal industry in the long reign of James VI.

By the decade 1681–90 output had reached 475,000 tons, a fourteenfold expansion in production in a little more than 120 years. Expansion at this great speed brought a whole series of problems to the industry, the main difficulty in the early stages being to keep pace with demand. Because of complaints of a dearth of fuel, Parliament and the Privy Council repeatedly intervened during the sixteenth and seventeenth centuries to prohibit the export of coal though it was never able fully to enforce the ban. It is certain that all markets were expanding rapidly, and that the expanding coal industry, as money was sunk in bigger collieries and deeper pits, had to meet all sorts of problems such as the supply of capital, supply of machinery for pumping and winding, supply of transport.

By the end of the sixteenth century the needs of the coal industry already awakened the interest of minds that were fertile in invention. John Napier of Merchiston, for example, great sixteenth-century mathematician, inventor of logarithms, about 1595 worked out the machinery for pumping water from coal-mines, and had his scheme approved under the great seal of the King of Scots.

But the greatest problem of all was the supply of labour for the pits to meet the sudden enormous expansion of the market.

2. SLAVERY BY ACT OF PARLIAMENT

In the year 1606 the Scottish colliers were made into slaves.[1] The Act of Parliament which accomplished this and thereby solved the man-power problem of the coal-owners was in force for nearly two centuries, from 1606 to 1799, and its victims could still be met in the times of our fathers.

The dissolution of the monasteries and other causes had cast upon the countryside those for whom there was neither work nor keep, a multitude that fell into vagrancy and beggary. Laws, exceedingly harsh, were enacted against these vagrants. The first Scots Poor Law of 1579 ordained that a convicted vagrant might have his sentence of stripes or ear-branding commuted into servitude to an employer, who would publicly undertake to keep him at work for a year, while his children might be seized and kept in bondage till they were eighteen in the case of girls and twenty-four in the case of boys. By an Amending Act of the Scots Parliament in 1597, the children might be kept in life-long bondage—'strang beggaris and their bairnes be employed on common works, and their service mentioned in the Act of Parliament 1579 be prorogat during their lyftime'. These general Acts were

---

[1] Following the older usage, as given in the documents quoted or consulted, I have retained the term 'slave'. But Ashton and Sykes in their *Coal Industry of the Eighteenth Century* (1929) queried whether this term was correctly applied and tentatively suggested instead the use of 'collier-serf'. J. U. Nef, however, in his *Rise of the British Coal Industry* (1932) retains the old term, and indeed in this respect compares the Scottish coal-mines with the cotton plantations of the Southern States of the U.S.A. before the Civil War. This conflict of recent authorities suggests the need for a careful examination of the range of conditions comprised under each of the three historic forms of servitude. When writing *The Miners* (1949) I regarded it as analogous to the 'second serfdom' of Prussia and elsewhere in the seventeenth century.

never fully operated in most industries, largely because enforcement depended on the parish Kirk Sessions which administered the Poor Law. For these bodies, the first expression of popular representation in contrast to Parliament which was in the hands of the nobility, did not take kindly to enforcing such harsh statutes.

In one case, however, the situation was entirely different. In the coal-pits, and the associated salt-pans, the shortage of labour was acute. So the Lords of the Articles, themselves often great coal-owners, found a means to bypass the resistance of the Kirk Sessions in the Act of 1606. This Act had five main provisions. First, no one was to hire any salters, colliers or coal-bearers without the leave of their master, duly written or attested. Second, if any workman, being a salter, collier or coal-bearer, left for other service without such a testimonial or leaving certificate, his first master could, within a year and a day, proceed to reclaim him. Third, the new employer was forced to surrender him, within twenty-four hours, under penalty of a fine of £100 Scots for each time of asking. Fourth, a deserting workman was to be deemed a thief (he had stolen himself away from his master), and as such punished in his body. Fifth, Parliament gave 'power and commission to all masters and owners of coal-heughs and salt-pans to apprehend all vagabonds and sturdy beggars to be put to labour'. Of this new Act the masters of coal and salt took full advantage: and it was strictly enforced by the Privy Council, on which sat some of the more powerful coal-masters.

A new Act of Parliament (November 6, 1641) ratified the Act of 1606, extended its scope, and, since experience had shown that 'the giving of great fees hath been a means and way to seduce and bring coal hewers from their masters', made it unlawful to offer any greater sum than 'twenty marks in fee or bountith'. This Act also deprived the colliers of their customary holidays and ordained that they must work the full six days, week in, week out; on grounds given in the following words:

because the said coal hewers and salters and other workmen in coal-heughs within this kingdom do lie from their work at Pasch [Easter], Yule [Christmas], Whitsunday and certain other times in the year, which times they employ in drinking and debauchery to the great offence of god and prejudice of their master, it is therefore statute and ordained . . .

The Yule holiday, however, continued to be kept because, as is still the case in England, December 25 was the Quarter Day. But another Act in 1647 provided that

The Estates of Parliament considering that the observing of Yule day and other superstitious days is much occasioned by coal hewers and salters flitting and entering at Yule, therefore they ordain that the terms of flitting and entry of all coal hewers and salters shall hereafter be upon the first of December yearly

and added that those who observed Yule or 'any other superstitious days' would come under the penalties contained in 'the acts of parliament made against profanation of the sabbath'. Further, an Act of July 9, 1661, ordained that all the workmen in coal-heughs 'work all the six days of the week except the time of Christmas under the pain of twenty shilling Scot to be paid to their master for ilk days failing' and 'other punishment of their bodies'.

These laws were applied with severity also against any employer who took a runaway into his service. This occurred often in the years of the Civil War in England from 1642 to 1644 when the English Parliament's blockade of the Tyne and Wear ports had caused a sudden urgent demand for Scottish coal. Altogether the Act of 1606 was carried out in letter and spirit. It was devised to prevent a rise in wages when labour was scarce. But the Scots Parliament did more than attempt to check a rise in wages. It succeeded in making the colliers into an enslaved class, degraded below the level of the poorest free men.

3. THE COLLIERS AND THEIR FAMILIES

The condition of slavery in the ancient world was hereditary. Under Roman law the child of an enslaved man was born a slave. The same was true of the slaves of the Southern States of the U.S.A. before Abraham Lincoln in 1863 proclaimed their emancipation. In Scotland the statutory bondage of the colliers was not hereditary in law, but became so in practice. This came about in the following way. A man bound himself, either by taking service for a year and a day, or by taking arles, that is earnest-money—and there are examples of the arles being not in coined money but in kind. If he bound himself to a coal-master by thus taking arles he thereby enslaved himself. The custom grew up amongst the colliers of 'arling' their children to the coal-master, not when they were old enough to creep about in the coal-heugh but at their baptism. This 'arling', which was the sale of the future labour of the child in return for a sum of money and was witnessed by the minister and others present at the baptism, became a formal and regular custom, with a written record of the responsibilities undertaken by the coal-master for his part. Thus the child of the collier was sold into slavery. Lord Henry Cockburn in his often-quoted *Memorials* remarks: 'Wives, daughters and sons went on from generation to generation under the system which was the family doom'.

'Wives and daughters.' These words reveal another feature of Scottish coal-mining which was only found exceptionally elsewhere. The 'wives and daughters' were the coal-bearers who went down to the coal-face, took the coal to the pit-bottom and then in many a case climbed up ladders to the surface: and did this many times a day. If a collier had no wife or daughter to do this work, he had to rely on the service of one who was called a 'fremit' bearer. The coal-bearers, being 'wives and daughters' in the main, were as a rule not paid anything at all: they were just helping the head of the family. But fremit bearers had to be paid something however small. At Kincardine colliery[1] in Fife the bearer's wage in 1679 was only seven to eight shillings Scots, which comes to less than one English shilling a week.

A description of the collier's life was given by one who survived to give evidence before a Royal Commission in 1842:

Was first yoked to the coal work at Preston Grange when I was nine years of age; we were then all slaves to the Preston Grange laird.

Even if we had no work on the colliery in my father's time we could seek none other without a written licence and agreement to return. Even then the laird or the tacksman selected our place of work, and if we did not do his bidding we were placed by the necks in iron collars, called juggs, and fastened to the wall or 'made to go the

[1] Nef, *The Rise of the British Coal Industry*, Vol. II, p. 183.

rown'. The latter I recollect well, the men's hands were tied in face of the horse at the gin, and made run round backwards all day.[1]

The degradation into which seventeenth-century legislation had thrust the colliers was added to by laws in the first half of the eighteenth century. Thus in the Act of 1701 'for preventing wrong imprisonment against delays in Tryals' (usually known as the 'Scotch Habeas Corpus Act') colliers were expressly excluded.

This legal and social degradation was matched by the low esteem in which the colliers came to be held by the rest of the labouring population. The colliers came to be looked upon by the urban population as something almost less than human. They were herded together in miserable hovels in villages that were equally miserable and cheerless. They were almost completely shut off from association with their fellows in other occupations. All sorts of lurid stories were told of these dark and grimy people: and the ordinary respectable tradesman would have been horrified at the idea of social mingling with these harshly exploited toilers. In Fife the dead collier was not allowed to lie in the same burial-ground as the free labourer: no one thought then that this 'despised and rejected' section of the working-class community would one day become the 'corner-stone' of the country's economic prosperity and in the forefront of working-class advance.

Slave labour in the end, however, became uneconomic and defeated its own ends. For with the rapid growth of the demand for coal, especially from the new ironworks of the Industrial Revolution, more labour was needed for the pits. Because of the unwillingness of workers to submit to slavery if there was any other livelihood open to them, they could only be induced to become colliers at all by the payment of wages higher than those elsewhere.[2] Even apart from this, economists like Adam Smith in *The Wealth of Nations* argued that 'the work done by slaves, though it appears to cost only their maintenance, is in the long run the dearest of any', because there was no incentive to work efficiently or regularly.

---

[1] Children's Employment Commission (1842), Mines.
[2] Professor John Millar in *Observations concerning the Distinction of Ranks in Society* (1771), says Scottish colliers earned 12s. to 13s. a day as against 9s. for colliers in Newcastle and 4s. to 6s. for ordinary labourers in the Scottish mining counties, p. 238.

4. THE EMANCIPATION

There was a growing agitation in the eighteenth century for the suppression of the African slave trade. There was also a strong sentiment for the abolition of Negro slavery in the British colonies, evidenced by Dr. Samuel Johnson, Tory as he was, 'when in company with some very grave men at Oxford' giving the toast 'Here's to the next insurrection of the Negroes in the West Indies'. In the case of the Scottish colliers no such humanitarian agitation is recorded.

It seems that any claims[1] put forward for the humanitarian movement must be dismissed: and the credit for abolition of the colliers' bondage must be put to the account of developing economic factors. This is borne out by the circumstances of the parliamentary Bill introduced in March 1774[2] by the Lord Advocate of Scotland, Sir Alexander Gilmour. The Bill was 'prepared at the instigation of the Earl of Abercorn and other coal-masters' who proved more powerful than those proprietors of coal-pits who sent in petitions against it. In the preamble the primary reason that prompted its promoters is plainly given as that

there are not a sufficient number of colliers, coal-bearers, and salters, in Scotland, for working the quantity of coal and salt necessarily wanted; and many new discovered coals remain unwrought; and many are not sufficiently wrought nor are there a sufficient number of salters for the salt works, to the great loss of the owners and disadvantage to the publick.

It is added only as a secondary consideration that its effect would be to 'remove the reproach of allowing such a state of servitude to exist in a free country'. The Bill proposed to liberate all persons working as colliers: but an amendment was carried that 'no person who shall begin to work' in the industry should be bound 'in any way or manner different from what is permitted by the Law of Scotland with regard to Servants and Labourers'. Thus the statute (the Bill re-

[1] Nef, *op. cit.*, Vol. II, p. 164.
[2] The Statutes at Large, Vol. XXXI, cap. xxviii, pp. 50–3.

ceived the Royal Assent on May 5, 1774) set forth that after
July 1, 1775, new entrants would be free, but that colliers
and salters already in the industry would be set free by stages
and would have, as it were, to work their passage to emancipation. Thus those under twenty years of age were to be set free
after seven years' service—i.e. on July 1, 1782; those between
twenty-one and thirty-five after ten years, i.e. on July 1,
1785; those between thirty-five and forty-five after seven
years, provided that they had 'instructed a person as an
apprentice if required so to do by the master or lessee . . . in
the art or mystery of coal-hewing', in default of which condition they must serve three more years. Those over forty-five
were to be freed in three years. Wives and children were to be
freed when the husband and father was freed: while, once
freed, the collier straightway got the benefit of the Habeas
Corpus Act of 1701. If, however, any one of them were found
taking part in a strike to raise wages or leaving the colliery
before their day of liberation, they would have to serve two
additional years as a penalty.[1]

The somewhat grudging release afforded by the Act of 1774
was reported to have caused great joy amongst the colliers,
who always kept July 1 as a holiday to commemorate the
day of this liberation.

Twenty years later, however, it became clear that the Act
of 1774 had been largely ineffective in freeing the old hands
and their families. For one thing, the collier in order to
establish his right of freedom had to sue his master in the
Sheriff Court, a procedure not too easy for the unlettered.
For another, there were the possibilities of postponement under
the statute through incurring penalties or not serving out their
time. But the main reason was that so many of them had
fallen into an oppressive debt slavery, chiefly through the
continuance of the custom of 'arling' their children at baptism

---

[1] IX. Provided always that in case it shall be proved to the satisfaction of the said
Sheriff, that the person so applying by petition has, subsequent to the passing of this act,
been guilty of entering into any unlawful combination with the other colliers or salters to
leave off working, in order to distress or injure the proprietor or lessee of such coal or salt-
work, or in order to compel him to increase the wages or allowances usually paid for the
said work: or that the person so applying shall have wilfully deserted the said works; then,
and in that case, the person guilty of such offences shall not be intitled to the benefit of the
said act until the expiration of two years after the respective periods at which, in terms of
this act, he would have been intitled to his freedom, if he had not been guilty of such
offences. (The Statutes at Large, Anno 1773, Vol. XXXI, pp. 50–3.)

to the coal-master. Instead of being treated as earnest-money, that is, as a gratuity as a token of service, arles came to be treated as a debt, which the collier had to pay before he could get free of his master. The amount of arles was considerable and being often added to by loans to tide over times of distress or sickness, amounted to as much as from £20 to £40 in most cases. No collier could readily pay back such a sum: for there could be no habit of thrift among them. No new master would take them on at the cost of first reimbursing their old master for what was now treated as a debt. The colliers and their families remained bound to their old masters. The emancipation, like Dead Sea fruit, had turned in their mouths to dust and ashes.

The second Act, which put an end to bondage in Scotland, was passed half a dozen years after the French Revolution in the Constitution of 1793 had proclaimed the equality of man, to be followed by its victorious armies liberating the feudal serfs of the Rhineland and Lombardy. It was at a moment too when the slave trade from Africa had come under the attention of Parliament. But there were other motives: it had been found 'impossible to keep the colliers strictly in servitude, and difficult to obtain labour for the pits', and that the colliers 'worked only three or four days in the week instead of six . . . and lastly, that they frequently enlisted in His Majesty's Army and Navy'.[1]

Much can be learned about the conditions of life of the colliers in these last years of their servitude, of the scarcity of their labour despite the relatively high wages, and finally of their secret societies, from two pamphlets[2] published in 1793 in Edinburgh. Both are written from the standpoint of the coal-owners and both exhibit much hostility to the colliers. The first pamphleteer is much concerned with the behaviour and the high wages of the colliers; and he proposes 'bounties' to increase their numbers and 'so to diminish their at present most extravagant wages'.

He is aware of the evils of the 'truck' system, against which

---

[1] R. N. Boyd, *Coal Pits and Pitmen* (1892), p. 10.
[2] The first (indexed in the British Museum catalogue under Archibald Cochrane) is entitled *Description of the Estate and Abbey of Culross. Particularly on the Mineral and Coal Property. Wherein is given an Account of the Coal Workings at Culross Since the Year 1572.*

Acts of Parliament were subsequently passed but which took even then over fifty years to eradicate:

An abolition of the dirty and mean practice of many of the Scots Owners of Collieries acting as Sutlers, and supplying their workmen, frequently at an advanced price with Oatmeal, Salt Herrings, Salt Beef, Cheese, Butter, Candles, Soap and such articles; receiving besides a bonus or gratuity from the Oversman of the Colliery, or some other person, as a share of the profits on retailing Small Beer and Whiskey, the favourite beverage of the lower classes of the people in Scotland. . . .

This pamphleteer of 1793 is bedevilled by fear of Jacobinism. He ends his pamphlet by a passage which displays equally his fears and his prejudices:

There is a great similarity between negroes and colliers, in colour, in manners; and the likeness would be still greater were they emancipated.

The second pamphleteer[1] in his description of the 'colliers in a state of slavery', speaks of them as

Destitute of all principles of religion and morality; perfectly indifferent to the opinion of the world, they had no motives of emulation to incite their industry. Hence they lived in dirty hovels, a few loose boards and straw formed their beds, a pot and pan, with round stones, or timber stools, to sit on, the whole furniture of the house.

He blames these colliers for the custom of bearers which, if not instituted by the employers, had never been discountenanced by them—as is shown by the 'arling'. He says:

The manner of treating their wives and daughters, of making them bearers in the pits, of employing them to carry coal on their backs; of *mixing the sexes in the pits*, did not contribute to cultivate or humanise their manners.

The scarcity of colliers is emphasised and the colliers themselves are blamed for it. But the most interesting passages are those in which he describes the hidden organisation of these statutory slaves (the brotherings) and also the three-day week and their recompense:

They have among them too a practice which makes any reformation of their manners very difficult. They have among them what they call *brotherings*: It is a solemn oath, or engagement, to stand by each

[1] *Considerations on the Present Scarcity and High Price of Coals in Scotland.* Edinburgh, 1793.

other. In the west country, where this practice is universal, they have some *watch-word*, by sending round of which they can lay the whole *of the collieries in the country idle*. . . .

If a collier from England, or from any other place, who is not of the brotherhood, comes among them, he is immediately obliged to enter into the Society, and take this oath, or they will not allow him to work. The case is, that they are generally united, and if the majority in the pit agree to make an *idle* day, *the rest must do the same*. If they offer to work they are severely fined, or obliged to leave the work, by this means a pit seldom works above *three days* in a week.

When in 1799 the Lord Advocate brought in a Bill to amend the Act of 1774, coal-owners petitioned against it, but without success. There were adverse clauses in the Bill which brought a petition from the colliers. The colliers of Lanarkshire resolved on resistance, collected a subscription of 2s. per man from 600 of their number, sent deputations to collieries in other districts of Scotland, and employed Mr. Wilson, of Cowglen, a law-agent in Glasgow, to conduct the opposition to the Bill, with the result that the objectionable clauses were removed.[1]

Under the Act which became law on June 13, 1799,[2] all colliers bound at that date became free. Wages in each county were to be fixed at intervals by justices of the peace. Combinations amongst colliers were to be punished by fines: of debt slavery it was laid down that 'no diligence or action shall be competent for any sum or sums of money hereafter to be lent or advanced to colliers or other persons employed at the collieries'—except advances for support in sickness, when the coal-owners were given the right to withhold part of the wages, not exceeding one-twelfth, to cover such advances.

The miners themselves not only kept the anniversary of their first emancipation as a holiday but also showed that they knew how to use their freedom. 'Many of the colliers', writes Robert Bald in 1808, 'have of late, particularly within these eight years, betaken themselves to the work of common labourers at half their original wages.' They never forgot their bondage.[3] To them there was a special meaning in

---

[1] James Barrowman, 'Slavery in the Coal-Mines of Scotland', *Transactions of the Federated Institution of Mining Engineers*, Vol. XIV, 1897–8, p. 276.
[2] The Statutes at Large, Vol. XLII, Part I, cap. lvi, pp. 247–50.
[3] My father used to tell me how in his youth he had met an old man who had been a bondsman in the Fife coal-field.

Barbour's *Bruce*, as they heard it read in their villages, with its stirring lines:

> Ah, freedom is a noble thing!
> Freedom makes man to have liking!
> Freedom all solace to man gives!
> He lives at ease that freely lives!

Soon, however, the Scottish colliers were to find that 'all solace' was not theirs and that they had changed but the form of their servitude.

CHAPTER II

CHILD LABOUR AND CHARTISM

I. EARLY COMBINATION

THE colliers, emancipated from legal bondage in 1799, found that as free men they were, together with other workers, subject to new oppressive laws. The Combination Acts passed in 1799–1800 forbade the workers to combine together to better their conditions of life. Other laws both before and after restricted the mass of the working people from political activities that were dreaded by the rulers of the country. It was a period of wars, revolution and repression. The American War of Independence had ended in 1783. From about 1784 onwards for some sixty years there was the huge expansion of industry, especially in Britain, that is called the Industrial Revolution. The French Revolution began in 1789; and the French wars lasted for some twenty-three years up to Waterloo in 1815. After Waterloo the repression hardened for several years. After the Reform Act of 1832 the activities of the working class developed in the Chartist movement as well as in Trade Unions and Co-operative Societies. All these changes that transformed the face of Britain make up the first stage of modern European history up to 1848. The rising class of manufacturing capitalists saw no reason for anything but rejoicing in these changes. But there were many who saw the seamy side, and not only amongst the men of action or agitators such as Robert Owen and William Cobbett. Poets raised their voices in protest, often aimed at the ruling dynasty. Robert Burns in 1787 could write:

> The injured Stuart line is gone,
> A race outlandish fills their throne;
> An idiot race, to honour lost;
> Who know them best despise them most.

Another Scot, Lord Byron, was even more biting ('A worse

king never left a realm undone') in his 'Vision of Judgment' (1822). Others, like Shelley, saw that the evil lay deeper than the rapacity of the royal family or the squandering of riches by the fundholders and the households of the nobility: and the poet's call to revolt:

> Rise like lions after slumber
> In unvanquishable number—
> Ye are many, they are few

was soon to be echoed in the early trade unions and in the movement of the Chartists.

Within this period falls the twenty-five years of the Combination Laws which made strikes or trade unions a crime to be met by heavy penalties. Nevertheless there were strikes and even, in 1817, a collier's trade union. We learn about this temporary union of 1817 from evidence given to the Royal Commission on Trade Unions fifty years later. It was said to exist 'all over Lanarkshire and Ayrshire', conducted openly and 'contended with the employers by strikes'. Unions, whether open or secret, were against the law at that time. But according to the witness, the colliers got round the law by the ingenious method (revealed in the report of the Trade Union Commission of 1867–8) of meeting in public and changing their officials at every meeting. They thus evaded the existence of an actual board of office-bearers, which would have brought them 'within the meshes of the law'.

The first union amongst Scottish miners, after the repeal of the Combination Laws in 1824, was founded by operative colliers from twenty-seven pits around Kilmarnock meeting on October 25, 1824. That same year 1400 Ayrshire miners were on strike for over two months. Though this Ayrshire union disappears after the strike, we may be sure from this time onwards, if only from the evidence of other coal-fields, that there were few years without strikes: and that the strike committees often grew into short-lived unions. Throughout the island local unions were spreading in the second quarter of the century and combinations of these were springing up.

The workers at this time struggled against the new Poor Law of 1834 and the other measures to reshape national and local government in a way that would suit the new capitalists and ensure the subjection of the new proletariat. They fought for Factory Acts and inspection of mines, against long hours and child labour, for education and the freedom of the press. This economic and social struggle was the basis of a new political movement, the demand for the People's Charter.

In the same year that the six points of the People's Charter were first worked out (in February 1837) there came a great economic crisis, the burden of which employers tried to lay on the shoulders of the workers. This in turn led to the first wide-spread strike movement of colliers in Scotland. The strikes were organised by local or district unions, where these existed beforehand, and elsewhere strike action led to the formation of unions. Of the former, in the remote south of Lanarkshire, we have an example in the year Victoria became Queen. This is witnessed by a notice posted at a colliery near Douglas Water:

NOTICE

To Labourers

WHEREAS the Factor on Lord Douglas' Estate, the Factor on Carmichael Estate, and the Tacksman, Robert Swan, as well as the public at large, have suffered much loss and inconvenience by the Colliers at Ponfeigh and Rigside running to such an extreme with their union, as to allow no person unconnected with it to go into the Pits to work the Coal, and also threatening them.

Notice is hereby given,

That they are now determined to put a complete stop to it, and in order to effect this, from 50 to 60 Weavers or Labourers are immediately wanted, to whom Mr. Swan will pay ten or twelve shillings a week, till they learn to work the Coal and can earn more. On Thursday and Friday last 2 Labourers went into the Pit, and in eight hours put out 3s. 4d. worth each. A man with a boy of 16 years of age went in at the same time, and put out 6s. worth. Those having families will get free houses, which will all be cleared of the old Hands by Wednesday the 19th, or Thursday 20th instant at farthest.

Those wishing for work to apply as early as possible to Robert Swan, Coalmaster, Rigside.

Colliershall, 15th April, 1837.

The ruthless wording of this notice shows how determined the masters were to root out trade unionism. But the main cause of disputes in Lanarkshire was the question of the 'darg' or amount of output that could be reasonably expected from a day's work in return for the wages paid. It had long been the custom amongst the colliers to meet a reduction of wages or other worsening of conditions by a reduction of output, called the 'wee darg'. The 'wee darg' recurred for another generation after 1837 and, though in an altered form, could be found till nearly the present day whenever conditions called it forth. The 'wee darg' was a normal 'instinctive' reaction to any unfair bargain, especially when trade unions were repressed or not recognised, so that collective bargaining could not take place. This was the case in the winter of 1836–7 when the darg had been reduced.

In the spring of 1837 the coal-masters resolved to put an end to restriction. The colliers resisted. The strikes in some parts lasted as long as four months. But the coal-masters were ruthless. They seized the opportunity of the economic crisis which had thrown thousands of handloom weavers and others out of work to bring in as blacklegs the workless weavers and starving peasants from Ireland who had recently got work as labourers in the pits. We learn from a hostile source seven years later an admission of how in Lanarkshire a strike was provoked:

In 1837 we insisted on the men breaking through the rule by which they restricted their labour. They stood out against it for four months when they gave in. (Mr. Charles Baird, one of the managers at Shotts Works, Lanarkshire.)

Another spokesman of the Bairds of Gartsherrie told Commissioner Tremenheere:[1]

At that strike 200 of our men turned out. We brought in Irish labourers who had been working in the pits as roadsmen. In three weeks we had the output of coal increased. We were obliged to protect them day and night. The other men were very savage and in one instance, not at our works, threw a policeman down a pit, and cut the pit ropes.

How was it that the colliers could come out on strike and remain out, without strike funds, for several weeks, let alone

[1] *Report of the Commissioner appointed under the Provisions of the Act 5 & 6 Vict. C. 99.* London, 1844.

for several months, at a time of economic crisis? Apart from the spirit of stubborn struggle that will glow in men who believe that they have been wronged, the answer is partly to be found in the use made of the friendly benefit societies which were found amongst the colliers as well as other trades.

Though the Scottish strikes of 1837 were defeated, the spirit of the colliers was not cowed. Together with other workers they took part in the next three years in the Chartist agitation. In Glasgow, then a considerable coal-field, the national campaign for the Charter opened on May 21, 1839, with a demonstration attended by over 200,000 who, stepping out quickly marching six abreast, took about 100 minutes to pass a given point. The great petition for the Charter was rejected by Parliament that summer while the Government endeavoured to crush the movement by wholesale arrests of scores of Chartist leaders. This drove the movement underground: the workers everywhere were filled with resentment; and at Newport in Monmouth on November 3, 1839, there was an armed rising. Those who took part in it were mainly miners. Thereafter the repression became harder and the arrests multiplied till over 500 of the best Chartists, mainly miners and metal-workers, spinners and weavers, were held in gaol. It was in the tense atmosphere created by these events that Parliament met in the year 1840.

2. THE CHILDREN'S EMPLOYMENT COMMISSION

Much of our knowledge of conditions in the coal-mines at this period comes from the reports of the Children's Employment Commission, appointed by Parliament on the motion of Lord Shaftesbury in 1840. This Commission's terms of reference were to enquire into 'the employment of the children of the poorer classes in mines and collieries, and in the various branches of trade and manufacture in which numbers of children work together'. It came into existence partly because the Tory landlords and aristocrats, hostile to the new rising capitalist class which had taken the control of Parliament out of their hands after the Reform Act of 1832, were glad to put a sprag in their wheels; in this way Shaftesbury, himself a Tory landowner, became the leader of the philanthropic campaign of the aristocracy for the ten-hour day against the Whigs and their allies, the manufacturers. There was, however, another important factor. Ten days before the Commission was appointed Parliament had learned of the formation in Manchester of the National Charter Association, an independent working-class political party, the first of its kind in any country.

The officers of this Commission were instructed to enquire into the ages and number of children employed in mines, the hours of work, meals, nature of employment, working conditions, accidents, holidays, hiring and wages; they were also to examine their physical and moral condition, including any provision made for schooling and religious instruction. Evidence was taken from the employers, the children themselves, parents and adult workers, as well as from doctors, teachers, clergymen and others in the districts concerned. It was only by this means that facts were brought to light which could never have been discovered by the examination of the coal-owners alone. As the Commissioners themselves report: 'It is in general with extreme reluctance that this class of witnesses acknowledge that Children begin to work in the pits even as early as seven years of age'.[1] On the hours of work, too, coal-owners often enough stated them to be much less than the Commissioners finally accepted as correct. For example, many of the coal-owners in one coal-field represented the regular hours of work in pits to be only from six to seven per day; 'but', says the Report, 'no manager, agent or underground steward assigns less than 10, and most of them say it is 11 and upwards, with which latter statement that of the colliers agrees'.[2] The children, however, worked longer than this. 'The Children themselves state that they work 12 hours, and according to the representation of several of them they are often in the pit 13 hours.'

The four fact-finding Commissioners set out their summarised conclusions in studiously restrained phrasing, which today, nevertheless, conveys a sense of horror at the condi-

[1] Children's Employment Commission, Vol. I, p. 13.
[2] C.E.C., Vol. I, p. 108, par. 413.

tions they described. Here are half a dozen of the thirty or so paragraphs of their conclusions.

1. That instances occur in which Children are taken into these mines to work as early as four years of age, sometimes at five, and between five and six, not unfrequently between six and seven, and often from seven to eight, while from eight to nine is the ordinary age at which employment in these mines commences.

10. That at different ages, from six years old and upwards, the hard work of pushing and dragging the carriages of coal from the workings to the main ways, or to the foot of the shaft, begins; a labour which all classes of witnesses concur in stating requires the unremitting exertion of all the physical power which the young workers possess.

11. That, in the districts in which females are taken down into the coal mines, both sexes are employed together in precisely the same kind of labour, and work for the same number of hours; that the girls and boys, and the young men and young women, and even married women and women with child, commonly work almost naked, and the men, in many mines, quite naked; and that all classes of witnesses bear testimony to the demoralising influence of the employment of females underground.

19. That in all the coal-fields accidents of a fearful nature are extremely frequent; and that the returns made to our own queries, as well as the registry tables, prove that of the workpeople who perish by such accidents, the proportion of Children and Young Persons sometimes equals and rarely falls much below that of adults.

26. That . . . this employment, as at present carried on in all the districts, deteriorates the physical constitution; in the thin-seam mines, more especially, the limbs become crippled and the body distorted; and in general the muscular powers give way, and the workpeople are incapable of following their occupation, at an earlier period of life than is common in other branches of industry.

27. That by the same causes the seeds of painful and mortal diseases are very often sown in childhood and youth; these, slowly but steadily developing themselves, assume a formidable character between the ages of thirty and forty; and each generation of this class of the population is commonly extinct soon after fifty.

The evidence for these findings was collected by Sub-Commissioners; Thomas Tancred for the West of Scotland and R. H. Franks for the East. As for the West, the report shows that in general the employment of women and children underground was not a marked feature there, bad though conditions of the miners otherwise were. Indeed, he tells that it has been 'one of the rules of the colliers' union that no females should be allowed underground', and adds that 'the temptation to employ them arises from their wages being lower than that of males. Nowhere in the West of Scotland, however, do they bear out coals on their backs, as I understand is the case in Fifeshire and the Lothians.'[1] This passage is one of the few references to trade unions. But a document enclosed with his report shows in its opening clauses what were the harsh conditions imposed on colliers in an effort to stamp out the unions:

REGULATIONS to be observed at AYR COLLIERY, and to which every man or boy employed at it, shall be understood to be bound, whether he has signed them or not. (August 3, 1837.)

1. Every one hereby declares that he never belonged to, or that he has now renounced being a member of, any union or association of working men, and he binds and obliges himself never hereafter to be a member of any such.

2. That if, in violation of the above rule, any one should be found to belong, at any time, to any such union or association, he shall not only instantly be compelled to renounce it but shall also forfeit one month's wages, and be liable to pay the proprietor £5 sterling.

3. That there shall be no meetings of colliers or oncost (men) held above or below ground. If there be any grievance to complain of, each collier or oncostman is to complain to the manager for himself alone.

Altogether, the evidence collected by Sub-Commissioner Thomas Tancred shows how strong in 1837 had been 'the combination', as the union in each district was called, and what a rueful memory of it remained in the minds of those who had for the time being broken it up. Though the combination had been defeated, the colliers were by no means reconciled to their lot. On the contrary they were now more and more adhering to the revolutionary outlook of Chartism: witness the iron-works clerk who told Tancred that

The School fees about here are 3d. a week reading, 4d. a week writing and arithmetic. There is no reading-room, mechanics' institute, musical band or any other public amusement amongst the colliers, but they join in clubs of 12 or so, and take in papers, chiefly Feargus O'Connor's *Northern Star* and the *Glasgow Patriot*, also a few of the other papers not of Chartist opinion; but the one-half are not given to read anything.

[1] C.E.C., Appendix I, p. 324.

The engineers and mechanics were also mostly Chartists. The strength of the combination, the form of its district organisation and the method used to keep the pits from being swamped by cheap labour comes out clearly from the following description:

Four years ago the combination was in force, and then any man not a regular bred collier by birth had to pay £4 and even regular bred colliers at successive stages, as they become half men, etc., had to pay 5s. for each step. No man could make a bargain about work with his master unless by leave of the 'house', i.e. the committee who met for a certain district. At the time of the association all the women were put out both of the coal and iron-stone pits, but now they are coming in again.

The Sub-Commissioner for the enquiry in the East of Scotland, Robert Hugh Franks, was a social investigator of high calibre. While Tancred records fully enough some fifty interviews, only some of which are with colliers and their children, Franks recorded no less than 429 interviews, the vast majority of which were with the children themselves. In investigations, covering over 100 collieries in the three Lothians, Stirlingshire, Fife, Clackmannan, he showed that roughly a quarter of the workers employed (2256 out of 9090) were children under thirteen years of age. The further east the coal-field, the higher the proportion of child labour becomes.

3. WOMEN AND CHILDREN UNDERGROUND

Under the heading Nature of Employment R. H. Franks began with the *coal-bearers*, 'women and children employed to carry coal on their backs in unrailed roads with burdens varying from ¾ cwt. to 3 cwt.' This degrading labour, called by him 'barbarous and cruel', was only to be found in the Lothians, 'the remnant of the slavery of a degraded age'. He was determined to show beyond any possible cavilling the horrible nature of this employment: and for this purpose he gave extracts from the evidence of the coal-bearers themselves.

Janet Cumming (No. 1), 11 years old, bears coals:

I gang with the women at five and come up at five at night; work *all night* on Fridays, and come away at twelve in the day. I carry the large bits of coal from the wall-face to the pit-bottom, and the small pieces called chows in a creel. The weight is usually a hundred-weight; do not know how many pounds there are in a hundred-weight, but it is some weight to carry; it takes three journeys to fill a tub of 4 cwt. The distance varies, as the work is not always on the same wall; sometimes 150 fathoms, whiles 250 fathoms. The roof is very low; I have to bend my back and legs, and the water comes frequently up to the calves of my legs. Have no liking for the work; father makes me like it. Never got hurt but often obliged to scramble out of the pit when bad air was in.

Agnes Moffat (No. 23), 17 years of age:

Began working at 10 years of age. Work 12 and 14 hours daily. Can earn 12s. in a fortnight, if work be not stopped by bad air or otherwise. Father took sister and I down; he gets our wages. I fill five baskets; the weight is more than 22 cwt.; it takes me five journeys. The work is o'er sair for females. Had my shoulder knocked out a short time ago, and laid idle some time. *It is no uncommon thing for women to lose their burthen (load) and drop off the ladder down the dyke below.* Margaret M'Neil did a few weeks since, and injured both legs. When the tugs which pass over the forehead break, which they frequently do, it is very dangerous to be under a load. The lassies hate the work altogether, but they canna run away from it.

From this and the other child witnesses we can gather the nature of the interview as conducted by the Sub-Commissioner. He apparently asked first their age, the length of their working day, the nature of their work, the weight of coal that they bore on their backs, the distance and height they had to travel, how and when they were fed, whether or not they liked the work and, sometimes, what wage they got. Then he asked about their schooling, if any, and finally tested them for scriptural and general knowledge. 'To learn the Questions' means to learn the Presbyterian *Shorter Catechism*.

In Sir John Hope's great pit at New Craighall, then employing nearly 500, the Sub-Commissioner interviewed no child bearers; but it was here that he found old colliers who could recall the days when they were slaves.

In the parish of Lasswade Sir George Clerk, Bart., M.P., of Penicuik owned the colliery of Loanhead, where there were only twenty-seven adult males out of a total of ninety-three employed. Here the Sub-Commissioner interviewed several coal-bearers of different ages. The name of one child interviewed at the Loanhead Colliery was misheard by the Sub-Commissioner as Ellison; but it must obviously have been the familiar Scots first name of Alison. She had gone down the pit at the age of eight.

Ellison Jack (No. 55), 11 years old, coal-bearer:

I have been working below three years on my father's account; he takes me down at two in the morning, and I come up at one and two next afternoon. I go to bed at six at night to be ready for work next morning: the part of the pit I bear in the seams are much on the edge.

I have to bear my burthen up four traps, or ladders, before I get to the main road which leads to the pit bottom. My task is four to five tubs: each tub holds 4¼ cwt. I fill five tubs in 20 journeys.

I have had the strap when I did not do my bidding. Am very glad when my task is wrought, as it sore fatigues.

I can read, and was learning the writing; can do a little; not been at school for two years; go to kirk occasionally, over to Lasswade; don't know much about the Bible, so long since read; knows many of the Questions.

On Alison Jack's evidence Sub-Commissioner Franks made the following explanation and comment:

A brief description of this child's place of work will better illustrate her evidence. She has first to descend a nine-ladder pit to the first rest, even to which a shaft is sunk, to draw up the baskets or tubs of coals filled by the bearers: she then takes her creel (a basket formed to the back, not unlike a cockle-shell, flattened towards the neck, so as to allow lumps of coal to rest on the back of the neck and shoulders), and pursues her journey to the wall-face, or as it is called here, the room of work. She then lays down her basket, into which the coal is rolled, and it is frequently more than one man can do to lift the burden on her back. The tugs or straps are placed over the forehead, and the body bent in a semicircular form, in order to stiffen the arch. Large lumps of coal are then placed on the neck, and she then commences her journey with her burden to the pit bottom, first hanging her lamp to the cloth crossing her head. In this girl's case she has first to travel about 14 fathoms (84 feet) from wall-face to the first ladder, which is 18 feet high: leaving the first ladder she proceeds along the main road, probably 3 feet 6 inches to 4 feet 6 inches high, to the second ladder, 18 feet high, so on to the third and fourth ladders, till she reaches the pit-bottom, where she casts her load, varying from 1 cwt. to 1½ cwt. [into the tub. This one journey is designated a rake; the height ascended, and the distance along the roads added together, exceed the height of St. Paul's Cathedral; and it not infrequently happens that the tugs break, and the load falls upon those females who are following. However incredible it may appear, yet I have taken the evidence of fathers who have ruptured themselves from straining to lift coal on their children's backs.

In the same parish of Lasswade at the Dryden Colliery the Sub-Commissioner interviewed two children of the Kerr family, the ten of whom dwelt in a single room, five of them huddled in one bed. The first, a twelve-year-old, was a fremit bearer on days when her father was not working. The Sub-Commissioner remarks on her evidence: 'No scriptural knowledge; very acute beautiful child; did not appear above 10 years of age'.

Jane Kerr (No. 64), 12 years old, coal-bearer:

I get up at three in the morning, and gang to the work at four, return at four and five at night. It takes us muckle time to come the road, and put on our clothes. I work every day, for when father does not work, the master pays me 6d. a day for bearing wood for him.

I never get porridge before my return home, but I bring a bit of oat-cake, and get water when thirsty. Sister and I can fill one tub of 4¼ cwt. in two journeys. Sister is 14 years of age. My sister and brothers do not read, but I did once go to school to learn reading when at Sir John's work; have forgotten all the letters.

The Ladder Pit in which I work is gai drippie, and the air is a kind of bad, as the lamps do na burn sa bright as in guid air. My father straps me when I do not do his bidding. The work is very sair and fatiguing. I would like to go to school, but canna wone (go) owing to sair fatigue.

In Dryden Colliery the Sub-Commissioner met one of the few boy coal-bearers.

Alexander Kenny (No. 67), 10 years old, coal-bearer:

Worked below eight months; likes it fine; am thinking nobody told me to say so. It is better than going to school, as I do not get the licks that teacher gave me at Craighall, where we came from.

Was at school four years, and could read the Testament; nearly forgot it now. Master used to teach us the Questions. Knows God and that if we are wicked we shall be burnt up to char. There are two bawbees in a penny, and four in two pennies. Father gives me a bawbee on pay-day; I buy sweeties with it. I don't know what countryman my father is, but he is a collier.

In the parish of West Linton, Peeblesshire, just across the shire boundary from the Midlothian coal-field, the Sub-Commissioner found Harlaw Muir and Coaly Burn, two bearing pits of which the Rev. J. J. Beresford was leaseholder and heritor. In these, where out of fifty employed there were less than a third adult males, and no less than twelve females under thirteen years of age, the first witness, a sixteen-year-old girl, had to travel 200 yards underground and up a fifty-foot turnpike stair under a load of 2 cwt.: and, on occasion, had to do this thirty times a day. Franks remarks that she knew 'a few questions in the Child's Catechism, but very destitute of any useful information', which is not altogether surprising after some years of fourteen hours a day at this occupation.

Margaret Watson (No. 115), 16 years of age, coal-bearer:

I was first taken below to carry coals when I was six years old, and have never been away from the work, except a few evenings in the summer months, when some of us go to Carlops, two miles over the moor, to learn the reading: reads a little.

I never was taught to sew, much more shape a dress, yet I stitch up my pit clothes.

We often have bad air below; had some a short time since, and lost brother by it; he sunk down, and I tried to draw him out, but the air stopped my breath, and I was forced to gang.

The second witness was the youngest coal-bearer that Franks interviewed. He described her as 'A most interesting child, and perfectly beautiful' and added: 'I ascertained her age to be six years, 24th May, 1840; she was registered at Inveresk'.

Margaret Leveston (No. 116), 6 years old, coal-bearer:

Been down at coal-carrying six weeks; makes 10 to 14 rakes a day; carries full 56 lbs. of coal in a wooden backit. The work is na guid; it is so very sair. I work with sister Jesse and mother; dinna ken the time we gang; it is gai dark. Get plenty of broth and porridge, and run home and get bannock, as we live just by the pit. Never been to school; it is so far away.

When the Sub-Commissioner went to the East Lothian collieries, he found them to be much the same. Typical was this woman from Penston Colliery in the parish of Gladsmuir:

BEARERS OF COAL IN SCOTLAND

WOMEN COAL BEARERS, SCOTLAND

Isabel Hogg (No. 131), 53 years of age, was a coal-bearer:

Been married 37 years; it was the practice to marry early, when the coals were all carried on women's backs, men needed us; from the great sore labour false births are frequent and very dangerous.

I have four daughters married, and all work below till they bear their bairns—one is very badly now from working while pregnant, which brought on a miscarriage from which she is not expected to recover.

Collier-people suffer much more than others—my guid man died nine years since with bad breath; he lingered some years, and was entirely off work 11 years before he died.

You must just tell the Queen Victoria that we are guid loyal subjects; women-people here don't mind work, but they object to horse-work; and that she would have the blessings of all the Scotch coal-women if she would get them out of the pits, and send them to other labour.

On this witness, the only adult here quoted, Franks makes the following comment: 'Mrs. Hogg is one of the most respectable coal-wives in Penston, her rooms are all well furnished, and the house the cleanest I have seen in East Lothian'.

The Sub-Commissioner, in leaving the work of the BEARERS, says that

to this labour, which is at once so repulsive and severe, the girls are invariably set at an earlier age than boys are to their peculiar labour, from a notion very generally entertained amongst the parents themselves, that girls are more acute and capable of making themselves useful at an earlier age than boys.

The labour in which children and young persons were employed, 'next in severity to the sore slavery of coal-bearing', was coal-putting, in which the sexes were more equally distributed. PUTTERS dragged or pushed the carts containing coal, from the coal-wall to the pit-bottom, the weight varying from 3 to 10 cwt. The boxes or carriages in use were of two sorts, the hutchie and the slype. The hutchie was an oblong square-sided box with four wheels, usually run on a rail. The slype was described in evidence as a wood-framed box, curved and shod with iron at the bottom, holding from $2\frac{1}{4}$ to 5 cwt. of coal, and adapted to the seams through which it was dragged:

The lad or lass is harnessed over the shoulders and back with a strong leathern girth, which behind is furnished with an iron hook, attaching itself to a chain fastened to the coal-cart or slype, which is thus dragged along. The dresses of these girls are made of coarse hempen stuff (sacking) fitting close to the figure; the coverings to their heads are of the same material; little or no flannel is used, and their clothing, being of an absorbent nature, frequently gets completely saturated shortly after descending the pit, especially where the roofs are soft.

Where the seams were narrow and the roofs low, the lads and lasses dragged on all-fours, as one boy (witness) said in the evidence, 'like horses'. These slypes were used in those parts of mines where rails were not laid (the dip and rise preventing) or where the floors were soft from wall-faces to main roads. 'It is extremely difficult', says Franks, 'to give a sufficiently clear illustration of this miserable occupation.'

The coal-hewing itself was considered man's work. But 'man' in these pits included young male children from ten years and upwards; as witness this twelve-year-old coal-hewer with his working day of fifteen to sixteen hours:

Alexander Reid (No. 7), aged 12:

I have worked two years at Sheriff-hall, and go below at two or three in the morning, and hew till six at night; after that I fill and put the carts on the rails to pit-bottom. . . . The pit I work in is very wet; we often work in slush over our shoe-tops. When first below I used to fall asleep; am kept awake now. *It is most terrible work;* I am wrought in a 30-inch seam, and am obliged *to twist myself* up to work on my side; this is my every-day work except Friday, when I go down at 12 at night, and come up at 12 at noon, etc.

When R. H. Franks paid a visit to East and West Bryants Collieries, parish of Newbattle ('the Most Noble the Marquis of Lothian, heritor'), he interviewed the teacher at the village of East Houses, and the manager who said:

I see that no particular advantage would arise from excluding women from the pits, as they are used to the work, and fit for nothing else, and it might increase the price of coal 2d. to 2½d. per ton.

But even where coal-bearing had been abolished, the children underground did not find their lot cast in pleasant places. Here, from the village of East Houses, is the life of a trapper:

Thomas Duncan, 11 years of age:

I open the air-doors for the putters; do so from six in the morning till six at night. Mother calls me up at five in the morning and gives me a piece of cake, which is all I get till I return; sometimes I eat it as I gang. There is plenty of water in the pit; the part I am in it comes up to my knees. I did go to school before I was taken down, and could read then; Mother has always worked below; but Father has run away these five years.

Knows that twice 6 makes 12, and that 4 times 7 makes 20. Did read the Testament, in which Matthew says Christ was crucified; does not know what crucified means. Knows that he shall die, because many people do so in the East Houses. I get 3s. a-week, and take it home to Mother; sometimes she licks me and sometimes she gives me a baw-bee, which I spend in scones or sweeties.

East Houses is in the parish of Newbattle whose monks six hundred years before had little notion of what they were setting afoot when they got a charter for their 'coal-heughs'.

4. 'POORTITH CAULD'

The instructions of the four Commissioners were limited to children and young persons. Franks delved deeper than this, enquired into the wages and conditions of the mining community as a whole, and got facts and opinions both from employers and employees.

In Stirlingshire, Franks had noted colliers complaining of a great fall in real wages: that is, their daily earnings were less than they had been a few years before, while prices, so the older people told him, had risen since the beginning of the century. At the Carron Collieries, James Waugh, a coal-hewer aged 60, said: 'When I first wrought as a full man I could earn 3s. a day, no one can do much more now, and then my 3s. would get me flesh at half the price, and oat-meal at two-thirds its present price'. At the Still Colliery of Haggs in the parish of Denny 'Mr. Matthew Hay, Tacksman' said that he employed fifty men and boys, no women ('coal work is not fit for them'), and added:

The colliers are not so well off as they were formerly: they now take away 3s. 9d., before 5s. Having been a practical collier myself for 25 years before I took the lease of the Still Colliery, I feel much assured that the neglect of education, and the destitution, arise from the state of the markets; many who used to clothe their children well have not clothes for them even to go to Kirk in. Other tradesmen have not to contend with the difficulties colliers have. Bad air, machinery out of order, want of demand at certain seasons, and many other causes, render the demand for labour uncertain.[1]

Franks himself took pains to gather evidence on this. His investigation showed that average weekly earnings had fallen from 20s. in 1812 and 25s. in 1822 to 16s. by 1841, and meanwhile the prices of such staple foods as wheat and oatmeal were actually rising.

Under the heading 'Moral Conditions' Franks reported on day-schools and Sunday-schools, teachers (not salaried but paid by fees, '3d. weekly' on the average), the 'crying sin of intoxication', the progress of temperance principles and provisions for the poor. On this last subject he enquired into

the means by which the collier population is supported in cases of destitution, arising either from sickness, want of employment, or old age; and in so doing we may distinguish between—1st, the assistance which is derived from the parish;[2] 2nd, that to which colliers are entitled from the self-constituted benefit and other societies which are frequent in that community; and, 3rd, the customary charity of coal-proprietors and wealthy families in their particular district.

The first fell far below provisions of the Poor Law in England against which Chartists campaigned because of its harshness. In Scotland the 'means test' of those days was such that, says Franks, 'the parish withholds relief in almost all cases where the applicants have even one child at work in the pit'. And he goes on to say:

Few colliers are any burthen on the parish, for whilst they have any children at work they are supported by them; nor indeed are they generally a burthen to any one for very long, for death amongst colliers is not generally the close of a lingering existence, but a break-up of physical strength and constitution, and we have shown that nearly one-third of the population is afflicted with disease. That a greater portion of the support of enfeebled and aged parents is derived from the labour of the children will be found continually evidenced by the witnesses.

[1] C.E.C., App. I, p. 481, No. 240; pp. 485–6, No. 270.
[2] These include—(1) Collections at the church doors; (2) Other voluntary contributions; (3) Sessional funds; (4) Assessments.

Of one coal-field parish, where thirty-five families were destitute, the Sub-Commissioner quotes the statement of Dr. S. S. Alison, laid before the Poor Law Commissioners: 'I do not think more than 5s. per week of parish-money is spent on all these 35 families'—185 individuals. The Sub-Commissioner was frankly astonished at the defect in the Scots Poor Law, which had no legal provision for those who were destitute through want of work, and says of it that

its obvious tendency, as at present administered, is to force youthful labour into the pits at an early age, in order to raise support for indigent parents who receive either inefficient relief or no relief at all.

The unemployed or sick collier had to look to his own Benefit and Friendly Societies. These ordinarily had funds for sickness,[1] superannuation and 'Life Assurance', i.e. funeral benefit to support 'the needy as well as the unfortunate collier'.

Lastly the Sub-Commissioner 'adverts' to 'the private charity of the proprietors of collieries, and of other wealthy families in the district'. He handles this subject delicately, saying: 'the very nature of the subject prevents the possibility of our attaining any accurate estimate'.[2]

For all his dismay at the meagre provisions of the Poor Law, Franks was not one to have any sympathy with the advanced movement of that period. On the contrary he speaks of 'the mischievous purposes of the Unions', and is relieved to think that they have not been able to extend their operations 'to any great extent in the Lothians nor the East of Fife'.

It was clear to the Commissioners that conditions in Scotland and in particular the East of Scotland were on the whole considerably worse than in the English coal-fields. What they found in Scotland was a mining community of a peculiar kind. For at that time the colliers and their families still bore the birthmarks of that condition of legal bondage from which they had so recently emerged.

[1] 97. Upon the regular contribution of small payments, and compliance with the rules of these societies, the members ordinarily derive the following benefits,—viz. for sick aliment, for the first 13 weeks, 5s. per week; for the second 13 weeks, 3s. per week; for the third 13 weeks, 2s. 6d. per week; superannuated members, 1s. 6d. per week; these, of course, vary according to the funds and payments of the different societies. (C.E.C., App. I.)

[2] C.E.C., App. I, pp. 402–4.

5. THE ACT OF 1842

The Royal Commissioners signed their report in April 1842. So great was the interest and horror aroused by its disclosure of conditions underground that by the first week of June Lord Shaftesbury was able to bring in a Bill in Parliament with good hope of success. The main provisions of the Bill were to exclude women from work underground, and children under thirteen from work in the pits; to prevent anyone under the age of twenty-one from being in charge of a winding engine; and to appoint inspectors of the collieries above ground. 'As for subterranean inspectors, it is altogether impossible,' said Shaftesbury, 'and, indeed, if it were possible it would not be safe.'

The Bill was favourably received on its first reading and when the Committee stage began on June 22, its sponsor was able to present petitions from colliers thanking the House of Commons. But now the coal-owners, who had sung dumb at the introduction of the Bill, organised an opposition. This opposition was not successful in the Commons Committee (though Shaftesbury as a result of deputations from mining districts there accepted an amendment limiting the age for the descent of boys into the pit to ten instead of thirteen); but it held up the third reading for a week until Lord Palmerston, as Prime Minister, wound up the debate by announcing the Government's full support. When the Bill reached the House of Lords the opposition to it had become formidable. Here the Marquis of Londonderry, whose family's fortunes were built on the exploitation of the colliers, was 'the strongest and the fiercest spirit'. He roundly attacked the Commission as guilty of gross exaggeration and a few days later he was announcing in the House of Lords that if this measure ('in its present form it would entirely prevent the working of many of the most important coal mines in the country') were to come before their Lordships, he would fight it clause by clause.[1] On second reading in the House of Lords (July 14,

---

[1] To this there was one exception. His Lordship had no females working in his pits: and he did not propose to contest everything in the clause which would deprive his commercial rivals of the services of women underground. (See Boyd, *op. cit.*, pp. 68, 74.)

1842) the Marquis of Londonderry interrupted the mover with the remark that 'some seams of coal required the employment of women': and then moved the total rejection of the Bill. Right up to the third reading Londonderry continued his furious opposition.

The Bill, much weakened in its two months' passage through Parliament, became law on August 10, 1842. It provided that no women or girls, or boys under ten, were to be employed underground: that wages were not to be paid at or near a public-house; and that proper persons be appointed by the Home Secretary to visit and inspect mines and collieries. The penalty for breach of these provisions was derisory, being a fine of not less than £5 or more than £10 for each offence. In this diluted form the measure was received with indifference by the colliers, who had now under the guidance of the Chartists begun to believe that their own activities would do more than the parliamentary efforts of philanthropic aristocrats. As a consequence there began throughout the country a great movement of the colliers to which we must now turn.

6. UNIONS IN THE 'FORTIES

The forties of the last century were marked by economic crises and by famines, of which those in Ireland were the most conspicuous examples. Under these conditions there was a continuing response to the agitation for a People's Charter with its six points of democratic parliamentary reform: (1) Universal manhood suffrage; (2) Annual Parliaments; (3) Ballot vote; (4) The payment of Members; (5) Abolition of property qualifications; (6) Equal electoral districts. Despite the many prosecutions for seditious libel launched against the Chartists, their influence and organisation continued to spread. Chartism undoubtedly played a big part in stimulating the formation of trade unions: and its national character helped in arousing the desire that the miners should be mustered in a single national association. In 1841 there was formed at Wakefield the MINERS' ASSOCIATION OF GREAT BRITAIN AND IRELAND; 'the most gigantic union that ever was known at the time, and had for its leaders some of the ablest men, Martin Jude being at its head', says Fynes in his *History of the Durham and Northumberland Miners*. The Miners' Association developed rapidly towards the end of 1842 when a series of movements of the miners is found in most of the coal-fields. They were not content with Lord Shaftesbury's Act of 1842 which left many of their grievances completely unsatisfied. Moreover, they were beginning to become more active in the fight to remedy their grievances and more resentful of the treatment to which they were subjected. There were tumults in many coal-fields and soldiers were brought in at the request of the mine-owners. There were frequent strikes in 1842, some of them in Scotland. In the county of Clackmannan, for example, there was a strike, lasting six weeks, for a rise in wages, which had gone down according to the admission of Mr. Craich, the manager of the Alloa Colliery, from 5s. a day in 1836 to 'hardly 2s. a day for a good collier'.

We have seen that Sub-Commissioner Franks stated of the year 1841 that the unions had made little headway in the East of Scotland. Two years later the tide had turned. Commissioner Tremenheere mournfully records in 1844 that in the Lothians:

Delegates from the Miners' Association have for some months been engaged in urging them to join that body. It is understood that many of the Lothian colliers have already become members, either openly or covertly, and subscribe to its funds.

By the beginning of 1844 the Miners' Association of Great Britain and Ireland drew up an Address to the coal-owners. In this, after setting out their desire for 'an amicable adjustment of all differences' instead of a strike 'which we feel inclined to believe is equally disadvantageous to you as to us', they put forward a 'specific and simple plan'. This was to fix a uniform price list, to which cost the masters should 'add what they deem a proper and reasonable return for their capital'. For, they considered,

that, as we risk ourselves and you your money to dig from the bowels of the earth a commodity on which it may truly be said the existence of Great Britain as a nation depends, it is not too much to request that the price of that article shall be such as to give ample remuneration to both the labour and capital employed.

Something of this kind must be done. We have had to submit this year to a very great reduction in prices, and this we opine, if you as coal owners get once into the path of ruinous competition by underselling each other in the market and then endeavouring to reduce the wages to still keep a market, is a process which is alike ruinous to both parties.

On March 25, 1844, a National Conference of the Miners' Association of Great Britain and Ireland was held in the Mechanics Hall, Trongate, Glasgow. Over 70,000 miners were represented from coal-fields in England and Scotland. But a great strike beginning the next month in Durham and Northumberland tried the resources of the national organisation. In the course of the long strike, Fynes tells us:

A request was sent from Scotland for a deputation from Northumberland and Durham to hold a meeting at Dunfermline, as some of the English viewers had been there recruiting men. The deputation went, and a meeting of the spirited inhabitants of the above borough was held in the Masons' Hall on June 5th, 1844. Long before the time for taking the chair (7 o'clock) the spacious hall was filled. The greatest excitement was displayed in consequence of the soldiers being under arms, ready to act at a moment's notice, as were also the police. The magistrates were sitting, and the sheriff of the county was in his carriage in the street near the place of meeting.

What was the meaning of all this preparation and display?

Why, it had been bruited about that the English delegates had come from the Miners' Association into the town to make a riot, and, as a matter of course, burn the town and murder the inhabitants. What silly creatures these authorities must have been to have believed such a very ridiculous story. But the real truth of the matter was that their object was to overawe the speakers, and thus prevent the meeting being held. The meeting, however, was held, and passed off in a peaceable manner.

Whatever the degree of organisation in Scotland, it was weakened, as was every other coal-field, by the defeat in the end of the five months' struggle of the Durham and Northumberland miners. The Miners' Association of Great Britain and Ireland now took up vigorously the question of safety and in connection with one particular disaster made successful representations to the Home Secretary, through the medium of W. P. Roberts, the Chartist Solicitor. This activity, at the end of 1844, later broadened out and April 1847 is the date of their comprehensive petition to Parliament on safety, inspection, education, truck and true weighing.[1]

In this year we get a glimpse of how union districts operated in Scotland from the reports of Tremenheere, who it must be remembered was regarded by Martin Jude and other miners' representatives as hostile to trade unionism. He reports in 1847 that the Miners' Association, though numbering only half the membership it had in 1844, still claims 'upwards of 30,000 members in Lanarkshire, Ayrshire, Lancashire and Staffordshire to which are to be added those who are in Union in Wales and in other mining districts', and quotes a local official, William Cloughan, as follows:

I am clerk to the Union for the Holytown district, Lanarkshire. Including all in Union in the county of Lanark, there are more than 18,000, colliers, miners, drawers and pitmen of all description. The day's work is restricted to 26 or 29 cwt. according to the seam and the distance the coal has to be drawn. The men can do this day's work in eight hours. The restriction has had the effect of bringing into, and keeping in employment all the young hands, and any evil it has done, has been to prevent some of the younger colliers getting into other employments. . . .

In his next report Tremenheere makes reference to a big strike in Lanarkshire in the year 1847, saying:

All experience seems hitherto to have been lost upon the colliers and miners of this district, in regard to strikes. Notwithstanding the complete failure, as usual, of the one which occurred last autumn, during the months of July, August and September, threats have already been held out to the masters of another.

The strike, however, was not successful in that year of acute economic crisis. The next year, 1848, has been called from events in Europe the 'Year of Revolution', and it marked the last of the large-scale petitions for the People's Charter.[2]

---

[1] See *The Miners: Years of Struggle* (1953).

[2] There has been a tendency to regard Chartism as negligible after 1848. True, it diminished: but its liveliness was shown by John Saville's *Ernest Jones: Chartist* (1952). How widespread was its influence amongst colliers can be partly judged from facts furnished by the horrified Tremenheere, who states in his 1851 report that he went to a bookshop in Newcastle-upon-Tyne and got the owner to give him a list, with quantities, of papers sold by him. This he confirmed, from further enquiry, as correct. He then examined them all and gave the following classification: nine 'Infidel and Chartist' papers with a circulation of 1720; one 'Chartist Only' with a circulation of 600; four 'hostile to our present Institutions and of an immoral tendency', with a circulation of 1656; and only three, with a circulation of 888, which he could describe as 'Religious and Moral and containing useful Information'.

The Miners' Association of Great Britain and Ireland fell to pieces in the economic crisis of 1847–8; efforts to revive it were fruitless and a similar blight had fallen on the district unions both in England and Scotland. The early 'fifties represented the lowest point of mining trade unionism in the nineteenth century. To those who were then at the head of the Miners' Association and to its members it would seem as though all their work had been in vain: and to them the future would look darkly unattractive. But they had served a useful purpose.

For the history of the working class, like the history of life itself, has been a record of 'trial and error'. But each new development profits from the lessons of what has gone before, and already in the coal-fields new men and new ideas, shaped from the lessons of the past, were preparing to take the stage. One such man, who was later to represent a very great advance in the organisation and outlook of the miners, was at that time growing up and coming to manhood. He was a young miner who was destined to become the foremost leader of the British miners and, for a period, of the whole trade union movement. His name was Alexander McDonald.

CHAPTER III

THE COUNTY UNIONS

I. AN OUTSTANDING LEADER

IN the trade union headquarters of the Scottish and other coal-fields there are sculptured reliefs, busts, statues and other memorials to the memory of Alexander McDonald, the outstanding leader of the Scottish and afterwards of the British miners. Born in the parish of New Monkland in Lanarkshire on June 21, 1821, Alexander, eldest of seven boys, entered the pits at the age of eight. His first job was in an ironstone mine at Dykehead where he had to work from fourteen to seventeen hours a day. He worked continuously as a miner for sixteen years and thereafter for a year or two in spells of several months at a time. In later years he told a Royal Commission of his laborious early life as a putter. In that badly ventilated mine there were working with McDonald twenty other young boys: forty years later he was the only survivor. These intolerable conditions brought a strike in Lanarkshire in 1842; after which McDonald, who had played a leading part, was victimised, or in his own words 'at the close of the strike I was one of those that was selected as a victim for the tyranny of the employers'. He was twenty-one at the time: but he had already become a man of mark. His schooling had been guided by his mother. He told the Royal Commission, 'I could read the Bible when I was five'. Then he was sent to the Parish School and after he went to work in the pits he was sent to evening-school. He and his brother 'travelled three or four miles after we came out of the pit at 7 or 8 o'clock in the evening to a little village school for the children of farmers' labourers engaged in agricultural pursuits during the day'.

His thirst for knowledge grew, he set himself task after task and finally won his way to a university education—without grant or scholarship, and solely by his own exertions:

I moved to Airdrie for the purpose of attending evening-classes during the winter—going to them privately at night to get a knowledge of Latin & Greek. For the last three years I did not work in the winter season. I went to college (Glasgow University) in 1846— 3 sessions in the winter season. I paid for this with the savings I had effected previously and with what I earned in the summers. Class fees cost me £55 to £60—and lodging for 6 months.

These uncommon exertions brought him offers of work as a mine manager. He took charge of mines in 1849 and 1850 but his spare moments were still occupied 'in agitating the grievances of the mining population and endeavouring to ameliorate their condition'. He opened a school in 1851: but after five years he left teaching to devote his whole time to agitation on behalf of the miners. This he was able to do, having made a modest fortune by speculation; later he was helped from time to time by free-will offerings from the miners.

What were the changes sought by McDonald? He himself in a speech in 1873 gives the answer:

It was in 1856 that I crossed the border first to advocate a better Mines Act, true weighing, the education of the young, the restriction of the age to twelve years, the reduction of the working hours to eight in every twenty-four, the training of managers, the payment of wages weekly in the current coin of the realm, no truck, and many other useful things too numerous to mention here. Shortly after that, bone began to come to bone, and by 1858 we were in full action for better laws.

These activities as agitator and organiser were to make him the national leader of the miners and of British trade unionism (thrice chairman of the parliamentary committee of the Trades Union Congress); and finally, along with Tom Burt, pioneer Labour representative in Parliament from 1874 till his death in 1881. But to appreciate his work in Scotland we must now turn to the situation in the coal-fields when the tide of Chartism was on the ebb and the second half of the century had begun.

2. THE COAL AND IRON MINERS' ASSOCIATION

Trade unionism was at a low ebb and was limited to combination in each pit or group of pits, with occasional conferences of delegates from a wider area. Colliery conditions were bad from 1851 onwards, while wages had fallen as low as 2s. a day and were nowhere above 2s. 6d. even in the rapidly expanding field of Lanarkshire. The tone of depression is well shown by a circular which delegates from Lanarkshire districts decided to send to each employer.

Respected Sir,
     We, the workmen under your charge, solicit that you will take our case into consideration, and grant us an advance of one shilling a day, as the wages now earned by us are quite inadequate to keep us in that state of society to which we are entitled. Hoping, Sir, that you will take our case into serious consideration, we, your workmen, will certainly feel grateful. (*Glasgow Sentinel*, August 28, 1852.)

The circular was drafted by John Muir of Rutherglen who had a big influence in Glasgow's fifteen collieries; and eighteen months later he addressed the miners on their successive advances 'from 9s. a week to an average of 18s. or 20s.' and added, 'I must congratulate you for not having recourse to strikes'. But these advances, due to a seller's market, did not last much beyond 1854. Early in 1855, wages were cut by 1s. Appeals for a rise were unheeded. By the end of the summer the miners could bear it no longer: big meetings were held; strikes, beginning in Holytown in mid-September, spread through the coal-field, and within a fortnight had been successful. This rapid and spontaneous series of strikes, at a moment when iron prices were rising, was the overture to a new and important development in the history of the Scottish miners.
     On October 13, 1855, a large advertisement in the *Glasgow Sentinel* began with the following letter addressed 'To the Coal and Iron Miners of Scotland':

Fellow Workmen,
     The coal and iron miners of Lanarkshire have just passed through another ordeal. They solicited, several months since, the Masters to give a rise of wages, such as they thought the trade could yield. The petitions were unheeded, the demands unanswered. Knowing that our cause was just we struck work, and after, in some instances, a protracted, and others, a brief, struggle, our masters yielded and we are now about to enjoy the fruits of our perseverance and patience.
     During the time of our cessation from work our sentiments were fully interchanged. We saw that our divided condition served well the masters, if they were in any instance wishing to resist a just demand. We accordingly agreed that in order to obviate this state of

matters, our own anarchy should be overthrown and that we should again lay, if possible, a basis whereby all the coal and iron miners in Scotland might unite to save themselves from either being treated unjustly or oppressively.

To this end a general meeting of delegates was held in the Lyceum Rooms on Thursday 4th and on Monday 8th instant, for the purpose of forming articles for our own Association; and placing them before you for your consideration. Delegates were present from the Wishaw, Holytown, Cleland, Airdrie, Coatbridge, Baillieston, Maryhill and Glasgow Districts.

The letter, sent from Airdrie, was signed by Alexander McDonald as Interim General Secretary of the Association and was followed by draft rules. These were adopted at the beginning of November 1855. The rules began with Article 1:

That we, the operative coal and ironstone miners, reddsmen and drawers of Scotland, do form ourselves into one General Association, having for its principal object the protection of each other's rights and privileges.

A further score of Articles contained various provisions including payment of 1s. 6d. entrance fee and thereafter 1d. a week; a General Secretary, to be paid a yearly salary (unstated); and the stipulation usual at this time for members to conduct themselves 'in a quiet and discreet manner' at meetings and elsewhere, and 'not to violate the law of the land either by words or deeds or by threats or intimidations to any person' on pain of expulsion.

The new Association quickly spread from North Lanark to the other coal-fields: representatives were present on November 28 from Fife, Midlothian, and districts of Ayr, Renfrew, Stirling and West Lothian. By the end of 1855 the Association appeared to have struck deep roots. It opened up the prospect of an all-embracing organisation which would lift the organised miners of Scotland above the level of separate local or district combination.

The first activity on the agenda of this new Coal and Iron Miners' Association was the organisation of protest against the Special Rules under the Coal Mines Act of 1855. These, in addition to the first Seven General Rules that were to be the basis of all subsequent mining legislation, could be issued by employers and when passed by the Secretary of State would have the force of law. A number of employers had run riot and had devised Special Rules that were absurd or oppressive. McDonald organised a protest of the new Association, travelled to London, lobbied Members of Parliament, got thirty of them to back him up and obtained an interview at which one of them put the case against the Special Rules to the Home Secretary, to whom was submitted a written 'Requisition of the Miners of Scotland'. At the same time McDonald knew it was necessary to keep up a mass agitation, and in his published letter to the miners of Scotland on February 19 from London, he urged them to assemble in their districts and to 'tell your masters . . . calmly and fearlessly that your rights as men you shall protect'. In another passage in the same letter he says: 'from the little experience I have had in the lobby of the House of Commons, I believe there is not a wrong that you now labour under that could not be redressed, if you were united to one another'. It is clear from this how McDonald saw the future of the new Association. But there came an unexpected obstacle to these plans.

At the end of March 1856 the employers intimated a 20 per cent cut in wages. Strikes began at once, at first in West Lothian and Stirlingshire and then in the shires of Lanark and Ayr. The Lothians and Fife were not affected, but they were able to send help in money.

By mid-April there were 30,000 miners idle. Some of the masters yielded. The others not only refused arbitration, which the miners were asking, but called for additional police protection to enable them to bring in blacklegs. Moreover, advantage was taken of religious differences to try to split the ranks of the miners. The militia was embodied for the first time in twenty years, and the yeomanry were called out. These, together with the police, were poured in great numbers into the colliery districts. Miners with collecting boxes were arrested. At Maryhill on Saturday, April 26, 1856, the speakers impressively urged prudence and lawfulness. The meeting passed a resolution against the bringing in of police, and condemned Captain Smart, a police officer, who had that day said: 'All the police force have strict orders to detect all beggars, and in particular you miners, if you solicit assistance for your distressed poor, even by subscription sheets from persons willing to subscribe for that purpose'. At the beginning of May 1856 a moving appeal 'to the United Trades of Scotland' was issued by McDonald, who said: 'We cannot think to forego a fifth part of our wage when it was well known that even that wage was too little'. It stood at 18s., for 'no coal or iron miner works more than 4½ days per week', working ten to fourteen hours per day. The letter ends:

Take from us the 4s. 6d. a week and you reduce us to about 13s. 6d. This we deem sufficient to keep us at starving point but not in a state to keep ourselves in a proper position in the community, in that state of society to which we ought to aspire as free and honest men. To resist this unjust demand we have already subjected our-selves to great privations; still greater await us. These we are prepared to meet in the same stern manner that they are offered to us. By the end of this week fully 500 families will be thrown out of their homes. Find a shelter and a home for them we must. Provide for the really necessitous we must. We therefore appeal to you in this struggle of labour against capital, to ask for your sympathy and aid, and we trust that should a struggle come to your lot it would be ours to stand by you in your day of trial. We will respond to any call then with gratitude.

Yours, on behalf of the Miners of Scotland,
A. McDonald, General Secretary.

Not only the Scottish Trades but many of the general public were thoroughly sympathetic, including even some of the yeomanry who had been drafted in to keep order. To a miners' conference in Glasgow on May 2 it was reported that 'a small detachment sent to a village recently have offered out of their 7s. 6d. per day pay to give 2s. to the men on strike'. But without strike funds it was an unequal contest. By the end of May the strike was coming to an end.

The miners, after a lengthened, a determined, and a most painful struggle have been compelled to succumb. Starvation and misery have done their work and the submission of the refractory workmen has been accomplished

wrote the *Glasgow Sentinel*. (June 7, 1856.)

Thus ended one of the biggest and hardest-fought strikes of coal and iron miners in Scotland. In the hour of defeat, future prospects depended on how well the lessons of this defeat were learned and how soon internal weaknesses were remedied. On June 10, 1856, a General Conference of coal and iron

miners' delegates met in Glasgow to review the situation, and
to work out plans for 'the better organising of the mining
body'. McDonald read an Address from the United Trades
Committee, which ended with the words:

> You could by unity of action crush every attempt to oppress or
> enslave you. Your weakness has lain heretofore in your want of
> organisation, the want of foresight in the organisation of your labour
> and also the substance derived from that. Let the many strikes you
> have engaged in be your monitors. Let your grievances stir you to
> action. Let your jealousies be forgotten. Have each man confidence in
> his fellow workman and organise at once for the maintenance of your
> rights as citizens and the sweeping away of those oppressions you
> complain of as men. You will have our aid and sympathy in your
> every movement if they be conducted in that orderly manner that has
> marked your conduct in the last strike.

It was clear that one of the weaknesses had been the lack of
a central fund for the Association. All were willing to continue
the Association, but most wished the greater part of the money
to remain in the districts. Finally by a large majority, it was
carried that each member should pay 6½d. per fortnight, of
which a halfpenny was to be for the districts, which of course
had each power to raise a larger amount to deal with its own
internal affairs. They had now to begin the effort to build up
the union in earnest, but unfortunately this effort had to be
made in the hour of defeat and when the masters were dis-
charging men for joining the Association. In 1857 things went
from bad to worse. In the latter part of 1856 and throughout
1857 McDonald kept visiting district after district, especially
Ayrshire and Lanark, striving to keep up the spirit of the men,
but despite all he could do, the miners' organisation was in a
very depressed state for the whole of 1857 and until well on in
1858. Further wage cuts were imposed. In the early autumn
of 1858 McDonald, speaking at a meeting in Maryhill, said:

> wages are said to be three shillings a day ... but take ten days per
> fortnight (and off-takes), this left one pound one shilling and sixpence
> to maintain a family of perhaps seven or eight for fourteen days.

That autumn of 1858 an endeavour was made to rebuild
the Association. A new set of rules was drafted. With regard
to dues, the members were in future to pay 1d. a month.
It was clear from this that the Association had small resources.

It had also little power, as each district was to manage its own affairs. McDonald began the new year 1859 with a message in which he said: 'As the year 1858 progressed, a nucleus of Association was formed, and now those that profess to be in the union number ten thousand men'. McDonald might well use this cautious phrasing. In fact the contributions did not come in regularly. In May wages were cut to below 3s. a day and by mid-1859 there were less than 1500 miners paying their 1d. a month. Thereafter there was a further falling off. After four years of effort in Scotland the Coal and Iron Miners' Association had little more to show than an empty shell.

McDonald at the end of 1859 indomitably sought to build up within the shell of the Association a 'Scottish Miners' Amalgamated Society' on the model of the Amalgamated Society of Engineers, with an array of friendly benefits. The proposal was eagerly welcomed by delegates to a conference held on January 2, 1860. But the Society never came into being. Indefatigably McDonald carried on and brought forward in the autumn of 1860 a proposal for a Law Protection Society. A fund was raised and used for prosecution of employers who were not carrying out the law, and it continued in existence for some few years.

McDonald sought at this time—and indeed for the rest of his life—to direct the attention of the miners to the amelioration of their conditions through parliamentary and legislative activities. He had already in 1856, by assiduous lobbying in the House of Commons, gathered the support of some few score Members of Parliament. He now sought to extend the range of subjects on which this nucleus of public opinion in Parliament might become interested, and at the same time he adjured the miners, day in and day out, to press for better laws that would remove the worst of their grievances. Ventilation was bad, pits were mismanaged, the workers were not given true weight, the Truck Acts were not enforced, hours of labour were long. He linked the demands for the removal of these specific grievances with stirring appeals to the miners to liberate themselves. He played an immense part in bringing about the Mines Act of 1860 and still more in ensuring that it was carried into effect against the opposition of employers. It was this Act which provided for check-weighers or, as they were called, justice men, as well as for more inspectors. Though he pressed these and other necessary measures, McDonald was bitterly disappointed in the meagre response to his work. His success in London in 1860 was shorn of its glory by the failure of his Scots miners to take advantage of the new Act. Despondently he announced his retirement. Perhaps he half hoped that such a step might rouse the men, and in fact many meetings were held 'expressive of regret' and various small collections for him were taken.

Meantime in 1861 wages went even lower and touched 2s. a day. McDonald, however, did not finally give up; and when in 1862 organisation at last began to improve and with rising coal prices there was an advance in wages, McDonald once more got a conference called to revivify the Association and once more put forward a code of rules. By December 1862 there were signs of a marked revival of district organisation.[1] But within four months this fair prospect had vanished. A reduction of 6d. a day was demanded and 5000 miners were locked out. Others were on strike. By the autumn of 1863 organisation had collapsed in all districts except around Kilmarnock. At the end of the lock-out, the result had been (as McDonald recorded a year later): 'The destruction to a large extent of their union which then numbered 10,000 or 12,000'.

[1] West of Scotland districts (December 1862):

Banked	District	Number in union	Wages per day
£94	Hurlford, Kilmarnock, Galston	1300	4s.
£12	Johnstone	140	3s. 6d.
£5	Paisley	180	4s.
£27	Dreghorn	200	4s.
£14	Jordanhill	60	4s.
£75	Larkhall	500	4s. 6d.
£29	Falkirk	483	4s.
£10	Armadale	500	4s. 6d.
£35	Govan	273	4s. to 4s. 6d.
£3	Nitshill	36	3s. 6d.
£16	Hamilton	150	4s. 6d.
£10	Balamock	79	3s. 6d.
	Springfield and Huntershill	300	3s. 6d.
£200	Wishaw	700	4s. 6d.
£2	Kenmure No. 9	20	4s.
	Keppoch—16	30	4s.
£12	Baillieston	450	4s. 6d.
	Holytown (320 on strike, money exhausted)	500	3s. 6d.
	Glasgow (each pit or work (13 of them) bank their own—£20–£40 each)	1000	4s. 6d.
£544		6901	

3. THE FREE COLLIERS

But though the union, which McDonald and others had so ardently advocated, was reduced to a mere shadow, the colliers maintained their feeling of gathering together to express their common interests: and in the autumn of 1863 this began to show itself in a new form. In September there appeared the first mention of a new but short-lived type of organisation—or rather a revival of an old secret society, side by side, and inextricably mixed up with the existing association. This was the Free Collier or 'brothered miners' movement. James Simpson of Falkirk, its 'Grand Master', was the leading spirit. McDonald's attitude towards Free Collierism, it appears, was that of a man thankful for some sort of organisation in Scotland at a time when his own efforts were more and more required in national work. For this autumn McDonald had at last succeeded in bringing together all the established unions in the English coal-fields to form a new organisation representing the British miners as a whole. The earlier promise of improvement in the affairs of the Scottish Association had not materialised, and it was James Simpson—advocate of admission of the employers into the Free Colliers' lodges, and strict exponent of the rules and degrees of their mystery—who attended, as co-delegate with McDonald, the first Conference of the new National Association of Coal, Lime & Ironstone Miners of Great Britain at Leeds in 1863.

By the first week of November this new movement had spread so far that in summoning a miners' conference for a fortnight later (to report on the Leeds Conference) McDonald said that 'information will be given at the meeting as to the formation of Free Colliers' Lodges'.

This was the beginning of a strange development which swept over mining areas in Scotland and nowhere else; which, though short-lived, endures tenaciously in the memory of the miners. Again and again at the present day an old miner can be heard recalling with pride that his father had been a 'Free Collier': or a younger man will say, 'I aye mind my granny telling me that, long before there was a union, my grand-father had been one of the Free Colliers of Fife'.

By December 12, 1863, it is announced that Grand Master James Simpson and Chaplain Colin Maxwell are organising meetings in Bo'ness and elsewhere around Falkirk to form lodges and the following statement is published:

> The object of the formation of these lodges is for the purpose of settling all disputes that may arise between employer and employed, so that the system of strikes may be abolished, which have been ruin-ous to the community at large. Further they are not formed or con-fined to the collier or miner alone, for all classes of a respectable char-acter—yea the master—will be admitted as soon as the servant, which already has been the case in the Grand Lodge of Scotland.

A week later the kind of ceremonial language that was spreading is shown by the heading 'Funeral of a Free-born Collier' described as a 'brother of King Robert the Bruce Lodge, Bo'ness'. Many of these observances and formal pro-nouncements were probably a borrowing from the Free Masons. On March 2, 1864, McDonald was at an 'Ayrshire Miners' Festival' in the New Corn Exchange Hall of Kil-marnock, where food was taken, songs sung, and James Simpson, 'Grand Master of Sir William Wallace Lodge, Falkirk', declared in his speech that

> he appeared there as representative of 1,000 free-born colliers in the counties of Stirling and Linlithgow, determined to persevere in pro-moting their physical, social and moral improvement.

Each month thereafter in 1864 more lodges were opened. Some explanation of this tendency comes out of an April con-ference to 'devise means for better organisation among miners of Scotland' where a deputation from Dalry stated that there were 'no men willing to speak at meetings for fear of employers' and that they 'wished to form a lodge of Free Colliers to remedy this situation'.

It seems clear, therefore, that in this period of extreme weakness of the union, the miners were readily turning to this substitute form of gathering. There was no antagonism to the union as such, and still less to its Secretary, McDonald, as appears from the following report of its activities in the beginning of May:

Demonstrations at Bo'ness of King Robert the Bruce Lodge No. 2 accompanied by Hope Lodge No. 3 headed by R.W.M. of the Grand Lodge of Free Colliers in Scotland.

The procession proceeded eastward, all in due order, both with sociability and regularity, walking round the suburb of Bo'ness and Grange, with the banner of the Grand Lodge of Scotland flying in front, and the banner of King Robert the Bruce Lodge flying in the rear, with nearly 300 Free Colliers walking respectively under their banners.

After returning from the West and the procession near to a close, they made a counter march at the gate. The procession and the Chair of the Hope Lodge having gone out first, by the counter march the chair and procession of King Robert the Bruce Lodge went into the lodge first. The like was never seen in Scotland before, for two lodges of Free Colliers to be walking in brotherly love, such as is now.

When the brethren entered the lodge they appointed Brother Robertson R.W.M. of King Robert the Bruce Lodge as Chair Man, & Brother Campbell S.G., as croupier. Refreshments were supplied by Brother Sneddon, Hamilton Arms Inn.

The brothers were very sorry that Mr. Alexander McDonald could not attend. The toasts were drunk to the health of Brother Alex. McDonald and likewise the Grand Master of Scotland and every brother belonging to the order, the health of her Gracious Majesty Queen Victoria, the Prince of Wales and all the Royal Family, also the Army and Navy, the health of Mr. Campbell, of the Glasgow Sentinel etc. etc.

Songs . . . composed by some of the brethren were sung. The lodge having been closed in due form . . . dancing commenced and all ended in harmony and love at a Quarter to four A.M. (*Glasgow Sentinel*, May 7, 1864.)

In September 1864 the news of the Free Colliers in Fife is of the 'Brotherhood extending rapidly in the Ancient Kingdom'; and in East Lothian, where 215 miners are for forming a lodge: and of Midlothian where 325 joined. By the end of the year 1864 there were found 1122 members of the 'Free Brotherhood' in Midlothian, and 1200 in Fife. These were counties in which there had been but little trade union membership for several years. It must have seemed that the light shining from Falkirk was now to spread to all dark places. There seemed the fairest prospect for the Free Colliers.

But at the beginning of 1865 there was a rift in the lute. Attacks are made on the Free Colliers, who, however, are regarded by the new British Association as the only body from whom they can receive affiliation fees on behalf of the

Scottish miners. Finally in January 1866 when organisation was very weak in the Scottish coal-fields, McDonald, alluding to the fact that many had become Free Colliers, said that it 'must be a living thing from now on or be buried at once'. He criticised them for doing nothing but hold balls, saying that they 'called themselves grand what-nots and did not contribute a penny to any fund calculated to do good to the miners'.

The Free Colliers do not seem to have played any effective part in 1867 or 1868. There are brief notices that this or that lodge will meet—in the case of the Lord Abercorn Lodge of Brothered Miners in Wishaw, 'to consider the utility of getting their flag painted'. What decision they came to on that February evening is unknown: for by June 1868 it is announced that the Lord Abercorn Lodge is dissolved. It had set itself in opposition to the Grand Lodge at Falkirk. But of Falkirk too and its Grand Master Simpson there is no longer any record. While in various parts of the country there continues to be mention that meetings of the Free Colliers (or Brothered Miners) have been held, the whole movement which three years earlier had been functioning as a sort of substitute for the union is now on the wane. It seems in these late 'sixties to have persisted in Fife with more vigour and less ceremonial than elsewhere. But there too the Free Colliers go out of existence.

These bodies with their lofty titles and merry tuneful gatherings, their ceremony and their mystery, had caught the fancy of the Scots miners, when temporarily sunk below the level of trade unionism. They had been accepted, in default of anything better, by the Executive Committee of the British Association, including its President, McDonald. Their proceedings, however full of music and colour, were hardly likely to be an effective substitute for the arduous and serious duties of a trade union: and ineffective they proved to be. But these sentimental gatherings, with their solemnities and their mirthful evenings, were to remain in the memories of the miners for a couple of generations. And today this memory may give a hint to harassed local secretaries of how to get fuller meetings by combining pleasure with business.

4. FIFE AND OTHER COUNTY UNIONS

With the end of the 'sixties there came a turn for the better in the working-class movement. Voting rights had been gained in 1867. The Trades Union Congress, first called in 1868, was regularly held after 1870. For three successive years of its parliamentary committee McDonald, acknowledged as the leader of the British miners, was Chairman. The year 1870 opened with McDonald going throughout Scotland advocating 1s. advance in wages, shorter hours and amendments to the Mines Regulation Bill then before Parliament. The campaign prospered. By June 3 McDonald estimated that 60,000 miners had got 6d. a day advance. By late April many meetings had decided to start an eight-hour day on May 16: and McDonald issued a call for a one-day strike:

... to fully arrange both the rate of output and hours I would take the liberty of suggesting that you would suspend labour in every colliery, in every district, in every mining county in Scotland on the 13th or 14th of May....

The response came first in Lanarkshire and the Lothians and sundry pits elsewhere. But the summit of achievement was the shorter hours movement in Fife, which by means of a stay-down strike, secured on June 5, 1870, an eight-hour day. It was the first coal-field in Europe to win the eight-hour day: and this outstanding victory was marked for seventy-five years thereafter[1] by an annual gala in commemoration. This victory also marked the beginning of a firm trade union organisation in Fife.

Who were the leading men in this first permanent county organisation of colliers in Scotland? Apart from Alexander McDonald, the leaders were Penman, Dingwall and Cooke. In the course of the struggle of 1870 it was agreed to establish a central fund with permanent officials and an Executive Board. McDonald toured Fife in February 1871, bringing in pits that had stood aloof, and on February 16 the Fife and Clackmannan Association was definitely formed, with

[1] Not extinct but since 1947 merged in the gala of all the Scots miners, now held at Edinburgh.

McDonald as 'Corresponding Secretary'. Two years later the leading spirit, Richard Penman, had died. He had been refused work by the employers and suffered much for his activities. But his work survived him. His place was taken by Henry Cooke, who remained Secretary until his death in July 1880.

In the spring the new Union Board of Fife set a gala day on June 5, 1871, to celebrate the first anniversary of the eight hours victory. They sent a letter 'To the Coalmasters of Fife' which said:

We, the miners of Fife kindly invite all our masters to come to our meeting on that occasion. By their complying with this invitation, it will be but hastening the time, that is not far distant, when master and servant shall meet on one common platform to settle the differences that exist between us.

At the gala, held in Kirkcaldy, there were apparently no coal-owners present! But twenty colliery districts, each represented by more than 100 miners, together with wives and sweethearts, were there. A flute band led a march from the coastal collieries while an extra train for Oakley and Clackmannan men was chartered. There were six brass bands and one flute band, and ten banners in the mile-long procession which marched to the Corn Exchange for the meeting. Local factory owners had to close down for the day. Nothing like it had been seen in Kirkcaldy for over a generation. McDonald was presented with a purse of sovereigns. There were races on the shore, games and dancing. Following the gala, an advance of 6d. a day was gained in Fife; miners flowed into the union.

Other districts began to be organised and in December Mid and East Lothian decided to form a Board. At the end of the year 1871 Fife proudly announced that they had £52 : 14 : 2 in the bank. It was a small beginning but an earnest of greater things to come. McDonald, reviewing the situation as a whole, said that things were better for miners and workmen generally than for years past and were likely to remain so for some time ahead. His words proved true. For in 1872 wages rose rapidly and to levels never before reached; at first from 4s. 6d. and 5s. up to 6s.; by August there were collieries paying as much as 9s.; while those miners working the eight-hour day were getting 7s. and 8s. but in some cases going as high as 9s. 9d. It was a transformation from the persistently low wage levels of a generation.

Meantime the eight hours agitation went on: and endeavours were made to spread the eight-hour day from its stronghold in Fife into counties and districts which had not maintained the shorter hours campaign of 1870.

Last but not least the great Mines Act of 1872 for which McDonald had carried on a persistent campaign was passed into law. It was a year of personal triumph for McDonald who saw the causes for which he had fought so long and so strenuously—for higher wages, for shorter hours, for safety in mines, for union organisation—all advancing at one and the same time. There was a grand presentation to him in November 1872, following the passage of the new Mines Act. A Scottish presentation of £680 with a silver casket ('to keep the siller in') formed part of a total British presentation of £780, which as Normansell of Yorkshire said was the 'greatest ever presentation to a man in his position'.

But the most important feature of the year was the growth of trade union organisation in Scotland. Fife led the van; and here by June 1, 1872, they recorded with precision 4046½ members with £1200 in the bank and were reaping in full measure the reward for the struggle that had won the Fife miners the eight-hour day and the formation of a solidly-based county union.

Other districts too were moving forward in organisation. By the late autumn of 1872 the coal-owners were becoming uneasy alike at the high degree of organisation and the high wages. In November notices of reductions were given in nearly every part of the Scottish coal-field. At conferences in November and December McDonald's strategy was adopted: firstly to ask for an all-Scotland discussion with leading employers, and secondly, if this failed, to accept reductions of 1s. but to strike wherever the reductions were of 2s., the strikers (7000 out of 45,000 miners) to be maintained by those at work.

The market, however, was too good for the coal-owners to face the prospect of prolonged stoppages to enforce wages reductions: and the majority were again getting 9s. a day in the early months of 1873. The price of coal was rising at an unprecedented rate; yet there was considerable agitation amongst the employers that wages had risen to heights hitherto unknown; and much talk about 'importing Chinese' who, as far as one knows, are then spoken of as cheap mining labour for the first time. It was not to be the last time. Indeed, from the early 'seventies onwards a vision of the sons of this ancient civilisation, skilled, thrifty, and accustomed to live on a little rice in the conditions to which they had been thrust down by generations of exploitation, exercised a remarkable fascination on mine-owners.[1]

Meanwhile there was a new development. For the first time the representatives of the organised miners met the Scottish employers in conference in summer 1873. It had never happened before: and it did not happen again till the end of the century. The employers on this occasion withdrew notices of wage-reductions. This 1873 meeting of both sides, however temporary, is of importance, in that Lord Elcho, who brought it about, was an active proponent of arbitration in industry. In this he had the support of McDonald and of the miners. At this stage it was the employers who fought shy of arbitration as an interference both with the 'immutable laws of political economy' as well as with their own rights as property owners. As for the Government, there was to be no question for another twenty years and more of 'State interference' in an industrial dispute.

In this springtide of trade unionism of 1872–3 McDonald rejoiced in the strength of the Scottish counties and districts. To strengthen them further was always his argument. All the other devices he had tried at different times in the past score of years having failed, he now saw hope in the organisation of Lanarkshire and the West of Scotland, district by district,

[1] The British owners of South African mines thirty years after this succeeded in having 'indentured Chinese labour' brought to the Witwatersrand gold-mines of Johannesburg: and the question of this 'Chinese Slave Labour' was to play a big part in the Liberal and Labour propaganda in the General Election of January 1906. Ten years later the coal-owners, still intoxicated by this vision, proposed in 1915 to the Home Office, which adopted the suggestion, that the loss of man-power in the mines through the over-recruitment to 'Kitchener's army' should be met by the importation of cheap Chinese labour. It was rejected utterly by the British miners' unions and had to be dropped. But hankering for Chinese labour did not finally die out for another thirty years. Since 1949, however, when it was announced that 'China had stood up', this eighty-year-old vision at last faded away: and the Chinese people are no longer compelled to sell their labour cheap.

but only if they had a central Federal fund and Federal officials. The discussion on federation began in April 1873: rules of the proposed Federation were adopted on October 11. On October 25 the following were elected as officers of the Federation: Alexander McDonald, President; John Drinnan of Shotts, Vice-President; Sam Hughes of Maryhill, Treasurer; William Scobie of Baillieston, Secretary. This seemed a fair beginning. But, as it turned out later, this Federation was never consolidated. Once more McDonald could ruefully repeat the lines of Burns:

> The best laid schemes of mice and men
> Gang aft agley.

Buoyed up by all these recent developments, McDonald set himself to make the forthcoming November Conference of the British miners as epoch-making as elaborate preparation and careful and full reporting could contrive. It was to give new life to all trade unions of miners in Great Britain. It was to be such as would demonstrate the strength of the colliers' local and national organisation.

The organised parts of the Scottish coal-fields were well represented at this conference:

Scotland	Strength of the Districts	Financial Strength £
Fife and Clackmannan ..	5,339	6,750
Stirling and Linlithgow ..	5,300	3,729
Mid and E. Lothian ..	2,000	1,500
Larkhall	2,000	1,400
Maryhill	1,800	3,700
Wishaw	1,500	927
Den	330	300
Dalry	720	420
Total	18,989	£18,726

Henry Cooke of Dunfermline and John Gillespie of Falkirk were the leaders of their county unions. Another prominent figure in 1873 was the Secretary of the Mid and East Lothian Miners' Association, David Moffat, one of whose grandsons held a similar position seventy-five years later, while his older grandson was the Scottish miners' President from 1942 onwards.

In January 1874 McDonald had been once more elected
Chairman of the parliamentary committee of the T.U.C. at
its Sheffield meeting. Within three weeks thereafter McDonald
had been elected to Parliament for North Staffordshire and
at last had gained entrance to that chamber in whose lobby
he had for twenty years so often waited patiently to induce
this or that member to take up questions affecting the well-
being of the miners. Increasingly from February 1874 onwards McDonald was absorbed in the regular duties of a
Member of Parliament while more than ever he was in request as a speaker at miners' meetings and meetings of other
workers all over Britain and also in the United States. Therefore he was no longer able to be present at more than a few
of the Scottish meetings. But he seldom failed to send a letter
of advice to each conference that had important matters on
its agenda.

5. STRIFE IN THE SCOTTISH COAL-FIELDS

The selling price of coal, at its zenith in 1873, came
tumbling down in the early months of 1874. A series of wage-
cuts of 10 per cent, 20 per cent, 30 per cent and even 40 per
cent were announced: and their announcement met with
immediate resistance. Strikes broke out: and there was much
talk of a general strike in the central coal-fields. The employers, however, in their different groups had put forward
different reductions. McDonald saw a chance of keeping
them divided. He had been reckoning up the prospects of the
coming struggle and was much concerned lest the Scottish
miners should throw away what seemed to him the best
tactical moves. He therefore proposed, in a printed letter to
the miners, that reductions of 1s. should be accepted, and
reductions of more than a shilling should be resisted: and that
big strike levies should be raised for those resisting. He argued
this proposition very eloquently, all the more so because in
Lanarkshire the existing leaders had been thrust aside, there
were unofficial strikes and a demand for a general strike of
miners to resist all reductions whatsoever. McDonald saw the
danger of disunity being followed by collapse, and he ended
his letter with the words:

If we are to have districts acting on their own account, which can only lead to ruin; if we are to have men, who are not the leaders—I mean the recognised leaders—leading men away into small desultory parties, instead of meeting the difficulty in the core, to these at once I am willing to resign all control. Any failure now, any unwise act will, if done by you be charged to me. If my advice is taken and the advice of all the Delegates that act in Conference is taken, then no contumely, no reproach, no vexatious accusations will we care for if supported by you unitedly. In your hands, by unity in paying and in action, lies a certain victory; in your hands, by desultory and foolish conduct, lies a certain and ignoble defeat. I trust the former—UNITY —will be your watchword and your rallying cry.

Yours respectfully,
ALEXANDER McDONALD.

McDonald's advice was rejected. He himself became unpopular in Lanarkshire, and was hissed at a conference in April 1874. Strikes began and a series of stormy meetings were held at Powburn Toll.

By June the scattered strikes were proving unsuccessful. Miners and their families were camping in the fields in Lanarkshire, sending out spasmodically to collect aid from working men. Finally they had to succumb to the wage-cuts. By the end of the summer wages generally were about half what they had been nine months earlier. The figure of 5s. became fairly general, but many pits were working at a lesser figure. In that summer of 1874 there were in the *Glasgow Herald* constant attacks upon McDonald for precipitating strikes and causing a drop in coal prices and lack of trade. There were also constant attacks upon him from certain sections of the miners for not supporting their resistance to any reduction. The *Glasgow Herald* was dealing with the McDonald they had known for a score of years as an agitator, who strove through union to win strikes, and through strikes to build the union. But McDonald had for some time been entering upon a new phase, in which he pinned his faith to conciliation, on the crystallising of conciliation into a sliding-scale, and where this solution to conflicts was not feasible, to avoid disputes by arbitration. And these new themes in his speeches had been noted by some of the colliers. McDonald was not the only one. Twenty years later the Webbs were to note how many of the trade union leaders of the 'seventies won union recognition from the capitalists 'only at the cost of adopting the intellectual position of their opponents'.[1]

With the defeats of the summer of 1874 those who had been foremost in leading the strikes against reduction lost much of their credit. McDonald was able to call a Delegate Conference at Glasgow on September 18, where he reviewed the changed situation, and drew the lesson that they must now have a proper union in the west, with voting based on numerical strength, with circulation before meetings of matters to be discussed and with regular benefits such as funeral benefit. The advice was sage enough—if only there had been enough trade unionists to carry it out. Unfortunately the defeat of the ill-organised strike movement of spring and summer 1874 had led to a most serious falling away in the West of Scotland.

6. THE FIFE AND CLACKMANNAN LOCK-OUT OF 1877

The downward tendency of wages which set in with the opening months of 1874 continued. By April 1875 the position in every coal-field had become so serious that the Miners' National Union (not a new body, but the new title of the British organisation) called a Special Conference. The delegates (including Cooke from Fife, Gillespie from Stirling and Drinnan from Shotts) were unable to find a workable solution. The downward process went on. Where unions had been strong, they were weakened: where they had been weak, they ceased to exist. It was only in the East of Scotland, formerly so backward, that the county unions of the Lothians and Fife were able for the time to maintain their footing.

In Fife and Clackmannan proposals for wage-cuts led to a threat of strikes in April 1876. The Fife Board appointed a deputation to meet the owners, who were willing now to meet county union representatives. In the end the proposed wage-cut of 15 per cent was halved. This, as in Stirling when they agreed to accept all reductions down to a *minimum* of 4s., was therefore an organised retreat, in contrast at that time to Lanarkshire, where in May 1876 wages had been driven

---

[1] *The History of Trade Unionism* by Sidney and Beatrice Webb (1894 edition), p. 324.

down to 3s. in some pits so that the darg which two years earlier had brought in 11s. 6d. now brought in only 3s. 4d.

Thus when in the spring of 1877, with the oncoming of economic crisis, there was a further proposal to reduce wages, the Fife men were able to offer an organised resistance. All the elements of a clash of forces were present. 'Masters and men stand to each other in stern and hostile attitude.' (*Glasgow Sentinel*, May 12, 1877.) The dispute began in Clackmannan, where on one morning at the end of March 1877 the colliers found placards posted up at all the works intimating that the miners' wages were to be reduced by 10 per cent, and in future they would be charged for house rent and coal. The workmen were determined to resist. The county union took the matter up and decided on a strike of three pits: whereupon the masters threatened a general lock-out.

On May 19 the masters decided on a lock-out to enforce the reduction: by May 26, 4000 men had ceased work, of whom 700 struck work, while the rest were locked out. With the beginning of June the lock-out was general. It lasted fourteen weeks ending in a substantial victory for the men. It was the biggest dispute, conducted in an organised manner, that had taken place for over a generation. It was the first big dispute between a well-organised county union and the federated employers. The keenest interest in it was shown by the Miners' National Union, which in its long history made this one of the few occasions when it called a levy from all other British miners affiliated. The support was not given lightly. It is highly probable that the British leaders felt mining trade unionism in Scotland to be at stake. For if Fife and Clackmannan had suffered defeat, it might have meant the end of effective union organisation, as had been in their experience the result of the defeats two and three years earlier in other parts of Scotland. The Fife lock-out of 1877, with the substantial victory of the men,[1] may therefore be considered a landmark in the history of the Scottish miners.

[1] On December 22 the Fife and Clackmannan miners rejected the sliding-scale offered by the employers, their principal objection being that no minimum wage had been fixed. The Board of the union told the employers that, given a minimum, they would be willing to reconsider the whole question.

7. THE BLANTYRE CALAMITY

How little the Mines Act of 1872 availed to end the dreadful tale of colliery disasters was shown five years later by 'The Blantyre Calamity', the most serious explosion ever known in the Scottish coal-fields. In the morning of Monday, October 22, 1877, at Dixon's Collieries, High Blantyre, a few miles from Glasgow, an explosion of fire-damp wrecked the workings and caused a loss of over two hundred lives. The pits, worked by the 'stoop and room' system as pillar-and-stall was called, were 130 to 155 fathoms deep; and had been opened up in 1873 and 1876. It was a 'fiery mine' and was locally known to be such. 'Had I not been long idle', ran the evidence of William Eadie at the subsequent enquiry, 'previous to going to the Colliery, and the rent becoming due, I would not have gone down the pit.'

When the news became known of this terrible calamity, there was an immediate assembling of miners from all the neighbouring pits. Two thousand of them marched along the road to Dixon's Collieries, with the intention of descending the mine *en masse* to try to rescue their comrades, if any were still alive. When they were marching along the road they were met by Alexander McDonald, M.P., also hastening to Blantyre, who addressed them and counselled them not to go on with this plan, which he felt would only endanger more lives. The miners listened and were persuaded. But their attempted action was a measure both of the feelings of horror caused and of the unflinching bravery of the working miners.[1]

The conclusions of the official enquiry were clear enough: 'that the Coal Mines Regulation Act 1872 was apparently not complied with' in many respects. Alexander McDonald,

---

[1] A traditional song is still sung about this disaster, describing how
'all the women and children
With pale anxious faces they haste to the mine,
When the truth was made known the hills rang with their moaning;
Two hundred and seven young miners were slain.

Now husbands and wives and sweethearts and brothers
That Blantyre explosion they'll never forget;
And all you young miners that hear my sad story
Shed a tear for the victims who're laid to their rest.'
From A. L. Lloyd, *Come All Ye Bold Miners* (1952).

THE BLANTYRE COLLIERY EXPLOSION, 1877
Calling for volunteers for the exploring parties

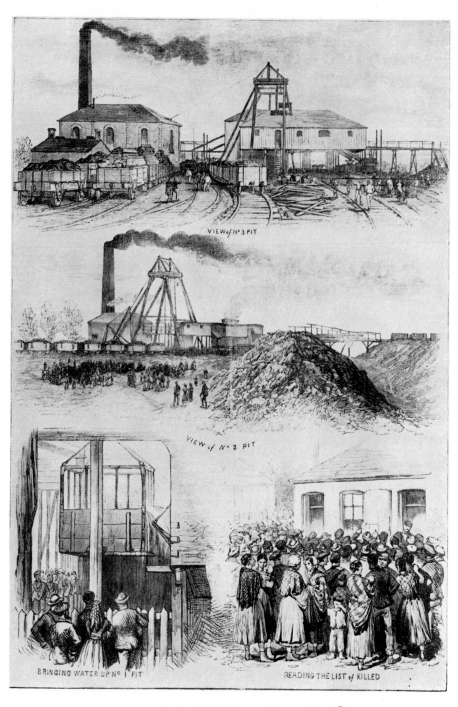

VIEW of Nº 3 PIT

VIEW of Nº 2 PIT

BRINGING WATER UP Nº 1 PIT

READING THE LIST of KILLED

THE BLANTYRE COLLIERY EXPLOSION, 1877
Scene of the disaster

M.P., whose pertinent questioning of witnesses was openly resented by representatives of the employers, assiduously gathered evidence as to previous conditions in the pit. It appeared that over two months earlier an explosion of fire-damp had given warning of the condition of the mine: 'on 20th August when some roof fell, an explosion followed, and two persons named McInulty who were working near with open lights got burned, one of them fatally'. The evidence of the survivor, Andrew McInulty, ran as follows:

Andrew McInulty deposed:

I live at Dixon's Row, Stonefield. I am 17 years of age. I was down No. 2 Pit at six o'clock one morning, three months ago last Monday. I went down with my brother Joseph McInulty, who had a contract for working out the stoops. I was engaged in laying rails with my brother, and while we were so employed the gas exploded at my lamp, which was a naked light. That was about eight o'clock in the morning. Both my brother and myself were severely burned. My brother died at ten o'clock that same night in consequence of the injuries he had received. I was burned on the hands, arms and back. I was working about half a stoop off the level road, eight yards from the stoops. All the workmen I saw about the place were using naked lights. No one told me to be careful with my light, as there was gas about the mines.[1]

There was dissatisfaction with the results of the public enquiry, which was not followed by any prosecution. Several times Alexander McDonald raised the matter in Parliament, but he was unable at that stage to get any further steps taken or pledges to improve the law.

If McDonald was dissatisfied, so too were the miners of Lanarkshire and of Scotland as a whole. Public meetings were held, strong resolutions passed, a memorial (censuring the conduct and views of the inspectorate) sent to the Home Secretary, and all this to an extent which was bound to have some effect on the Government. The effect on the inspectorate

[1] Seventy years later Andrew McAnulty (as his name is now spelt) told me from his vivid memory the details of the first explosion and showed me his scorched right arm with its shrivelled sinews. Later accidents deprived him of the sight of one eye and injured his feet, so that both in his body and in his trade union and political experience he was a living epitome of the miners' struggle. At the age of twenty-seven he became a member of the Executive of the short-lived Scottish Labour Party, which Keir Hardie formed in 1888. One of the founders of mining trade unionism in Lanarkshire, he was first a delegate to the Miners' National Conference in March 1893, a foundation member of the Communist Party in 1920, and after 1926 was the President for several years of the Lanarkshire Miners' County Union.

was no doubt salutary. But the greater effect of a successful prosecution against owners or managers was not forthcoming. For at this time, as for many long years afterwards, there was an apparent reluctance to put on their trial those who were found in enquiries to have been responsible for grave breaches of the law.

8. MCDONALD'S WORK IN PARLIAMENT

Alexander McDonald's entry into Parliament, together with Burt, aroused hopes and fears. It was assumed that he and Burt would be primarily functioning as 'the voice of the miners'. This he assuredly did. Never before had a Home Secretary been so persistently questioned at question time, and urged in debate, on matters not only legislative but administrative affecting the lives and livelihood of those engaged in a particular industry. It was not the miners only for whom he spoke, but also the seamen and the railwaymen. Safety in mines, railways and ships was his constant pre-occupation. Accidents and disaster found him insisting on the most searching examination, and upon the punishment of those culpable. For example (for the first half of the year 1877), he is always calling for prosecutions to make sure that the Mines Act of 1872 does not become a dead letter: and by July 2, he extracts the following admission from the Home Secretary:

With regard to the 32nd section of the Mines Regulation Act, he was afraid the managers of the mines had been in the habit of looking at it somewhat as a dead letter, and he had therefore twice during the present year ordered an investigation into the conduct of the manager of a mine under that section, for the purpose of showing the managers that it was not a dead letter, and that if they broke it they would be liable to be punished with the loss of their certificates.

Himself having been a working miner, and having gone through other grades including for a short period a manager's job, he was exceptionally well qualified to keep everyone responsible up to the mark, from Secretary of State down to district inspectors and mine managers. No question is too small for him to take up: for example he asks again and again: Why is there delay in H.M. Inspection of Mines

Reports? Why is it later than the previous year? When will it be out? Does the Home Secretary or his officials not realise that working men have a special interest in these reports and that they might be made available at the earliest moment? There can be no doubt that this sort of questioning effected small reforms and minor improvements at the time and kept the civil service on its toes of expectation, beside having a deterring effect on tendencies to evil-doing, corruption or sloth.

But McDonald spread his wings more widely than these subjects and questions would indicate. He was by no means the conventional Liberal. From time to time McDonald would speak with a boldness which few but the Irish Members could emulate on subjects where most Members of Parliament kept obstinately silent. For example, he opposed a Grant to the Duke of Connaught on his marriage, saying:

There was no question which was so freely and thoroughly discussed by the working classes as that of the continual demands which were made upon the country to maintain Members of the Royal Family apart from the heavy Civil List of Her Majesty. He hoped this would be the last grant of the kind, for he believed they were sapping the foundations of the throne. (*Hansard*, July 31, 1878.)

McDonald spoke out hardily, denouncing the system of a secret service, in the discussion on the estimates of £24,000.[1]

Scotland, years ago, suffered greatly from the existence of such a Service, and the name of one person—Castlereagh—was still thought of with detestation by working and middle class people in that country.

Secret Service money had also been used for the very worst purposes in England. During the Chartist agitation from 1838 to 1840, it was clearly shown that such money was employed for the purpose of fomenting insubordination and rebellion among the people. Then unfortunate victims who had been lured into rebellion by Government money were sent to distant lands for considerable periods. (*Hansard*, May 24, 1878.)

McDonald was an ardent defender of the Irish people against oppression. When Gladstone's Cabinet in February 1881 brought in their coercion Bill (Protection of Persons and Property (Ireland) Bill) McDonald fought against it in its various stages and on February 25 he rose to utter a protest.

---

[1] It was the same as the figure of the previous year (1876–7) of which only £14,900 had in fact been expended. This was less than the figure of seventy-seven years earlier (in 1800) when the secret service vote was £112,000 and much less than the figure of seventy-seven years later when in the estimates of 1952–3 the secret service stood at £4,500,000.

He (Mr. McDonald) felt bound to protest against this Bill. He had
voted against it because it suppressed the liberties of a whole people
on account of the action of a few; because it left the people of Ireland
in the hands of the informer, the spy, and the paid partisan; because
it cared nothing for the morality of the people, so long as they promoted their own objects; and because it came from the hands of the
so-called Liberal Party, with which he had been associated all his
life.

In general, while behaving with fearless independence on
such questions as those recounted above, McDonald like
most of the trade union officials was a convinced Liberal.
This meant that on all matters where he had no clear and
conscious backing from the working class he represented or
where the matter lay beyond the range of his experience he
was content to put his trust in the Liberal leaders. For
example in matters of foreign policy, while against oppression
of subject people, McDonald had no such keen insight and
native grasp of international principles as was possessed by the
Chartists of his early manhood, let alone the formidable grasp
of his contemporaries in the First International. Despite his
journeys to the U.S.A. or perhaps because of them (for his
advocacy of miners' emigration 'in order to become farmers'
was like an echo of Feargus O'Connor's last land settlement
schemes) he never attained any real comprehension of what
was happening in Europe.[1] It is not, however, for the defi-
ciencies in his make-up that McDonald is to be remembered,
but for all the remarkable work that he did. When his work
ended with his death in 1881 there was great grief amongst the
miners.

Today, a century after the miners responded to McDonald's
fiery agitation[2] and formed the Coal and Iron Miners'
Association, we may see some reasons why this first effort at
a single union for Scotland proved unsuccessful, why the

[1] For this and in general for allowing the working class to become 'nothing more than
the tail of the great Liberal Party', Marx and Engels had much the same opinion of
McDonald as they had of other trade union leaders at that time. (See *The Correspondence
of Marx and Engels*, ed. D. Torr 1934, p. 356, and *Marx-Engels Briefe am Bebel*, etc. 1933,
p. 226.)

[2] Mr. A. J. Youngson Brown in his article on 'Trade Union Policy in the Scots Coal-
fields 1855–1875' (*Economic History Review*, August 1953) gives useful material on
McDonald's standpoint in the eighteen-seventies on industrial relations. But he seems to
make the assumption (not substantiated in his article) that this 'class harmony' standpoint
was also fully typical of McDonald in his earlier stages; and also to miss the significance of
the Fife miners establishing the shorter working day in 1870.

Association so frequently collapsed on to its parochial units and why these too disappeared in hard times. First, with highly competitive collieries, there was an extremely localised outlook amongst colliers, for whom bonds of trade union feeling, strong in the pits, became feebler beyond their own parish; thus only one of these early county unions proved permanent. Second, the labour force itself, especially in the rapidly expanding industry of Lanarkshire where permanent organisation broke down again and again, was made up largely of new recruits from the landless peasantry of Ireland. These immigrants might rise in sudden strikes, but they needed time to acquire steadiness and capacity for sustained trade union activity. Lastly, McDonald's own wide ranging interests, ambitions and activities, while benefiting British miners as a whole, did not lead him to settle down to the humdrum and limited tasks of a miners' agent in those days. For all his remarkable personality, McDonald appeared to many as a brilliant adventurer, whose eloquence, adroitness and far-reaching schemes aroused admiration but did not always inspire the implicit trust that was accorded to lesser figures. This was the testimony of the oldest surviving Scots miner who had known McDonald, conversed with him and often heard his inspiring speeches. Said old Andrew McAnulty,[1] 'McDonald was an adventurer, a poseur. He used the miners to help him to win a great place in the world. But, mind you, at the same time he helped the miners and did them a lot of good.'

[1] In an interview in October 1947.

CHAPTER IV

THE GREAT STRIKE OF 1894

1. KEIR HARDIE AND THE FEDERATION OF 1887

THE county and local unions, built up in the period of
Alexander McDonald's main activities, reached their highest
point in the year 1874, 'the springtide of trade unionism'. This
growth of mining unions was not to last. It was blighted by the
great economic crisis, the worst of the nineteenth century, which
occurred in 1877 and reached its greatest depth in 1879. Wages
were cut everywhere, victimisation was widespread; in locality
after locality union organisation was destroyed or driven underground, and its records mostly lost. By 1880 the Fife and
Kinross Miners' Association alone survived.

Alexander McDonald himself died in 1881. In the county
of Fife Henry Cooke was still Secretary up to his death in
July 1880: and it fell to John Weir, appointed Secretary in
September 1880, to hold together the only surviving county
union. In Mid and East Lothian Secretary David Moffat was
victimised and compelled to leave the Lothians: he crossed
over into Fife, where at Lumphinnans he sought to gain a
livelihood for his numerous family. The first years of the
'eighties were indeed a barren period of trade unionism,
defeated and routed in most of the counties of Scotland. The
revival that began in 1886 is associated with various names
and famous amongst them, Keir Hardie.

James Keir Hardie was born at Legbrannock, near Holytown, August 15, 1856. With his parents he early removed to
Glasgow, where, when but a few months more than eight
years old, he began work, first as message boy, and afterwards
as a rivet heater. After two years his parents returned to the
country, and young Hardie entered the pits at Quarter as a
trapper. With the exception of two years spent in the quarries
about Hamilton he continued in the pits till he was twenty-
three, when he and his brothers were refused further employ-

ment. He then set up as a small shopkeeper, and while thus engaged he was in 1879 elected Secretary to the miners' union of Hamilton (an attempt to form a Lanarkshire Miners' Union), a post which he filled for fully two years. But during this time he fell foul of Alexander McDonald: and at the beginning of 1881, having received an invitation from the miners of Ayrshire, he went to that county to act as Agent and Secretary. An unsuccessful strike for wages in Ayrshire in the winter of 1881–2 wrecked the prospect of an effective union for several years. In 1882 Hardie got work as sub-editor of a local paper, *The Cumnock News*. When the Ayrshire Miners' Union was resuscitated largely through his efforts in August 1886, he was at once appointed Secretary. Three months later he also became Secretary of the newly-formed Scottish Miners' National Federation. The new Scottish body at once distinguished itself by the publication of *The Miner. A Journal for Underground Workers* whose first number of January 1887 contained an article by Thomas Burt, M.P.

From the beginning Keir Hardie was always interested in Labour journalism and in politics. Even when he had not yet left Liberalism behind, he was striving for working men to be chosen as representatives of the Liberal Party. It was as part of his wider political outlook that he conceived grandiose plans beyond the scope normal in most trade union agitators of the 'eighties. Thus he always looked to the need of organisation extensively and on a wide scale rather than to the detailed work of local trade unionism. When he had succeeded in rebuilding the Ayrshire Miners' Union, he pressed beyond this immediately for a wider Scottish organisation; and as soon as the revival showed itself in the English counties, he was a leader and eager participator in national conferences covering the United Kingdom.

The Scottish Miners' National Federation was formally constituted on October 5, 1886, with Keir Hardie as Secretary. It had connected with it local organisations with an aggregate membership of 'about 25,000' which were expected to pay a halfpenny per month per member into the Federation fund. The first issue of *The Miner* states:

The Federation has no power over the internal management of any local organisation; neither has it power to proclaim a strike, or enforce a levy for the support of men on strike. Nevertheless, it is of great value as a means of securing concerted action over the length and breadth of Scotland; of having justice done to members of local associations; in having the mining laws amended, and securing the return of miners' Candidates to St. Stephens. It acts the part of the 'Guide, the Counsellor, the Friend', and as its merits come to be appreciated in this capacity, so it will come to be prized. (January 1887.)

Thus introduced with a flourish of trumpets, the new Scottish organisation for a time blazed like a meteor in the skies. The English trade unions had great hopes of it. The connection with Scotland, rather frayed after the death of Alexander McDonald in 1881, was maintained by Keir Hardie's almost regular appearance, usually representing the Ayrshire miners, at national and international conferences, in the course of the next seven years. Under the leadership of the flamboyant personalities of Chisholm Robertson and Keir Hardie, the new Federation made a splash in 1887.

At its first annual meeting Chisholm Robertson from the chair said that this Federation had done well:

Although scarcely one year old, with a partial membership, its influence in the lobbies of the House of Parliament is an acknow-ledged fact; especially for the past few months, it is able to show a record of work in justification of its existence. That the Federation has played a conspicuous part is undoubted, in the many necessary, important and desired amendments which have been drafted to the new Mines Bill. The indomitable pluck and perseverance of the deputies sent to Westminster, armed with the concentration of power which a Federation gives, has had a splendid and telling effect, as was shown by several members of Parliament taking part in the debate, short as it was, favourable to the miners' amendments, who would have kept absolutely silent if not against, had it not been for the fact that in a great many cases the miners' grievances and con-siderations were in a great measure forced upon them. (August 5, 1887.)

From Keir Hardie's Report, which was read to the dele-gates and by them adopted, we learn that the National Federation began with twenty-six districts and 23,570 members and finished the year with some fifteen districts and 13,000 members—a loss due to the failure of local organisa-tions. Clearly, the mortality of the district unions was serious, eleven out of twenty-six within a single year. On this Hardie stated that 'Wherever county organisations have been formed, these continue to thrive and prosper, the whole of the failures having occurred with the district Unions'.

Wages were reported as very low, ranging from 2s. 6d. to 4s. per day, the average being about 3s. 3d., and the Report says: 'Work, however, is very unsteady, and thus the earnings of the men cannot be more than 12s. per week'. They were not alone in this respect for the same story came from the other coal-fields. From the first the policy of the new Scottish Federation had been five days a week, and eight hours a day, with a set wage. This it had not been found possible to apply generally. Hardie himself wanted a compromise, stating:

My own impression is that in order to secure uniformity, and solely as a matter of expediency, we ought to recommend eleven days a fortnight with the darg or set wage, and the eight hours. Hitherto the difficulty has lain in getting the men in the East to come to ten days, and this has been made the excuse for the men in the West going back to twelve days, and in many cases long hours and big dargs. The compromise I suggest, however, would place all on an equality, and secure united action; this, after all, being the greatest desideratum.

The Report goes on to argue for 'playing the pits' as a means to get higher wages:

What is wanted is the adoption of a policy which will bring the supply of coal going into the market well within the demand. Thus and thus only can wages be got up. The leaders in England are slow to learn this, though the educational process now going on among the men, with poverty for a teacher, will probably show good results before long. What we aim at meanwhile is to get the miners of the United Kingdom to be idle for a fortnight or so all at the same time.

Characteristic of Keir Hardie's personal standpoint were the following passages:

The formation of a Labour Party in the country has hitherto been looked upon as a dream of the enthusiast. It would appear as if the miners of Scotland were to have the credit of transforming it into a reality. Resolutions have been passed at various large centres in favour of this being done, while in some constituencies candidates have been selected. The Labour Party will be a distinct organisation from the Trades Unions. It will be Conservative enough to preserve everything that is good; Liberal enough to reform what is capable of being reformed; and Radical enough to uproot and destroy whatever is altogether wrong. I hope and expect to see something definite done at the annual meeting.

The concluding paragraph runs:

Ours is no old-fashioned sixpence-a-day agitation. We aim at the complete emancipation of the worker from the thraldom of wagedom. Co-operative production, under State management, should be our goal; as never till this has been obtained can we hope for better times for working people.

It will be seen from this Report that the Scottish Miners' National Federation was rather a propagandist association than the type of federal body that is usually signified by the term 'Federation of trade unions'. It was like a Scottish edition of the Miners' National Union which for seven years had retained little connection with its former Scottish affiliations. But there was no rivalry. Keir Hardie attended any United Kingdom conference whenever it was called from 1886 onwards, but after 1887 as representative only of Ayrshire. For the new Federation did not last out a couple of years. Its membership dwindled: and presently its name was known no more.

But the Federation of 1886–7 in its short-lived burst of activity had stimulated the growth of trade unionism. When it disappeared it left behind several new county unions. Thus apart from the Fife and Kinross Miners' Association formed in 1870, there were:

Amalgamated Section of Scottish Miners and Oilworkers (1886).
Ayrshire Miners' Union (1886).
Forth and Clyde Valley Miners' Association (1886).
Clackmannanshire Miners' Association (1887).
Mid and East Lothian Miners' Federation (1889).

In addition there was a number of local unions at Blantyre, Larkhall and other parts of the great Lanarkshire coal-field: but these were not yet federated and were not to join in a single county union until 1896. Information about the membership of these organisations is fragmentary. The minutes of various British miners' conferences over the period 1887–94, however, show that only the Fife organisation with 5000 to 6000 members could be called a really established union, able to pay regular affiliation fees: the others reporting between 1000 and 2000 members. When these successive conferences led to the formation of the new Miners' Federation of Great

Britain in 1889, Fife held aloof, and it was Chisholm Robertson (Forth and Clyde) and then Keir Hardie (Ayrshire) who
represented Scotland on the M.F.G.B. Executive.[1] The
Scottish organisations affiliated, however, showed considerable fluctuation, several making a fleeting appearance for a
year or so, and then dropping out.

2. THE SCOTTISH MINERS' FEDERATION

The victory of the English miners of the Federated area in
the great lock-out of August to November 1893 stimulated
a desire amongst each section of the Scots miners to have done
with the casual and fleeting association of the past few years
and to be linked up permanently with their English brethren.
Applications for affiliation from a number of county and
district unions in Scotland were considered by the M.F.G.B.
Executive, which suggested to the Scots that all the districts
in Scotland should form one Federation and then join the
M.F.G.B. in one body. The Scots delegates were willing: and
next day (January 17, 1894) the Annual Conference of the
M.F.G.B. agreed to accept the Scottish associations on this
condition. It was agreed that the Scots should call a Delegate
Conference of the different Scottish districts on January 31,
1894, to draft a constitution for the new Federation. The Scots
were as good as their word. Meetings were held. Each trade
union agreed and within another ten weeks the Federation
came into being.

The Scottish Miners' Federation as set up in March 1894
comprised all the then existing county and district unions
except that of the Shale Miners. The membership at the date
of formation was 26,783. The Federation was immediately
affiliated to the M.F.G.B. and this parenthood (together with
the objects of the M.F.G.B.) was set forth prominently in the
rule-book, preceding the rules themselves. The objects were:
To consider trade and wages questions; to secure mining legislation, the eight-hours day and proper compensation; and to
watch all public enquiries into accidents.

The rules provided for affiliation of county and district

---

[1] After 1890 Keir Hardie ceased to attend. He was elected M.P. for West Ham in 1892.

associations (but no section of a county, where a county association or federation existed, could affiliate). There were to be four officers, in addition to a management committee of at least five members elected at a yearly conference, and no officer or committee member could be elected if his organisation was more than two months in arrears. Voting at all conferences was to be by the number of members represented. The contribution was to be 1½d. per member per quarter. The provisions on strikes read as follows:

16. (a) That upon ten per cent. of the members of a district being involved in a dispute, a Conference shall be called immediately to consider the question, and if the Conference resolve that a stoppage of work should take place, Federation support shall be granted, according to Rule. (b) Where less than ten per cent. of the members of a district are affected by a dispute, such district shall, in the first place, deal with the case. In the event of the district agreeing to a stoppage of work, and such stoppage continuing for four weeks, a Conference shall be called at the request of said district, and upon the Conference endorsing the action of the district, the Federation shall be responsible for the future support and conducting of the dispute.

17. That the Conference shall have power to raise levies to enable the Federation to provide for cases of lock-out or of strike, and all levies shall be deemed arrears.

18. That in cases of lock-out or of strike the first week's payment shall fall due on the ninth day of the stoppage. The amount of the allowance shall be at the rate of seven shillings per member per week, or such other sum, less or more, as a special Conference shall decide upon.

Each organisation in the National Federation was to vote according to the will of the majority of its members, except on questions of national working policy, when a ballot was to be held and 'that policy adopted which has the largest number of votes throughout Scotland'.

3. WAGES

Wages throughout the great depression of the 'eighties had been very low all over the British coal-fields, but even lower in Scotland than in the rest of the country. Scottish wages were calculated on the basis of 1888, which was reckoned for coal-

getters at a figure of about 4s. a day. From the beginning of
1888 onwards, there was an improvement in trade. Advantage
was taken in the English coal-fields of this improvement in
trade and rise in coal prices to push up the level of wages. In
the central coal-fields of England, the joint wages movement
of nearly a dozen of the largest county and district associations
for wage-advances resulted in their staying together and in the
formation, as has been noted, in November 1889 of the
M.F.G.B. By the middle of 1890 they had secured a 40 per
cent rise on their 1888 basis, which was considerably higher
(well over a quarter higher) than the Scottish basis.

In Scotland, as far as changes in wage-rates were reckoned,
there were three main areas. In Lanarkshire a sliding scale
had been adopted in 1887, but had been terminated in 1889;
and thereafter, the changes in wage-rates applied to the
counties of Lanark, Ayr, Stirling, Dumbarton and Renfrew
which were all grouped together as West of Scotland. A
second division was Fife and Clackmannan. Mid and East
Lothian made the third division.

The downward tendency of hewers' wages, after the peak
years of 1890 and 1891, was interrupted in 1893. Profits were
growing and, in 1893, growing rapidly. There is little doubt,
however, that this was mainly due to the great lock-out of the
English Federated area, which enabled the Scottish coal-
owners that year to do good business. But with the resumption
of activity at the end of 1893 in the central coal-fields of
England, the amount of trade available (and it was dropping)
had to be competed for by all the coal-fields. It was certain,
therefore, that the employers in Scotland were likely to demand a reduction. The miners in Scotland had been greatly
cheered by the success of their English brethren in with-
standing for seventeen weeks the lock-out that ended in
November 1893. The English employers in the Federated
area had not succeeded in their demand for a 25 per cent
reduction, and the matter had been settled by the agreement
to establish a Conciliation Board.

Lanarkshire, by far the largest county in output, had most
of its district unions at this time linked together in a county
federation, and Robert Smillie (Secretary of the Larkhall
Miners' Association and Chairman of the County Federa-

tion), already showing promise of those characteristics which made him one of the most respected leaders, was President of the Scottish Miners' Federation. John Weir, Secretary of the Fife and Kinross Miners' Association, the only old-established county union dating back to 1870, became Treasurer, and R. Chisholm Robertson, Secretary of the Stirlingshire, Forth and Clyde Miners' Association, became Secretary. There was a tremendous contrast between these two men. John Weir, a douce ultra-respectable Fifer, was a well-known Liberal in politics, one of the early 'Lib-Lab' school whose policy in general dominated the mining areas of the country. Chisholm Robertson, on the other hand, was a stormy petrel in the Scottish mining areas. He had become a convert of Keir Hardie's and one of his most active supporters in the 1888 parliamentary election contest at Mid-Lanark. He was intolerant of 'Lib-Labs'. This intolerance led to bitter dissensions between him and the other leaders of the Scottish unions. His conduct on many occasions was questionable and ill-calculated to secure harmonious relations in the Scottish Executive. Latterly there were rumours and even accusations of 'Tory gold' being used by Robertson to bring about the defeat of Liberal candidates. But his position became more and more difficult—until he left Scotland for far-off Australia and passed out of the ken of the Scottish miners.

The new Scottish Federation was made up of county or district associations in each of which only a minority of the men employed were organised, and each of which had very little in the way of funds. What there was earlier had mostly been exhausted or brought very low by two strikes in the previous year. The Scottish employers were well aware of the condition of the units that had come together to form a Federation for the purpose of joint affiliation to the M.F.G.B. Within a few weeks, the West of Scotland employers had demanded a reduction of 25 per cent. In Fife they had asked for a reduction of 15 per cent. It was certain that in the third grouping, Mid and East Lothian, the employers would sooner or later take similar action. Faced with this, the Scots decided to see what help they could get from their English brethren. Accordingly, Robert Smillie was appointed to put the case before the Executive Committee of the M.F.G.B. at its next meeting, which was held in London on May 9, 1894. There, Smillie reported that there were 30,000 men idle in Scotland against a reduction in wages of a shilling per day or 25 per cent off the standard, and that, for the same reason, more men would be out the next day. In the districts affected (Lanark, Ayr, Stirling and West Lothian) the owners had refused to meet the miners' representatives. The unions were not very strong, but were gaining. On May 7 the Scottish Federation had met, and decided to advise the men to remain out until after the M.F.G.B. Executive meeting. The M.F.G.B. Executive decided to call a Special Conference on the Scottish dispute.

Pending the Special Conference of the M.F.G.B., the West of Scotland men went back to work. Thirty-five thousand had been out for five days. The Special M.F.G.B. Conference held at Carlisle on May 29–30, 1894, representing 200,000 miners, was attended by fifty delegates, of whom fourteen were Scots. These fourteen claimed to represent 31,500 union members in Scotland. Reports generally showed that trade was bad, with house-coal collieries in Yorkshire working only one and a half and two days a week, and other English counties ranging from two days up to five, with an average of three to four days per week. In Scotland, on the other hand, the reports showed also that although trade was bad in some parts, but nowhere so bad as the main English counties, in others it was fairly good.

In these circumstances, both in the Federated area of England and in Scotland, what policy was to be adopted? The M.F.G.B. had a quite definite and somewhat rigid principle of action: it gave support to any district which resisted reductions and it disaffiliated any district which failed to make a fight against reductions. Its watchword was 'An injury to one was an injury to all'. Any failure to fight against a reduction not only injured the district immediately affected, but was reckoned to be an injury to every other district, as it was a temptation to the coal-owners in these other districts to make an attack on wages. This policy of mutual aid was now applied in the case of Scotland. Accordingly, W. Parrott of Yorkshire moved, and Tom Greenall of Lancashire seconded, the following resolution:

That all districts belonging to this Federation where reductions in wages have recently taken place, be requested to give a proper notice for the same to be returned; and we are favourable to a levy being made to support them. (May 30, 1894.)

John Weir said that the Scottish delegates had decided to recommend the men to strike, would do their utmost to bring the men out, but could not promise great things; and if they did not come out to the expectations of the Federation the men would be blamed, not the leaders. Robert Brown, Secretary of the Mid and East Lothian Miners' Association, said: 'the Scotsmen are very indignant against the reduction, and if they do not fight now they never will'. Robert Smillie said they had already agreed to fight.

We will go back and ask the men to come out and fight. We will not say that the British Federation will find them support, but we will tell them that unless they come out and fight, their leaders cannot go back to the Federation. We shall at once take a ballot, and if the ballot is favourable, will then give notice where required.

The ballot was taken in the first week of June, and, as John Weir reported to the M.F.G.B. Executive Committee on June 15, resulted in 25,617 for strike; 14,490 against, a majority of 11,127. For the first time, and as the result of a ballot vote, all the Scots miners would be on strike at once.

4. THE STRIKE BEGINS

On Tuesday, June 26, 1894, the Scottish miners came out on strike. On the first day there were over 60,000 on strike and within a few days thereafter over 70,000. Of these, little more than 30,000 were members of the union. Thus, in every district except Fife, where the old-established county union had organised a majority of about two-thirds of its 10,000 miners, union members were in a minority: the average was one union man to every two non-union men.

In these circumstances, it was a remarkable testimony to the solidarity of feeling amongst the Scots miners and of their new-found determination to resist the shilling reduction, that all should have come out on strike together. It was also a demonstration of their faith in the power of the M.F.G.B. which had so successfully withstood demands for reductions in a period of falling trade. Few of those who came out on strike, without any guarantee of support for their wives and families, and in most cases without resources of their own other than a weekly wage, can have imagined that they were entering on a struggle that would go on for month after month. It meant that, amongst the trade unionist minority and the non-unionist majority alike, the traditions of the struggles carried on for over fifty years were strong enough to inspire them all to embark on what an outsider might have thought a hopeless endeavour.

But precisely this overwhelmingly strong proportion of non-unionists among the strikers gave rise to immediate difficulties. The M.F.G.B. had agreed to call levies to support the strike, by which they certainly meant the strike of the 30,000 trade unionists. Thomas Ashton, the M.F.G.B. Secretary, as soon as the news of the strike ballot had come through, had called on June 15 for a 6d. levy.

A week after the Scottish strike had begun, R. Chisholm Robertson wrote to the M.F.G.B. pointing out the over-whelming number of non-unionists on strike and the urgent need to give them also financial support to continue the struggle; a 6d. levy would not, in his opinion, meet the case. Secondly, he asked for a National Miners' Conference to be called and held in Scotland, where they could have first-hand information, and take part in demonstrations in the largest centres 'to encourage the miners to act properly at this momentous crisis'. The M.F.G.B. Executive discussed this letter very fully, and came to the conclusion that they could not take any steps about what should be given to non-unionists; but they did decide not only to send off the amount of the first levy (which was £5600) and to approve Thomas Ashton's action in having called a second 6d. levy; but decided also that the third levy be 1s. per member, 'and the same be called weekly'.

Meanwhile a problem had arisen in Scotland as to how the money received from the M.F.G.B. levy was to be divided among the men on strike, unionists and non-unionists. The M.F.G.B. decided that the various districts in the Scottish

Federation should receive the funds in proportion to the number of trade union members, not the number of men on strike.

A Special Conference for all districts in England, Scotland and Wales was held in the Primitive Methodist Schoolroom, Prudhoe Street, Newcastle-on-Tyne, and brought together nearly a hundred representatives of 284,000 miners in trade unions. Out of a number employed of 464,000, there was thus a trade unionist proportion of some 63 per cent. Of course, not all coal-fields were represented. Nobody came from South Wales; nor from Somerset, which, having accepted a reduction, had been at once excluded from the M.F.G.B. The total number of underground workers at this time (for these alone in the main were catered for by the trade unions) was 555,000. Sam Woods, who was another of the 'Lib-Lab' Members of Parliament, the Vice-President of the M.F.G.B., took the chair on the first day, which began with a closed session on the strike in Scotland. Smillie explained the situation, gave the figures of 70,000 on strike, of whom 30,000 were trade unionists; and that 'they were never so unanimous before as in this struggle, and they were determined to struggle on until some arrangement could be made which would be acceptable to the Federation of Great Britain'. Muir, successor to Keir Hardie as Secretary of the Ayrshire Miners' Federal Union, said that twelve months before not one-half of the present number in his county were members of the union; but looking to the future, they had decided to pay all round. Weir said that in Fife they had not recognised non-unionists, but wanted to help them as far as possible. This question of the unionists and non-unionists cut across the discussion and across the resolution moved by Harvey of Derbyshire, seconded by Chambers of Leicester:

This Conference, after hearing the reports from Scotland with regard to the Scotch strike, considers it to be the duty of all mining counties in England and Wales to render them all financial help possible; and trusts that it will be sufficient to enable them to contend for what we consider their just rights; and would recommend those outside the Federation to pay one shilling levy per member per week, along with the Federation members. (July 12, 1894.)

This was carried unanimously. So Smillie gratefully said:

'What we have heard will send us back with brighter hope and with doubled effort to win the struggle. The men and the women as well are as determined as ever to persevere.' It was understood that the M.F.G.B. would pay for members only, but it was left to each Scottish district or county 'to dispose of the funds so paid from the Federation as, according to the judgment of each Executive of each district, they may think best'.

5. NEW SIGNALS FROM ENGLAND

The strike had gone on for a little over four weeks when there took place in England a change in wages which was to have a big effect on the Scottish struggle. The Board of Conciliation for the Coal Trade of the Federated Districts, which had not been fully constituted for half a year after the Rosebery Settlement of the great English lock-out of August to November 1893, had at last met and on July 19 had agreed on a 10 per cent reduction in wages from August 1, 1894. Wages were to remain at this new level till January 1, 1896, after which they could not fall, but might vary upwards to 45 per cent above standard during the life of the Board which would last till August 1, 1896. The Miners' Federation leaders, having maintained wages at 40 per cent above standard for four years, in the latter part of which trade was declining, had now no alternative to accepting a cut of 10 per cent; but at the same time they had prevented any further reduction in the following seventeen months.

Clearly, this would have an effect on the Scottish struggle. For the M.F.G.B. policy was to maintain a measure of uniformity in wages: and they could not very easily accept a reduction in England and at the same time call levies and pour out money to resist a similar reduction in Scotland. On the other hand, the Scottish coal-masters had enforced a much bigger reduction than the English masters in the Federated area. The M.F.G.B. leaders could therefore, and indeed must therefore, in accordance with their policy, support the Scots in a struggle for uniformity.

Would there be any possibility of persuading the Scottish

coal-owners to follow the same path as the English coal-owners? It seemed to them worth trying. They approached the Scottish owners, who, however, refused to have any dealings whatever with the M.F.G.B. The British Executive thereupon advised the Scots that wherever the men on strike in Scotland could settle at any colliery for a return to work on the lines of the settlement made by the English Conciliation Board (i.e. 6d. a day reduction, instead of 1s. a day) they should do so, and the Scottish leaders were requested to advocate this policy. But instead of the Scottish vessel following the signals from the British flagship and making a tack to windward, the navigators burst into a long and heated discussion among themselves. Eventually, after bitter argument, the majority of the Scottish Executive took the decision to

Recommend to the Miners of Scotland the advisability of conforming to the advice of the Executive of the Federation of the Miners of Great Britain by accepting the minimum wage for a period of eighteen months—this wage to be the rate ruling at the time the strike began, with half the late reduction of one shilling per day restored.

They believed that a considerable number of owners would settle for 6d., and in any case they believed that the new tactics were best.

Secretary Chisholm Robertson stood out against this. He insisted that the fight should be for the full amount; and he savagely attacked those who had accepted the M.F.G.B. recommendation; and he was even more violent in his denunciation of the officials of the M.F.G.B. But while he was almost alone on the Scottish Federation Executive Committee, he had considerable support among the men, and was, moreover, a more practised orator than any of his colleagues. A miners' conference in August rejected the Executive's proposals and decided to continue on strike for the shilling, and to inform the M.F.G.B. that they would not budge until the owners agreed to a meeting.

When the M.F.G.B. came to consider this, they also had to consider a number of press reports of speeches by Chisholm Robertson, not only advocating a contrary policy, but attacking the M.F.G.B. Executive. The M.F.G.B. thereupon sent a delegation to attend the next Scottish Conference,

BLANTYRE NO. 2 PIT, LANARKSHIRE, 1953

NEWCRAIGHALL COLLIERY, LOTHIANS, 1953

as a result of which a ballot was to be held for or against the
M.F.G.B. policy of an offer to the owners to accept the Conciliation Board terms. The delegation reported that the other
agents were quite willing to advise their men to carry out the
Federation policy, but Chisholm Robertson was reported only
the day before the conference, at a mass meeting at Coatbridge, to have described the M.F.G.B.'s action as 'a brazen-
faced piece of impertinence', designed 'to make it impossible
for them to gain the result for which they had been suffering
for nine weeks'.

When the M.F.G.B. Executive received this report, and also
learned, according to Ashton's record, that 'the Scottish
Miners' Federation were very much dissatisfied with the
actions of Mr. Chisholm Robertson the Acting Secretary',
they took the unusual step of refusing to recognise him as
Secretary, and deciding to send all further communications
on the dispute to the President.

The ballot resulted in reversing the men's previous decision
by about 4000, and a further conference agreed to carry on
the fight on the basis laid down by the British Federation.
Meanwhile settlements had been made with one or two small
employers. The M.F.G.B. Executive therefore decided to urge
the Scottish owners to settle on the basis of this compromise;
meantime the levy to assist Scotland should be continued and
a Special M.F.G.B. Conference called to consider the dispute.

By the middle of September, when the strike had lasted
over eleven weeks, things began to take a turn for the worse.
The use of the police by the authorities at the instance of
the mine-owners was now more open and unrestrained than
before. On this a vivid contemporary comment was made by
Keir Hardie, now an M.P., in the *Labour Leader* which he
edited.

The Miners' Strike has entered on a new phase. The police have
been invoked on the side of the masters, and right brutally are they
performing their task. . . . The authorities, seeing the apparent
helplessness of the miners' plight, have yielded to the solicitations of
the employers and brought the forces of law and order into play in
the interest of property. In the first instance the authorities brought
policemen from Lancashire when there was not the slightest indications of disturbance. The very sight of these men was a source of
irritation; but when, prompted probably by their superiors, they

commenced to wantonly bludgeon peaceful and unoffending strikers, as we can prove was the case, some measure of retaliation was inevitable.

Keir Hardie then recounted what had happened in districts of Lanarkshire:

At Coalburn, the pickets were informed by the police that they were on private ground, whereupon they turned to go away. Meeting another picket going in the same direction, they stopped them to warn them not to proceed further. While so doing, the police swooped down upon them, plying their batons unmercifully. . . .

Sixteen men playing in a band in a field near Motherwell were charged by four mounted and a large number of foot police and beat unmercifully. Here is a quotation from the *Mail* report:

> One poor soul at the time the processionists were chased at the Logan Rows, and the police laying on him with their staves, he all the while crying, 'Oh, for God's sake, have mercy on us'. The English policemen were shouting 'Get out of this, you Scotch b——s'.

We ask the working men of the country how long they will tolerate this state of affairs? A handful of men claim the mines, the minerals and everything else besides. They reduce the wages of 70,000 colliers is. per day, leaving them less than one pound per week for their labour. The colliers ask for a Conciliation Board to decide whether the proposed reduction is justifiable, and the reply is three months of starvation, concluding with scenes like those above described. Nothing save a nation of cowards would tolerate such proceedings, and our great regret is that the miners were not prepared to give as good as they got in these *mêlées*.

Keir Hardie demanded a 'full, searching and impartial inquiry' into the whole proceedings, and ended his editorial with these words:

We demand that the workers shall, as in the sight of heaven, enter into a covenant, one with the other to know no rest nor slumber till the last vestige of the hateful system which enslaves them and ranges the power of the community against them has been swept away for ever. (September 22, 1894.)

6. THE M.F.G.B. MEETS AT EDINBURGH

In the three weeks before the Special Conference of the M.F.G.B. met at Edinburgh on Thursday and Friday,

September 27 and 28, the strike struggle had been weakened by defections in the ranks following on the quarrels between the leaders. Between one-fifth and one-sixth of the men who had been out had returned to work on the employers' terms, were 'working blackleg'. The dissensions among the leaders, more bitter than before, were played upon by the hostile press, and had proved an additional factor in the falling off of the levies from the English districts.

At the conference, Smillie reported on the facts of the Scottish strike, pointing out that the press reports were deliberately misleading. For ten weeks the strike had been practically solid. Now 2500 men were working on the Federation terms, 10,000 were working blackleg, leaving 55,000 in the field who had not gone back to work. He explained also that they had approached the owners, on the Federation's advice, four months previously, but the owners refused. A month before the Special Conference a meeting had been held with eight or nine non-associated coal-masters. The miners offered to return on the Federation terms, but the employers would only discuss the owners' terms. They offered, however, if the men went back on their terms, to try and get a Conciliation Board formed, and to guarantee no further wage reduction till the next year.

After this the Chairman of the conference read the M.F.G.B. policy resolution (of August 7—see earlier, page 80) which recommended the Scots to settle wherever they could with coal-owners to resume work on the Federation terms (i.e. 6d. a day reduction, but *not* 1s. a day). These Federation terms had been finally adopted by the Scots on August 31. A meeting thereafter had been arranged with the non-associated coal-owners. Then on September 12, an anonymous circular had been passed round the coal-fields repudiating the Federation terms. Immediately Chisholm Robertson was charged by John Wilson of Broxburn as being the author of the document, a charge which led to accusations and counter-accusations, embittering more than ever the relations between Robertson and the majority of the Executive Committee.

Smillie then spoke again. He said that the Scottish Delegate Conference of a day earlier (Wednesday, September 26) had resolved to recommend to the M.F.G.B. 'the absolute necessity of keeping the Scottish Miners on strike until the Federation terms are conceded'. He referred to the fact that at the Carlisle Conference four months earlier, some very hard things were said about the organisation and fighting power of the Scots miners. 'And Mr. Parrott said something about the Scotch leaders—that they could talk and that was all they could do—they couldn't organise.'

We promised, at that time, *to do our level best to bring them out,* and to fight the battle to a successful issue. In no country in the world before have 70,000 men been brought out, 40,000 of them non-unionists, and for eleven weeks no black-legging whatever....

Our men are determined to continue fighting if they can be kept from starving. I have done something to keep the battle going on and to obtain the Federation terms; but I believe you all feel, after your seventeen weeks' experience last year, that there is a point beyond which human endurance cannot go, and we know that it has almost been reached in the Scotch strike. You know, as we know, and the public know, the Scotch miners were not prepared with funds to fight with. They had nothing to begin with, and unfortunately they had not big banking accounts to draw upon.... They are prepared to go on fighting if it is possible for the English Miners and trade-unionists to say 'We are prepared to keep you from starvation so long as you continue this struggle'.

This speech had the immediate practical result that the English delegates proceeded to give reports district by district as to the amount of help they had given and hoped to give. Parrott of Yorkshire told first how the previous year's lock-out had left many of them in debt, and how trade had been bad; and then said:

Thousands of our men have during the summer months only been working one or two days a week. In some cases after they had paid their sick clubs and other things they had very little left to find food with. But although they have done so badly, they have done their best to pay the shilling levy in order that your women and children should have some bread during this severe war. I want you to remember this, especially those of you who have thought that the Miners' Federation has not done much.

On the morrow the Scots delegates, having met in the meantime and discussed the matter in view of the reports from the English districts, moved:

That the British Miners' Federation, recognising the absolute necessity of keeping the Scottish miners on strike until the Federation
terms are conceded—these terms being half of the last reduction of
one shilling per day, and that such wages remain for two years;
reaffirm its former resolution to secure for them all possible support
over the area of the British Federation. (September 28, 1894.)

After some discussion the resolution was put and carried
unanimously. Robert Smillie, President of the Scottish
Federation, then moved the following resolution:

That this Conference of the British Federation, in view of a solution of the Scottish Coal Strike, permits the Scottish Federation to
enter into provisional agreements with any owners who may be willing to grant the terms of the Federation—restoration of the half of
the last reduction with a two years' guarantee—in the event of the
majority of the owners granting the above terms.

After this had been seconded by Robert Brown of Mid and
East Lothian, Chisholm Robertson moved an amendment:

That in accordance with the decision of the Scottish Miners' Conference, and with the terms fixed by the Miners' Federation of Great
Britain, no conditional guarantee shall be approved of by this Conference to be accepted by the Miners at any colliery in Scotland as a
settlement of the present Strike.

Fifty-four votes were recorded for the resolution and four for
the amendment. The policy was now settled, both as regards
support from the English districts and as regards tactics.
The last business of the conference was to discuss a resolution regretting the 'wild and reckless speeches of Mr. R. C.
Robertson, reflecting on the M.F.G.B. and on its leaders',
and formally endorsing the Executive's action against him.
This was moved by Ned Cowey of Yorkshire, who quoted
some of the statements complained of:

'I do not know', Mr. Robertson says, 'if the Englishmen stop
sending us their miserable pittance of one shilling and one and threepence a week, then the Lord help us and have mercy upon us.' A
greater insult could not have been given to men who have been paying as our men have been paying. . . . I visited 10,000 men the other
week, who had worked eight days in eleven weeks in Yorkshire, men
who were going home with 4s. a week and paying one and sixpence
a week out of it, and then were told it was their 'miserable pittance'.

Chisholm Robertson defended himself savagely and a highly

acrimonious debate followed, in the course of which he called John Weir 'a white-livered liar' and Weir replied in the same strain. A compromise amendment to hold a ballot vote of the Scottish miners on Robertson's conduct was defeated, and the resolution was carried by a vote of 48 to 3.

So ended the Edinburgh Conference of the M.F.G.B., which despite the dissensions and personalities amongst a number of the Scottish delegates, registered considerable progress in the development of organisation in Scotland as well as in England.

7. THE STRIKE ENDS

When the Executive Committee of the M.F.G.B. met a fortnight later, telegrams received by its secretary Ashton showed that the strike in the West of Scotland had collapsed. John Weir reported that on Monday, October 8, at a meeting of the Scottish Federation it had been decided to ballot the men still on strike on the question of resuming work or continuing the strike. The Fife miners had held a meeting on Tuesday, October 9, but refused to ballot and decided to continue the strike. He thought there would be about 10,000 miners in Scotland who would still continue to fight. After hearing this the Executive resolved:

1. That this meeting cannot see its way to allocate any further money to districts where the bulk of the men have resumed work, but in those districts where the bulk of the men have not resumed work, we continue to grant assistance; whilst at the same time leave whatever arrangements are made in the hands of the Scottish trade unions.

2. That each district continue to get all the levies they can for the Scotch miners on strike.

By that time £74,551 : 13 : 7 had been forwarded by the Federation; and from levies received later, another sum of £1500 was sent by decision of the Executive Committee at the end of the first week in November 'for disposal in the various districts to assist them in carrying on the work of the Scottish Federation'. The strike in Scotland had lasted on in Fife for a fortnight after the rest of Scotland, but by October 22 they too had gone back to work. In this area, the strike had lasted for seventeen weeks.

After the strike was over Keir Hardie published an article in the *Labour Leader* on October 20, 1894, headed 'A Friendly Chat with the Scotch Miners', in which he wrote:

Why have fifty mineowners power to starve 70,000 miners into submission?

I want to try and help you to find an answer to this question. But first of all let us go over in detail what you were contending for. Six months ago the wages of miners in the West of Scotland ranged from 5s. 3d. to 6s. for the 'masters' darg'. The 'masters' darg' is the number of tons or cwts. which the masters admit to be a full day's work for a collier and varies according to the thickness of the seam of the coal. The average number of days being worked by you did not exceed four per week and this through no fault of your own.

Thus your gross earnings averaged from 21s. to 24s. per week, from which, deductions for pick sharping, oil, powder, etc. fell to be made. About midsummer, the masters took a shilling per day off your wages which brought them down to 17s. and 20s. and you came on strike to have the shilling restored and also to have a Conciliation Board formed to settle disputes. Both these demands were resisted by the employers, whereupon you, unwisely as I think, agreed to modify your wages demand and accept 6d. and a Conciliation Board. But your employers refused this also, and in the end you were defeated.

Clearly, Keir Hardie considered that his old associate Chisholm Robertson had been right in opposing the policy of the English leaders. He went on to answer the fundamental question posed at the opening of this article.

All through the strike the forces of the law were used to protect black-legs and to imprison and fine those who even dared to look at them, or say boo to them. Honest Labour struggling for a living wage, was batoned and imprisoned whilst black-legs were protected and glorified into the saviours of Society. The Press of the Country was against you and day by day published exaggerated reports about men going to work, in the hope of inducing you to do the same. The Government, when appealed to, either pleaded that it could do nothing, or took the side of your opponents. The pulpit—when it did not openly take the side of the masters—was with few exceptions, hostile to you. To sum up:—on one side were the miners, their wives and children; on the other, fighting against you, were hunger, the masters, the law, backed by policemen and soldiers, the Government, the press and the pulpit all arrayed against you. There is but one answer.

All these are rich and you are poor.

Mindful from his own experience and from a half-century's

history in Lanarkshire and Ayrshire of the danger of defeat turning into rout, Hardie ended as a trade union leader should, with a warning to close the ranks. To this he added (what few miners' leaders would then have done) a final argument for independent labour representation.

Just one word in conclusion. Don't forget your trade union. Nothing can absolve you from your duty to your union. Be a consistent member; pay your contributions regularly; loyally carry out the decisions of the union. But after you have done all this, carry your principles to their logical conclusion by acting politically as you do industrially. It is foolish to form a union to fight the coalmasters and then send one of these masters or his friend to make laws for you. The class which makes the laws can do as it pleases. . . .

This summing up of the great strike of 1894 by Keir Hardie, then almost at the peak of his powers as a writer (and before he had begun to be influenced by Ramsay MacDonald), showed how he could combine acute trade union perceptions with socialist argumentation, and at the same time drive home his immediate objective of independent working-class representation in Parliament. Just as the final word on the great English lock-out of 1893 was given by William Morris writing on 'The Deeper Meaning of the Struggle', so Keir Hardie gave the needed final word on the great Scottish strike of 1894.

CHAPTER V

CONCILIATION ON TRIAL

I. AFTERMATH OF THE GREAT STRIKE

BY the end of October 1894, the miners in every part of Scotland had gone back to work—in most cases on the employers' terms. By the end of December 1894, percentage wage-rates above the level of 'the 1888 basis' (roughly 4s. a day) had gone down in Lanarkshire by 25 per cent (i.e. roughly 1s. a shift), in the Lothians by 20 per cent (nearly 10d. a shift) and Fife by 12½ per cent (or about 6d. a shift) from the heights of 50 per cent and 40 per cent at the beginning of the year. The county unions and districts had no funds. The miners, unionists and non-unionists, had come out on strike together, but now, defeated in the struggle and cast into disarray by the dissensions of the leaders, they suffered an inevitable set-back. Trade union membership fell rapidly in 1895. At the end of 1895 and in 1896 the employers made further slashing cuts in wages, and trade union membership fell further. It seemed as though the Scottish miners were in a vicious spiral of wage-cuts and falling union membership; and all the while the total number of both underground and surface workers was growing and with it the Scottish output of coal. It is true that trade union membership in these years suffered a fall in all the British coal-fields, but a comparison with the M.F.G.B. figures shows that its Scottish unit had suffered far more severely than the average.

Year	Scottish Miners' Federation	Miners' Federation of Great Britain
1894	35,900	185,126
1895	20,920	161,971
1896	17,950	155,436
1897	15,700	148,562

Scotland had been poorly organised in 1894, when much

less than half of the underground workers were in the unions. By the end of 1897, less than a fifth of these were organised. In that year the outlook might have seemed bleak, but there were reasons for hope. In the first place, the Scots miners had struggled together as one force, and the memory of that fellowship in struggle could not be extinguished, and what had been done once could be done again. Secondly, they had fought as part of the M.F.G.B., had been supported by it, and in the fire of the struggle had fully grasped the fact that the common interests of the coal-miners in all parts of Britain called for unity and for trade union organisation representing that unity; and that whoever played upon national feelings to separate or to set them against their English or Welsh brethren were playing the game of the employers. Thirdly, the feud with Chisholm Robertson and his Stirlingshire or Forth and Clyde Union, though disastrous enough in all conscience,[1] had the positive effect of drawing the other unions closer together and overcoming the age-long difference between the East and West of Scotland. Fourthly, the strike experience in the biggest of the Scottish coal-fields had taught the miners there the need for better organisation and closer unity; and the process that had begun when the Lanarkshire Miners' County Federation came together in 1893 as a rather weak link between the districts was now to be carried forward into the creation for the first time of a Lanarkshire County Union.

2. LANARKSHIRE ORGANISES

All the coal-fields of Scotland were expanding during the nineteenth century, but Lanarkshire more than any other.

[1] At the end of 1895 Chisholm Robertson's Forth and Clyde Valley Association dropped out of the S.M.F. as a result of a dispute about excess expenditure of strike pay; a little later William Webb, the new Secretary, applied for readmission, and this was granted in 1896 on the understanding that charges that the Scottish Executive had dealt hardly with these members were withdrawn. But Chisholm Robertson, now irreconcilable, continued the feud and ran a rival association for several years. The end came in 1900, with a debate between Robertson and Smillie at successive meetings of the Glasgow Trades Council on the question: 'Is R. Chisholm Robertson a proper person to occupy the position of President, Glasgow Trades Council, or act as official in any respectable Trades Union?' Smillie won the debate. A verbatim report, entitled *The Smillie-Chisholm Robertson Controversy*, was printed in 25,000 copies by the Scottish Miners' Federation. Fifty years later, old miners remembered Robertson with detestation—except in Stirlingshire, where his personality was still recalled with admiration.

Here had been the centre of Alexander McDonald's work. Here he had given his best towards the organising of the miners, agitating and educating wherever he went. But while thriving districts grew up in Lanarkshire, loosely linked together in conferences of district delegates, some-times under the auspices of the nominally existing Scottish Coal and Iron Miners' Association, there was never a county union. Glasgow, at that time, as well as being an engineering and shipbuilding centre, could also be described as a pro-sperous coal-field. It became the centre for Renfrew, Dum-barton, Stirling and especially for the Lower Ward (the north) of Lanarkshire. When this early form of organisation went under in the late 'seventies, there was nothing to take its place. While Fife had remained continuously as an organised nucleus with its county union ever since 1870, and while the brief revival led by Keir Hardie in 1886 had brought with it county unions in Ayr, West Lothian, Stirling and, in 1887, Clackmannan, to be followed by Mid and East Lothian in 1889, in Lanarkshire it was different. Local unions had come to life again in 1886. But these were not all of them simply revivals of the older district unions of Lanarkshire. Some of them were in the Upper Ward; while in the Lower Ward, its fitful organisation was undertaken sometimes by the other Lanarkshire districts and sometimes by the Forth and Clyde (Stirlingshire) Union. The lack of effective continuing organi-sation in Lanarkshire was the crucial weakness of the Scottish coal-fields.

The pioneers of these new local unions of the 'eighties had been such men as Andrew McAnulty of the Blantyre Miners' Association (one of the stalwarts who lived to see a single union for all the Scottish miners) and Robert Smillie of the Larkhall Miners' Association. Others of a similar character took the lead in the miners' associations of Bellshill, Hamilton, Holytown and Shotts. But it was not a miner who was the moving spirit in bringing about organisation through the county as a whole: it was William Small, a shopkeeper, one of the early socialists, who was particularly concerned with the fearful exploitation to which the miners were subjected.

There is no man that earned such esteem among the miners of Lanarkshire. As a socialist agitator he understood fully the importance of trade union organisation. He set himself the task to educate as far as he possibly could the miners with the new ideas that were beginning to spread amongst the working class as a whole, and even as he taught them to organise them. While organising them he acted as their representative and carried on all their correspondence with the mine-owners and with the Home Office. He had carried on this arduous work for years before the Lanarkshire Miners' County Federation was formed in 1893, when he was immediately chosen as its first Secretary, on a salary of two pounds a week. The Lanarkshire Miners' County Federation began in the latter part of 1893. By June 1894 it had thirteen fully functioning units: and by the end of 1894 there were twenty-one. It was his work, together with that of Smillie, McAnulty and the other younger men, that built up the Lanarkshire Federation into something more than a name and made it the foundation for a county union. William Small was the teacher, instructor and guide of a generation of the young lions of Lanarkshire.

In 1896 Robert Smillie was appointed agent for Lanarkshire with a view to the formation of a county union, the local unions in Lanarkshire being favourable; and the new county union was soon in being. The collieries in Dunbartonshire which had been part of the Lanarkshire Federation, however, now formed themselves into a small separate county union, the Kirkintilloch and Twechar Miners' Association. Smillie too was a socialist, and on terms of the closest comradeship with Keir Hardie all his life. It was amazing during this period the number of meetings that were held in the miners' villages of Lanarkshire. Night after night, whatever the weather, one or other of these young ardent socialists was on the job. But not only were there speeches: pamphlets and periodicals and in particular Keir Hardie's *Labour Leader* were widely circulated and eagerly read by the miners. Thus while the older established and at that time better organised East of Scotland remained strongly Liberal, in the West, especially in Lanarkshire, it was socialist enthusiasm and agitation that went hand in hand with trade union struggles to build up the new organisation.

Of what nature were these local unions, or in some cases,

district unions, which were thus linked up in the Lanarkshire Miners' County Federation? In most cases they were not pit unions, but unions based on a small mining town that had grown up within walking distance of two or three, or as many as twelve to fifteen pits. In the latter case, of course, as organisation grew better, there would be a tendency to have not one but two or three miners' lodges in that same locality. The active leaders of the Lanarkshire Miners sought to have those who would be a focus of trade unionism chosen as checkweighers. The owners, well aware of this, would often put difficulties in the way of such elections; and for many years the miners felt a serious grievance, both that the law as regarded checkweighers was not clear enough and required to be amended, and secondly, that insufficient as it was, the law was not in practice carried out. Thus one of the preoccupations of these local unions, and later of the county unions, was the struggle over the election of checkweighers. It may be worth noting here that the present President of the Scottish miners (Abe Moffat) was himself a checkweigher and was removed from his position by the action of the Fife Coal Company who used the law to have him interdicted from anywhere on or near the pit.

3. THE SCOTS AND SOCIALISM

The Leicester Annual Conference of the M.F.G.B. in 1897 is of particular interest because it was there that the strong and vocal Scottish delegation (ten out of fifty-four delegates) clashed sharply with the older leaders on the issue of Socialism. The Scots all heard Ben Pickard, in his presidential address, lay down the rules and principles of the Federation. After emphasising the rule on strike policy as the sheet-anchor of the Federation, he referred to 'the principle of the living wage' and said that the Federation was against a sliding scale, 'neither does it believe in a Wages Board working under similar conditions to a Sliding Scale; or where it has an independent Chairman to step in between the two parties with power to determine what the wages of the workmen shall be'. Then Pickard declared in his concluding remarks that he was against several of the motions that had come from Scotland. Very sternly he warned the delegates that at this conference they had to decide 'whether or not we are to work under a new law of Socialism instead of the old principles of Trade Unionism'. Yes, it was the case, the Scottish Federation with about one-tenth of the total M.F.G.B. membership, had sent in full half of the motions on the week's Agenda; and amongst them the most contentious. This was the socialistic proposal:

That to secure the best conditions of industrial and social life it is absolutely necessary that the Land, Minerals, Railways, and instruments of wealth production should be owned and controlled by the State for the people.

This was moved by John Wilson of Broxburn. After Smillie had seconded, 'iron-man' Pickard (speaking as a delegate) opposed, and then Ned Cowey moved the following motion from Yorkshire as an amendment:

That representatives to the Federation Conferences and all Congresses act on Trade Union lines as in the past, and not on Socialistic lines. (January 6, 1897.)

Cowey and his supporters mainly argued that, while not utterly opposed to Socialism ('I am a Socialist to a certain extent, but I am a " possibilist ". . . . If possible and practicable, I am willing to bend every nerve I have got to carry it, but I am not willing to expend my strength for nought'), he felt the trade unions had enough to do and that the motion was 'impracticable'. Seven out of the ten Scots spoke in the debate, amongst them James Cook of Clackmannan, who, although now retired, still takes a lively interest in all that affects the life and well-being of the miners. Only John Weir from Fife was in mild opposition to his brother Scots on this matter.

The animus of the Yorkshire amendment was made clear by Pickard both in a presidential speech before the vote ('it has been admitted in this Conference that this resolution is the core of the Independent Labour Party as enunciated by its leaders, and we have had gentlemen saying in here yesterday that they will support that rather than support trade

unionism') and also in a heated intervention earlier which
is recorded in the minutes as follows:

THE PRESIDENT: It was stated—and I may as well give the place—
it was at Rothwell in Yorkshire—that Trade Unionism was played
out, and that we have to look to Socialism for any good in the future.

A DELEGATE: That is an individual opinion.

MR. COWEY: It was given among our members.

THE PRESIDENT: I am not going to blame Mr. Keir Hardie, but he
laid down the principle.

MR. SMILLIE: Did Keir Hardie lay down that principle?

THE PRESIDENT: You know he did.

MR. SMILLIE: I know he did not. He is as good a Trade Unionist as
there is in this place.

THE PRESIDENT: I don't want to compete with Mr. Keir Hardie as
a Trade Unionist. All I can say is—if Mr. Keir Hardie is a better
Trade Unionist than any man in this room, we all ought to follow
him.

MR. SMILLIE: I did not say better.

THE PRESIDENT: Yes, you did. I say Mr. Hardie and Mr. Tom
Mann have laid down manifestoes before to-day, and those men, too,
who are connected with your 'Clarion'—they have laid down the
principle that Trade Unionism is played out.

MR. GREENALL (Lancashire): It is not true. Tom Mann has never
laid down the principle. I unhesitatingly say that no one can prove
that Tom Mann said so.

THE PRESIDENT: It appears it is not Trade Unionism we are debating; we are debating now individual opinions.

MR. GREENALL: Let us not mind Tom Mann and Keir Hardie.

THE PRESIDENT: Look here, some of you are followers of him, and
when a delegate tells you that his man is as good or better Trade
Unionist than any man in this room, I say follow him if he is. Don't
follow any man in this room, or any number of them. Go preach your
doctrines where they are more acceptable. I believe in Trade Unionism, and I believe I am as good a Socialist as any man outside who
cries down Trade Unionism. I am making a statement which is true,
as those who have read the manifestoes from time to time can verify.
I am not a manifesto man, telling everybody my society is better than
everybody else's. All I can say is, if this is the Socialistic idea of how
we should debate and carry on our business, I want us to be saved
from it as a Federation.

MR. COWEY: I want to know, are we not here as Trade Unionists?
(Cries of 'Yes'.) Then what has Socialism to do with this business?
Who pays our wages? Trade Unionism. Every man here is paid from
Trade Unionism, and paid to come here as a Trade Unionist, there-
fore Socialism has no footing here. (A Delegate: Where do you
separate them?) Trade Unionism is Trade Unionism, and Socialism

is Socialism. They are two different factions, and it is a hard thing to serve God and Mammon.

The Scottish resolution was overwhelmingly defeated by 137,000 to 18,000 while the Yorkshire amendment (now voted on as a separate motion) was carried by 134,000 to 21,000. But the delegates wanted to make it clear that they were opposed at that time only to the last portion of the Scottish Resolution ('and instruments of wealth production should be owned, etc.') and so they proceeded to vote by 97,000 against 6000 for the Lancashire and Cheshire motion that 'In the opinion of this Federation it is essential for the maintenance of British Industries to Nationalise the Land, Mines, Mineral Royalties, and Railways of this country'. Yorkshire on this abstained from voting. Throughout all this discussion it was clear that while some of the 'Lib-Lab' leaders were bitterly anti-Socialist, others were of the opinion that until organisation in the coal-fields, especially the Scottish coal-field, was better developed, it was premature for the Miners' Federation of Great Britain to try for any further aims than those already set down in its rules and objects.

4. A NEW ERA

The end of the nineteenth and the beginning of the present century marked significant changes. At the beginning of the reign of Victoria 'free competition' had been the feature of industry as a whole, and this had continued through the times that are called mid-Victorian. It was the heyday of competitive capitalism. In the last quarter of the nineteenth century there had been increasing signs of change, with the growth of larger and larger units in one industry after another as well as in the banks and the consequent squeezing out or subordination of the smaller competitors. Monopoly was growing. Monopoly conditions meant the weakening or disappearance of the free market, in that a dozen or a score of large firms dominated an industry and were in a position to fix prices amongst themselves.

Monopoly did not grow in the same way in each country. In Britain the staple export trade of coal which had for so long

DEMONSTRATION FOR 8-HOUR DAY, c. 1900

Speaking: John Robertson. *Seated*: Keir Hardie, R. Smillie and others

VETERANS OF THE INDUSTRY
Andrew Connor, Lanarkshire, 1953

been dominant in the world market, was slow to change. The capitalist organisation of the British coal trade did not exhibit any such transformation as the far-reaching Westphalian coal syndicate in the Ruhr or the corresponding giant organisation in the coal-fields of Pennsylvania. Yet the firms were growing fewer in number and larger in size. This was seen in Scotland in areas where the iron-masters were at the same time coal-owners, but it was also found in the districts mainly producing for export.

The export of capital was growing in comparison with the export of goods; international trusts were spreading everywhere; colonies had been seized all over the world and in particular the continent of Africa had within a generation been divided up between the European Powers. The Great Powers who had seized the colonies were getting ready to redivide the spoil and the only method known to them for redivision was the method of war. The first of the lesser imperialist wars was being waged by the British Government against the Boer Republics of the Transvaal and the Orange Free State in South Africa from 1899 to 1902. This, incidentally, caused in 1900 an upward leap in the price of coal and a consequent increase in the wages of the colliers all over Britain.

At home Keir Hardie and those associated with him had been successful in getting a number of trade unions to join with three socialist bodies (the Independent Labour Party, the Social Democratic Federation and the Fabian Society) in the formation of a Labour Representation Committee in 1900, and this federal organisation for electoral purposes was six years later to change its name and to take on the title of The Labour Party. From this the M.F.G.B. stood aloof and its leaders for the most part still remained within the Liberal fold. This was true also of parts of Scotland. In Fife, for example, John Weir was an outstanding Liberal leader or, as the phrase went in those days, a Lib-Lab. Yet in Lanarkshire most of the younger agents were keen socialists, followers of Smillie and of Keir Hardie; and they hoped for great things from the new Labour Representation Committee. Meantime they had to pay much attention to the spread of trade union organisation, to the campaigns for shorter hours, a better Mines Act and improved conditions generally. Above all, they had to deal with the question of wages.

5. A CONCILIATION BOARD

For several years there had been an endeavour to get some regular method of wage settlement for Scotland as a whole. But the Scottish coal-owners had been unwilling to meet as a body the representatives of the men. In Fife, for many years well organised, there had been regular joint meetings of the two sides. But in Lanarkshire, for so long poorly organised or where organisation reached a high pitch only to fall away, the Lanarkshire Coal-masters Association would not meet either the Lanarkshire Federation from 1893 onwards, nor from 1896 onwards would they treat with the Lanarkshire Miners' County Union as fully representative of the men on all questions of wages and conditions.

By the end of 1898 the circumstances had begun to alter. A successful fortnight's strike in that year in Lanarkshire had made it clear that a memory of the defeat of the great strike of 1894 would no longer deter the miners from taking action to enforce their claims. As the market price of most kinds of coal was rising steadily, and as trade generally was good, there was no desire on the part of the coal-owners to provoke a strike. Finally, an end was in sight of the poor organisation which so long afflicted the Scottish coal-fields. Consequently when the Scottish Miners' Federation approached the coal-owners for a discussion 'to arrange some settlement of the wages question in order to prevent any dislocation of the trade in the future', this was agreed to, and in March 1899 a conference of representatives from 'the coal-owners of Scotland and the Scottish Miners' Federation' was held in Glasgow. Andrew K. McCosh, representative of William Baird & Co. Ltd., then the largest firm in the coal trade, was appointed Chairman, and Robert Smillie Vice-Chairman. The miners were claiming an advance of 6d. a day, and in Lanarkshire (where there was no joint negotiating machinery) this was necessarily backed by a threat of strike action.

There was much sparring and protracted argument both on principle and detail. In the end the owners offered $6\frac{1}{4}$ per cent for four months, i.e. 3d. a day, or half what the men had asked. 'Threepence a day!' exclaimed the leaders who had nodded agreement when Smillie in asking for 6d. had said it ought to have been a claim for eighteen pence. In the end they agreed to put it to a ballot of the men, but refused to recommend acceptance of such an offer. But the men accepted.

The object of the miners was:

(1) union recognition;

(2) collective bargaining on wages for the whole of Scotland;

(3) within any framework of bargaining (such as a Conciliation Board) a minimum wage—the 'living wage' principle of the Miners' Federation.

The men did not want a Conciliation Board unless a minimum were fixed—and to this the owners had a strong objection. However, after a series of further conferences of coal-masters and colliers in May, June, July, they got so far as to make an agreement to stabilise wage-rates for another six months. In October 1899 they agreed to set up a Conciliation Board.

Its object was to regulate miners' wages. It made the year 1888, when wages were roughly 4s. a day, the basis (equal to 100). Wages were calculated in percentages on this basis, 1s. being equal to 25 per cent. It laid down a minimum wage of $31\frac{1}{4}$ per cent above the 1888 basis (or 5s. 3d.) and a maximum of 75 per cent above the 1888 basis (or 7s.). If either party desired to change the rate of wages, a meeting of the Board must be called within fourteen days. In case of disagreement the meeting should be adjourned for fourteen days, and if there was still no agreement a neutral Chairman could be called in by agreement of both parties, whose decision would be final and binding.

The decision had been to set up a Conciliation Board for an experimental period of six months. There was then hard bargaining between owners and miners' officials on the subject of a renewal and, if it should be renewed, under what conditions this renewal should take place. Coal prices were

rising very high: and this made the owners ready to renew
the Board in order to avoid any stoppages should any
differences arise. The miners wanted a higher maximum and
higher minimum as well as an immediate advance in wages of
50 per cent on the 1888 basis. Eventually, after several
meetings, agreement was reached on July 31, 1900, just
before the Board expired, that it should continue for another
year. The maximum and minimum were increased to 8s. and
5s. 6d., and an increase in wages was granted of half the
miners' claim. But they soon lost more than this rise; for
between February 1901 and September 1901 wages were
three times reduced through the medium of the Conciliation
Board, till they stood at 50 per cent or roughly 6s. a day.

At the time of rising coal prices and high profits the owners
had agreed to setting up a Conciliation Board, in order to
avoid stoppages; but it was not the kind of Conciliation
Board that they liked. The owners looked back to the 'seventies and 'eighties, when they had been able to impose sliding
scales in which wages varied automatically with the market
price of coal; when the market price sank very low, wages
correspondingly might fall below the bare level of subsistence. A Conciliation Board of a kind that would embody
this relation between market prices and wages was their
object.

The Board was due to expire on February 1, 1902. The
owners were willing to continue only if certain conditions
were fulfilled. They wanted a fixed relation between prices
changes and changes in wages, precise figures of tonnage
and prices to be made available, and the ending of casual
stoppages, especially on non-unionism. After much discussion, it was in the end agreed on May 26, 1902, to continue
the Board subject to three months' notice on either side and
to accept a newly defined basis for its decisions. 'The net
average realised value of coal at the pit bank for the time
being, taken in conjunction with the state of trade and the
prospects thereof', was to be considered in fixing miners'
wages. A rise or fall of $6\frac{1}{4}$ per cent in wages on 1888 basis for
each $4\frac{1}{2}$d. per ton rise or fall in prices was to be taken as
'reasonable'; the base selling price was taken as 6s. $6\frac{3}{4}$d.; and
a procedure was laid down for the owners to compute the

average value of coal and for the miners to appoint independent accountants to check their figures.

But this was in practice a sliding-scale agreement: and
one purpose of the M.F.G.B. at its beginning had been to get
away from the whole system of sliding scales. It was this
reason that had kept the South Wales miners out of the
M.F.G.B., that they were tied by 'a rotten sliding scale'.
Now the Scots had submitted to an agreement which had
some of the undesirable features of a sliding scale. It is true
that it was cautiously worded: the price of coal was only 'to
be considered' in fixing miners' wages; and this and the use
of the word 'reasonable' did leave some scope for argument
between the parties. So the leaders of the M.F.G.B. accepted
what the Scots had done. The alternative would have been a
struggle for which they were not prepared.

During 1902 Sheriff Jameson, as independent Chairman,
awarded two reductions each of $6\frac{1}{4}$ per cent (or 6d. in all).
The miners were now down on the Conciliation Board
minimum of $37\frac{1}{2}$ per cent (or 5s. 6d.). Six weeks later the
Scottish Miners' Federation claimed an increase of $12\frac{1}{2}$ per
cent (or 6d.) which would have wiped out the two cuts of the
previous ten weeks. Sheriff Jameson in his award of November 28, 1902, gave them $6\frac{1}{4}$ per cent (or 3d.). Thereupon the
owners, feeling that greater precision was needed in the interpretation of the Wages Agreement of May 26, 1902, asked for
further meetings: and on December 16, 1902, a 'Minute of
Interpretation' was recorded which laid down a precise
sliding scale relating wages arithmetically to the price of coal.

Within seven months the miners were brought down once
more to the minimum and remained on it for a twelvemonth,
till the owners raised the question of ending the wages agreement in order to bring in a new and lower minimum, and in
June 1904 gave three months' notice to terminate it.

6. THE MINERS' FEDERATION OF GREAT BRITAIN ARE WARNED

The Scots miners were in a difficult position. Across the
Border the English Conciliation Board had recommended a

reduction of wages. It was not a favourable moment for a long strike struggle. On the other hand, the attitude of the Scottish coal-owners was clearly intended to pave the way to a cut in wages below the minimum, and how far below yet remained to be seen. In any case a destruction of the wages agreement cut right across the established policy on which the M.F.G.B. had been built up. So the Scots decided to call upon help from across the Border. They informed the M.F.G.B. Secretary who circulated the information to all districts to put them on the alert. The Scots meanwhile staved off the critical hour by delaying action on points of procedure.

Next, at the request of the Scottish Miners' Federation Conference, a Special (London) M.F.G.B. Conference was held on July 29, 1904 (Enoch Edwards in the chair), with seventy-three delegates, of whom twenty came from Scotland. Smillie explained that the coal-masters' move to end the wages agreement would most certainly be followed by a demand for reductions that would bring wages far below the minimum, and thus affect the general M.F.G.B. policy for a 'living wage'. The Scottish Miners' Conference, he said, had instructed their delegates to move that the famous 20th Rule[1] of the M.F.G.B. be now put into force.

This would have meant a declaration there and then that all the coal-fields organised in the M.F.G.B. would come out on strike to support the Scots against the prospective abolition of the minimum. The English and Welsh delegates asked many questions and showed themselves averse from any such immediate decision. This came out in many of the speeches, but was most clearly shown in the utterances of the President, Enoch Edwards. In February of that year Ben Pickard had died and his successor was now faced for the first time by a difficult situation. He had not the tenacious, determined and fighting character of Ben Pickard, but was rather of a gentle and persuasive nature, and was always endeavouring to smooth over difficulties and to find accommodation between different points of view. But he unmistakably voiced the reluctance common to most of the English and Welsh

---

[1] Rule 20 ran as follows: That whenever any County, Federation or District is attacked on the Wage question or any action taken by a general Conference, all members connected with the Society shall tender a notice to terminate their contracts—if approved of by a Conference called to consider the advisability of such joint action being taken.

associations to proceed to immediate action, rule or no rule. They had only that summer accepted wage-cuts that brought them near enough to the minimum in both the English and Welsh Conciliation Boards: while in Yorkshire a legal case similar to the Taff Vale judgment had taken away over a hundred thousand pounds from their funds and reduced them nearly to beggary. In these circumstances the division of opinion was acute.

Eventually the business committee (acting for the Executive) moved that the resolution on action to protect the minimum wage, passed at the Glasgow Conference, should be put to the miners' branches 'in order that a decision as to the policy to be adopted to protect the minimum wage in Scotland may be arrived at at a future conference'. With this motion the Scottish delegates were far from satisfied. They wanted something more drastic, and Smillie moved the following amendment:

That this Conference, having heard the statement of the Scottish Miners, that the Scottish coalowners were going to attack the present minimum wage, would advise the miners in the Federation of Great Britain to carry out the Resolution at the last Annual Conference by stopping work in the event of the reduction of the minimum wage in Scotland being enforced. (July 29, 1904.)

Both Smillie as mover and John Weir as seconder of the amendment argued very strongly that the delegates were bound by the resolution of the previous Annual Conference.

The opposite view was clearly put by the President, who asked Smillie to withdraw his amendment so as to get a unanimous vote. Smillie refused, declaring that the motion struck at the fundamental principle on which the Federation was built. The amendment was defeated by 40 votes to 28 and the resolution was then carried by 41 to 23.

When the adjourned Special Conference was held at Southport on September 1, 1904, Smillie informed the conference that the owners had now openly told them that the minimum wage was too high and must be reduced—by how much they did not say.

A very long discussion took place. The delegates from all the districts in England and Wales reported that their members were prepared to stand by the Scots in their efforts to maintain the minimum rate of wages. Thereupon it was unanimously decided to appoint six representatives of the M.F.G.B. (including Smillie and Brown from Scotland) to meet the Scottish owners to ascertain their terms and try to prevent a reduction.

The meeting was duly held on September 16. Enoch Edwards began by pointing out that the Scottish Conciliation Board Minimum, at 5s. 6d. a day, was already considerably lower than that in the English Conciliation Board area; and he went on to declare that the men were determined to enforce the minimum wage even at the cost of operating the 20th Rule and calling a strike. Finally the owners agreed to have another meeting of the Scottish Conciliation Board, at which the wage reduction need not be mooted at all. Arising from this negotiations were resumed, and finally on December 1, Smillie reported to the M.F.G.B. Executive that they had arrived at proposals which both sides had agreed to recommend. The new proposals were that the starting point in the relation of the market price of coal and wages should be 6s. 10d. instead of 6s. 6$\frac{3}{4}$d.; and that wages should be advanced by 6$\frac{1}{4}$ per cent (or 3d.) for every 4d. advance in the selling price of coal above 6s. 10d., instead of 4$\frac{1}{2}$d. The owners had given up their demand for a wage-cut, and had received instead an alteration in the sliding scale to their advantage.

7. A CRISIS BUILDS UP

Wages remained on the minimum of roughly 5s. 6d. a day, not only in 1903, but now under these new stipulations throughout the year 1904 and in 1905. In December 1905 the Conservative Prime Minister, A. J. Balfour, resigned, and was succeeded by the Radical Sir Henry Campbell-Bannerman, who was confirmed in office, with an overwhelming majority, as a result of the General Election of January 1906. At home the advent to Westminster of twenty-nine members of the Labour Representation Committee (which then changed its title to Labour Party), together with some fifteen representatives of the Miners' Federation of Great Britain, seemed a portent. It led to the passing of the Trade Disputes

Act of 1906, and then to the Eight Hours Act for coal-mines in 1908.

It was at this time that there began to be noticeable a rise in consumer prices and consequently a fall in the value of the pound sterling. But neither then nor for seven years was any account taken of this in the regulation of wages.

In 1906–7 coal prices were rising and the miners made a series of claims for increased wages, which were granted in part, though not in full, through the Conciliation Board and the neutral Chairman. Wages, which had been stationary at 5s. 6d. a day from the summer of 1903 to December 1906, rose in less than a twelvemonth to 7s. 6d. a day by December 3, 1907. In addition to wage increases, the union in April 1907 demanded a new agreement under which the minimum wage would be 6s. a day. The owners, however, refused: they wished to renew the existing agreement, subject to six months' notice, and with a new provision that would make the calling-in of the neutral Chairman automatic if the two sides failed to agree: they wanted, in effect, a compulsory arbitration system. By the end of 1907 the high-point had been reached and prices began to ebb once more. It was now the owners' turn to ask for successive reductions, which they obtained to such effect that by July 1908 wages were down again to 6s. 3d., a cut of 1s. 3d. A further demand for 3d. a day reduction, refused by the miners' side, was then confirmed by the neutral Chairman, Lord Ardevall, thus bringing wages in March 1909 down to 6s. a day—the amount which two years earlier the Scottish miners had declared to be their future conception of the minimum. Consequently when at a Board on May 10, 1909, the owners claimed 12½ per cent reduction, Smillie not only refused, but intimated that they would not consent to call in the neutral Chairman on this matter. Wages at 6s. a day (50 per cent on 1888) were, he declared, the minimum that a miner should receive and no concession from this standpoint was possible. This refusal meant a crisis of the Conciliation Board.

When wages came tumbling down in the spring and summer of 1908 the Scots took precautions. They informed the M.F.G.B. Executive Committee that in accordance with the general policy expressed at United Kingdom Conferences for

steps to be taken to raise the basis rates, they proposed not to
agree to any reduction which would bring wages below 50
per cent over 1888, i.e. roughly 6s. a day. The M.F.G.B.
Executive and successive M.F.G.B. Conferences endorsed
this attitude and pledged the Federation to support the
Scottish miners to secure or defend a 6s. minimum. In May
the M.F.G.B. Executive decided to send its officers to meet
the Scottish Conciliation Board if required. This strong
backing enabled Smillie to be grim and unyielding in his
attitude. The owners retaliated, by giving three months'
notice to end the existence of the Conciliation Board and the
minimum wage, unless the union would agree to a wage reduction or submit the matter to an independent chairman.
They added that 'after three months we shall be at liberty
to take any action even beyond the $37\frac{1}{2}$ per cent that we may
think desirable and expedient'. The deadlock was complete.

8. THE MINERS' FEDERATION INTERVENES

From mid-June 1909 onwards the coal-masters were considering what reduction should be demanded and enforced
by lock-out notices. Before this could be put into operation,
they received letters and telegrams from Thomas Ashton
proposing (as arranged with the Scots many weeks earlier)
a meeting of M.F.G.B. representatives with the coal-owners
and the miners of Scotland and strongly urging that lock-out
notices should be withheld until after such a meeting. This
proposal, agreed to with some reluctance by the Scottish
owners, at once staved off the critical moment and also gave
the Scots an opportunity of utilising the occasion of the
M.F.G.B. Special Conference on the Eight Hours Question
on July 1 to bring the Scottish Wage Question sharply before
their English and Welsh colleagues. Smillie (in the chair)
brought out the imminence of the crisis by reading out a
circular that had been issued by the Scottish coalmasters. Its
last clause ran:

We further undertake, in the event of notice being posted at the
collieries and a strike ensuing, that the conduct and settlement thereof shall be left in the hands of the Committee, and, further, we under-

take to make no concessions to our workmen and to keep our pits idle so long as required by the Committee.

The delegates unanimously decided that if the Scottish owners pressed their claims the M.F.G.B. Executive should call a Special Conference to discuss a general stoppage under the 20th Rule. The joint meeting of the M.F.G.B. officials with the owners, held on July 7, did not break the deadlock, and two days later fourteen days' notice was given to the miners throughout Scotland.

The miners, unless they submitted, would, according to Thomas Ashton's reckoning, be locked out from all the pits in Scotland by July 26, 1909. Therefore the M.F.G.B. officials called a Special Conference on the Scottish Miners' Dispute (Minimum Wage) on July 15 and 16, at which it was agreed to ballot all members of the Federation as to whether the 20th Rule should be put into force, which meant a general stoppage, in support of the Scottish miners' stand for the 6s. minimum.

9. WINSTON CHURCHILL INTERVENES

Few working-class issues since the days of the Dockers' Tanner had aroused so much feeling and agitation as this question of the Miners' Minimum Wage. The Government was forced to take a hand. At that time what would now be a duty of the Minister of Labour was the function of the President of the Board of Trade, and the then President of the Board of Trade was Winston Churchill. He asked to see representatives from the Miners' Federation of Great Britain and from the Scots. A civil servant[1] records that 'Mr. Churchill became alarmed'.

A joint meeting of the Scottish owners' and miners' representatives, together with Wm. Abraham, W. E. Harvey and Thomas Ashton representing the Miners' Federation, was held at the Board of Trade on July 22, with Winston Churchill in the chair. 'In his opening address', stated Andrew McCosh five months later, 'the President, who frankly admitted that the Scotch coal trade could not go on paying a minimum wage while working at a loss, threw out the suggestion that an

[1] Lord Askwith, in *Industrial Problems and Disputes* (1920), p. 131.

inquiry should be held whether there were any conditions in the shape of a *quid pro quo* to the coal-owners which would enable them to agree to a new minimum wage, and, if so, what these conditions were.' The full meeting was continued for a time; and then it was agreed that each party should elect four or five of their number, with the three representatives from the Federation, to act as a sub-committee, with Mr. George Askwith, K.C., a permanent official of the Board of Trade, in the chair. The sub-committee met, and met again all the next day, July 23. Eventually, when Smillie put forward a proposition[1] the owners said that they must have time to consider, and that it would be necessary to lay the matter before their larger constituency. For while the Scottish miners' representatives possessed plenary powers to settle on reasonable terms, the owners did not possess such powers. They also demanded that the next meeting be held in Glasgow.

Winston Churchill, however, could not leave London at that time, so G. R. Askwith, K.C., took his place as chairman at Glasgow. The Glasgow meeting, held on July 27, 1909, had only one positive result, that the lock-out notices were suspended for one week to enable deliberations to continue.

The next day, Wednesday, July 28, the M.F.G.B. Special Conference reassembled. It was felt as a tense situation, both by the delegates and by Winston Churchill, waiting at the offices of the Board of Trade. First Ashton read the result of the ballot vote that had been taken as to whether Rule 20 should be put into operation. There was a large majority in every district in favour. The full totals were 518,361 for and 62,980 against. This was a majority of over six to one. No doubt could remain as to the consequences if a settlement were not reached. If any of the Scottish owners, or if anyone at the Board of Trade, had thought there was an element of bluff in the attitude of the Miners' Federation leaders, they were now disillusioned. The conference then heard a report

---

[1] 'As a result of the meetings in London, after many hours of discussion, the miners' representatives offer to take the minimum wage of 50 per cent, and accept the recent scale basis price, viz. 7s. 1.45d. and 7s. 5.45d., as representing that wage. If the coalowners do not agree to this they are willing to submit it to a Neutral Chairman mutually appointed, or, failing agreement, to be appointed as the Committee might decide, whether the basis selling price as representing 50 per cent on 1888 rates should be increased or reduced to any extent not exceeding 4d. per ton. Also that the Arbiter should determine whether the price of 4d. per ton as representing $6\frac{1}{4}$ per cent should be increased.'

from W. E. Harvey, M.P., on the discussions, supplemented by Robert Smillie for the Scots; and then unanimously passed the following resolution:

That unless a satisfactory settlement is arrived at tomorrow with regard to the Scottish dispute, notice be served at every colliery in all districts to cease work, the notices to terminate on the last day of August.

Conference adjourned to the next day, Thursday, July 29, to enable their chosen representatives to attend the meeting called by Churchill at the Board of Trade. This met at 11 o'clock Thursday morning. Meetings of the whole of the representatives, of the sub-committee, of the parties meeting separately and meeting the President of the Board of Trade and Mr. Askwith, continued the whole of that day from 11 A.M. to 8 P.M.

Meantime the M.F.G.B. Special Conference met at 3 o'clock on the Thursday, waited, adjourned till 7 o'clock, and then adjourned till next day. The discussions went on at the Board of Trade throughout Friday, July 30. Negotiations proceeded, different kinds of meetings being held constantly the whole of the day until past 7 o'clock, when agreement was reached. The agreement was accepted by the Executive Committee and then put before the Special Conference that same evening. There was some discussion in which Cairns of Northumberland protested that by the terms the Scots had put themselves in the hands of the arbiter and had 'mortgaged the future for the six shillings'. But when the vote was taken he was the sole dissentient. The following resolution was adopted:

That having heard the proposed terms of agreement, this Conference hereby confirms and ratifies the same, and thanks our representatives for their services in the matter. (July 30, 1909.)

The agreement was signed at 9.30 the same evening at the Board of Trade. But Smillie would not put his name to it. Its principal points were:

(1) The principle of 50 per cent on 1888 as the minimum wage (i.e. the 6s. minimum) was conceded.
(2) The price of coal to which this minimum would correspond

and the new sliding scale to be based on it were to be determined by an Arbiter, and the new price should not be lower than the recent basis price.

(3) If the ascertained prices for a period of months did not warrant the 6s. minimum, then for the same number of months afterwards any increased percentage to which the miners became entitled would be reduced by $6\frac{1}{4}$ per cent.

(4) The Conciliation Board should continue, but a neutral chairman would be obligatory, whose decisions would be final and binding. He would be appointed by the two sides, and failing agreement the Speaker of the House of Commons was to be called in to decide the nomination.

The two sides of the Conciliation Board met again on August 23, 1909. Their main business, even before they set up the rules of the renewed Conciliation Board, was to choose an arbiter. They had to think a bit about it, if they were to avoid having an arbiter imposed. Smillie's proposal was the Lord Chancellor, Lord Loreburn, but he refused. It was then the turn of the coal-owners' nominee, who accepted immediately—it was Lord Balfour of Burleigh, who had been in Salisbury's Conservative Cabinet till 1903 as Secretary for Scotland.

When the arbitration took place each side produced arrays of figures and arrays of arguments as never before in the history of the Conciliation Board. For the employers McCosh made much of the recent mining legislation which they said had worn a hole in their purses. Smillie brought up the rising cost of living and the range of high dividends enjoyed by a considerable number of coal-owners in the lean years. On a series of points it was decided to call in accountants to go further into the figures of the coal trade. Finally, Lord Balfour of Burleigh on May 23, 1910, having heard the parties six months earlier, stated in his old-fashioned way that 'being now well and ripely advised on the matters submitted to me, and having God and a good conscience before my eyes, I do hereby give forth and pronounce my final sentence and Decree Arbitral as follows:—The basis price for the minimum wage of 50 per cent above the basis of 1888 shall be 7s. 5.45d. per ton'. The subsequent steps were set out by which each $6\frac{1}{4}$ per cent change in wages would correspond to a given change in 'the value of coal'. It meant that after ten years of

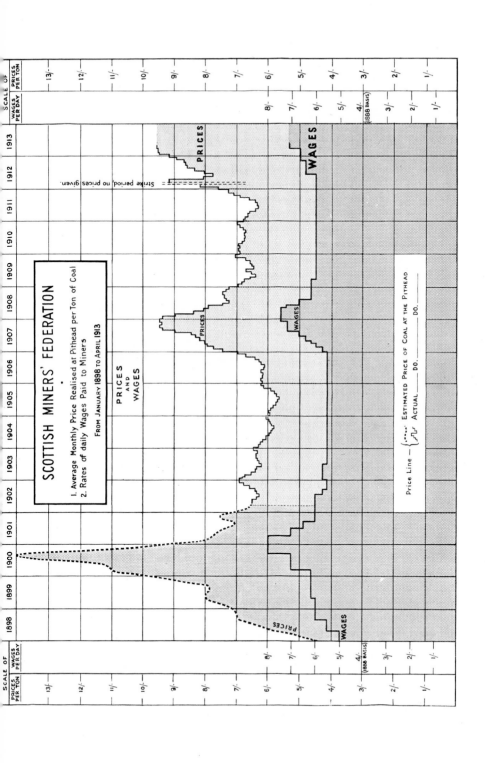

SCOTTISH MINERS' FEDERATION

1. Average Monthly Price Realised at Pithead per Ton of Coal
2. Rates of daily Wages Paid to Miners

From January 1898 to April 1913

PRICES AND WAGES

Price Line — { ⋯⋯ Estimated Price of Coal at the Pithead _____ Do.
               ᒧᒧ Actual _____ Do. _____

conciliation the Scottish miners' wages were tied, as a generation earlier, to a sliding scale.

The Scots had been eager at the beginning of the century for a Conciliation Board. But step by step the owners had got it changed into something that was no longer simple collective bargaining, but a complicated machinery through which the selling price of coal held down the miners' standard of living. Moreover, by the latest agreement and Arbitral Award, the owners had established the principle that they would be recouped for 'losses' suffered in months when they were precluded from forcing wages below the minimum. This principle had also been achieved by the owners in the English Conciliation Board the same year. Twelve years later the same principle was to be vastly extended, in connection with quarterly ascertainments, in every coal-field in Britain. At the moment, in the Scottish as well as in the English Conciliation Board, the owners had brought wage movements to a standstill, and had trussed up the negotiators for the miners.

CHAPTER VI

THE GREAT STRIKE OF 1912

I. THE POLITICAL BACKGROUND

BY the time King Edward VII died, in May 1910, the first consequences were beginning to become apparent of the growth of monopoly capitalism and the political tendencies linked with it, in particular the diplomacy of successive British Governments. With the Triple Entente of Britain, France and Russia organised against the German-headed Triple Alliance, Europe became an armed camp. In this setting, one international crisis after another brought Britain and Europe to the brink of general war. The Agadir crisis, the war of Italy on Turkey, the wars in the Balkans, were summer lightnings that preceded the greater storm. The dividing up of colonies and the armaments race continued apace. There was, in consequence, a growing fear of the increasing war danger expressed at international conferences of the Miners' Federation as well as at conferences of the Socialist International.

At home there was a steep rise in the cost of living and a growing awareness amongst the organised workers that their strength, if united, was now such as could yield them better wages and conditions. But how was that strength to be made effective? What form of organisation? What kind of activity would yield the results they desired? These questions were agitating the minds of many.

Great hopes had been reposed in the Labour Representation Committee when it returned to Parliament twenty-nine members in 1906, to be joined under its new title of The Labour Party by most of the Miners' Federation M.P.s by 1909. These hopes seemed at first to be justified. When in 1906 the Trade Disputes Act was passed reversing the Taff Vale Judgment which had crippled the activities of the trade unions; and when after more than fifteen years' agitation the Eight Hours Act for Mines had been passed in 1908; when in

1908 also the Labour Party had applied for admission to the Socialist International and had been admitted, it seemed a token that the Labour Party, which as yet had no socialist programme, would, nevertheless, move more and more rapidly in the direction of a socialist outlook, based on a Marxist attitude to the class struggle.

But against this there were to be set other facts, symbolised by the choice as Chairman of the Labour M.P.s (or Party Leader as he would later be called), in succession to Keir Hardie, of a leading cotton trade unionist, D. J. Shackleton, who shortly after resigned his seat, and accepted a post as Labour adviser to the Board of Trade. His successor was Arthur Henderson, President of the Ironfounders' Association, a capable organiser, but definitely not at that time a socialist. In 1910 he was followed by G. N. Barnes of the Amalgamated Society of Engineers, who later moved right out of the working-class movement. He in turn was succeeded by Ramsay MacDonald, up till then Secretary of the Labour Party—a man even then prone to petty electoral intrigues outside Parliament and ambiguous policies within Parliament. Under this leadership the Parliamentary Labour Party proved unable to respond to all the hopes reposed in it, and there was considerable disappointment among the organised workers.

On the other hand the Liberal Cabinet, headed after the death of Campbell-Bannerman in 1908 by H. H. Asquith, was sufficiently aware of the gradually changing mood of the working class. They continued the policy of the Liberal Imperialist League in foreign affairs, while they promoted a series of social measures which to some extent took the wind out of the sails of the Labour Party. The effect, if not the intention, was to retard the movement of the organised workers towards an active policy of class struggle and a socialist outlook. The chief exponent of the Liberal social reforms of these years, which ante-dated the 'Welfare State' by a third of a century, was the Chancellor of the Exchequer, David Lloyd George, with the young Winston Churchill as one of his lieutenants. Lloyd George not only brought forward social measures, but at the same time, especially after 1909 when his Budget imposing land taxes was rejected by the House of

Lords, plunged into campaigns whose oratorical vigour and apparently implacable hostility to the landlords and the leading Tories, left the parliamentary or public speeches of Labour M.P.s far behind. There is no question but that the campaigns of Lloyd George, the social measures he proposed and his 'tax the rich' propaganda won the applause of many workers; and ordinary people when they saw this David apparently fighting, at any rate in words, against the Goliath of landlordism and toryism, were thrilled and emotionally bound to the liberalism in which so many of them had been brought up.

So far from attaining any advance of a kind corresponding to the forward leap in the first years of the century, the Labour Party in January 1910, contesting seventy-eight constituencies, came back forty strong with a net loss of five seats. In December 1910 the Labour Party contested only fifty-six constituencies and returned with forty-two Members. There was loss of enthusiasm for a party which was not as yet capable of challenging effectively the two main capitalist parties. Consequently, particularly amongst those workers who refused to be seduced by the fine phrases of Lloyd George, there began a search for some other means of attaining an improvement in their conditions of life. They began to feel that by their own action, within the framework of the trade unions they had built, they might find a means to get that advance which it had proved impossible to wring out of the parliamentary calendar.

What applied to the workers generally was true of the coal-miners in particular. With the M.F.G.B. embracing every coal-field after the accession of Northumberland and Durham in 1908 and 1909 respectively, the miners had become conscious of the potential strength of their organisation, but were unable immediately to see how that could be made effective in order to improve their conditions or to withstand the result of the rise in the cost of living. Their earlier plan, devised by Ben Pickard in the 'nineties, of bringing all wage negotiations under one national Conciliation Board, had been frustrated. They had to reckon with negotiations in five separate main Conciliation Boards, the results of which largely governed the wages in the smaller areas as well. In more than one of these

Boards a point had been reached where the detailed arrangements entered into with the owners had tied them up for years ahead. This was the case, for example, in the Scottish Coal Conciliation Board, where the wage level, having reached the minimum of 6s. a day early in 1909, remained unaltered and unalterable in the succeeding thirty months although the cost of living was rising during this period.

Output was steadily rising towards the zenith year of British coal production of nearly 290 million tons, and the coal trade appeared to be fairly prosperous. This prosperity seemed to be confirmed by an inspection of the profit and dividend figures of at any rate the larger companies. There was no obvious way out of the difficulty in which the miners found themselves, tied as they were to agreements reached earlier in several of the Conciliation Boards.

There were, however, other matters which in the opinion of some of the miners' leaders lay outside the scope of the Conciliation Boards' agreements, amongst them the question of Abnormal Working Places.

2. ABNORMAL PLACES

It could easily happen that a hewer, paid by piece-work, might find that conditions of the place where he was working had changed and become 'abnormal', with the result that he was unable to deliver more than a small quantity of coal, for which small quantity he was given a corresponding payment which might be half or a quarter of that which he could normally expect to get. He might even find that he had produced no coal at all though he had toiled the whole day. In such a case a manager would give him a small allowance, but there was no fixed rule about it; and it fell to be a matter of individual bargaining between the management and the man concerned, in which case the man was often at a serious disadvantage. W. E. Harvey of Derbyshire, at the Edinburgh M.F.G.B. Annual Conference on October 6, 1910, said:

Of course, the difficulty there is, is to prove that there are abnormal conditions. In many cases there is no difficulty at all. Nobody will admit that a fall in a stall is normal. Nobody will admit that an inundation of water in a stall is normal, or when the coal gets thinner it is a normal condition. Where another difficulty comes in, is the want of backbone in the men to claim their wages and not be put on one side.

At the end of that discussion it was carried unanimously:

That the miners of Scotland, England, and Wales be requested to meet their respective employers and demand a fair living wage to be paid to all miners working in abnormal places failing to get which, that a National Conference be called with a view of further dealing with the matter. (October 6, 1910.)

A series of M.F.G.B. Conferences during 1911 dealt with this issue. There was some difficulty in ascertaining the exact position in all pits and districts. Although the districts most severely affected (such as South Wales and Lancashire) were impatient and pressed for immediate action, the conference as a whole moved cautiously, giving every opportunity for all districts to meet their owners and attempt to secure a settlement.

Scotland was less acutely affected by the issue than some other districts, mainly because the miners there worked on daily notices. This position, though disadvantageous to the miners in most respects, made it slightly easier for a man to deal with underpayment as a result of an abnormal place, since he could simply refuse to work in that place the next day. Nevertheless, the Scots also suffered and shared the general sense of grievance.

At the fourth Special Conference of the M.F.G.B. on the issue, in July 1911, the Scots reported that they had met the owners and failed to reach agreement. The Scottish owners had agreed in principle that a man working in an abnormal place where he could not earn wages was entitled to a fair wage, but they refused to establish machinery to determine whether the place was abnormal in any particular instance. The Chairman of the M.F.G.B., Enoch Edwards, proposed that a national settlement should be sought for. Smillie, speaking as Vice-President, pointed out the need for unanimity and supported the Chairman's suggestion of getting the employers into a national discussion. He said:

If the owners refuse then I think we could be unanimous that the time has come, not in the interest of 50,000, or of 20,000, but in the interest of all, to declare a general strike. This is of some importance, because some of us anticipate what a general strike means. It may mean causing misery to hundreds of thousands not concerned with the coal trade. We should do everything we can to avoid it; everything we can to avoid it in the interests of tens of thousands of men and women and children who will suffer, because the land-owning class will not be without their dinners on the morrow of a stoppage as many of our people will. We should exhaust everything in reason before we decide on a stoppage. If we exhaust everything in reason we should have public opinion behind us in our action, and we would have the right to say to the Government that private ownership has failed, these men who have made millions out of the mines of this country have refused to pay a fair wage for fair work, and now we cannot see our way to resume work on the terms of private ownership of mines, cannot allow this system of private ownership to continue any longer. (July 28, 1911.)

The Executive's course was adopted by a vote of 82 against 54 for the Lancashire proposal of an immediate national strike ballot. A discussion with the owners resulted only in pushing the question back to district negotiations, and convinced the M.F.G.B. delegates that they would have to merge the question of abnormal places in a wider claim for the minimum wage. Consequently the M.F.G.B. Annual Conference decided:

That the Federation take immediate steps to secure an individual District Minimum Wage for all men and boys working in mines in the area of the Federation without any reference to the working places being abnormal.

In the event of the employers refusing to agree to this then the amended 21st Rule of the Federation be put into operation to demand the same. (October 6, 1911.)

All districts were also instructed to meet their own employers on the issue and report to a Special Conference on November 14, 1911.

3. THE SCOTTISH CONCILIATION BOARD

In Glasgow on November 6, 1911, in the Central Station Hotel, there was held a Conference of the Members of the Conciliation Board. They were to consider the resolution for a minimum wage passed by the M.F.G.B. Annual Conference on October 6, 'without any reference to the working places being abnormal'. Smillie explained to the Scottish owners that, because the owners at the national meeting had refused to agree to set up machinery to ensure that men unable to earn wages through the abnormal condition of their working place should be paid fair wages, the M.F.G.B. had passed the resolution to take action under Rule 21.[1]

'What is Rule 21?' asked Chairman Andrew McCosh: and thereupon had it explained to him very coolly by Smillie that it usually meant the calling of a conference which might decide to take a strike ballot: but that under this last M.F.G.B. resolution, if the employers refused to concede a minimum wage, Rule 21 would be operated, 'which means a general stoppage shall take place in order to demand the same'. The intention of the first part of the resolution, however, was to ask the employers in each district to agree that their own district rate should be applied to each individual workman:

Our meeting with you to-day is to ask you that every person work-ing at the coal face should be secured in return for his eight hours' work underground at the coal face at least 6s. per day. . . . If he failed to earn wages because the coal was thinner, harder, wetter, or any-thing of that kind, then he must be made up to at least 6s. per day. If he failed through overcrowding of a colliery or a section to earn his wages, then he must secure at least 6s. per day for every day he is in the mine. If he failed through a breakdown in the machinery to earn full wages, then he would be entitled to be paid at least 6s. per day. That is what is meant by the individual minimum rate of wages. (November 6, 1911.)

Smillie went on to demand a standard wage for oncost men throughout Scotland: for firemen a minimum of 6s. a day; for roadmen 5s. 10d.; and for ordinary oncost men 5s. 9d. Lastly Smillie proposed there should be a standard wage for boys, beginning as 'a half-man's wage' and rising at a fixed rate each half-year until at eighteen each would get a man's wages. In dealing with this claim he made reference to a recognised custom in the past in the West of Scotland and elsewhere which he called 'the system of bens':

I know it has been recognised in the west of Scotland that when a lad started at twelve, or thirteen, he was a half ben, and when he

---

[1] This was the old Rule 20, renumbered Rule 21 in 1910.

came to fourteen he was entitled to three-quarters, and when he came to sixteen he was recognised as a man's ben, and we always claimed that he was entitled to a man's wages at the face. If he was working with his father, then they were entitled to get two men's wages at the face. (November 6, 1911.)

In making all these claims Smillie contended that they were not going beyond the Scottish agreement (by which they were bound up to July 1912) but 'asking merely that the terms of that agreement would be carried out'.

At last the Chairman expressed the feelings of the indignant coal-owners by saying:

The gist of the whole of this is that you are asking us to give you a very large advance in wages, an advance in wages that would entail great additional cost on the collieries. Now, I maintain that as long as our agreement lasts, that is an impossible position. If it is insisted upon, then it is practically tearing up the agreement. I cannot conceive of your putting these demands forward unless you intended that they were to take a large amount of money out of the colliery owners' pockets and put it into the pockets of their workmen. That is what it comes to. (Scottish Conciliation Board, November 6, 1911, p. 36.)

Finally the coal-owners turned down flat the demand for an individual district minimum wage for coal-face workers. The demands for oncost men and lads they said they would discuss at a future meeting, but gave no hint of any concession.

Meantime the coal-owners in the Federated area of England had, in a guarded form, conceded the principle of the minimum wage. On this, at the M.F.G.B. Special Conference of November 15, several county associations in the Federated area desired to delay the moment for action until they had exhausted all possibilities of peaceful settlement. Against them and for immediate action were South Wales, Lancashire and Northumberland, and some smaller districts. Durham, however, was also for delay, and so was Scotland. Smillie, desirous as M.F.G.B. Vice-President of reaching the maximum of agreement, said:

I personally believe that no power on earth can prevent a national strike; because the Welsh employers will not give way on that question and the Scottish owners will not give way, it is bound to come. Whether we declare it here today or leave it for some future occasion, it will come.

Accordingly the M.F.G.B. Special Conference decided to adjourn for some five weeks 'so that further efforts may be made to bring about a satisfactory settlement'.

When the adjourned Conference of the Members of the Conciliation Board of Scotland met, this time in the North British Station Hotel, Chairman Andrew McCosh at once gave the reply of the coal-owners:

We cannot agree to the demand for an individual district minimum wage for all miners working at the coal face. We adhere to the agreement made at the Board of Trade on 30th July, 1909. . . . We cannot agree to the standardisation of the wages of oncost men and boys and youths on the lines proposed. We adhere to the agreement made at the Board of Trade on 30th July, 1909. (December 14, 1911.)

The owners were willing, however, to have permanent machinery set up to deal with disputes on abnormal places 'where the dispute affects twelve or more miners': further they would recommend the classification according to age and experience of boys and youths working at the coal face. 'That', said McCosh, 'is the length that we are prepared to go.' That ended it. For though the conference went on discussing sundry details of wages paid in the past to different grades, there was really nothing more to be said. One thing only of interest emerged, namely, that the proposed national joint meeting would not be held, the United Kingdom coal-owners having decided against it on the ground that 'no useful purpose would be served'.

4. THE MINIMUM WAGE CLAIMS

When the adjourned M.F.G.B. Special Conference, held on December 20, 1911, learned that the minimum wage had been rejected in so very many of the district meetings and that the owners would have no further national meetings, there was no further talk of delay. The delegates were incensed. They felt they had been 'humbugged'. Without more ado the votes were taken for a ballot of all the members in the coal-fields. When the returned ballot papers were reported to the M.F.G.B. Special Conference at Birmingham on January 18, 1912, the result was a four to one majority for a strike to

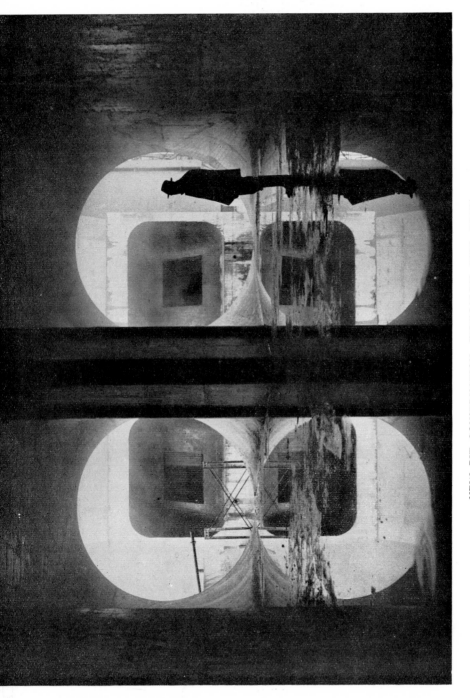

NEW PIT CONSTRUCTION, KIRKCALDY, FIFE, 1953

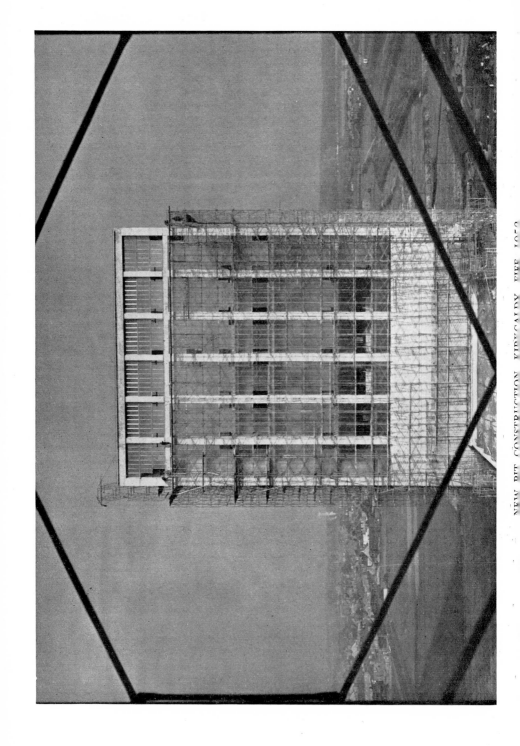

NEW PIT CONSTRUCTION KIRKCALDY PIT 1952

enforce the claim for a minimum wage. In Yorkshire there was a six to one majority: while in Scotland there was a five to one majority. In the long series of Miners' Federation Conferences in the previous fifteen months, the delegates from Yorkshire and Scotland had appeared to their fellow delegates to be lagging behind, as against the proposals for early and drastic action coming from South Wales, Lancashire or Northumberland. But when it came to the ballot vote of the members, it was precisely these two where there was the biggest majority for a strike. In Scotland there were 60,611 votes cast for a strike and only 12,035 against. The total vote of all coalfields was 445,801 in favour and 115,921 against. There was a total poll of 561,722 out of some 862,000 underground workers. The remaining 300,000 would be made up of miners who did not cast their vote, miners outside the union, and the considerable number of craftsmen underground who belonged to other trade unions than the county associations.

The next step was for each district to fix its own minimum to go into the schedule of claims. These were agreed at the adjourned Special Conference of February 1 and 2, and any question of an advance in wage-rates was dropped. The schedule of claims set forth the minimum day wage-rate for coal-getters. The rate, as has been noted, varied from district to district. Of the larger districts Scotland was lowest, with its claim for 6s. a day. Yorkshire and Nottingham stood at 7s. 6d., or a quarter as much again. South Wales and Derbyshire ranged above 7s. and up to 7s. 6d. The only large district whose rate came nearly as low as Scotland was Durham with its claim for 6s. 1½d. The mere setting out of this schedule of claims must have brought home to many a Scottish miner how much leeway they had to gain in order to come up to the general level of the larger coal-fields. The ground had been lost in the later part of the nineteenth century, especially in the failure to maintain their union organisation in the early 'eighties.

When all these detailed preparations had been carried through the coal-owners of the U.K. were now prepared to meet the miners' representatives, who at each successive conference or meeting in January and February had passed resolutions leaving the door open for further negotiations if the coal-owners so desired. A joint meeting took place at the Westminster Palace Hotel on February 7: but the coal-owners would not budge; they refused the claim. The M.F.G.B. representatives put forward a resolution regretting the refusal to accept the principle of the individual minimum wage, said they had no wish to cause 'a serious rupture in the coal trade of the country' and were willing to meet the coal-owners again. With the assurance of the coal-owners' chairman that this would receive 'the most careful consideration', the conference came to an end. The negotiations had broken down. Throughout the country it began to be realised that in twenty-one days there would be a general stoppage of all the pits in the country, a situation which had never occurred before.

Meantime the Scots had taken a step to improve the general level of wage-rates as from a period over three months ahead. For they, on January 29, through the Conciliation Board, gave six months' notice to terminate the existing wage agreement, their reason being to raise the minimum wage to 7s. a day. The owners held that the claim on which the national strike was approaching for an individual minimum wage and for standardisation of oncost wages would be a breach of the existing agreement. They demanded reference to a neutral Chairman on this point, but the miners' side refused, and there was a deadlock.

5. GOVERNMENT INTERVENTION

In face of an impending coal strike of a magnitude never known before, there were demands that the Government should intervene. In those days before the first World War there had always been reluctance on the part of governments thus to act, except through the medium of the Labour Department of the Board of Trade. It is true that, breaking with all traditions and breaking also with his own cherished notions of non-intervention, Prime Minister Gladstone had intervened in the great lock-out of the Federated area in 1893, but the intervention had come only after nearly three months' lock-out. This time Prime Minister Asquith took action ten days before the strike was due to begin, and offered mediation. It was agreed that he should put his proposals before the entire Conference of the M.F.G.B., which went to the Foreign Office to hear the Prime Minister. To emphasise the importance of the occasion, the Prime Minister was accompanied not only by the President of the Board of Trade, Sydney Buxton, but by the two leading members of the Government next to himself, David Lloyd George, the Chancellor of the Exchequer, and Sir Edward Grey, the Foreign Secretary.

The Government's proposals for settlement of the dispute were as follows:

1. His Majesty's Government are satisfied, after careful consideration, that there are cases in which underground employees cannot earn a reasonable minimum wage, from causes over which they have no control.
2. They are further satisfied that the power to earn such a wage should be secured by arrangements suitable to the special circumstances of each district. Adequate safeguards to be provided to protect the employers against abuse.
3. His Majesty's Government are prepared to confer with the parties as to the best method of giving practical effect to these conclusions, by means of district Conferences between the parties, a representative appointed by the Government being present.
4. In the event of any of the Conferences failing to arrive at a complete settlement within a reasonable time, the representatives appointed by His Majesty's Government to decide jointly any outstanding points for the purpose of giving effect in that district to the above principles.

With the first two of these proposals the Miners' Federation could agree. The third proposal cut right across their demand for a national settlement on the schedule of claims. Their objection to this would apply consequently to proposal No. 4 to which, on other grounds, they were bound to be opposed, as it meant instituting that compulsory arbitration of which they had always been determined opponents. On the other hand, the majority of British coal-owners were agreed with those four points and at once accepted them. A minority of the coal-owners were resolutely against—in South Wales, Scotland and Northumberland. In short, the Government, while proclaiming loudly enough its belief in the justice of the men's cause and its acceptance of the principle of the minimum wage, had put forward proposals that were acceptable to the great majority of the employers and unacceptable to the miners.

After the Prime Minister had made his statement on the morning of Tuesday, February 27, and it had been agreed that a committee of twenty should act for the whole conference and go into details during that afternoon and evening, there was a realisation amongst most of the delegates of what they were up against. On the next day, February 28, they heard the report from Enoch Edwards and then reaffirmed their policy, repeating:

that there can be no settlement of the present dispute unless the principle of an individual minimum wage for all men and boys employed underground is agreed to by the Colliery Owners.

Meantime discussions were going on at the Foreign Office. The miners' conference continued in session, getting reports from time to time. When, on February 29, they learned first of all that the Government would not budge from their proposals, and second that these proposals, although accepted by a majority of the coal-owners, had been turned down by a minority of the coal-owners, they realised that there was little possibility of averting a bitter strike struggle. Robert Brown, speaking for Scotland, said:

I believe that we have come to a point when it is absolutely essential that we should not deviate one iota from the position we occupy. I am aware of the gravity of the situation, but those who are refusing our claims are responsible for it. We are in the right as miners. . . .

We know this, that no one else can go below and take the position of the miners; the Government may interfere, but they cannot produce coal. They cannot bring any power to bear upon us if the men stand firm, and I believe they will stand firm all over the country. It is a common saying that one man can take a horse to the water, but twenty men cannot make it drink. They can open the mines, but they will not be able to work them.

We stand to win, we are going to be the pioneers of the minimum wage; we are going to lay the foundation. We will not rest content with a 6s. minimum in Scotland. Once get the foundation laid, it will only be a question of time when we shall seek to obtain a wage of 8s. for men below ground.

We are making this the great charter of the working class for every man to have a minimum wage at the end of the week, and I hope that this Conference will not deviate from the position we have taken up, and we must not budge for anybody. (February 29, 1912.)

Robert Brown was voicing not only the opinion of Scotland but of others as well. That night throughout the whole of Britain pitmen were coming out of the pits not to return there for many weeks. The great Minimum Wage Strike had begun.

6. THE WHEELS STOP

On Friday, March 1, 1912, a strange silence fell: no seams were being worked underground in Britain. No coal was being wound to the surface. For the first time in a hundred years, or rather for the first time in seven centuries, there was an utter cessation of work. In the villages the coal-miners were standing about discussing the situation. The coal-owners had failed to meet their claims. The Government, they felt, had given them words only, saying the minimum wage demand was just in the abstract, but refusing to consider the adoption of their concrete and detailed claims. After discussions that had gone on for the better part of two years in their own ranks, after over a year's discussions with the coal-owners, there was nothing left now, they felt, except to take the action decided upon by their ballot vote. They knew that before them lay a period when they would be on very short rations, and when the trouble their wives or mothers had in providing for the needs of their families would be doubled or trebled.

Each district of the M.F.G.B. had its own funds out of which strike pay was paid at a rate that varied from one coal-field to another throughout the country. Though the families of the owners had no anxieties of this kind to face, nevertheless the owners were, some of them, rather anxious about the outcome of the great struggle that had begun. For one thing they had confidently expected that a good number of miners would continue working, and as the weeks of the strike wore on, some of them never lost the expectation that there would be a breakaway and a return to the pits. It is true that there were cases here and there where strike pickets had to go out in order to peacefully persuade any who wanted to return to work against taking any such step, and except in the case of one pit in North Wales, the efforts of the pickets were almost uniformly successful. The great majority of the coal-owners entertained no hopes of a breakaway; they were content to wait till the miners were worn down. As they waited they had the satisfaction of seeing the price of coal rise very rapidly and large stocks of coal, laid in at many collieries during the winter months, being sold at very high prices. This was another reason that made the owners feel they could afford to wait. It did not, however, make the public feel the same, and a protest against this rise in prices was voiced in Parliament where it got short shrift from Asquith.

Meantime throughout the country it was not long before the effects of the coal strike began to be felt in institutions and households, in industry and in transport. There were fewer trains, fewer steamers. Railwaymen, dockers and seamen were stood off by their employers and, having no unemployment insurance to rely on, were dependent on the small friendly benefits of their trade unions. Throughout that month of March 1912, the pulse of industry was slowing down. From all quarters there began to be demands for action from the Government, but Mr. Asquith and his colleagues let a week pass by without any action. They, too, had decided to wait.

To this general atmosphere of cessation of activity and of waiting expectancy there was one notable exception—the newspapers of Britain took up an entirely different attitude. There was no single daily paper then which represented the interests of the miners or any other section of the working class or that stood by the principles of trade unionism or co-operation. On the contrary, so violent and apparently so unscrupulous was their attack on the million miners who, with their families, constituted more than one-tenth of the whole population of Great Britain, that they stirred up a feeling of class antagonism that had been absent in the speeches and statements of many of the miners' leaders. Nearly twenty years earlier there had been a great lock-out in the Federated area, and on that occasion several newspapers had espoused the cause of the miners. No such attitude was taken up by any of the leading daily newspapers in 1912. It was not, however, a matter of editorial opinion, but of false reports that roused the indignation of the most pacific-minded members of the Federation Executive. In the Executive Committee meeting held at the end of that first week of March a strongly worded resolution of protest was passed. Whether under the influence of the press in misreporting and incitement of class feeling against the miners, or moved by their party sympathies or (in the case of coal-owners) by personal interests, the Conservative Members of Parliament were asking questions in the House of Commons and demanding that more and more police should be drafted to the mines.

After nearly two weeks had gone by the Government arranged a joint meeting of coal-owners' and coal-miners' representatives under the chairmanship of Mr. Asquith, on March 12 to 14, and during the same period the M.F.G.B. was meeting in Special Conference. The meetings led to nothing. The representatives of the miners remained willing to 'meet the owners at any time for the purpose of securing a settlement'. The effort was fruitless. The attempt at mediation failed. The story has been told in detail elsewhere[1] of how the Government, on March 19, introduced in Parliament the Minimum Wage Bill which affirmed the principle of the minimum wage, but set up district machinery to give effect to the principle and did not insert the district figures (as made by the miners) in the Schedules of the Bill. On the same day also the tendency for methods of repression to be used were signalised by the decision to arrest Tom Mann. The arrest of Tom Mann and prosecution of the printer and publisher of his journal *The Syndicalist* for the 'Don't Shoot' leaflet was raised in debate in the House of Commons by Josiah Wedgwood, who stated that since the trial of William Cobbett in 1831 'prosecutions of the Press of this nature have ceased'. He pointed out that such as Tom Mann, a working-class leader, had been singled out for arrest and trial, while no action was taken against Sir Edward Carson and other Ulster Conservatives who had been making seditious if not treasonable speeches. George Lansbury followed Wedgwood, saying: 'I cannot respect the law which discriminates between Privy Councillors and men who have to earn their daily bread'. He referred to a statement in that morning's Tory newspapers and declared:

[1] See *The Miners: Years of Struggle* (pp. 90–122).

... that the Government are going to use the forces of the Crown, and, generally speaking, they are going to be marched about the country for the purpose of over-aweing the miners. I am going to do everything I can to make the miners realise that they have a right to sell their labour on their own terms, without being dictated to by Governments, and if any Government think they are going to put down unrest and crush out this spirit of unrest by taking hold of a tiny little journal like the 'Syndicalist' they are making the biggest mistake that any Government has ever made in our time. . . . You call upon one set of the working classes to murder another set of the working classes, for the soldiers are drawn from the working classes, if you set out to shoot down their fathers and their mothers. You know perfectly well that you are calling upon them to murder their loved ones. It is nothing else. I am sure I am not here to say that I approve of that. I hope that British soldiers will have manliness and pluck enough to say, 'We are ready to defend the country if need be against foreign invasion, but we are not ready to shoot down our brothers, our sisters, our wives, and our friends in defence of the capitalists, who are trying to starve us into submission'. (*Hansard*, March 25, 1912.)

The Attorney-General, Sir Rufus Isaacs (afterwards Viceroy of India where he was responsible for great severities of repression), elaborately explained that the freedom of the press was not in danger, in that the prosecutions were set going under the Incitement to Mutiny Act of 1797—which Wedgwood had described as a most reactionary measure, fought against at the time of its passage by Sheridan and Charles James Fox. The Attorney's reply was much interrupted from the Labour benches, particularly on his arguments to escape the charge of class discrimination. Thereupon Keir Hardie rose, and, saying that Isaacs had 'been reasoning on a false basis', he went on:

What has happened at this moment? One prominent Labour leader is in gaol, and from every part of the industrial field come resolutions of protest demanding a general strike until he is released, calling upon Labour Members to stop the proceedings of this House until something is done. That is what your prosecutions are leading you to.

Lastly referring to the 'Don't Shoot' leaflet, Keir Hardie said:

To-night we are discussing the prosecution of men for no other offence whatever than that they have gone to the soldiers and said, 'Comrades, when your brothers are fighting for better conditions—conditions for you yourselves when you return to work—do not shoot them down, even if your officers command you to do so. Take the consequences of refusal to shoot them down, but do not murder your brother and your comrade who is fighting your cause as well as his own'. (*Hansard*, March 25, 1912.)

It is not necessary here to recount the progress through Parliament of the Minimum Wage Bill, or what the Miners' Conference for a time hoped from it, or of how they found that their hopes had been in vain and that they had been deluded; or of how the Bill was finally carried against the opposition of the Miners' M.P.s and the whole Labour Party by the combined votes of Liberals, Conservatives and Irish Nationalists. The Bill became law on March 29, and the M.F.G.B. Conference decided they must take a vote of the men whether or not to continue the strike. The ballot paper put the question:

Are you in favour of resuming work pending settlement of the minimum rates of wages in the various grades by the district boards to be appointed under the Mines Minimum Wage Act?

By ballot returned on April 3 the miners decided to continue the strike by 244,011 to 201,013. In Scotland the majority for continuing the strike was 30,473 against 23,186. The Executive Committee and, on April 6, an M.F.G.B. Special Conference took the view that the majority was not great enough and that the strike should be ended. By mid-April the pits were once more at work. The strikers went back with an ill grace because the pit-men felt the Government had cheated them of an assured victory. This dissatisfaction amongst the colliers, so many of whom had previously voted for Liberal candidates in parliamentary elections, was soon to be expressed as a change of political outlook. Asquith, Lloyd George and Sir Edward Grey had been very clever indeed in the way they ended the coal strike, but in so doing they over-reached themselves. The long-term policy they had learned from W. E. Gladstone, of endeavouring always to retain a large section of organised labour within the ranks of Liberalism, had been exploded by their immediate policy towards the miners in 1912. Anyone ten years later would have been able to look back and say they were 'hoist with their own petard'.

7. WHEN SCOT MEETS SCOT

Under the new Act the two sides had to foregather and take the first steps towards the setting up of a Joint District Board, which would come into being when 'recognised' by the Board of Trade.

After a prolonged wrangle as to whether the Scottish miners were entitled to have a lawyer, James Macbeth, as Secretary to their side (they eventually won the point), the Joint District Board continued its sessions day after day for ten days between May 9 and May 30, while sub-committees were meeting on the intermediate days. Smillie and Macbeth argued for the miners' schedule of claims and against the set of figures proposed by the coal-owners. The employers put forward counter-arguments. One example out of these ten days must suffice. On May 16 Adam Nimmo, after remarking that 'Mr. Smillie is putting forward his claims on an entirely arbitrary and capricious basis' and 'in ignorance of the existing rates', said:

If I were to assume for a moment that he put them forward with a due and proper knowledge of the facts as existing in the Scottish coal trade, then we could only assume that he was bent upon a policy of plunder and rapine which I think would be unexampled in connection with any trade. (May 16, 1912.)

Later he said that 'it would entirely and absolutely ruin the whole Trade altogether'.

Smillie, after recalling that on seven different occasions he had been present at the advertised funeral of the Scottish coal trade but that 'it is still alive and kicking', remarked on the familiar argument that unless a reduction in wages was granted or an increase in wages refused, 'the Scottish coal trade was doomed and would have to close up'. He then told how in 1909, being told 'of the parlous state of the Scottish coal trade', the Scottish Miners' Federation extracted the figures of some public companies, with interesting results:

In spite of all the bad trade for the last ten or fifteen years and the terrible ravages made by wages and legislation, and the rapine and plunder that are going on, the shares of many of the companies were higher in value when we got these figures out, as follows:

Coltness Company, the £1 shares were standing at £2 : 19 : 6; Fife Coal Company, the £1 shares were standing at £5⅞; the Lochgelly Coal Company, £10 shares were standing at £22⅙; John Wilson, the £8½ shares were standing at £24; Merry & Cuninghame, £10 shares at £14⅛; Shotts Iron Company, £1 shares at £2 : 2 : 6; Wilsons & Clyde, £3 shares at £10 : 15 : 6.

The position in which the shares of a company stand usually is a fairly good indication of the state of the profits earned by that company. I put these figures before you to reassure you, for the sake of patriotism, that the Scottish coal trade is not anything like dead up to the present time. (May 17, 1912.)

The two sides failed to agree on the first minimum rates of wages. They failed to agree on the district rules. So under the Act it fell to the three joint-chairmen to settle. Their Award caused great dissatisfaction amongst the miners. For similar reasons there was dissatisfaction in other coal-fields. Soon an M.F.G.B. Special Conference uttered a strong protest and called on the Government to take action to remedy the defects in the awards. A deputation went on July 15 to Prime Minister Asquith, from whom they got back no change. Indignation grew and was voiced in a resolution expressing 'strong dissatisfaction' at an M.F.G.B. Special Conference,[1] and mentioned especially the following:

(a) The fact that with few exceptions no award has provided for the paying of 5s. per day to the low paid wage workmen;

(b) in many instances the Independent Chairmen have not had reasonable regard to the average wages of the piece-workers in fixing the minimum wage;

(c) those awards which require 100 per cent of attendance at work to qualify for the minimum wage;

(d) the serious delay of many owners in paying the arrears of wages due under the awards. (August 16, 1912.)

Nothing of any importance was done to remedy these defects. Consequently the miners, roused by the great strike struggle and soured of Liberalism by the behaviour of the Government, now turned more and more towards a forward policy. In preparation for any coming struggle they began to strengthen their forces and to look round for allies. They may have felt

[1] Smillie presided. He became president of the M.F.G.B. after Enoch Edwards' death in June 1912.

themselves worsted and cheated. All the more, this experience had the effect of welding them more closely together both within Scotland and throughout the British coal-fields.

While the discussions were going on in the newly constituted District Wages Board a meeting of the members of the Conciliation Board was held in Glasgow on May 20, following on a letter from the miners asking for a meeting to consider a demand for 25 per cent increase in wages. The employers to begin with said they were willing to consider weekly pays in future. As regards the application before them, they could not grant it. At the adjourned meeting on June 4, the new Chairman, Adam Nimmo, repeated their rejection of the application and then said:

We consider that the strike which took place following upon the demand for an individual minimum wage was in breach of the agreement, and that by that strike the agreement, in so far as it bears upon wages and values of coal, was really torn up. Further, we have today the individual minimum wage which has been introduced into the situation, and which has introduced a new and entirely disturbing factor. We further do not think that the scale of wages in the agreement can now be regarded as operative. We do not see our way, in view of the whole altered circumstances, to be bound by that scale.

When this statement was made it seemed to open up a prospect of a bitter quarrel. Later in the discussion old Andrew McCosh, now the ex-chairman, amplified the employers' standpoint in the following remarks:

The position we are in is this, that on account of the strike prices have been rushed up, and we are altogether in an abnormal state. Then we have this minimum wage upon us. As you know, it is to be retrospective, and whatever is to be the award, I do not think you gentlemen look for any reduction in wages thereby, at any rate. Then we have in a short time the new Mines Act coming into force, which undoubtedly will add very considerably to the cost of the collieries. We have also the Insurance Act coming into force, which will add to our cost.

VICE-CHAIRMAN SMILLIE: And to ours also.

MR. McCOSH: But you get the benefit, and we do not. You are to get 9d. for 4d., you know.

The disagreement was finally referred to a neutral Chairman, Lord Hunter, who gave his award for a 12½ per cent increase. Lord Hunter took the somewhat unusual step of appending to this award a Note in which he explained how he had reached this decision as an interpretation of existing agreements and the prices figures of the coal trade. In the course of this Note, however, he refused to deal with the alleged breach of agreement, saying that it was not his business. He also ruled out the miners' contention that prices during the strike should be taken into account.

Thereafter for a year or two longer the course of the Conciliation Board resulted in small successive advances in wages.

8. GROWTH OF THE SCOTTISH MINERS' FEDERATION

The Minimum Wage strike of 1912 was outstanding in the history of the miners' struggle. It played a great part in the further development and strengthening of the Trade Union movement in the mining areas. This applied particularly to Scotland. Membership figures of the Scottish Miners' Federation began to mount. From the 50,000 mark in 1900 it had risen to 78,700 in 1910; but after the great strike the figure for 1913 leapt to 87,200. By 1914 the Scots were paying to the Miners' Federation of Great Britain on the basis of no less than 90,000 members, or nearly thrice as many as a score of years earlier. As boys and women were paying half dues and each two of them counted as a full member, the actual number organised was greater than the figures returned to the M.F.G.B.

At the same time the numbers employed in the coal-mining industry were growing, especially in Fife and the Lothians, both absolutely and in relation to the number in other trades. But the rate of increase in organisation was ahead of the increase in the number employed. By 1913 there were 38 per cent more miners than at the opening of the century, but those organised had increased by 74 per cent. In 1900 less than half the number were organised; by 1913 more than six out of every ten were in the Miners' unions, while many were enrolled in the colliery craftsmen's organisations and in other craft or general labour unions. By the eve of the 1914–18 war miners with their wives and families must have made up nearly a fifth of the total population of Scotland.

Within a few months after their experiences in the great strike, the Scottish miners had taken a significant move: this was to seek to strengthen the loose federation in which the eight county associations were linked. To bring them into a closer structure a scheme was prepared in the shape of a new constitution. This, after a ballot, came into force on October 31, 1914, and new officers were elected. The most spectacular change was in the name, which was altered from Scottish Miners' Federation to National Union of Scottish Mineworkers. However, this did not mean, as it might seem, that the existing eight district unions comprising this body were now dissolved and merged into a new union. The districts continued as separate unions, but with a closer degree of federation. The great strike of 1912 had driven home the need for unity: and thereafter the virtues of unity were hymned at every conference. In practice a generation was to pass before this aim could be realised.

9. THE SCOTTISH MINERS' HOUSES

The same year of 1912 saw the fruits of a dogged campaign by the Scottish Miners to force attention to the housing conditions under which they were living. Deputations from the Scottish Miners had met the Secretary of State for Scotland in 1909 and again in 1911 to press for an investigation of housing in the mining areas of Scotland. But it was not till after the shock of the 1912 strike that an enquiry, in the form of a Royal Commission on Housing in Scotland,[1] was undertaken. It was 1918, on the eve of Lloyd George's 'Homes for Heroes' campaign, before it had reported; the publication of the volumes of evidence was not completed until 1921.

Housing in Scotland in recent times was described by a Secretary of State for Scotland as 'shocking' and 'a disgrace to Scotland'. But great improvements have taken place during the past fifty years. At the beginning of this century the housing conditions particularly in the mining areas were

[1] Cmd. 1831 of 1918.

appalling, and far worse than in the most wretched industrial areas of England. The industrial revolution of 1780 onwards had brought housing problems, which became more difficult as the nineteenth century unfolded. In the twentieth century there was a falling-off in the building of houses. The number of builders in Scotland fell from 124,000 in 1901 to 96,000 in 1911. This in turn had meant not only too few houses for the people but that 'arrears of shortage had been fast accumulating', to quote the Commission Report.

The dozen Commissioners included David Gilmour, Secretary of the Lanarkshire Miners' County Union, and the head of the Fife Coal Company, Charles Augustus Carlow. From the volumes of evidence presented by the Commission we have space to cite only their horrifying description of 'A Mining District'.

The 'Miners' Row' of inferior class is often a dreary and feature-less place, with houses, dismal in themselves, arranged in monotonous lines or in squares. The open spaces are encumbered with wash-houses, privies, etc., often out of repair, and in wet weather get churned up into a morass of semi-liquid mud, with little in the way of solidly constructed road or footpath—a fact which adds greatly to the burdens of the overwrought housewife.

The houses vary greatly in construction, but a large number are of two types. The older is either a 'single-end' or 'but-and-ben', according as it has one or two rooms. It has only one door, and the solid back wall is pierced only by the smallest of windows, if by any, so that through ventilation does not exist.

Many of the older houses show the faults of their class—leaky roofs, damp walls, and uneven and broken floors—the last a source of particularly bitter complaint. In addition, there are faults not found outside mining communities, the chief being broken plaster and fissures in the walls, where 'subsidence' has been serious, while in the worst houses in the West of Scotland the only place for the storage of coals is below the bed. The impossibility of domestic cleanliness and order where this is the case needs no enforcement.

What a nightmare it was for the miner's wife with a large household, living under these conditions, may be imagined from the following description:

If the workers in a house ate on different shifts, the task of the housewife is complicated by irregular meals and sleeping-hours. If the pit is a wet one, the miners' soaking clothes must be left at night by the kitchen fire; and as the kitchen is a sleeping apartment even where there are one or two other rooms, the steam and gas which are given off as the pit clothes dry are highly injurious to the children, who may be in one of the two large beds nearby. In the absence of baths at the pithead or in any save the newest houses, the miner on his return must take his bath in the scullery (if there is one), or in the inevitable publicity of the kitchen. With this accumulation of difficulties to contend with, the standard of cleanliness and neatness attained in many houses (though by no means in all) is a matter for genuine surprise and admiration. In the numerous cases, however, in which water has not been introduced into the houses but must be fetched from a standpipe at the end of the row, a high standard of cleanliness cannot be looked for.

The sanitary conditions described were a menace to the health of the miner and his family:

The dreary and unkempt surroundings of many rows have been already referred to, but a word must be said as to the nature of the outhouses which fill the intervals between the rows. Occasionally there is a properly constructed common washhouse, but in the older villages more often only such makeshift and ramshackle washhouses and coal-sheds as the miners have run up for themselves. But the chief of these unsightly structures are the privies. In the West of Scotland this often is a 'privy-midden', which has only in comparatively recent times been expelled from the cities and still unhappily retains its place in the mining villages. It is a large erection, open on one side, where ashes and all other household refuse are thrown in, and closed (though often not adequately closed) on the side which serves as latrine. It is the only sanitary convenience in many rows; and it is so impossible to keep clean, so foul-smelling, and so littered with filth of all sorts, that no decent woman can use it, while if the children do so, it is at grave risk to their health of body and mind. Another case, one degree less bad, is that of the range of separate privies—one for each three or four houses in the row. Here things may be better if they are well kept, but the difficulty of keeping them well is enormous; and often locks are forced, and doors may even be wrenched off.

This appalling general picture of the miners' houses is borne out as being typical in every coal-field. In a passage summing up what the Commission regarded as necessary, we find these startling remarks:

2233. The last census showed that thousands of one-room houses continued to be occupied by families; that overcrowding reckoned even by the most moderate standard is practically universal in the one- and two-room houses; that, in spite of protest and administrative superintendence, domestic overcrowding of houses and over-

OLD STYLE MINERS' HOUSES, LUMPHINNANS, FIFE

NEW HOUSING, CROSSHILL-MEADOWS ESTATE, ARGYLL

PITHEAD, OLD STYLE : BARONY COLLIERY, AYRSHIRE

PITHEAD, NEW STYLE : COMRIE COLLIERY, FIFE

building of areas have not been prevented. To our amazement, we found that, even if we take overcrowding to mean more than three persons per room, we should, to secure even this moderate standard for Scotland, have to displace some 284,000 of the population. But this is not all. We conclude that, at least, 50 per cent. of the one-room houses and 15 per cent. of the two-room houses ought to be replaced by new houses. In brief, merely to relieve existing overcrowding, and replace houses that should be demolished, some 121,000 houses are required, and, if an improved standard is adopted, as we recommend, the total number of new houses required would approach 236,000. For such gigantic figures our Report submits full justification. On this point the Commission is unanimous.

Among the causes of the particularly bad housing in Scotland found by the Commissioners two may be noted, each of them rooted in the past—the peculiar Scottish system of land tenure, and the colliers' old slavery.

What changes took place in the next generation? For this we have to turn to the report on the Scottish Coalfields,[1] drawn up by a committee set up on July 27, 1942, of which the Solicitor-General for Scotland was chairman. Amongst its dozen members were James Barbour, formerly President of the National Union of Scottish Mineworkers; Alexander Cameron, Secretary, Mid and East Lothian Miners' Association; Peter Henderson, Miners' Agent, Fife, Clackmannan and Kinross Miners' Union; and William Pearson, Treasurer, National Union of Scottish Mineworkers.

The Committee estimated that, in all, some 33,500 new houses were needed: and they looked for this need to be met by local authorities with assistance from the Exchequer 'after the end of the war in Europe'.

Examining the general conditions of miners' houses the Committee found 'from our own observation' that since 1917 'there has been some general improvement', but that there was considerable room for further improvement. They had inspected the older type of miners' rows, by which the Royal Commissioners thirty years before had been so much depressed; and especially noted examples from Ayrshire (Auchinleck), Fife (Glencraig and Lumphinnans), Lanarkshire (Blantyre), Midlothian (Niddrie) and Stirlingshire (Cowie).

The Committee expressed their admiration in warm terms

[1] Cmd. 6575, Scottish Coalfields, Scottish Home Department, 1944.

for the efforts of the miners' wives:

We have been in some of the worst of these miners' rows. With roads in a wretched condition—no attempt on the part of the local authorities to keep them in repair—in wet weather mud often up to the ankles and with everything around looking sordid and tawdry. Yet in stopping at one or other of these hospitable houses for a cup of tea we gazed around in wonder and admiration at the amount of beauty these housewives had, by dint of hard work, provided even in these wretched rooms for their husbands and their children. Furniture, floors, brass-work, steel facing of the fireplaces were all bright and shining with the polish and the labour that had been used to great and good effect.

These changes, however, were an outcome of a later war. In 1912 few miners who had struggled so hard for wages and for better housing imagined that within two years the gathering storm would break, and they would be plunged into the strains and stress of the first World War.

CHAPTER VII

WAR AND ITS SEQUEL

I. THE WAR OF 1914–18

THE war between the Triple Alliance headed by Germany and the Triple Entente of Britain, France and Russia, began at the end of July 1914. Beginning as a mainly European war which many confidently expected to be over by Christmas 1914, it spread to every continent and lasted for over four years. It was interrupted by the Easter Rising in Ireland of 1916 and by the Russian Revolution in 1917. It ended with the defeat of Germany; the dismemberment of the Ottoman and Austro-Hungarian empires; and the addition of vast territories of Asia and Africa to the British Empire. Its total cost in human lives was put at over thirty million men, women and children. For the capitalist countries the course of the war marked the entry into a prolonged period of general crisis. For the peoples and for the working classes it marked an abrupt turn in history. Like all the other organised workers in Britain, the miners were to be profoundly affected by the opening of this epoch of wars and revolutions.

The attitude to war of the Scottish Miners had been elaborated before the war broke out. Along with other sections of the M.F.G.B. they had taken part in the International Miners' Congresses, where in successive meetings they had dealt with the war danger and passed resolutions in favour of peaceful means of settling disputes between governments. As part of the Labour Party they were committed to the policy resolutions of the Socialist International. With an increasing sense of urgency as the danger of war between the Triple Alliance and the Triple Entente grew nearer, the International Socialist Congresses of Stuttgart in 1907, of Copenhagen in 1910 and Basel in 1912, had laid down the policy to be followed by all working-class organisations and affiliated parties. The policy, or, as the resolutions said, 'the duty', was first, to do the utmost to prevent war; second, if war nevertheless broke out, to intervene to stop the war, which entailed opposition to their governments; and third, to use the crisis arising from the war to rouse the people and end the rule of the capitalist class. All sections of the Socialist International and of the British Labour movement had thus the duty of trying to prevent the outbreak of war. A manifesto on behalf of the British section was signed by Arthur Henderson, the secretary of the Labour Party, and by Keir Hardie, summoning the workers to oppose the war-mongers and the ruling class (August 1, 1914):

Workers, stand together, therefore, for peace! Combine and conquer the militarist enemy and the self-seeking Imperialists today, once and for all.

Men and women of Britain, you have now an unexampled opportunity of rendering a magnificent service to humanity, and to the world!

Proclaim that for you the days of plunder and butchery have gone by. Send messages of peace and fraternity to your fellows who have less liberty than you. Down with class rule! Down with the rule of brute force! Down with war! Up with the peaceful rule of the people!

But when, despite all efforts to prevent it, war broke out, the majority sections of the labour movement in Britain and in the other countries at war did not, with the exception of Russia, oppose their governments. Before the end of August in every other country they were supporting their governments. Minority sections endeavoured to oppose their governments and to struggle against the torrent of war fever in which the workers were swept along in that autumn of 1914. In Britain the minority was found within the trade unions and the socialist organisations which made up the Labour Party as well as in smaller bodies. Typical of the minority was the manifesto of the Independent Labour Party indicting the foreign policy of the British Liberal Government, the armament race and the practice of secret diplomacy. It ended with the words:

In forcing this appalling crime upon the nations, it is the rulers, the diplomats, the militarists who have sealed their doom. In tears of blood and bitterness the greater democracy will be born. With steadfast faith we greet the future; our cause is holy and imperishable, and the labour of our hands has not been in vain.

Long live Freedom and Fraternity! Long live International Socialism! (August 13, 1914.)

In the late autumn of that year 1914 along with James Middleton[1] the author visited Keir Hardie in Nevill's Court, off Fleet Street. It was the only time that the author had a prolonged conversation with the Scottish miner who had been a founding member of the M.F.G.B., the founder in 1893 of the I.L.P. and also the chief founder in 1900 of the Labour Party. For him the war was a calamity which threatened to wreck his whole life's effort for working-class independence, socialism and peace. Before another year was out he had died, broken-hearted. In that winter the author also had many talks with Robert Smillie who shared Keir Hardie's attitude.

Smillie was in an awkward position. He was President of the Scottish Miners' Federation, within which both his life's record and his position as President of the M.F.G.B. had lent him great prestige. He had been unchallenged leader for over twenty years in Scotland; and had sought to influence the miners and the miners' agents, to wean them away from Liberalism and towards support of socialism and peace. Now, suddenly, he found himself in a very small minority on this last great issue, both within the Executive Committee of the M.F.G.B. and, what was more galling, within the Executive of the Scottish Miners' Federation.

For some years he had relied much on the younger men who were socialists, in the Social Democratic Federation (which had become the British Socialist Party) and in the Independent Labour Party. But the British Socialist Party had for long time been under the domination of H. M. Hyndman who was supporting the war, and twenty months passed by before the anti-war minority (in Scotland led by John MacLean and William Gallacher) had become the majority. Consequently at the outbreak of war some of the miners' agents belonging to the British Socialist Party had followed the lead of H. M. Hyndman. Amongst these was Smillie's chief lieutenant, John Robertson, Chairman of the Lanarkshire Miners' County Union. The difference inside the

[1] Then Assistant Secretary of the Labour Party and afterwards for many years its Secretary.

Executive about the war at times grew bitter enough; but as the war developed the miners both in Scotland and throughout the United Kingdom were glad to have as their chief spokesman one whose first concern was the interests of the working people.

By the end of the first six months of the war there was a serious shortage of coal output, mostly due to high numbers of miners enlisted. Coal-owners pressed for an extension of hours by the suspension of the Eight Hours Act, which the miners vigorously resisted as being no solution to the problem. The matter had become urgent by February 1915, when 17 per cent of all the miners had enlisted. In Scotland the percentage was still higher at 21·3 per cent, and by August 1915 nearly one in four of the Scottish miners had joined the forces. A Home Office Departmental Committee was set up on which three miners' leaders figured, including Robert Smillie. Its report in May warned against further recruitment, opposed more employment of women and children and urged employers to 'co-operate with the representatives of the workmen' on any questions likely to produce friction. In July 1915 a conference of both sides met with the Home Secretary as Chairman; output was short of 3,000,000 tons a month despite efforts by the men, and the cry for suspension of the Eight Hours Act was again raised. At this Robert Smillie appealed for an increase, so that 'the grates of the poor should not be empty' that winter, and that every effort should be tried rather than allow the suspension of the Act.

The cost of living had soared, and the M.F.G.B. put forward a claim for a 20 per cent increase to meet the rising cost of living. After the owners had offered 10 per cent and notice had been given to terminate all existing Conciliation Board agreements, the Government stepped in to secure district negotiations. Scotland fared better than most, achieving an 18½ per cent rise.

Before 1915 was out another question which was to have increasing significance at a later stage had reached a conclusion. Under the influence of Robert Smillie the embryo Triple Alliance of railway, transport and miners' unions, first suggested at the Miners' Annual Conference of 1913, following the stormy experiences of 1910 and 1912, was re-formed, and brought into full existence. Robert Smillie became Chairman. It was the firm protest of the Triple Alliance the next year which scotched proposals to introduce Chinese labour which it was feared would threaten under-cutting of wage-rates.

Such was the general picture of the first eighteen months of the war. From 1914 onward the minutes of the Executive Committee were regularly printed and circulated. From these we find that over half the items reported are pit disputes or grievances. Sometimes they would be settled without lock-out or strike: but the General Fund accounts for 1915-16 show that strike payments were made in every main county except the Lothians, amounting for the twelve months to £7621, or nearly half the expenditure.

In February 1917 an event took place which was to have consequences of very great importance in the future struggle of the miners. Lloyd George announced that henceforward, for the duration of the emergency, there would be State control of the mines. This did not amount to nationalisation, but was merely State control over output and distribution. The first charge on the industry remained the profits of the coal-owners. These were guaranteed out of a national profits pool, to which the Government contributed heavily from excess profits tax proceeds. But State control had also strategic advantages for the miners; it destroyed the whole argument of the owners that wages could not be settled on a national, but only on a district, basis: it thus struck at the root of the owners' refusal to negotiate nationally. At the same time, it was to give added impetus to the miners' demand for nationalisation.

This came to the fore in the Annual Conference of the Scottish Miners held in August 1918, when John Robertson moved an important resolution on the nationalisation of mines. His speech was at the same time a strong plea for the miners to concern themselves with political action. The resolution ran:

(a) That in the opinion of this Conference the time has come when this country should no longer be dependent for its coal supply on a small number of capitalist colliery proprietors, coal-merchants and dealers, among whom there is an increasing tendency to combinations and price arrangements, by which the consumer is made to pay a quite unnecessary price for coal; and that the Government should at once take over all coal and other mines, work them as a national enterprise, and appropriate to the nation all rents and wayleaves.

(*b*) That in organising the nation's coal supply on the basis of production for use instead of production for profit, due arrangements should be made for the participation in the management, both local and central, of the employees of all grades.

(*c*) That the Government Coal Department might undertake the supply for export and shipping, the Local Authorities, and all industrial consumers of any magnitude; delivering the coal for domestic consumption to any railway station at a uniform fixed price, as unalterable and as uniform as that of the postage stamp. (August 16, 1918.)

Other resolutions of a directly political kind carried at this conference were in favour of Home Rule for Scotland; release of Tom Mooney, an American trade union organiser 'framed' for his activities; and the release of John MacLean. John MacLean, Scots teacher, one of the anti-war minority of the British Socialist Party, was internationally famous: Lenin before the October Revolution of 1917 had named MacLean as one who held unswervingly to the pre-war decisions of the Second International, and called him one of 'those isolated heroes who have taken on themselves the arduous mission of being the forerunners of the world revolution'. The British authorities had taken action against MacLean, and at this conference a motion—moved by Joseph Young, seconded by Andrew Clarke—was carried almost unanimously, declaring:

That we protest against the action of the Authorities for the imprisonment of John MacLean and that we take action along with other Trade Unions to try to get him released. (August 16, 1918.)

This was the last conference for a number of years over which Smillie presided. The M.F.G.B. in that summer of 1918 carried through extensive changes in its organisation and policy. In future there were to be two whole-time national officials. By the time the year 1918 ended Smillie had become the full-time salaried President of the M.F.G.B., which entailed his resignation as Scottish President (a post held by him nearly a quarter of a century) and also from the post of President of the Lanarkshire Miners' County Union.

At a monthly conference of Lanarkshire council delegates, on December 28, 1918, Smillie made a farewell speech. To it

James Tonner[1] replied that every miner in Lanarkshire felt proud at Smillie's success: 'His election to the highest rung in our movement will enlarge his activities and redound to the welfare of the whole Trade Union movement'.

The full-time President of the M.F.G.B. was already busy working on a series of post-war demands which were put to the Government in January 1919.

2. THE SANKEY COMMISSION AND AFTER

There were four such demands. The first was a claim for a 30 per cent advance on total earnings exclusive of the war wage. Other points were the six-hour day; certain questions affecting demobilisation; and—of great importance—State ownership of the mines, with joint control and administration by the State and the miners. This was presented as embodied in a draft Bill, the Nationalisation of Mines and Minerals Bill. When the Lloyd George Coalition Government refused these demands, a ballot of the British coal-fields resulted in an overwhelming majority to secure them by strike action. In Scotland the ballot showed 77,130 in favour of a stoppage and 14,601 against, or a vote of 84 per cent in favour, as compared with the average for Britain as a whole of 85.4 per cent.

To avert this, Lloyd George offered a Royal Commission of which half the members would be appointed or approved by the Miners' Federation and promised that whatever the Commission recommended would be carried into effect. Among the questions into which the Commissioners were to enquire were wages; hours; the social conditions of the miners; and, most far-reaching of all, the future organisation.

Any scheme that may be submitted to or formulated by the Commissioners for the future organisation of the coal industry, whether on the present basis of joint control, nationalisation, or any other basis.

These were startlingly comprehensive terms of reference. Even so there was considerable hesitation among the miners, who had had experiences of delaying tactics by previous Governments. Finally Lloyd George was obliged to agree

---

[1] James Tonner, miners' agent and subsequently President of the County Union.

that an interim report should be forthcoming from the Commission in less than a month. Thereupon, after keen debate, a Miners' Conference on February 27 decided to postpone strike notices for three weeks.

The Coal Industry Commission began on March 3, 1919, with Mr. Justice Sankey as Chairman, three Government nominees, three representatives of the coal-owners, and six members appointed, or approved by the M.F.G.B. Robert Smillie was one of these. For a fortnight the evidence heard was closely followed by an aroused public; for the first time they were getting a comprehensive picture of the state of the industry and the conditions of the miners. It was a startling picture; disclosures of swollen profits wrung from low wages paid to miners and high prices charged to the public; disclosures by experts of waste and inefficiency in production and distribution; and disclosures by Government officials of wartime profiteering.

But it was not only the economic facts which startled the public. For on March 14 and 15, when the M.F.G.B. witnesses were examined, the conditions of the miners' lives were brought into the full light of day. Chief amongst the miners' witnesses was the Scottish President, John Robertson. He gave comprehensive evidence on the miners' standard of life; on health, education, accidents, and, above all, on housing. Indeed, after hearing the evidence on housing, Mr. Justice Sankey in his Report was forced to the conclusion that

There are houses in some districts which are a reproach to our civilisation. No judicial language is sufficiently strong or sufficiently severe to apply to their condemnation.

It was no accident that it had been the Scottish President who gave the main evidence on this subject. Miners' housing conditions in 1919 were no better than in 1912; if anything, they were worse, for the war had interrupted any replacement that might have been in progress. Even in England and Wales over-crowding was bad enough, affecting four out of every ten persons in certain mining villages of Durham. But housing conditions among the Scots were appalling.

Typical of conditions prevailing was the description[1] given

[1] Royal Commission on Housing in Scotland, p. 139.

by the Lanarkshire Miners' Union of Rosehall rows, Whifflet.

They consist of four long parallel rows of single-story hovels; most of them have not rones to carry the rain from the roofs. Rainwater simply runs down the roof and then runs down the walls, or falls off as chance or the wind decides. There are no coal-cellars; coals are kept below the beds. There are no wash-houses. Water is supplied from stands in the alleys. The closet accommodation is hideous. A number of these hovels are built back-to-back.

Although the publication of all the evidence of the Scottish Housing Commission was not to be completed for a full two years after the Sankey Commission, John Robertson had it all at his finger tips; he had lived there.

A Royal Commission limited to housing in Scotland had followed one great strike of miners; the threat of the next great strike, hard upon the terrible years of war, had produced a Royal Commission with very much more comprehensive terms of reference. The whole future conduct of the industry was in issue. Before the Sankey Commission, private owner-ship of mining was in the dock. The indictment was in-escapable. The case for nationalisation was overwhelming.

On March 20, three reports of the Sankey Commission were presented to Parliament. There was a Majority Report signed by the six Commissioners appointed, or approved, by the M.F.G.B.; a Minority Report signed by the three repre-sentatives of the coal-owners; and the 'Sankey' Report signed by the Chairman Sankey and the three Government nominees.

The Sankey Report recommended the limitation of hours of work underground to seven as from July 16, 1919, 'and subject to the economic position of the industry at the end of 1920', to six hours as from July 13, 1921; with a $46\frac{1}{2}$ hour week for surface workers; and a 2s. wage increase. A tribute to the case on miners' social conditions was tacitly acknow-ledged by a recommendation that 1d. per ton should be col-lected and 'applied to improve the housing and amenities of each particular colliery district'. Finally, the Sankey Report made the momentous recommendation, declaring that

Even upon the evidence already given, the present system of ownership and working in the coal industry stands condemned, and some other system must be substituted for it, either nationalisation or a method of unification by national purchase and/or by joint control.

Comprehensive investigation of schemes to effect this were to be carried out in a second stage of the Commission.

There and then in the House of Commons the Government announced that it was adopting the Sankey Report 'in letter and in spirit'. The miners took a ballot, which was declared on April 15, and 90 per cent were in favour of acceptance. Strike notices were withdrawn. Lloyd George's Government had succeeded in averting a general stoppage.

For two months the Commission was at work on the second stage. When the Commission reported on June 20, seven of the thirteen Commissioners were in favour of nationalisation as the best method of unification. Behind the scenes manœuvres began; weeks passed; the Government suddenly raised the price of coal by no less than 6s. a ton. The miners noted these signs that Lloyd George would go back on his promise. Tension grew and the attitude of the Scottish Miners is reflected in the proceedings of the 26th Annual Conference.

In his opening address the new President, John Robertson, M.P., said that 'it is remarkable that not even the report by the coal-owners' members of the Commission defended the existing system of private ownership'. He continued:

One would have expected the Coalowners to defend the present system, but they did not. Joint management of the workers, baths, better housing, share of the profits, they were prepared to offer. The bait was not sufficiently enticing for the miners. Nationalisation is coming, not for the benefit of the miners, but for the benefit of the whole community. (August 13, 1919.)

The first resolution at this conference, passed unanimously, demanded that the Government should implement the recommendations of the Sankey Commission and nationalise the mines. Robert Smillie, who was received with enthusiasm, made a speech which both referred to his policy in the past and to the need of strike action if Lloyd George and Bonar Law, who was Chairman of the Tory Party, were to bilk the miners. Referring to the Coal Commission's Report, he said:

We hear of its being wrong to adopt direct action for political purposes. I want to put it to you: If the Prime Minister and the Government invite us to take part in a Royal Commission, and then allow their capitalist friends in the House of Commons to frighten them and prevent them carrying out the recommendations of the Commission —which was practically a promise of Mr. Bonar Law for the Government—it will be the duty of organised Labour and of the miners themselves to use their industrial power to force the hands of the Government.

Hardly had the delegates dispersed when Lloyd George, on August 18, 1919, announced the Government's policy—to reject nationalisation.

Although the miners were ready to take strike action, and although they secured the assent of the T.U.C. to join with them, 'if and when' it was considered necessary, the T.U.C., when it came to the bit, decided to limit itself to political propaganda. So the year 1919–20 left the miners baulked in their major aim of nationalisation. The Government's promise had been broken; and apart from the Seven Hours Act (seven hours plus winding time) and the wage increase (which was not to last) the most the miners received from the whole Sankey Commission and controversy was the Welfare Commission's activity, financed by a penny a ton levy. Nevertheless, the evidence put forward and the whole of the circumstances of its creation and conduct made the Sankey Commission a landmark. The main deposit left by Sankey was not material: it was the conviction in the minds of the colliers that private ownership was detrimental to the coal industry and ought to be abolished.

3. THE YEAR 1920

The twelve months that followed were to prove a testing time for the miners, not least the Scots. How was their organisation shaping, and in what ways was their outlook hardening as the turbulent days began to approach? First, as to numerical strength the Scottish miners reached the highest point of their history. The increase in membership was such that by the end of May it was decided to raise the figure of members affiliated to the M.F.G.B. from 90,000 to 110,000.

It may be assumed that the total number organised by mid-summer of 1920 was something approaching 120,000. On May 14, 1920, the Executive had decided to accept the Scottish Oil Workers 'as a separate entity'. In the same month a Committee was appointed 'to draw up Rules for a National Union'. This was the period when in the trade union movement as a whole there was a rapid growth of both federations and amalgamations. One curious example of this tendency was an application to affiliate to the National Union of Scottish Mineworkers from the Associated Blacksmiths' and Ironworkers' Society of Great Britain and Ireland. The Executive Committee, however, on September 27, decided that this application must be refused. Nevertheless, the exact frontiers of the influence and organising power of the Miners' unions was never defined with any extreme strictness. Occasionally they went well beyond their frontier, as in the case of the Ayrshire Miners' Federal Union; about this time and for many years afterwards the Ayrshire men had a large number of rope workers in one of their branches. The rope workers had been on strike, had been helped to win by the aid of the miners and had themselves requested to be enrolled in the union that had won them the victory. On the other hand, this absence of strict definition of frontiers led sometimes to quarrels with other unions, and always in the course of the next twenty-five years to frequent and prolonged discussion with craft unions whose members might be found working in or about the pits.

Their general outlook on industrial and political questions was shown that summer, first by their Executive decision to affiliate to the 'Scottish Home Rule Association' (June 14, 1920). Shortly after the Executive took action supporting Home Rule for India too. That summer, the Government seemed on the point of declaring open war on the young Soviet Republic. This had resulted in the formation of Councils of Action. The Scottish Miners' Executive

decided that we recommend the Conference of Delegates today to adopt a policy of hostility against the Government should they declare war against Russia. (August 9, 1920.)

Such was the mood as seen in the Executive minutes that

summer. But dominating all other interests was the storm blowing up over wages.

The cost of living had been steeply rising and negotiations were opened between the M.F.G.B. and the Government for a pay increase. When the Government made a counter-offer of about two-thirds only of the miners' figure, there was a ballot in April which recommended acceptance nationally by 53·97 per cent. The Scottish vote was 54,708 for and 51,564 against acceptance, or 51·48 per cent in favour. But immediately afterwards the Government clapped a huge increase on to the price of coal, especially household coal; the Government was manipulating prices, and had in view the preparation of public opinion for the decontrol of the mines. At the same time the cost of living leapt to 142 per cent above pre-war. The M.F.G.B., after debate in the Executive and in conferences, put forward a demand for a further increase which they linked with a cut in domestic coal prices. When this was rejected by the Government a strike ballot was taken at the end of August 1920. This showed a majority of 71·75 per cent for a stoppage, Scotland voting in favour by 72·40 per cent.

The response was practically complete. The strike, known as the Datum Line Strike, lasted two weeks or a little more, was conducted nationally and concluded nationally on terms which linked wages with total output. These terms gave advances in wages, provided total production rose above a certain given tonnage, called the Datum Line;[1] these were not to last beyond the winter of 1920–21.

4. THE GREAT LOCK-OUT OF 1921

Meantime a world economic crisis developed in the later months of 1920 and ushered in the 'between the wars' period when unemployment in the coal-mining and other industries soon reached levels never known before. From March 1921 onward for twenty years unemployment was at the million mark, and far above it in the worst years. In the spring of 1921 the Lloyd George Government suddenly abandoned the

[1] *The Miners: Years of Struggle* (pp. 239–78).

control of coal-mines and this precipitated the great lock-out of 1921. In that great struggle, which lasted for three months, the outstanding features were the abandonment of the miners early in April 1921 by their allies in the Triple Alliance; the actions of the Government against the miners; and the mobilisation on the side of the coal-owners and the Government of every possible agency that could help in strike-breaking. Consequently this dispute was fought with more bitterness than the struggles of 1920 or 1912 or those of the early 'nineties. In particular parts of the Scottish coal-field this bitterness resulted in dramatic events, especially in the county of Fife.

In the first week of April 1921 what the *Dunfermline Press* described as an 'ugly situation' developed in certain coal-field areas, into which large contingents both of the armed forces and of police were drafted. The miners were indignant at police, and later the military, being brought in from other districts. There were demonstrations and mass marches to those pits where managers and managerial volunteers refused to draw the fires. Disturbances were reported only from areas where these two factors were combined.

At Blairadam on Sunday, April 3, miners went to the Aitken Pit and interviewed the manager, Mr. Carlow Reid, who agreed to draw all the fires and have all work suspended. Yet two days later, on Tuesday, April 5, a charabanc of police arrived. The men rushed to the spot and delivered an ultimatum to the police, allowing them fifteen minutes to leave the village. This they finally did. Some windows were broken in the colliery office. The *Dunfermline Press* commented that after these scenes 'Kelty is taking the strike very quietly'.

In Lochgelly the men sent a deputation to the management at Nellie Pit, owned by the Lochgelly Iron and Coal Company, with a view to stopping work. The press describes the incident which followed:

The police were aware of the intention of the men and with commendable speed a detachment was rushed up to the colliery whither over 1,000 miners had already assembled. The miners, after counselling among themselves, appointed representatives to demand that the officials withdraw. This request, however, was flatly refused but the strikers did not yield, and continued to clamour for about 2 hours for the withdrawal of the workers. In view of the insistent demand made by the strikers, the officials ultimately agreed to cease work at 9 o'clock on Monday night.

In this district the stoppage was complete. Not a single member of the Miners' Union or Scottish Colliery Engine-men and Boilermen's Association was working at any of the collieries in the district. A large committee, representative of all employed in and about the mines, was formed, 'with a view to having unanimity of purpose'. At a mass meeting of the Glencraig and Lochore miners, T. Culbert, secretary of the local branch of the Scottish Colliery Firemen and Boilermen's Association, submitted a report of the Delegate Conference held in Glasgow a few days earlier at which it had been decided by an overwhelming majority to support the miners. Four days later another mass meeting of Glencraig and Lochore miners passed the following resolution:

That this joint meeting of Glencraig and Lochore locked-out miners demand that our National Executive cease negotiations with the coalowners and that the Government give effect to the findings of the Sankey Commission.

Descriptions of 'drastic action' at Kinglassie Pit may be given from the *Dunfermline Press*, telling its tale vividly, but entirely from the standpoint of the authorities and the mine-owners. Here 'several thousand strikers marched to the pit and ordered that the fires be drawn and the pit closed down within half an hour'. The company had called on the police but these were 'unable to cope with the large crowd'. The pit was therefore abandoned 'and strikers cut the telephone wires'. Again, at Oakley Colliery four or five hundred miners 'marched from Valleyfield to Kinneddar pit' and per-emptorily demanded 'an instant withdrawal of all labour from the colliery'. Here

on the manager being communicated with, he observed in effect that it would be hopeless to continue operations and he intimated that the colliery would be closed down within 24 hours. The deputation there-upon withdrew, after intimating that they would return with rein-forcements within 24 hours in order to ascertain that the manager had fulfilled his promise.

In some places the colliery companies called in the police before pickets arrived. This happened at Bowhill where it is clear that only a well-disciplined march by large numbers of miners averted 'an ugly situation'. The *Dunfermline Press* states:

Rumours that the men working the pumps at Bowhill Colliery were to be forced to cease work made it necessary late on Sunday afternoon for a large body of police under Supt. Cumming, Dunfermline, to proceed to the colliery. They were met by a force of strikers numbering about 2,000. The miners marched to the pit-head and informed the men employed at the colliery that within half an hour they must draw the fire and leave their work. The police were hopelessly outnumbered, and in consequence were unable to cope with the situation. The workmen therefore were obliged to leave. With their spirits raised by their success the strikers thereafter repaired to Kelty where similar tactics were adopted. Success again attended their efforts.

At pits round Cowdenbeath, however, determined preparations had been made to resist the men. For example, Blairhall Colliery furnaces had been restarted with 'volunteers' brought in from Glasgow. Moreover, it was widely known that one of the general managers of the Fife Coal Company, Mr. William Spalding, was himself firing at the Dalbeath Pit, Hill of Beath. Police and later military detachments were drafted in and there were major incidents, fierce baton charges and arrests.

The story starts quietly enough, with a mass meeting of strikers held in Cowdenbeath on Monday afternoon, April 4, from which small deputations were despatched to pits where it was known that furnaces were being kept going. These included Hill of Beath, Kirkford, Lumphinnans and Raith. The deputations returned to a report-back meeting that evening, with the news that only at Raith Colliery had some opposition been experienced. However, the following day, Tuesday, April 5, it was found that steam was being kept up at Hill of Beath and also at Kirkford, or No. 10, Cowdenbeath. Here under-managers were working to keep half the ten boilers at work; the winding engine was idle.

The miners held a mass meeting at the Empire Theatre; and while they planned a march to the Kirkford Pit to demand that the under-managers stop working as boiler-firemen, the Cowdenbeath Pipe Band paraded the High Street. When the meeting had ended, several thousand miners, headed by the band, and led by union officials, marched to the pit. Behind them the Hill of Beath Pipe Band headed another procession of Hill of Beath villagers; and in their ranks there 'were a fair number of women'. After the procession had reached Kirkford Pit, 'there was an ominous sound of escaping steam, a loud hissing noise proclaiming that the boilers were being "let off"'. The procession then marched on to Dalbeath Pit, Hill of Beath. Here they were incensed at finding, among managers and other officials, Mr. Spalding himself at work in fire holes. At this there were lively scenes, which the *Dunfermline Press* describes. Mr. Spalding was the object of the men's anger.

The strikers got hold of him, and after very rough treatment a consultation was held. Various suggestions were made but ultimately he was marched away from the pit-head, the police being powerless to deal with the crowd. Mr. Spalding was hustled along the road to Cowdenbeath and, at the bleachfield ponds, a suggestion to throw him in was made but was not carried into effect. He was hauled past his home in Bridge Street down to High Street. A brick was thrown which unfortunately struck a man named Wilson and made an ugly wound on his head. He was taken away for medical attention.

The police made an attempt to rescue Mr. Spalding but were unsuccessful and the march was continued, the victim presenting a sorrowful appearance. At the corner of Union Street a spirit of humour seemingly seized the crowd. Some miners hoisted him on their shoulders and he was derisively asked to make a speech. The police, now greatly strengthened, effected a rescue and got Mr. Spalding on a tram-car going towards the north end of the town.

A few of the police tried to keep the crowd back and an ugly situation arose. Baton charges were made and the crowd replied with stones. Several of the police were injured and in the baton charges several of the crowd, and unfortunately mostly those who were taking no part in the mêlée, were victims of the blows. This incensed the crowd, but gradually, though great excitement prevailed at the time, the streets resumed their normal appearance.

During this *mêlée* three members of the police force were injured, including a sergeant who had been one of a posse driven in from Lochgelly in a charabanc, the driver of which had also been hurt. One middle-aged miner was arrested, William Easton, whom the newspaper described as having 'for some time been actively identified with the Communist movement'. After the baton charge there was quiet until ten P.M., when the crowd reassembled and began to move up the High Street. At this there was a sudden outbreak of violence, for a posse of police seventy strong at the north end of the street drew their batons and were given the order to charge. Fierce scenes took place:

> This was followed by a wild scampering on the part of the strikers and the police with drawn batons swept down the street at a great pace and cleared it from end to end.
>
> The trouble, however, was not yet over. The strikers again assembled at the north end of High Street, while the police lined up further south for a second effort to quell the trouble. Apparently at a given signal, all the lights of the town were simultaneously switched off and the police, who had by this time formed a cordon across the street, moved northwards. This effort was crowned with success. In the darkness, and in front of the advancing constables, the crowd melted away, and quiet was restored. Until a late hour, however, the police continued to patrol the street.

Next morning, Wednesday, April 6, William Easton was brought before the Sheriff at Dunfermline and committed to prison for assaulting the police. That night there were further disturbances and shop windows and street lamps were broken. This was alleged to be the work of young lads who (like the Lochgelly police) 'do not even claim residence in Cowdenbeath, but whose places of abode are in the outlying districts'. A mass meeting of miners condemned their action, as did a meeting convened by the Labour Party and the Miners' Union. Next day, Thursday, April 7, even more police were sent in from Aberdeenshire.

Two days later, on Saturday, April 9, telegrams were sent to all Districts by the M.F.G.B., stating that since a conference with the owners was being opened unconditionally, all members were urged 'to abstain from all action which will interfere with the measures necessary for securing the safety of the mines, or will necessitate force by the Government'. In West Fife the mining population was smouldering with resentment and awaiting the outcome of the charges against William Easton, for whose legal defence the Fife, Kinross and Clackmannan Miners' Association had made arrangements.

The local press was filled with criticism of the locked-out men, and scare stories of 'extremists'. The *Kirkcaldy Times* of April 13, for example, declared that 'some extremists, no doubt imported from outside', and, 'for the sake of some weird political theory which can only be described as syndicalism', were 'stampeding' the West Fife miners. The journal continued:

That the miners of Fifeshire have been subjected to the preaching of extremists for some time past is well known. Just the other day, a friend showed me one of these extremist leaflets and I give it as an illustration of what has been going on:

BRITISH MINERS' REFORM MOVEMENT
(Miners' Section Workers' Committee)
Objects:

' To work for abolition of Capitalism and substitution of Communism which means ownership and control of means of life by the working class.'

Immediate Objects

1. Full wages during time of compulsory unemployment.
2. A five day working week and 6 hours working day.
3. Resistance to local and national reductions.
4. Abolition of piecework.
5. Abolition of income tax and other impositions on workers.
6. Full wage as compensation for accident or disablement.
7. Annual holiday with pay.

Nor was the local press alone in similar criticism.[1] Moreover the whole of the British press was on the warpath.

But for a week all remained quiet in Cowdenbeath, including the pits where the furnaces had all been drawn. Then, without warning, the town suddenly suffered what

---

[1] Mr. Andrew Clarke, J.P., the Secretary of the Mid and East Lothian Miners' Association, was not only disturbed by the action of the union members, but publicly came out against the policy of the M.F.G.B. He is reported as saying:

Passing through Dalkeith the other day, I noticed the words—'On the Verge of Beyond', exhibited at the entrance of the picture house. With a slight alteration—the substitution of 'disaster' for beyond—the legend exactly represents the condition to which the coal industry was reduced by the policy of the Miners' Federation in withdrawing the pumping men from the collieries and by the unprecedented expedient of the crowds of youths who visited the collieries and compelled the volunteers to desert the boiler fire holes and the engine houses. I do not blame the natives of Mid and East Lothian for the disaster. The policy was alien to the counties. It was dictated from without. It is the same policy as that which Lenin now admits has ruined Russia. (*Dalkeith Advertiser*, April 28, 1921.)

Mr. Clarke stood for the post of Secretary at the next Scottish conference, but was defeated, having the support only of his own Association.

amounted to an armed invasion. The *Dunfermline Press* says: 'On Wednesday, April 13, Cowdenbeath rate-payers woke up to find that the burgh had, overnight, been converted into what was virtually an armed camp'. In the early morning, motor-buses packed with soldiers and marines poured into the town and also into Lochgelly.

The officers commandeered for billets all the available hall accommodation, and at once posted guards in all the pits in the district. The soldiers are drafts of the Argyll and Sutherland and Seaforth Highlanders. Firing of the furnaces was begun at most of the collieries, the work being performed by managers and other officials. At each colliery where this work was begun, there was a mounted military guard, and wire rope barricading was erected all round each pithead.

In the small hours of the morning Fife County police swooped on Cowdenbeath, Lumphinnans and Lochgelly and arrested eight more men. The description of the arrests runs as follows:

Taking place, as they did, at a time when few persons were about and while the men sought for were asleep in their beds, the arrests were quietly effected. A motor char-a-banc in which a strong force of police was seated, conveyed the prisoners to Dunfermline, which was reached before day-break. In their passage through the streets of Dunfermline, the prisoners vociferously sang 'The Red Flag'. Pending their appearance at the Sheriff Court, the prisoners were incarcerated in the cells within the Court buildings.

The charges were those of 'forming part of a riotous mob, assaulting William Spalding, an agent of the Fife Coal Company, and 2 other officials of the Company, and obstructing the police'.

There was some demonstration as the prisoners were removed from the Court buildings to a char-a-banc which removed them to the railway station en route for Edinburgh. Against the occurrence of any possible disturbance, ample police provision was made. A crowd of sympathisers from Cowdenbeath were kept at a considerable distance from the Court exit. Shouts of encouragement were made to the prisoners who were told to 'cheer up' and made happy rejoinders as they were driven away down Guildhall Street.

That spirited scene was taking place on the eve of 'Black Friday', when J. H. Thomas was to announce that the railwaymen and the transport workers, the allies of the miners in the Triple Alliance, were not to support them by strike action.

The miners were isolated, and left to fight on alone. Negotiations with the owners were broken off.

From the beginning of the lock-out Lloyd George's Government had been making skilful propaganda use in Parliament and the press of the decision to withdraw the safety men by the locked-out miners; attention had been concentrated on the possibility of pit ponies being drowned. Certainly in Scotland too, most press publicity, in these troubled times, was reserved for the two pit ponies of Leven who were (it was alleged) drowned as the result of the men's refusal to allow pumping to be continued there. A Society for the Prevention of Cruelty to Animals was enlisted in the campaign against the miners: and one of their officials went round Buckhaven with summonses.

A publicity campaign continued around this. It was answered publicly by Tom Kennedy, newly elected M.P. for Kirkcaldy Burghs, first in a speech in London and on April 12 in the House of Commons, where he asked the Prime Minister to enquire into the matter and pointed out that the management was responsible for not bringing the ponies to the surface much earlier. By the time the management's responsibility for the incident was finally admitted in Parliament (May 9) the publicity aimed at courting public opinion against the locked-out miners by bemoaning the fate of the locked-in pit ponies had had a long run.

Week by week the struggle had dragged on. Government terms had been rejected at the end of April. Early in June by a 70 per cent majority the miners balloted against new terms of Government and owners, the percentage in Scotland rising to 78 per cent against. The men were feeling the pinch, although not all eight constituents were affected as neither the Scottish Oil Workers' Association nor the Scottish Shale Miners were locked out. Donations came in, but did not provide a great deal. It should be noted that even before the lock-out began there had been considerable unemployment amongst miners owing to the economic crisis.

On July 1 the long drawn-out conflict ended with a decision to return to work.

The struggle was over. The deferred Annual Conference was held on Friday, August 12, 1921. Hugh Murnin, the

President, was in the chair, and only necessary business was transacted. Robert Smillie, who was specially invited to attend, said:

The fight was not of the miners' choosing. It was forced upon us. Never in the history of industry and of Trades Unionism has a better army entered on a defensive fight. There was not a waverer in the million-odd miners from Campbeltown to Kent. Not only were the men and boys enthusiastic and determined, but their womenfolk were with them (Applause). It was a glorious struggle, and I congratulate our people on the great fight which they made. But I would not have been able to congratulate them had they accepted the brutal, impertinent terms offered to them by the employers.

I sincerely hope there will be no feeling in any part of the British coalfield that the mine workers have been defeated (Hear, hear). That would be the worst possible thing that could happen. The miners would have been defeated had they been forced to start at the end of fourteen weeks' stoppage on the terms originally offered to them. . . . The dispute originally was that Mine Owners offered to the Mine Workers a daily wage which was insufficient to keep body and soul together. That is what the fight was about, and what raised indignation in the hearts of the mine workers and their families. The miners have not to start on anything like the terms which the employers desired to impose upon them.

He then went on to deal in detail with the situation created by widespread unemployment. He said:

I am one of those who thought the Government was bound to pay Unemployment Benefit to Mine Workers during the Lock-out. They (the miners) were not on strike. It was not their fault that they were idle. . . . It was wrong, and the Government were wrong in refusing. The protest of this Conference must be strong (Applause).

In spite of Smillie's brave words, unemployment remained high and wages remained low. Many difficult months lay ahead: and it was not for nearly three years that conditions improved and a new spirit was manifest among the miners.

KINGSHILL NO. 3 PIT, LANARKSHIRE, 1953

BOTHWELL CASTLE COLLIERY, LANARKSHIRE, 1953

CHAPTER VIII

THE LOCK-OUT OF 1926 AND ITS AFTERMATH

I. A TROUBLED PERIOD

FROM the end of the great lock-out in the summer of 1921 the British miners were plunged into conditions worse than had been known for many years. The coal-owners had triumphed in the struggle that had been thrust upon the industry by the action of the Coalition Government in its abrupt stopping of all controls in the spring of 1921; they made full use of their superior position. At the same time economic crisis was deepening and the prospect of recovery from it kept receding. Unemployment was rife in every industry but particularly in the coal and metal trades; it went on for three bleak winters.

The fall of the Lloyd George Coalition Government in the autumn of 1922 precipitated a general election. The result was a Conservative victory, and a Conservative Cabinet, headed latterly by Stanley Baldwin. But Labour representation in the House of Commons was more than double the number returned in 1918. Of 142 Labour Members no less than 45 were miners' representatives. A year later the general election of December 1923 resulted in a considerable increase in both the Labour and Liberal representation, so that the Conservatives, though still the strongest single party in the House of Commons, had lost many seats and were easily to be defeated by a combination of the other two main parties. The figures were: Conservative, 258; Labour, 191; Liberal, 158; Others, 8. Scottish miners' candidates had done well.

For a time Baldwin clung to office, but following an adverse vote in the House of Commons, the Government resigned on January 21, 1924. The first Labour Ministry was formed by Ramsay MacDonald that day. This was expected to have a considerable effect on the position of the miners. It seemed to them that all they had striven for during these difficult last thirty months would now be gained and that their wrongs would all be righted.

The advent of the Labour Government came at a time of temporary boom in the coal trade, in part due to the occupation of the Ruhr by the French armies, with the result that most of the markets of that great coal-field were for a time supplied with British coal. The Miners' Federation of Great Britain in December 1923 had taken a ballot on a demand to revise the national wages agreement of July 1, 1921. The ballot, with a four to one majority, empowered the Executive to approach the coal-owners for a revision. When the coal-owners made no satisfactory offer, there appeared the possibility of a great mining dispute. Mr. Emanuel Shinwell, Secretary of Mines, then set up a Committee of Inquiry under the Chairmanship of Lord Buckmaster, a former Lord Chancellor. The Report of the Committee of Inquiry was favourable to the claims of the miners to a certain extent. It was said at the time this was partly due to the skill with which the material for the case presented by the miners had been prepared by the Labour Research Department which, on the initiative of the new Secretary, A. J. Cook, was once more[1] brought closely into connection with the M.F.G.B. The election of A. J. Cook in place of Frank Hodges, who had been given a minor post by Ramsay MacDonald in the new Labour Government, was itself a symbol of an awakening spirit of resistance in the coal-fields of Britain, for A. J. Cook had been a prominent member of the Minority Movement[2] and was indeed supported very strongly by that body which had members and strong adherents in every coal-field. It was in these circumstances that the coal-owners, following the Report of the Committee of Inquiry and faced by a more militant Executive, yielded and signed an agreement on June 18, 1924, for one year which gave better terms.

During that twelvemonth from the summer of 1924, A. J. Cook spent his week-ends addressing meetings in the coal-fields,

---

[1] In the period up to the end of 1921, the Labour Research Department (founded in 1912 by Beatrice Webb) had frequently been called upon for its services by the Miners' Federation.

[2] The Minority Movement, beginning in 1923, linked together all the various forward-looking agitations in the trade unions. It had wide influence in the Scottish coal-field and caused considerable dismay in the minds of the older officials.

in order to build up the moral unity of the miners. Cook's campaign for unity, extending beyond the mining industry, began to rouse echoes in other trades, especially where the Minority Movement had made headway.

The new agreement of the summer of 1924 had run for a few short months when the Labour Government was overthrown by a combination in the House of Commons of Tories and Liberals. Hardly had the 31st Annual Conference been ended in September 1924 than the chain of events began which led to what was to be called the 'Forged Letter' election. The result was a considerable victory for the Conservatives and a defeat for Labour and an overwhelming rout for the Liberals, whose Lobby combination with the Tories turned out a sorry bargain for themselves. The Liberals were reduced to less than forty seats in Parliament. The new Government was headed once more by Stanley Baldwin as Prime Minister. His Chancellor of the Exchequer was Winston Churchill, who could now sing:

> I turned a cat-in-pan once more
> And so became a Tory.

But now the temporary boom in the coal trade was beginning to fall away in the autumn of 1924. The coal-owners then made it unmistakably clear that they would not consent to a continuation of existing conditions. They wanted both a lengthening of hours and a lowering of wages.

In the spring of 1925, in the teeth of such expert economists as J. M. Keynes, Chancellor of the Exchequer Churchill announced the return of the Gold Standard. This had the immediate effect of diminishing British exports; and, indeed, presenting the prospect of ruining the export trade—unless costs could be cut by at least 10 per cent immediately. In the eyes of the employers the cutting of costs meant primarily the lowering of wages. This was made unmistakably clear in July of 1925, when Prime Minister Baldwin announced in a meeting with the miners' Executive that not only the wages of the miners but of all workers would have to come down.

Already J. M. Keynes had predicted that Churchill's monetary policy would cause greater unemployment and a lower standard of living. The coal-owners gave notice to end the twelve months agreement; and then on July 1, 1925, put forward proposals that meant a slashing reduction of wages and the sweeping away of the minimum wage. Thus the brunt of the coming general attack fell upon the miners, who were given a month's notice of a lock-out on July 31, unless they submitted. But the miners were determined to resist. They refused to negotiate until the owners' proposals were withdrawn; for, as the Trades Union Congress General Council stated on July 10, 'no self-respecting body of organised workers could negotiate on such terms'. Moreover, Cook's persistent campaign for unity had borne fruit. Negotiations (begun six months earlier) for an alliance of trade unions in transport and heavy industry were already in an advanced stage. This had an effect on a special Trades Union Congress, to which the miners submitted their case on July 24; and also upon the unions most affected, several of which decided to strike if necessary.

Meanwhile the Government intervention, both with miners and mine-owners, to avert a lock-out had been unsuccessful, partly because neither Baldwin nor Churchill would assume any responsibility for a situation to which their own policy had contributed. In the last week of July 1925 the situation became tense. Approached by a T.U.C. Special Committee, Baldwin declared as late as July 29 that 'the Government would not grant any subsidy'. The next day a conference of trade union executives empowered the T.U.C. to give financial support and to issue strike orders. That night of June 30 the strike orders were issued to railway and transport unions. They took the form of an embargo on all movements of coal after midnight of July 31. It was a refusal to handle blackleg work or materials. Thereupon the Cabinet beat a hasty retreat. Eight hours before the lock-out of all the miners was due to begin, Baldwin announced that the coal-owners had suspended notices, and that the Government would give a subsidy to the owners for nine months, up to May 1, 1926.

It was on Friday, July 31, that the Cabinet yielded; and the day of the T.U.C. success was thereafter called Red Friday. The miners, however, through the mouth of the M.F.G.B. Chairman, warned that it was not 'a glorious victory', but that 'it is only an armistice'. Nevertheless, Red

Friday was 'a glorious victory' for unity of purpose in the trade union world.

2. THE SITUATION IN SCOTLAND

The Scottish miners shared in the revival of trade union activity that mounted throughout 1924 and culminated, for the time being, in the high point of Red Friday in the summer of 1925. But before this they had gone through an exceptionally difficult period. First there had been the aftermath of the great lock-out of 1921, with real wages driven down below the level of 1914, and many pits idle. By October 1921 there were 22,000 men unemployed and 45,000 partially unemployed in the Scottish coal-field. Protests to the Government against the inadequate amounts paid to the unemployed, and demands for better conditions for them, met with little response. They had slightly better response to the frequent representations made to reduce the sentences that had been passed on various miners. Thus their minutes record this letter from the Secretary for Scotland regarding persons convicted of offences connected with the Coal Dispute in the earlier part of 1921:

I have now had under consideration the cases of persons sentenced to 12 months' imprisonment, and have felt justified in advising that the sentences imposed upon William Easton, John Whyte, and John Kent, and upon Archibald McInnes, Hugh Aitken, and John Evers be treated as sentences of 10 months.

Yours faithfully,
(Signed) ROBERT MUNRO.
(Minute 312, January 16, 1922.)

By the autumn of 1922, the Scottish Executive Committee were faced with a serious decline in membership. Lanarkshire announced a reduction of their dues-paying members from 47,000 to 25,000. Membership was nearly halved in less than two years; never in the history of the unions had there been such a catastrophic fall. The biggest districts were the hardest hit. Two unions ended their affiliation, the Enginekeepers and the Oilworkers. These were some of the problems confronting the Annual Conference held in Glasgow on Saturday,

September 16, 1922. The President, Hugh Murnin, was ill, and James Tonner, the Vice-President, presided.

The delegates had to consider yet another problem—the declining funds of the union. The effect of the severe period of unemployment following on the great lock-out of spring 1921 had dealt a serious blow at the funds. The General Fund had fallen from £6704 in 1921 to £3381 in 1922; and cash in bank on deposit and current account had fallen from £17,170 to £8980. There were heavy arrears outstanding, totalling nearly £17,000 of which Lanark owed £7120 and Fife £6694.

In this difficult situation the conference was unanimous in electing to the presidency Robert Smillie, who had held that position for some twenty years until he became President of the M.F.G.B. With his resignation from the M.F.G.B. presidency just before the great 1921 lock-out it was possible for him once more to take up the guidance of the N.U.S.M.W. But it was no longer the same Smillie. By the autumn of 1922 ill-health had had its effect. His forces were exhausted. This, however, was not immediately apparent, and in their difficult situation the delegates were very pleased once more to have Bob Smillie as their leader. Even amongst those who were to be most critical of his policy there was a recognition of his former greatness.

Scarcely nine months passed when Robert Smillie hastened to Morpeth to take part in a bye-election: this brought the number of seats he had contested to a round dozen within thirty years. Always he had been ready to fight, no matter how difficult the circumstances. At Morpeth he was successful. For the first time for over thirty years of contests the letters 'M.P.' appeared after the name of Robert Smillie. He was re-elected at the succeeding two general elections. These six years of parliamentarianism, during which he retained the presidency of the Scottish Miners for most of the time, did not have the result that many had hoped for. Had he reached Parliament at the beginning of his career, he would have been a worthy ally of Keir Hardie. Coming at the end of these years it did little to enhance his reputation; indeed, it was the ghost of the former Robert Smillie that sat mute upon the benches in the House of Commons. For the moment, however, there was great joy amongst the Scottish miners.

Smillie and those who thought with him were in favour of a single union for all Scotland. But there were obstacles in the path. In Fife there had been a sharp difference between the older officials, some of them cradled in the Liberal tradition, and the younger ardent Socialists in the coal-field, who carried on the resistance to the coal-owners in 1921 with the greatest stubbornness.

Combined with this there was, as always happens in a period of sharp class struggle, a demand for greater democracy within the union and for definite steps towards one single union for Scotland as a whole. In pursuance of this last the Fife miners had in 1920 made a new rule that their five county representatives on the Board of the N.U.S.M.W. should be chosen by democratic ballot vote of the members, instead of being appointed by the members of the Fife Board. Had this democratic decision been operated and carried through to the end in Fife, and had this democratic practice spread to the other counties, the history of the N.U.S.M.W. in the next twenty years would have been very different. What actually took place led to great trouble with the miners. A ballot was duly taken and it showed that Adamson, the General Secretary, and Philip Hodge, another official, were easily highest (with Hodge higher than Adamson); a second ballot resulted in a complete defeat of the other officials and in a victory for left-wing candidates, but on a rather low poll. On the ground that the poll was low, Adamson cancelled the results of the election and induced the Fife Board to re-appoint the five who had previously sat on the N.U.S.M.W. Executive Committee.

These procedures caused a division in the ranks of the Fife miners, an increasing number of whom came to believe that undemocratic methods had been used and (what was more important) would continue to be used to nullify any change they could hope for through the ordinary processes of democracy in the union. This fear seemed to be confirmed when, in 1922, an adherent of Adamson's in the chair refused to apply one of the Standing Orders of the union Board for taking 'the Financial Vote'. One thing led to another. The upshot was a split of the county union and the formation in January 1923 of a Reform Union with Hodge as secretary.

The Minority Movement, however, was in favour of unity. Smillie, too, and most of the Scottish Executive would have been glad enough to see an end to the internecine strife in the Fife area, more especially as in the midst of it all they were forced to allow the Adamson union to fall into heavy arrears. Thus from two sides there was a strong disposition to bring unity amongst the Fife miners. This, however, had little enough effect for the first eighteen months when the struggle in Fife grew more and more bitter.

From the beginning of 1925 onwards, however, the diehards in both the old union and the Reform Union had to encounter a growing desire for unity amongst the miners.

After Red Friday (July 31, 1925), the desire for unity grew stronger.

Robert Smillie summed up the situation at the Scottish Annual Conference held on October 6 and 7, 1925:

The owners undoubtedly thought that by giving notice and bringing about a serious crisis in the mining industry they would defeat the miners on the wages question and stampede the Government into withdrawing from the Statute Book the seven hours day. That attempt led to a most extraordinary knitting-up of all branches of the trade union movement, because the workers realised that if the mineowners succeeded in making a substantial reduction in wages and in abolishing the seven hours day it would not stop there, and employers in other industries would in all probability take similar steps.

The second day of the conference was largely devoted to an important resolution on the Government-sponsored Organisation for the Maintenance of Supplies (O.M.S.):

That we protest emphatically against the creation of the blackleg organisation known as the O.M.S., and in view of the fact that the miners had been singled out in the past for attention from the Navy and Army during industrial disputes, and also that the O.M.S. and kindred organisations will certainly be used against the miners in the coming industrial conflict, pledge itself to work against these organisations to the full extent of its power. (October 7, 1925.)

The resolution was moved by a young Lanarkshire delegate, William Allan, who had only recently come on to the Executive.

Supporting the resolution, Robert Smillie said that the O.M.S. was supposed to have been organised for a very high idealistic purpose—that if a general strike should take place it would be the duty of somebody to make sure that supplies were sent to the various districts. He thought it had been found that the Fascist movement was not going to get on in this country as it had done in Italy. Therefore, in the guise of protecting the people, they were building up this organisation. This movement, which had been established and was spreading throughout the country, was a menace and was organised in order to help the capitalist class to continue the enslavement of the workers.

To meet the urgent need for unity, it was agreed to call a special conference two months later. It was held in Glasgow on December 14, 1925, 'to consider the proposed new Rules for a National Union'. A new cleavage was revealed inside Scotland; two county unions had signified their opposition. First to object was Mid and East Lothian, who considered the new rules 'likely to be harmful rather than helpful in making for unity'. A week before the Special Conference Ayrshire wrote to declare itself 'not in favour of any change'.

The Special Conference opened with the reading of the two letters. Then the Chairman, Robert Smillie, M.P., addressed the delegates regretting these letters. He told of the early struggles of the miners fifty years ago, of the rivalry of the small districts, and how the county unions had discussed the hopes of having one national union for the whole of Scotland. Every county and district in Scotland had voted in favour of one national union; an organisation similar to that of Yorkshire, Durham, Lancashire or South Wales, with a central office and a permanent staff of officials. He said, 'It is the one dream of my life to see one National Union in Scotland'.

It turned out that Dumbarton was also against the proposed rules. Lanarkshire miners were divided, although it was they who had so frequently put forward the proposal for a real national union. James Hood and James McEwan, both of Ayrshire, moved 'that we do not consider any proposals for a national union'; this was defeated by 6 votes to 45. Fife and Stirlingshire were in favour of immediate acceptance of the proposed rules; but West Lothian, while favouring them, feared defeat and moved a delaying motion through James Doonan: 'That the rules be remitted back to districts and amendments to be sent in to the Secretary within the next three months'. To this Malcolm Turner of Stirlingshire, seconded by James Cook of Fife, moved an amendment that 'we adopt the present rules, as it might be more difficult to accept them six months hence'. The amendment was lost by 18 to 36, and the rules were accordingly remitted for amendments to be sent in within three months. But by the time half a year had passed, the Scottish miners were to be in throes of a greater struggle than had ever been known before.

3. GENERAL STRIKE AND LOCK-OUT

Ever since Red Friday, July 31, 1925, preparations had been going forward for an eventual struggle in the late spring of 1926. When the transport and railway unions, with the full backing of the General Council of the T.U.C., had imposed an embargo on all movements of coal, the Baldwin-Churchill Government had been compelled to acknowledge defeat. The price was a Treasury subsidy to the coal-owners so that wages might be kept up to the existing level for another nine months —a subsidy out of which it was believed amongst the miners that the coal-owners had done very well. This subsidy the Government were determined not to renew. With this subsidy they were buying time, time to prepare should there be any renewal of crisis. Consequently Red Friday was followed by the most thorough, far-reaching and extensive Government preparations including the patronage of a force of strike-breakers.

The preparation for it was to be both material and moral. The moral side of it, apart from speeches by Members of the Government and with their faithful following in the press, consisted first and foremost in the appointment of the Samuel Commission. When half the period had elapsed, Winston Churchill, in a programmatic speech as Chancellor of the Exchequer just before Christmas 1925, was able to announce that preparations were practically complete. The first four months of 1926 could therefore be devoted by the

Government to the testing and overhauling of their material preparations for dealing with any recurrence of Red Friday. The more complete the Government preparations, the less either they or the coal-owners were prepared to yield from their standpoint. On the side of the T.U.C. hardly any corresponding preparations appear to have been made. As the end of the nine months approached, signs of impatience were manifest, not only in Minority Movement conferences, where a lead was being given by Tom Mann, Arthur Horner and others, but amongst the rank and file of the trade unions generally. To these demands and questions leaders of the T.U.C. turned a deaf ear because, as was afterwards explained, they feared that by making preparations they might precipitate a crisis. Never has a great industrial struggle been precipitated with so much preparation on one side, so little on the other.

In the atmosphere created by the appointment and work of the Samuel Commission,[1] negotiations had been held over until its Report had been studied. There was thus out of all the nine months only a few weeks left towards the end of them for negotiations between the parties. It was not long before the miners realised the mine-owners would not budge. Then the General Council of the T.U.C. took a hand in negotiations, but without any tangible result. By April it was clear that there was deadlock between the miners and the mine-owners. Between the whole trade union movement and the Government there was also deadlock. In these circumstances a Conference of Executives was summoned to meet at the end of April. When that conference learned of the attitude of the coal-owners and heard the terms put forward by the Government, it became clear to them that the deadlock was complete. Accordingly at the eleventh hour (April 30, 1926) when the miners were due to be locked out that midnight in every coalfield of the country, the Conference of Executives felt they had no option left to them. On May 1, amid scenes of undoubted enthusiasm on the part of most, they decided that a whole series of the most important trade unions would call out their members on strike by the beginning of Tuesday, May 4—

[1] For the Samuel Commission and the political chicanery involved see *The Miners: Years of Struggle* (chapters 12–14).

unless a settlement could be reached. There remained that first week-end of May 1926.[1]

On Saturday, May 1, 1926, the coal-owners locked out the miners who were unanimous in refusing to enter the pits on the coal-owners' terms. In preparation for the lock-out a Proclamation by the King had been issued the previous day, putting into force the Emergency Powers Act of 1920. This gave the Government and the authorities everywhere special powers of arrest, search and imprisonment. The Act had been passed at the time of the miners' national strike in 1920, had been opposed by the Labour Party in the House of Commons and had then been ruthlessly applied against the miners in the great lock-out of 1921. This formidable engine, by which Britain for the time being was turned into what it has become fashionable to call a 'police state', was now put into operation. Not only the police force but the other armed forces and the whole of the apparatus of national and local government were put on the alert and endowed with special powers. All this, however, left the miners undismayed. Those of them who would have been working a Saturday shift took things very calmly on that morning of May Day, 1926. In the afternoon there were in Scotland and throughout Britain May Day demonstrations on a scale hardly ever witnessed before. While this air of calm brooded over the coal-fields, where there was no winding and every wheel was stopped, there were feverish negotiations and meetings at the headquarters of the T.U.C. and Downing Street. The outcome on the Sunday night was the sudden breaking-off of all negotiations by the Cabinet and an ultimatum to the trade union movement, for the coal-owners and the Conservative Cabinet had decided to have a 'showdown' with the trade unions of Great

---

[1] At a meeting of the Council of the Lanarkshire Mine Workers' Union on May 5, 1926, A. McAnulty, presiding, said, in giving a report of the conference held in London the previous week:

that the General Council of the British Trades Union Congress had undertaken negotiations and having failed to find a way out of the dispute, consulted a Special Meeting of the Congress on the question of supporting the miners in their fight against a reduction in wages, an increase in hours and district agreements, at which 1,500 Executive members of the different Unions were represented. That Congress had conferred power on the General Council to deal with the situation. During the negotiations, the printers employed in the 'Daily Mail' establishment had refused to consent to an article entitled 'For King and Country' being issued, and forthwith stopped work. This and the action of the General Council in calling a General Strike was construed by the Government as an overt act, as a result of which they broke off negotiations abruptly.

Britain.[1] Accordingly by Monday morning miners, workers of Britain, the whole people, and workers and governments throughout the world as well, knew that that night a General Strike would begin in Britain in support of the miners.

There followed the General Strike which shook the whole industrial life of Britain. The words of A. J. Cook in the pamphlet, *The Nine Days*, may aptly be quoted:

Tuesday, May 4th, started with the workers answering the call. What a wonderful response! What loyalty!! What solidarity!!! From John o' Groats to Land's End the workers answered the call to arms to defend us, to defend the brave miner in his fight for a living wage. . . .

It was a wonderful achievement, a wonderful accomplishment that proved conclusively that the Labour Movement has the men and women that are capable in an emergency of providing the means of carrying on the country. Who can forget the effect of motor conveyances with posters saying 'By permission of the T.U.C.'? The Government with its O.M.S. were absolutely demoralised. Confidence, calm, and order prevailed everywhere, despite the irritation caused by the volunteers, blacklegs, and special constables. The workers acted as one. Splendid discipline! Splendid loyalty!

The detailed story of the events that immediately preceded the General Strike, the record of what happened during it and the ignominious surrender by the General Council leaders that brought it to an end, have been told in detail elsewhere.[2] It is enough to say that the Scottish workers of all the trades called out played their part manfully during those nine days and that the whole apparatus of government was unable to quell the General Strike; and that the Scottish miners, making no reproaches, were ready to do their utmost to help the other

[1] Throughout the General Strike the eyes of all observers throughout the world were turned to Britain. One of the most acute and experienced observers, J. V. Stalin, was following it with close attention. To a gathering of railwaymen at Tiflis in his native Georgia the next month Stalin in a speech analysed what had happened and why it had happened.

Eight years later, in a conversation with the famous British author H. G. Wells, he made the following general remark that recalled these days of 1926:

The first thing any other bourgeoisie would have done in the face of such an event, when the General Council of Trade Unions called for a strike, would have been to arrest the Trade Union leaders. The British bourgeoisie did not do that, and it acted cleverly from the point of view of its own interest. I cannot conceive of such a flexible strategy being employed by the bourgeoisie of the United States, Germany or France. In order to maintain their rule, the ruling classes of Great Britain have never forsworn small concessions, reforms. But it would be a mistake to think that these reforms were revolutionary. (Stalin-Wells Talk. Verbatim Record. *New Statesman & Nation*, December 1934, p. 17.)

[2] *The Miners: Years of Struggle* (chapters 13 and 14).

trade unionists against threats of victimisation after their leaders had unconditionally surrendered.

The long drawn-out struggle of the miners which lasted for seven months was, up to that time, the greatest and longest struggle of the workers in a single industry in the history of Britain, indeed in the history of any country. It was a fight of the whole of the British miners of which the Scots were one contingent. At the end they stood together with their fellow miners in Durham, Yorkshire, Northumberland, Cumberland and the other great coal-fields south of the Border. It was a British, not a separate Scottish story. The main negotiations and decisions were taken in the Special Conferences of the M.F.G.B. All that need be related here are certain special features or incidents of the general struggle as it applied in Scotland.

As one week ran out after another the distress in all the coal-fields grew greater. The Miners' Relief Fund, amounting to over one million eight hundred thousand pounds, was a considerable help. All over Britain and all over Scotland work-shop collections were being made and donations were being paid in to the Miners' Relief Fund. But the biggest single contribution by far came from the trade unionists of the Soviet Union, who contributed well over a million pounds, outweighing all other contributions taken together both at home and abroad. At Rothesay and Dunoon, remote from the coal-fields, collections were being made for the miners by men and women, boys and girls, who carried a miniature miner's lamp. Similar collections were being made in the other sea-side resorts of Scotland. Away on the shores of the Black Sea in the little seaside resort of Yalta, the capital of the Crimea, collectors were going round amongst the trade unionists on holiday, raising money to support the miners of Scotland, England and Wales. Never will the miners of England, Scotland and Wales forget the generosity of those who contributed so largely to help them in their days of need.

Besides the main Miners' Relief Fund there were many local contributions forthcoming, but all taken together was little enough to sustain a mining community of several millions of men, women and children through nearly thirty weeks without earnings. Here and there starvation began to play its part, here and there men began to drift into the pits. Nevertheless, at the end of September, when the districts were about to reject the Government terms and had mobilised all their forces for stronger measures for struggle, the number who had drifted back was 3260 out of a total number employed in or about the coal-mines in Scotland in April 1926 of 140,000. This was an extremely small proportion after so many weeks of struggle. The number rose in the last weeks, but never got to the proportions of an effective breakaway. Though starving, the men stood together and stood by the union. When finally they were forced to go back in every district on terms imposed by the owners, the men submitted, but with a determination not to accept these terms as the permanent conditions of the industry.

4. LOCK-OUT SCENES IN SCOTLAND

Before the month of May was out, two weeks after the miners had been left to stand alone confronting Government and owners, local authorities administering poor relief to destitute miners' families were already groaning under a burden which was soon to become a problem to the Scottish Office, and to Whitehall. The Scottish Board of Health put out a circular for the guidance of parish councils under which the grant included 12s. per week to married women and 4s. for each child. But the composition of some local bodies was such that it took vigorous efforts by deputations from Councils of Action and Trades Councils to enforce payment of relief even on this meagre scale. In the cases where a more generous scale was operated at first, it was not long before the spectre of increase in rates brought the level down to the Scottish Board's rate and well below it.

In Hamilton there was a particularly sharp clash. While a deputation was waiting on the council protesting against any system of relief in kind, and demanding full cash payment, it is recorded that

a private conference of merchants, professional and business people is to be held on Tuesday evening to consider the whole matter, and, if necessary, to interdict the payments. If the payments are found to be illegal . . . the auditor will be called upon to surcharge and no doubt the bank will require to satisfy itself how it stands before making further payments. (*Hamilton Advertiser*, June 12, 1926.)

In some areas the 'city fathers' were indignant at having to give any relief at all. A strong resolution was forwarded to the Scottish Board of Health by the Avondale Parish Council, who only 'under protest' could bring themselves to pay out relief 'to the women and children of strikers in the mines industrial dispute, and who say they are destitute in the sense of the word'. For it seemed to them that there was 'no logical reason why one industry should be supported by other industries who are at present suffering at the expense of the present dispute'. They cut their scales to 10s. for women and 2s. for children.

Conferences were held of parish councils and joint deputations were sent to the Scottish Board to seek means of lifting the burden from the localities. The Association of Parish Councils of Scotland challenged the legality of the instructions of the Scottish Board of Health and decided upon a direct approach to the Government for grants.

As the weeks dragged on, the burden increased; no satisfaction was obtained. More and more local authorities found themselves obliged to reduce the scale of relief, to raise expensive loans, to induce the county to feed the school children, to tighten up in all directions. With the difficulties growing, the Government timed its next step. In the seventeenth week of the strike there appeared in the local press a full-length advertisement directed to the miners but aimed at 'public opinion'. It exhorted the Scottish miners to follow the example of a coal-field where there had been a partial return to work: 'Go back to work! The choice is Yours!' At the same time Mr. Winston Churchill made the significant statement that the Government 'could not be asked to take sides against arithmetic, or the obvious facts of the situation'.

These moves immediately had the desired effect—not on the miners, but in other quarters. The tendency to cut relief scales at once went further. Some councils cut all relief completely. Among these was Lanark Parish Council, which earned a sharp rebuke from the Scottish Board of Health on the ground that stopping payment to miners' dependents

PITHEAD BATHS, MICHAEL COLLIERY, FIFE

TILLICOULTRY DRIFT MINE, CLACKMANNAN

practically amounted to the council's refusing to perform one of the main duties laid on them by statute. When they maintained their refusal there was further correspondence, and an uneasy debate as to exactly who would be responsible for deaths from malnutrition. The following passages took place:

MR. BROWNLIE said there was not much danger of deaths from starvation; there was more danger from over-feeding.

THE CLERK said he had already attended to a number of cases that claimed to be destitute. . . .

MR. ROSS: There must be absolute destitution before we can relieve.

THE CHAIRMAN said that in cases of absolute destitution they offered the poorhouse. . . .

MR. CAMERON: Are you giving relief to miners' wives and children now?

THE CLERK: In another way. We employ all needful cases on the burial ground. If a person is entitled to ten shillings we get ten hours' work for that. That is put in as capital expenditure and spread over thirty years. No ratepayer can object to that.

Distress was now acute; yet nowhere could it be claimed that the Scottish miners were breaking their ranks. While much publicity was given to the usual inspired rumours of mass returns to work, the same issues of the journals would be carrying reports of mass meetings addressed by stalwarts like Andrew McAnulty and other leaders, which scotched the lie. Moreover, journals had week by week to repeat the rumours which carried less conviction for every repetition. Then came the inevitable new phase: the importation of 'miners from other districts' under provocative police guard.

Typical of the scenes is this from Blantyre, in a report which is in no way sympathetic to the miner:

Shortly after three o'clock on Wednesday a serious outbreak of disorder occurred at Blantyre, where strikers came into conflict with the police who were ultimately compelled to draw their batons and charge the mob, which numbered about six or seven hundred. On the police making their charge, the crowds scattered in all directions, and in a few minutes the police were masters of the situation. . . . (*Hamilton Advertiser*, October 23, 1926.)

Seven men were arrested; and the next day 'the largest meeting of miners ever seen in Blantyre' was held in a field by the colliery. There was, reports the local journal, 'a large force of police at the meeting, but at no time was their service required'.

The local journal describes events in the area of Holytown. Among the eleven arrested, who were charged with besetting, were two miners' wives. That same week the Holytown Parish Council were themselves 'beset' by a mass demonstration demanding the Board of Health scale relief instead of the reduced rate of 10s. for the wife and 2s. for child. While the Trades Council deputation went into the meeting, 'the crowd sang the Red Flag, but dispersed quietly'.

As the baton charges became more frequent and more and more police were drafted in, feeling ran higher and higher. As the weeks went on miners' leaders were prosecuted and severe sentences imposed. Fife provides an example of local affrays having a widespread effect and arousing bitter feeling in the mining villages. In the third week of September 1926 there had been a night raid and batoning by the police, with a number of casualties, at Glencraig. On September 20 a similar incident took place at Lochore. At Lochgelly the next night there was a meeting of several hundred miners. Among the speakers was James Stewart, Lochgelly town councillor, who had been Chairman of the Reform Union. That night he made a speech which led to his being charged under the Emergency Regulations for 'an act calculated to cause disaffection among the civilian population'.

Lively interest in this case was taken throughout Scotland, and for more reasons than one. First, because it marked a significant turn in the struggle. Second, because this was the first case during the lock-out in which the law had been invoked against a well-known miners' leader. Third, because the man in the dock had once been sitting on the magistrate's bench. Appointed bailie in 1921, at that time he was in all probability the only Communist in Scotland to be a magistrate. Unlike most who are elevated to this position, Stewart paid scant attention to the hints given him by the Clerk of the Council or the police, but used his own native wits as to how a working-class magistrate should behave. Stories are still told of how he astonished the police, the press and not least perhaps the panel (i.e. the accused) when the usual melancholy procession of cases came up. For example, the following dialogue took place when a little girl, charged with 'stealing coal', was brought before him.

> How auld are ye, my lassie?
> Just twal, sir.
> How auld is your wee brother?
> He's eight.
> It was gey cauld last week?
> Ay, it was gey cauld.
> Did ye take the coal, hen?
> Ay.
> Muckle?
> Just a bucketful.
> Did you take the coal to make a fire for your wee brother?
> Ay.
> What ye did was richt.—CHARGE DISMISSED.[1]

In 1926, together with other miners' leaders, this rugged kindly character had been tirelessly campaigning and addressing meetings throughout the strike, without coming into collision with the authorities. A police sergeant agreed that he had been present at no less than thirty meetings addressed by Stewart. On the night of September 21, according to the *Dunfermline Press* account of police witnesses, he had said:

[1] Again there was the case of a miner charged with wife-beating; Stewart interrogated him.

Where do you work?
In such-and-such colliery.
At the face?
Ay.
It's hot doon there?
Ay.
Conditions are bad?
Ay.
It's a Fife Coal Company pit?
Ay.
Ye maun feel things boiling up inside you, working under these conditions?
Ay.
Ye get angry?
Ay.
And then ye ought to be angry against the Fife Coal Company: and instead ye come hame and take it out of your wife, poor woman.
Ay.
Are ye sorry?
Ay.
Well, I'm going to bind you over, on one condition. It's May Day the morn. The condition is that you attend the May Day Demonstration, hear the speeches about the Fife Coal Company and sing the Red Flag. Do you accept the condition?
Ay.
See and be there; in the front row. Mind you, I'll be on the platform and I'll be watching for you.—BOUND OVER.

Well now, you know what I said to you last night about the casualty list at Glencraig. Well, there was another case of the same kind at Lochore last night. So far as my information goes, the casualty list is now about 20. There may be more. It is alleged the police were doped. You hear of the atrocities in China, but you have it as bad in Lochore. One case, a woman was batoned down, and had to get four clasps in her head. I understand this woman was away for chips, or something of that sort. To make things worse, this woman is within a fortnight of a very critical period of her life. The police went into houses and tables were upset. Now then, we will have to do something. We have a meeting at Lochore today and an inquiry will be held by parish councillors, county councillors and others. When we get full information we will put it in circular form. We will send a copy to the Chief Constable and all Members of Parliament. As I told you, as the struggle goes on, it will grow more intense. Well, then, we will have to do something to defend ourselves. I want you all to turn out at 4.30 A.M. tomorrow. I want all the women to stay in their houses.

The police witness was cross-examined as to what sort of people were to make up the enquiry:

WITNESS: Parish councillors, county councillors, etc.
MR. WATSON: All very responsible people?
WITNESS: Sometimes.
MR. WATSON: Officially!
WITNESS: Supposed to be.

In answer to further questions, witness said he did not regard 4.30 A.M. as an abnormal hour for holding a meeting, if they wanted to make arrangements for lawful picketing.

MR. WATSON: You did not regard the fact of the women being asked to stay away as anything very sinister?
WITNESS: Well, the last time we had trouble, the women left shortly before the thing broke out.
MR. WATSON: But if you are going to do peaceful picketing you are better to have men only?
WITNESS: Yes; I would think so.

The formal defence, which the Sheriff described as 'ingenious', was that the announcement that an enquiry would be held had prevented disorder since the people did not take direct reprisals against the police. After James Stewart had given evidence in his own defence, there was the following exchange on the subject of who it was who maintained law and order:

PROCURATOR-FISCAL: You said something about 'defending ourselves'. You don't require to defend yourself unless you are attacked?

ACCUSED, in reply, indicated that he did not use the expression in the sense suggested by the Procurator-Fiscal, and added: You will agree I have more sense than ask them to go and interfere with the men who keep law and order.

PROCURATOR-FISCAL: You will remember that there was a baton charge at Lochgelly, at the Jenny Gray Pit, and there was not a second required. That seemed to have had a soothing effect on the locality.

ACCUSED: No! when it did take place we immediately did all we possibly could to preserve law and order and we have that, as leaders of our people, by nothing occurring since.

However, the case ended with Councillor James Stewart being fined £10. A year later he was to be elected to the Board of the Fife union.

At the next meeting of the Fife County Council, members demanded an enquiry into the behaviour of the police, for 'there were numerous occasions when the provocative conduct of the police had led to the indiscriminate drawing of batons and the striking of men, women and children who had no part in the mining dispute'. This was opposed, the *Dunfermline Press* relates, by Earl Lindsay, Major Noel Baxter, Sir Thomas Erskine and Major Anstruther Gray. Another spokesman, Major Ross, declared that 'his own impression was that the police of the county of Fife were models to Scotland'. The enquiry was referred to the Standing Joint Committee: this decided that 'the action of the Chief Constable and police had been of a most exemplary character'.

During this struggle it was not dozens, but hundreds, of miners who were arrested under the Emergency Powers Act and clapped into gaol. Police note-takers and informers were busy. Not since the Scottish Chartists or even the Covenanters had there been such a cleavage between the mass of the people and their rulers, ruthlessly using their powers of repression against those who gave voice to the feelings of the miners.[1] This use of the police by the authorities in

---

[1] Miners coming into Dunfermline from the Fife coal-field could read on the house of the last Abbot of Dunfermline the carven words:

Sin word is thrall and thocht is free
Keep weel thy tongue, I counsel thee.

They scorned this craven sentiment, spoke their mind freely and suffered the penalty of imprisonment.

close touch with the mine-owners left the miners undismayed. They were steadfast in the struggle. They were united. They developed a powerful organisation to combat the use of the police. All over the Scottish coal-field there was seen the beginning of a new leadership, arising from the struggle and tested in it.

5. IN FIFE AND LANARKSHIRE

During the seven months' lock-out, when miners in Fife were standing together against the coal-owners and the Government, there seemed even less reason still for their being organised in two rival trade unions. Efforts were made by the N.U.S.M.W. Executive to bring the representatives of both unions together to negotiate, and in July 1926 a joint meeting, chaired by Smillie, agreed in principle on amalgamation, Hodge to continue as agent in the reunited union and the Reform Union to be dissolved. Finally, by early in March 1927, the amalgamation had been carried through. Peace had been declared, and the miners in that coal-field were again united in a single trade union.

Elections held during the year showed a growing swing to the left. Ballots for the posts of two miners' agents for the county and for five representatives on the Scottish Executive Committee were taken successively during the summer and autumn of 1927. There was plenty of time to do this: for, no elections having been held in 1926 during the lock-out, the N.U.S.M.W. Executive elected in 1925 were still in office and had been slow to fix a date for the 1927 Conference. Eventually they decided that the Annual Scottish Conference (at which the elections became effective) would be held in December 1927.

Meanwhile each successive ballot in Fife showed stronger support for those who had been prominent in the dissolved Reform Union, with less support for General Secretary Adamson and his close associates. The final ballot vote for the Executive showed that five candidates of the Left had been elected (three being prominent as Communists), while Adamson and the sitting Executive members had been defeated.[1] At the same time John McArthur and David Proudfoot were chosen as full-time agents against the two temporary acting agents, James Cook and Alex. Smith.[2] This result was not only remarkable in that it chose new men as Scottish representatives against the sitting officials (which very seldom happens in trade union elections), but also signalised a political cleavage. The cleavage ran between those who were for the fighting policy of which A. J. Cook was the most prominent advocate, and those who were already moving towards that kind of harmony with the employers known as Mondism.[3]

But an even more remarkable indication of the desire of the Fife miners for a sweeping change in leadership was shown when nominations were submitted to fill the four official positions in the N.U.S.M.W. By branch vote the existing N.U.S.M.W. office-bearers, including Smillie and other established miners' agents, were rejected and new left candidates elected.[4] The Executive of the N.U.S.M.W., however, when they had a formal letter from Adamson asking for the usual routine confirmation as agents of McArthur and Proudfoot, decided to delay confirming the appointments—a step the significance of which was to appear later.

The leftward swing in Fife was not an isolated event. After the seven-month struggle of the 1926 lock-out hard conditions were imposed in each coal-field of Britain. In Scotland the

[1] The figures were as follows:

Elected		Not Elected	
Philip Hodge	6886	Wm. Adamson (Gen. Sec.)	5609
J. McArthur	6577	J. Cook (temp. agent)	5040
D. Proudfoot	6445	A. Smith (temp. agent)	4791
Jas. Stewart	6043	J. Potter (M.F.G.B. Exec.)	4744
John Bird	5962	C. Tonner (Chairman)	4740

[2] The result in the second ballot, with the number of candidates reduced to six, was:

John McArthur	4896	Alex. Smith	4144
David Proudfoot	4889	Patrick Connolly	2354
James Cook	4710	D. J. Williams	2334

[3] Mondism was so-called because Sir Alfred Mond, head of the great monopoly Imperial Chemical Industries Ltd., and leader of a group of big employers, had first enunciated this policy. It had been given provisional welcome in the speech of the T.U.C. Chairman in September 1927, and was more fully accepted at the Swansea T.U.C. in September 1928. A few years later it was dropped—by the employers—after it had served their purpose at a particular period.

[4] The nominations, after two branch votes (forty-nine out of fifty-four branches taking part), were:

President: R. Smillie, M.P. (Lanarkshire), 21; J. Bird (Fifeshire), 28.

Vice-President: H. Murnin, M.P. (Stirlingshire), 18; A. Thomson (Stirling), 31.

Secretary: R. Smith (Ayrshire), 16; W. Allan (Lanarkshire), 33.

Treasurer: E. Hawke (Lanarkshire), 20; Dan Sim (Ayrshire), 29.

owners put forward proposals which even in the last weeks were rejected. When, however, the Miners' Federation declared the struggle over, then a Scottish Delegate Conference on November 27, by a vote of 50 to 6, accepted the owners' terms willy-nilly. But there remained a bitter resentment amongst the miners both against the owners and the Government. Part of this resentment was turned against the leaders elected in 1925: and, as we have seen in the case of Fife, the ballot votes were strongly in favour of a sweeping change in the Scottish office-bearers and Executive Committee, as well as such county posts as came up for election. The same tendency was seen in Lanarkshire, the largest county union. Whether the tendency existed in the remaining counties must remain a matter of opinion. It cannot be proved one way or another. For in the smaller counties no ballot or branch votes were taken. The existing boards of these county organisations themselves nominated the candidates for the Executive Committee of the National Union of Scottish Mineworkers.[1]

In Lanarkshire, however, votes of the membership were duly taken, and with a similar result to that recorded for Fife. Ever since mid-1924 the President of the Lanarkshire Miners' County Union had been Andrew McAnulty. He was to be joined on the Scottish and Lanarkshire Executives by a young miner in his early twenties. William Allan, like John McArthur from Fife, had in 1921 been one of the small band of full-time students in the Scottish Labour College organised and led by John MacLean. Even before he was twenty-five he had become a well-known and popular figure in the county. In the mid-summer 1927 elections William Allan was elected General Secretary of the Lanarkshire Miners' County Union, displacing the sitting Secretary, W. B. Small, by a vote of 5102 against 4311. There is no doubt that this caused a degree of consternation amongst the older agents and officials— except of course McAnulty for whom this meant an accession

[1] In the case of Dumbarton (the Kirkintilloch and Twechar Miners' Association) the old Secretary, Donaldson, had resigned in the spring of 1926: and there had been no successor elected. Instead, throughout 1926 and 1927 Smillie and others were frequently visiting Dunbartonshire to try to settle the conditions under which their small separate county organisation, consisting of rather less than a thousand trade unionists, would be absorbed into the adjacent county union of Lanarkshire. This was finally carried through, though not without some discussion with the Stirlingshire Miners' Association, in the autumn of 1927.

of strength. But when it came to the nominations in Lanarkshire for the office-bearers of the National Union of Scottish
Mineworkers the swing of opinion became even more marked.
Here could be no question of a personal equation entering
into the matter. For the Lanarkshire miners showed they
wanted to have a checkweighman from Bowhill in Fife, of
whom few could have any close personal knowledge, to be
the Scottish President instead of Robert Smillie whom they
knew so well.[1] When in addition to this the financial vote of
the Lanarkshire branches for their eleven representatives on
the N.U.S.M.W. Executive returned a majority of left-wing
candidates, it became clear that the change of opinion was a
landslide.

A landslide, generally desired by each side in parliamentary
elections and sometimes (as in 1906, 1931 and 1945) actually
taking place, is extremely infrequent in trade union elections.
Whenever it has happened it has usually indicated a high
degree of dissatisfaction with the existing office-holders and
committees: and, however disagreeable the outcome of the
vote may be to the persons concerned, it has normally been
accepted as the verdict of democracy.

6. STRIFE AND SCHISM

By the constitution the new Executive Committee would
take office at the N.U.S.M.W. Annual Conference. If,
however, the Annual Conference were postponed, then the old
Executive, elected in September 1925, would carry on
pending the day of their dismissal from office. The Annual
Conference, which was not held in 1926 on the ground that
there was a lock-out, had not been held at the usual time in
1927 but had been *postponed* till December. On November 4
the Executive Committee decided to call for a financial report

---

[1] The branch financial votes for the office-bearers were as follows:

President: John Bird,* £580; Robert Smillie, £542.
Vice-President: Alexr. Thomson,* £567; Hugh Murnin, £482; Jas. Doonan, £86.
Secretary: William Allan,* £788; Robt. Smith, £346.
Treasurer: Edward Hawke, £527; Daniel Sim,* £419; John Hunter, £187.

(Left wing candidate.)

(Lanarkshire M.W.U. Minute, November 2, 1927, p. 7.)

and meantime to *postpone* the Annual Conference. Seven weeks then elapsed without any Executive meeting. Meantime it had become clear that wherever the usual democratic ballot vote or branch vote had been taken, all the office-bearers elected in 1925 had been defeated, and many of the Executive members as well. Thereupon in mid-December there began especially in the West of Scotland a press campaign, which showed the alarm of leading newspapers at the defeat of those whom they had come to rely upon as moderates. Prominent in the capitalist press was the Glasgow *Evening Times*, which, apparently on hints given by Duncan Graham, M.P., suggested that the method of voting was unrepresentative of the true opinion of the Lanarkshire miners. That this was demonstrably false was pointed out by the Secretary of the union in letters to the newspapers. Duncan Graham immediately dropped his odd suggestion of 'unrepresentative voting': for of course it was by the same method that he had himself at one time been elected. It was, however, indicative of the fury with which the election results had been received that such a baseless charge should have been made: and Duncan Graham, who in the past had made some reputation by his defence of the miners in Parliament, did not add to it by this incident.

When at last the old Scottish Executive met on December 27, 1927, it was to consider a financial proposal that all districts in arrears should be given three months to pay up and that the Annual Conference be *postponed* to some date beyond three months. The proposal was put forward by a small sub-committee on which sat the Secretary and the Treasurer, neither of whom would have retained their position once the Annual Conference took place. This question of arrears had never been raised before in connection with the holding of Annual Conferences—not even in the case of a county like Fife which had been for seven years heavily in arrears.

It was at the following Executive meeting on January 13, 1928, that the unusual decision was taken by 11 votes to 4 not to approve in the normal way the appointment of John McArthur and David Proudfoot who had been elected as agents in Fife. The decision once more to *postpone* the conference aroused comment in the press. The non-union

Evening Times, which seemed to rely less on imagination than on informers within the union, told its readers that there was a scheme 'to dish the Reds'. Discussion was aroused in the coalfields. In Fife a vote by 24 branches to 14 demanded that the Annual Conference be called. In Lanarkshire a similar demand was put forward by 30 branches to 23. This meant that the existing representatives from these two largest counties, which together had a majority over all others, now had a clear mandate from their members. The mandate, however, could not be exercised at an early date: for the Scottish Executive was not called together for nearly two months. When it met on April 5, several representatives from Lanarkshire and Fife did not represent their members' views. It recommended a further *postponement* of the Annual Conference, and an approach to the M.F.G.B. to enlist its support.

On April 18 a sort of official-unofficial manifesto appeared. It was signed by most of the officials (already defeated in the ballot and branch voting), but in fact, not being a statement from the Executive Committee, it was fairly clearly an unofficial right-wing manifesto although using the heading 'National Union of Scottish Mineworkers'. Robert Smillie did not sign his name to it.

This manifesto put forward the need for a full enquiry into the financial membership position as the justification for repeatedly postponing the conference, and suggested that districts in arrears might be suspended and excluded from the conference. It then passed on to a sharp attack on the Minority Movement. It concluded by saying that the full facts would be placed before the Executive of the M.F.G.B.

It will be seen that this manifesto now raised an entirely new argument for refusing to accept the decisions of the membership expressed in ballots and branch votes. It was an argument of a kind fairly familiar to present-day readers who follow the news of Senator McCarthy and others in the U.S.A. The gist of the argument is that democratic majority decisions need not be accepted if the outlook and methods of the majority leaders are considered utterly repellant and evil by the minority, which believes itself more truly to represent the real opinion of the particular electorate.

The manifesto was given immense publicity in the press. A. J. Cook, however, refused to allow it to be printed in *The Miner*, the semi-official organ of the M.F.G.B. Explaining his reasons for this, Cook said:

In some of our districts where the men are suffering terribly from rationalisation the leadership, instead of rallying the miners to fight, are busy fighting the 'Reds', and refuse to allow the rank and file to decide on issues affecting their livelihood and the control of their own organisation. The Manifesto issued by these leaders attacking the 'Reds' in their district will not appear in *The Miner*. I would like to emphasize that in the M.F.G.B. every man on joining the Union has full rights to decide the policy and programme of the Union, to attend all conferences affecting the Union if chosen by his branch, and to stand for all positions in his Union, the only qualification being financial membership.

I regret to say that the policy now being pursued in Scotland appears to me directed towards the disruption of the Union and is likely to endanger the whole existence of the M.F.G.B. (*Sunday Worker*, April 22, 1928.)

With this 'Manifesto' in their hands a group then went as a 'deputation' to London to get support for their statement from the M.F.G.B. Executive Committee. Their action was strongly criticised by other members of the Scottish Executive.[1]

[1] For example, Sandy Hunter, Vice-President of the Lanarkshire Miners' County Union, said that when he differed from the 'Reds':

I never hesitate to show it, and never intend to do so. In the present situation in Scotland, however, I must state that I totally repudiate what is being done by the present officials. I have fought as vigorously as I can, and will continue to do so, against either the suspension of the annual conference in the Union, or the attempt to nullify the ballot votes which have already taken place. At no time do I remember all counties being free from arrears; and at no time, in the last twelve years, has there been any different system in electing officials.

He then went on to criticise the visit to London, saying:

The deputation to the M.F.G.B. has been one of the most barefaced and undemocratic actions I have experienced. I, a member of the E.C., had no say in sending it, nor did I have a say in who should compose it. To follow it up with the proposal of expelling Fife and also Communists from the Union, is simply bewildering. I have already said that I will fight as much as I am able against it. Instead of expelling men from the Union, we need more and more energy inside it. (*Sunday Worker*, June 3, 1928.)

McLaren, for ten years a member of the Scottish Executive and the only one on it who was not an official in one of the counties, said sharp things of

the various county officials, who zealously guard their own little prerogatives as if they were sacred. So blind are they, and so prejudiced, that they fail to see that it is the coalowners and their own tactics that are disintegrating the Unions, not the Communists.

I am not a Communist, nor do I agree with many things they say. What they do is quite a different matter: I have never yet seen them do anything outwith the rules of the union, neither have I seen them flout mandates of the men.

The M.F.G.B. Executive had now a majority in support of Mondism; A. J. Cook and his supporters were in a minority.[1] It did not give a blanket endorsement to the activities of the authors of the manifesto, but it did pass a resolution (May 17, 1928) condemning the 'Minority Movement and the tactics which have been adopted in the various coal-fields, and particularly in Scotland'. At the M.F.G.B. Conference of July 1928 this resolution was incorporated in the Executive Report, but discussion on the Scottish situation was ruled out by the Chairman, credentials having already been refused to two left-wing Scottish delegates (W. Allan and J. McKendrick). A semi-assurance was, however, given that M.F.G.B. officials should visit Scotland if the Report were accepted. But many delegates remained uneasy at the handling of the situation. This was voiced in various ways and from many quarters.[2]

At the same time a manifesto was signed by eighteen prominent members of the Federation and addressed 'To all miners' lodges'. It appealed to them to demand a ballot vote whether or not all mine-workers were 'eligible for membership and to declare whether members elected by majority vote shall take office regardless of their political associations'. The manifesto declared that 'a conference largely composed mainly of full time officials' had taken a decision which would break the M.F.G.B. and turn it from being 'a free and independent Federation of Mineworkers into the appendage of a particular political party'. This manifesto was signed, among others, by A. J. Cook; E.C. member S. O. Davies, Vice-President of

He went on to refer to the ignored ballot:

> The ballot vote turning myself down, as well as Mr. Smillie and Mr. Small, has been the same method adopted as long as I can remember. It was as democratic as any vote has ever been in this county. We have reached this stage now even in the Scottish E.C. that things are being done in its name without that full body being consulted. I knew nothing of the deputation to the M.F.G.B. or the proposed expulsion of Fife and the Communists until the press reported it. There can be no Scottish conference without Fife. Neither can there be expulsion of individual Communists. Those defeated in the ballot vote—and I am one—must stand down. If they refuse to do so, then they will require to be expelled from the Union if needs be. (*Sunday Worker*, June 3, 1928.)

[1] Outside the four office-bearers, Cook had supporters in the M.F.G.B. Executive and Conference, as well as in the coal-fields. On the wider issues of industry and politics, the Cook-Maxton manifesto which won assent from the then influential I.L.P.—though not from the Communist Party—infuriated the right-wing opponents of Cook inside and outside the Federation.

[2] For example, at the close of the conference, an M.F.G.B. Executive member, S. O. Davies, said: 'At last a definite official sanction has been given, by this Miners' Conference, to the process of excluding from any official position the elected representative of the rank and file—if that representative has the courage of breaking with the traditional petrified methods and ideas of the old school'.

South Wales, and Arthur Horner; E.C. member Harry Hicken, General Secretary of Derbyshire, and O. Wright, Financial Secretary; William Lawther and two other E.C. members of Durham; F. J. Hancock of North Stafford (E.C. member 1927–8); G. Woods of Lancashire and Cheshire (E.C. member 1927–8); and the Lanarkshire and Fife officials.[1] Amongst the signatories were a future M.F.G.B. President and Secretary. It showed that the cleavage in principle was of grave import, and not confined to Scotland.

7. ADAMSON'S BREAKAWAY

Meantime feeling was rising inside the Fife, Kinross and Clackmannan Mineworkers' Association. This was expressed in protests by the Board against the postponement of the conference and in angry demands by branches for the resignation of General Secretary Adamson for misrepresenting the members' minds at the Scottish Executive and the M.F.G.B. In May 1928 a financial vote at the Executive Board made James Stewart President. Another sign of the times was the election of the justicemen (or checkweighers) at Lumphinnans Number XI Colliery, where the brothers Abe and Alex. Moffat were elected by ballot vote out of a list of six candidates. In the minutes of the Board at which Stewart presided on June 2, the very last item on the agenda described how the Lumphinnans delegate Alex. Moffat stated that

he had been instructed to move the suspension of the Standing Orders in order to discuss the suspension of Mr. Adamson, and leave having been given to discuss this matter, the Chairman read the following letter from the Secretary of the Lumphinnans branch:

May 1, 1928

FIFE, KINROSS & CLACKMANNAN MINEWORKERS' ASSOCIATION

Branch: Lumphinnans
From 46 Mungall St.

I have to notify you that the above branch have instructed

[1] Three months later the three E.C. members, A. J. Cook, S. O. Davies and H. Hicken, were reported in the press to have been obliged under pressure to withdraw their names. Harry Hicken in a recent interview (October 1953), however, says this was not so.

Moffat to move the suspension of the Standing Orders to discuss complaint against Mr. Adamson, General Secretary.

Our complaint is as follows:

A month ago the members by a huge majority passed a vote of censure on Mr. Adamson and others for violating the mandate of the Fife miners at a meeting of the Scottish E.C., *re* question of National Conference. The miners passed this vote of censure because they were of opinion that Mr. Adamson had done something that was detrimental to the miners, and now since that time he has participated in a deputation to the M.F.G.B., a deputation which had no support either from the Fife or Scottish miners.

That deputation was able to get a resolution passed at M.F.G.B. which will, if put into operation, smash all or any organisation of the miners that is left in the coalfield.

We think this action of Mr. Adamson requires to be dealt with and ask the Executive if they agree with us to put Rule 8 into operation—suspend Mr. Adamson from office, and take a vote of the county as to whether he should be dismissed or not.

Yours faithfully,
ALEX. CAMPBELL, Secy.
JOHN GRIEG, Chairman.

After a very long discussion it was moved that Adamson be suspended and that a Committee of Inquiry be set up. Eventually it was agreed to delay consideration of the whole matter until the next monthly meeting. There appears to have been a certain reluctance on the part of the Fife Board to proceed to strong measures against Adamson: and of course the fact that a minority of the Board were old friends of Adamson played a part in delaying a decision. There was, however, no hesitation on Adamson's part in siding with measures against the union of which he was still General Secretary. For on July 23, 1928, he took part in a meeting of the Scottish Executive which unanimously[1] decided 'that the Annual Conference be held on 31 August 1928', and imposed financial conditions which would exclude Fife and Stirling from representation. The same meeting decided that they were empowered to exclude from nomination those of whom they disapproved. This done, they re-nominated the existing officials.

On receiving these decisions the Fife Board instructed the

[1] Philip Hodge, duly elected from Fife on to the Scottish Executive, had received no summons to its meetings. William Allan had been expelled from the meeting after an altercation with the Chairman.

President to take legal action to interdict the holding of the
N.U.S.M.W. Conference with the exclusion of Fife (a step
subsequently endorsed by the branches).[1] Adamson was
suspended from office and a ballot of the members taken on
whether he should be dismissed. Without awaiting the result
of the ballot, however, Adamson announced his resignation
and his intention to form a rival organisation.

Adamson was able to get together in his union (which he
adroitly christened the Fife, Clackmannan and Kinross
Mineworkers' Association) a small minority of the organised
workers in the Fife coal-field. The big majority remained with
the Fife, Kinross and Clackmannan Mineworkers' Association,
which, however, also had to carry the huge load of debt accumulated in the previous seven years of Adamson's secretaryship.

After the breakaway union had been started, the M.F.G.B.
Executive passed a resolution that they wished it 'to be
understood that the Llandudno resolution cannot be interpreted to imply the dismembering of individual members of
the Federation on account of their political beliefs or associations'. After an enquiry had been made by the national
officials into the split, the M.F.G.B. Executive expressed its
desire to assist in adjusting the differences and restoring unity
in the Fife coal-field and in Scotland generally. The M.F.G.B.
officials made a number of attempts to get the two opposing
sides together, visiting Scotland for the purpose, but were
rebuffed on each occasion by the Scottish Executive, who
vetoed such a meeting and informed the M.F.G.B. that they
considered the Fife question 'clearly a domestic matter' for
themselves to settle. The M.F.G.B., in fact, had served their
purpose, and they had no further use for it in Scottish matters
once they had attained their object. But the consequences for
the Scottish miners were to be disastrous.

8. RIVAL UNIONS

For years there had been a body of opinion, as we have
seen, favouring a closer structure; what was needed was not a

[1] Three days before the proposed conference an interim edict was granted by Lord
Moncrieff against the N.U.S.M.W.

View towards Bowhill Colliery
with Miners Cottages - Bowhill

Reg Forrester 15.6.1953

VIEW TOWARDS BOWHILL COLLIERY, FIFE, 1953

NELLIE PIT, LOCHGELLY, FIFE, 1953

loose federal structure of county unions, each of different levels of strength in numbers and vigour, but a single national union. To deal with coal-owners who were beginning to press hard, and with a view to negotiating a new national agreement, which would shortly be necessary, there was an added impetus to the views of those who had long believed that the county unions needed to be turned into one national union for Scotland.

The miners were fully conscious of the mounting problems —with unemployment and rationalisation schemes to bring it home in each pit. They needed to meet on a wider platform than that of their branches, and indeed their county unions. And yet it was precisely at this time that the old guard in the counties were so apprehensive of the rank and file that they were everywhere failing, and indeed in some cases refusing, to call normal conferences. Above all, the N.U.S.M.W. officials had not called an Annual Conference since 1925 nor published balance sheets of the falling membership's dues, because they would have to accept ballots replacing them as officials.

It was therefore not at all surprising that these two streams —the old demand for closer unification into one national union; and the discontent with the existing officials blocking activity—should flow together. There was set up a Save-the-Union Council composed of many elements from the seven counties. Its campaign was marked by a big meeting at Falkirk on October 13, 1928, which drew wide attendance. After that, a whole series of meetings and conferences was held in all the districts.

The final fuel to the flames came when, in February, Adamson's breakaway union was whitewashed. For at that very time it became known to the N.U.S.M.W. officials that the decision on the interdict was to be announced. Realising that as a consequence they would shortly be obliged to call the three-year-delayed conference, the Scottish Executive decided to summon immediately a Special Delegate Conference with the one item of business only: to alter Rule 4 in such a way as to disaffiliate Fife, Kinross and Clackmannan Miners' Association. This would then completely clear the ground for its substitution by Adamson's breakaway union.

Their decision was taken on February 11; the Special Delegate Conference was called for only seven days later. This haste led to widespread accusations of 'gerry-mandering', and for many it was the last straw. Two days before it took place, at a meeting in Glasgow held by the Save-the-Union Council, there were angry scenes; and a decision was taken to call an all-Scotland conference together.

The official minutes of the N.U.S.M.W. Special Delegate Conference to change Rule 4, at which seventy-two delegates were present, are brief, complex and uninformative. In particular, the statement by Philip Hodge of the position of the dues arrears of Fife, Kinross and Clackmannan Mineworkers' Association is not minuted at all. According to an article by him in the next issue of *The Scottish Mineworker*, however, he told the conference that he had written to the Secretary of the N.U.S.M.W. at the beginning of the year, suggesting a meeting to arrange payment of dues and arrears, and to adjust the actual numbers who should be paid for, but this offer was not accepted or even considered. He had also pointed out that according to the rules the members must be consulted before passing the new rule, but though this was admitted the rule was changed without the officials of a single district being able to say that they had consulted their members.

Following upon these events, William Allan, for the Save-the-Union Council, issued a manifesto denouncing the Scottish officials for their 'crime against the Scottish miners', and declaring that the old officials were incapable of organising, while the employers were already taking advantage of the situation with further vicious attacks on the miners' standards. It called for 'organisation on a Scottish scale to fight the coalowners and protect the interests of the men'.

A new 'Scottish Mineworkers' Union' must be built in order to carry on the men's struggles. The 'Save the Union' Council is preparing to take the necessary action to immediately achieve this. It calls on the (disaffiliated) F.K. & C.M.A. to co-operate with the 'Save the Union' Council in immediately carrying out a campaign in the various mining counties for a new Scottish Mineworkers' Union.

As a result of this manifesto, William Allan was suspended

from the Lanarkshire union, of which he was General Secretary; and he was also excluded from the Scottish Executive.

From now on there could be but one outcome. The all-Scotland conference called by the Save-the-Union Council took place on April 13. It was attended by 132 delegates, and the Fife Council came *en bloc*. A new union, the United Mine-workers of Scotland, was set up. Rules and a programme were adopted. William Allan became Secretary.

But it was to be many weeks later before the appointment of the Fife members—Messrs. Cation, White, Boyd and Alexander Moffat, who became Vice-President; for there was a struggle in the Fife union between the majority headed by James Stewart, Alexander Moffat, John MacArthur and David Proudfoot (President, Vice-President, Compensation Secretary and Agent respectively) and the General Secretary Philip Hodge. The latter, it was clear, was living still in hope of the M.F.G.B. officials intervening decisively and success-fully with the N.U.S.M.W. officials; and that Adamson would yet be abandoned in favour of the Fife, Kinross and Clackmannan Miners' Association. For month after month Philip Hodge continued to count on the N.U.S.M.W. being obliged to restore his union to its full rights, even after they had accepted the affiliation of Adamson's union, and the M.F.G.B. had retired from the field. Thus it was that for a certain time there were actually three groups competing to organise the Fife miners. But by October Philip Hodge had been brought low indeed; he asked to be allowed to join the organisation of his old enemy Adamson.

The breach was now complete, and was to remain so for half a dozen years. There is nothing to be gained from follow-ing the story of recriminations and rivalry which dragged on between the N.U.S.M.W. and the new U.M.S. Hence-forward the developments run on two parallel lines which were not to meet. Of the N.U.S.M.W. the record continues from their not very informative minutes. The activities of the U.M.S. were largely occupied with day-to-day struggles in the different pits in resisting wage-reductions which followed the ending of the national agreement in November 1929.

We may give one example from Lumphinnans which

appears typical. A strike had developed against the Fife Coal
Company in the Peeweep, Aitken and Mary Pits. The strike
committee included Alex. Moffat and Abe Moffat, who were
both checkweighers at No. 11 Colliery. After the strike had
ended, the Fife Coal Company served summonses to remove
them from their positions for their activities in connection
with the strike. The men immediately elected the two brothers
as Local Pit Inspectors; and a deputation interviewed the
General Manager of the Fife Coal Company, Mr. C. C. Reid,
to demand the withdrawal of the summonses. The subsequent
hearing, at which Mr. Reid gave evidence, is reported by *The
Scottish Mineworker* of November 9, 1929, as follows:

Alex Moffat, in the witness-box, stated that Reid wanted him to
agree to cease his activities and be a good fellow to the Company;
that he would drop all legal proceedings if Moffat would sign a statement (1) to act at the colliery as a checkweighman strictly in accordance with the Check-weighers Act; (2) cease all Communist activities
at the colliery; (3) admit that he was wrong in bringing the men on
strike, and now regretted his actions. Moffat pointed out that he
regarded that offer as a bribe, and would not sign such a statement
for all the Reids in the Fife Coal Company, and that he would rather
be removed as checkweighman by the Company for fighting them,
than by the men for betraying the workers in their struggle against
the Company.

In all of their evidence, the checkweighers did not retract from the
part they had played in the strike. The Sheriff held that the case was
proved against them, ordered their removal as checkweighers, and
granted the Company expenses of £3 : 3 : 0 against each of the checkweighers.

It was on the basis of local activities such as these that there
was built up in one mining centre after another a spirit of
active and militant trade unionism in these difficult years.

CHAPTER IX

THE WORLD ECONOMIC CRISIS

I. THE SECOND LABOUR GOVERNMENT

THE General Election, June 1929, from which the miners hoped so much, resulted in big gains for the Labour Party, lesser gains for the Liberal Party and heavy losses for the Conservative Party. Baldwin resigned and Ramsay Mac-Donald once more formed an administration. William Adamson, M.P. for West Fife, became Secretary of State for Scotland. The miners had looked forward to a Labour Government which they hoped would restore the seven-hour day, nationalise the mines and minerals, get rid of the harsh provisions (the 'not genuinely seeking work' clause) of unemployment benefit, and repeal the Trade Disputes and Trade Unions Act of 1927. MacDonald had promised to do various things for the miners; what he tried to do was less than what he promised; and what finally came out of it was less still. Given the situation of the coal industry, the strong position held by the coal-owners, the extreme weakness of the M.F.G.B. at that time and finally the composition both of Parliament and of the Cabinet, this is what might have been expected. In explanation particular stress was laid upon the fact that the Liberals, though they supported many Labour Government Bills, could at any moment join with the Conservatives and upset the Government. It is now known that it was the composition of the Cabinet which was an even bigger factor in preventing the miners from getting what they desired. Labour Party writers were in later years to make the severest criticism of the second Labour Government. The Labour Party official historian, Mr. Francis Williams, says:

The MacDonald administration failed lamentably in any true economic understanding of the problem. It stuck obstinately to a course

which was bound to end in political and economic disaster and lead
to a betrayal of all the principles of social and economic equity for
which the Labour Movement had struggled throughout its lifetime.
(*Fifty Years' March: the Rise of the Labour Party*, 1949, p. 337.)

The second Labour Government proved unable to bring
in the legislative measures that the miners had hoped for, but
it brought in and carried by a narrow majority in the House
of Commons the Coal Mines Act, 1930. From the miners'
point of view, the main provision of this Act was the seven-
and-a-half-hour day to take the place of the permissive eight-
hour day passed in the middle of the 1926 lock-out by the
Conservative Government. But mingled with the seven-and-
a-half-hour day was the vexed question of the spread-over,
which led to much heart-burning and difficulty in the coal-
fields and to differences arising between one district and
another. This 1930 Act, if compared with the programme of
nationalisation set forth in *Labour and the New Social Order* in
1918, or as recommended by the Sankey Commission of 1919,
or as reaffirmed in subsequent Labour Party declarations,
was something very meagre indeed as the fruit of a Labour
Government. Nevertheless, it was regarded by most of the
miners as a first upward step out of the morass of longer hours
and lower wages into which they had been plunged since the
end of 1926.

The Labour Government had come to office in a period of
rising prosperity on both sides of the Atlantic; it had been in
office for less than half a year when in the United States there
was a crash on the stock exchange. This was the first sign of an
economic crisis which, in a period of months, was to spread to
every country in the world—with the exception of the Union
of Soviet Socialist Republics.

The interesting feature of the crisis that began in late 1929
was that for three years previously there had not only been a
piling up of profits, but the piling up of theories that by the
American methods of production crises had been and would
be avoided. These theories, voiced primarily by the economists of the various universities in the United States, had been
taken up by socialist writers. The British policy of Mondism
was justified as being on similar lines as that which had
seemingly proved so successful in the United States. Even

H. N. Brailsford,[1] editor of the I.L.P. organ *The New Leader*, voiced the view that Henry Ford had superseded Karl Marx. It was not only the ordinary private owners and their managers, inspired by the profit motive, who had been behind the drive for 'rationalising' in the coal-mines ever since the year 1926. There was a crowd of writers and speakers who were promising the wonderful results that would arise from 'rationalisation' and from the methods that had been so successful in the United States in avoiding economic crises. Now the economic crisis had come. Here and there amongst the writers there were a few, but only a few, who recognised that all the propaganda had been false; and that periodic onset of crises was inescapable under capitalism, being, indeed, part of the very nature of capitalism. Beginning in the United States this was the longest, deepest and widest that had ever been known in the history of modern capitalism.

It began to be felt in Great Britain fairly early in 1930, and increased thereafter at a rapid pace. It was assumed that the Labour Government would be much better able to deal with the effects than any other, and hopes were raised when J. H. Thomas was put in charge of the major problem of unemployment. But he was able to do nothing that had any observable effect.

2. THE NATIONAL GOVERNMENT

As the crisis grew rapidly worse in the winter of 1930–1, the demand of the 'big-business' interests that the Labour Government should find a solution to industrial problems at the expense of social services increased. The clamour of the newspapers grew even yet more shrill. The Labour Government yielded. Philip Snowden, Chancellor of the Exchequer, appointed 'big-business' men to be a Committee on National Expenditure. To meet a prospective Budget deficit, this Committee, headed by Sir George May of the Prudential Assurance Company, suggested cuts amounting to a hundred million pounds, of which about two-thirds would be at the expense of the unemployed. A 10 per cent cut in unemployment benefit

[1] In an article entitled 'Ford *versus* Marx'.

was suggested. The crisis grew steadily deeper. The demand for a paring down of expenditure on social services came ever more insistently from the capitalist interests, both in Britain and in the United States. Finally, on the issue of the 10 per cent cut in benefit there was a split in the Cabinet on Sunday, August 23, 1931. On one side there was Ramsay MacDonald, Philip Snowden and also J. H. Thomas, together with the Lord Chancellor and other law officers. Amongst those on the other side were Arthur Henderson, George Lansbury and Sidney Webb. MacDonald went off to see the King, and after some hobnobbing with the leaders of the parties opposed to the Labour Party, the next day he coolly informed his colleagues that at the request of His Majesty he had formed a new Government together with the Conservative and Liberal parties. He himself would be Prime Minister and Snowden Chancellor of the Exchequer. MacDonald and his little bunch of followers had sacked the leaders of the Labour Party from their positions as Ministers; they abandoned the Labour Party and entered the ranks of its enemies. With the utmost use of publicity, it was announced that this step had been rendered necessary in order to maintain the pound sterling on the gold standard, and the public were informed that a General Election would take place in the near future.

Within a few weeks the new Cabinet had abandoned the gold standard which it had promised to maintain. The pretext for the behaviour of MacDonald, Snowden and Thomas was thus itself swept away. The General Election, on October 27, 1931, was carried through with the maximum use of every device that could alarm the electorate, and conjure up in their minds the spectre of a money inflation that would destroy all their savings and make their weekly wages depreciate before they were spent on the household needs for the week. Philip Snowden had for many years been a prominent anti-bolshevist, but now he uttered in his broadcasts scare stories and statements that Arthur Henderson and the other leaders of the Labour Party were worse than bolsheviks, for he described their policy as 'bolshevism run mad'.

The apostasy of MacDonald and Snowden, bringing about the betrayal of their party and of the principles they had so often proclaimed from the platform, was not, however, a matter of a sudden change. Their policy over a period of years had led up to it. It was Snowden who, at the end of the seven months' miners' struggle, made the preparations for Mondism by his specious demand for 'peace in industry', which had been fiercely answered by the miners' leader, A. J. Cook, in his pamphlet *Is It Peace?* ending with the words: 'Judas at least had the decency to hang himself'. More and more the policy represented by MacDonald, Snowden and Thomas had swayed Labour Party leaders in sundry localities and leaders of various trade unions.

The General Election resulted in a great loss of seats by the Labour Party, which came back to Parliament with its numbers reduced to fifty-two, while the number of Conservative seats rose to 471. If it had not been for the mining constituencies, and for a few of the big towns, the Labour Party in Parliament would have been brought nearly to extinction. The M.F.G.B. put forward forty-three candidates and lost twenty seats. In Scotland all the seven seats were swept away except that of Duncan Graham at Hamilton.

A coalition of the Conservatives, two of the three sections of the Liberal Party—but not Lloyd George and his group—together with the handful of MacDonald's 'National Labour', endured for another year, and then after a reshuffle, with the Tories dominating both in numbers and policy, went on until 1935. Then came a further reshuffle. Baldwin, tired of leading the orchestra as second fiddle, became Prime Minister.

Under the self-styled 'National' Government the economic crisis deepened; unemployment grew and the 10 per cent cut in benefit was carried through. The economic devices, of which the worst was the notorious Means Test, designed to throw the burden of the terrible crisis on to the shoulders of the working class, were accompanied by repressive measures against civil liberties. Of these repressive measures a particularly flagrant example was the imprisonment of Tom Mann. For this veteran was not charged with any offence but, under an Act of 1348, he was required not to make speeches to the unemployed. On his refusing to be thus muzzled (as any man of spirit, let alone Tom Mann, would have refused) he was sent to prison for six months. The miserable Ramsay MacDonald, when an appeal was made to him to end this scandal, refused to do anything. The Scottish Executive Committee passed a resolution to be forwarded to the Prime Minister:

That we, the Executive of the National Union of Scottish Mine Workers, on behalf of our members, protest against the action of the authorities for the arrest and imprisonment of Mr. Tom Mann, under an old and now obsolete Act of Parliament, as being a serious curtailment of the liberty of free speech. (December 24, 1932.)

For the miners' unions which had not yet recovered from the defeat of 1926, and in which the influence of the policy of Mondism had hampered recovery, it was a very difficult period. This may be shown by a single token. In the past, whether it was a Labour Government or whether it was the Government of Bonar Law or Baldwin, a deputation from the Miners' Federation of Great Britain was usually received by the Prime Minister and three or four other leading Members of the Government. Under the National Government, the M.F.G.B. leaders found that they could not have discussions with anyone higher than the civil servants in charge of the Department of Mines.[1]

3. EFFECTS OF THE SLUMP

The coal trade, which had been expanding in output and man-power at a rapid rate for a hundred years and had reached its highest output, of 287,000,000 tons, in 1913, had thereafter ceased to expand. The disturbed years of the first World War were followed by the loss of markets, the growth

---

[1] It is interesting to note that the first question which William Gallacher, M.P., was to put on first taking his seat in the House of Commons was on this subject. It runs as follows:

47. MR. GALLACHER asked the Prime Minister the reason why he did not receive the deputation of the Mineworkers' Federation of Great Britain in person, in view of the importance of the matters they were raising?

THE PRIME MINISTER: As the hon. Member is aware, there is a Government Department specifically concerned with the care of all matters in connection with the mining industry. In accordance with the accepted principles of public administration, the Minister in charge of that Department is acting on behalf of the Government in the matter.

MR. GALLACHER: As a matter of fact, is not the miners' case so strong that while the Department, on the plea of having no power, can evade the issue, the Prime Minister could not evade the issue, and did not dare to face it?

THE PRIME MINISTER: May I say, in answer to that question, that when a sentence is prefaced by the words 'as a matter of fact' it is always very remote from fact. (*Hansard*, December 5, 1935.)

of rival coal-producing countries, the substitution for coal of oil and hydro-electric power. Added to these were political policies which shut off the considerable Russian market; and, by the Dawes Plan, boosted the rival coal industry of Germany—policies supported in their purblind way by the coal-owners. The zenith year in output was 1913; in number employed—nearly a million and a quarter—it was 1920. Thereafter there was a slow drop in output and also in man-power. After 1926 output was still going down, while man-power began to fall with great rapidity. In 1923 there were employed in coal-mines of Great Britain 1,203,290, of whom no less than 966,136 worked below ground. By 1932 the total had fallen to 819,324. It was upon an already contracting industry, especially contraction of man-power, that the slump fell with such terrific force. But Scottish coal-mining was contracting in man-power even more rapidly than the British coal-fields as a whole, as will be seen from the following table:

Counties	1923	1932
Fife, Clackmannan, Kinross and Sutherland	30,936	19,928
Lothians (Mid and East) and Peebles	15,792	12,483
Lanarkshire, Linlithgow, Stirling, Renfrew and Dumbarton	80,108	38,585
Ayrshire, Dumfries and Argyll	16,431	11,362
Total: Scotland	143,267	82,358

Man-power shrank in these nine years in England and Wales by a little over a quarter: in Scotland by much more than a third.

How many miners were thrown out of work even before the slump reached its greatest depth? When the Census was taken in Great Britain in 1931, there were still a million who returned their 'occupation' under the heading of coal and shale mines: but of this million nearly a fifth also returned themselves as 'out of work'. By the middle of 1932, when the percentage of unemployed men was over 25 per cent (one man in four idle), the percentage of unemployment in coal-mining had risen to over 40 per cent (two miners workless out of every five).

Hunger drove most of the workless miners to seek supplementary poor relief (under a Poor Law then going through various changes of name and administration). It was the same with many other trades. Over two and three-quarter million persons between the ages of sixteen and sixty-four were 'unemployed' in the middle of 1932: by January 1933 about half of them were getting poor relief. In England and Wales poor relief totals in 1933 were twice as many as in 1914: in Scotland they were thrice as many.

Yet with all these figures we cannot tell the poverty and the misery in all the coal-fields, but especially in the valleys of South Wales and the mining counties of Scotland. For no statistics can measure the destitution in those dreadful years that smote the mining communities like a plague.

4. THE SLUMP AND THE COUNTY UNIONS

The effect of the slump in unemployment, and of Government policy in its restrictions on unemployment benefits, especially the Means Test imposed by the National Government in November 1931, was naturally reflected in the miners' trade unions. But these unions were no longer the powerful and united bodies that had made governments tremble between 1911 and 1921, and up to the year 1926. The agreements imposed in each coal-field after the lock-out of 1926 had been designed to break up the M.F.G.B. or to leave it largely as a paper organisation. The miners' county associations were now more separate from one another and tending more to express different and separate interests than at any time for forty years. Not satisfied with this the coal-owners had taken the further step of fostering 'non-political' unions (or 'yellow unions' as they were called on the Continent) in county after county in opposition to the M.F.G.B. organisations. In Britain they were usually called 'Spencer' unions because the first of the kind had been formed by George Spencer, M.P. (former Secretary of the Nottinghamshire Miners' Association), after he had been expelled from an M.F.G.B. Conference in the autumn of 1926. There was no effective attempt to build a 'non-political' union in Scotland.

For the coal-owners were content to enter into relations of conciliation with the existing county unions, whose militancy had been largely extirpated by the events of 1927 to 1929, as narrated in the last chapter. In Fife and in Lanark where the method of branch and ballot votes, which was not the practice to the same extent in the four smaller county associations, had given expression to the great militancy of 1926–8, a considerable number in 1929 enrolled in the United Mine-workers of Scotland, which also had its adherents in the other counties. From the standpoint of the year 1929 there is no saying what would have been the outcome of this situation of union rivalry in the coal-fields. But the year 1929 was followed in 1930 by the onset of economic crisis and its deepening in the years that followed. This upset all forecasts and created an entirely new situation and one that was most painful for the colliers, whether in work or out of work.

In the annals of this period of economic crisis it would be only a harrowing story to relate the details of the struggles between the rival unions or to revive an old quarrel by telling of the accusations, usually couched in the most vehement terms, of the militant organisation against the leaders of the old county unions, or the counter-arguments and denuncia-tions launched by the older leaders, many of them Members of Parliament and close followers up to August 1931 of the policy of Ramsay MacDonald, against the militants enrolled in the U.M.S. But it is important to show how each of them regarded the situation into which the miners had been plunged by the economic crisis, by the attitude of the employers, and by the action or inaction of successive governments.

First let us turn to the records of the old Scottish Executive. Here we must rely on the presidential addresses and resolu-tions of annual or other delegate conferences, apart from which nothing but the barest record is minuted, hardly more than a list of agenda items. At the long-delayed 'Annual Conference' held on March 28, 1929 (at which it was decided that 'present acting officials remain in office and Executive Committee' for another seven months), James Doonan was Chairman; for Robert Smillie had sent in his resignation the previous year and refused to reconsider his decision. Doonan said in the course of his remarks:

Trade, after a period of depression, is on the upgrade. Prices are going up. The ascertainments between October and January show that the price of coal has been increased by 9d. per ton. How far that increase is likely to continue is difficult to say. In the meantime if we want improved conditions we must have an improved organisation.

Conference carried a resolution unanimously which called attention to

The present serious conditions prevailing in the Scottish coalfield. Unemployment—low wages paid to many workers—breaches of the 8 Hours Act—excessive overtime—termination of the overtime agreement—and other encroachments on the improved conditions obtained when our organisation was strong. (March 28, 1929.)

At the next conference Doonan devoted two-thirds of his speech to a denunciation of the rival trade union. He dealt more briefly with the question of wages and hours, saying: 'We have continued to protest against the longer working day. Now that a Labour Government has been returned we look forward hopefully and with a measure of certainty to this measure being repealed.' Under the heading 'Unemployment' the conference record adds only this:

Delegates complained of the manner in which the workmen were being dealt with by the officials of the Labour Exchanges especially on the plea of 'not genuinely seeking work'. It was agreed to press the present Government to delete such a clause entirely from the regulations. (August 30, 1929.)

A year later, at the Annual Conference Chairman Doonan, after a passing hostile reference to the adherents of the U.M.S., said of the Coal Mines Act that it

fell short of many of the cherished ideals and principles for which the Miners' Federation stood. . . . The constructive parts of the Act by no means represented the contribution which the majority of the members of the Government would make to the reorganisation of the mining industry, but they represented the maximum contribution that could be made quickly to help the industry in the face of present political difficulties. (August 27, 1930.)

James Doonan's protest in 1929 against the longer working day and his deploring of the shortcomings of the Act of 1930 (which reduced the working day to seven-and-a-half hours) were later to be put to the proof. For some months after the Act had been passed, the vexed question arose of extra hours being worked under what was called the 'spread-over'. Against this the Miners' Federation took a decisive vote on November 27, 1930.

Seven months later the M.F.G.B. Executive Committee made the following remarks on this 'most reactionary measure':

The 'spread-over' was merely a subterfuge to cover the intention of the owners of continuing a working day of eight hours and of robbing the workmen of the shorter working day. It is therefore a negation of the principle of the shorter working day, and it also destroys a principle which the Federation has always regarded as of vital importance, namely, the principle of uniformity in relation to hours.

But they also stated that Scotland had 'continued to work the "spread-over" and in accordance with our decision[1] we now formally report this fact to the Annual Conference'. Already at the M.F.G.B. Special Conference on hours and wages (June 25, 26 and July 2, 1931), after Doonan had made a speech in which he referred to the arrangement that he and others of the Scottish Executive had made with the Scottish coal-owners, A. J. Cook, as General Secretary, had stated very forcibly:

Scotland in defiance of the Federation and the Government continued to work the 'spread-over' and did not face the situation as other people did, with a higher rate of wages. In relation to the rest of the coal-field there has been 8 hours per day in Scotland, when others have been working 7½ hours. It could not be allowed to continue, in the interests of the whole coal-field.

But even after that M.F.G.B. Special Conference the attitude of the Scottish Executive had caused anxiety both to the Minister of Mines (Emanuel Shinwell) and at the head-quarters of the M.F.G.B.

On July 9, 1931, Shinwell wired to the union:

Have seen statements in the Press that arrangements have been made to continue working in excess of seven and a half hours day,

---

[1] Ebby Edwards from the Chair at the M.F.G.B. Conference of June 25 had pointedly read out this decision:

That we regret that the Scottish Miners have not fallen into line with the Conference decision and express the opinion that there is no change in circumstances justifying a reversal of such decision, and make a further appeal to Scotland to be loyal to the Federation. (April 2, 1931.)

stop. Please enable me to deny that men have been advised to act illegally.

Doonan replied:

Men advised to continue working at existing wages and hours while negotiations proceed. Alternatives, viz.: Submit to reduction of 19 per cent on basic rates, or strike.

A similar enquiry as to whether Scottish miners were working the 'spread-over' came from A. J. Cook, who was informed that the union had agreed to 'continue day-to-day contracts on the old terms'. Cook replied brusquely:

Wire received. Executive Meeting today—note position and expects Scottish Miners to observe the law.

Seven weeks later, at the Annual Conference held on August 31, 1931, at the Christian Institute, Glasgow, where but forty delegates attended, President James Doonan referred to a recent dispute regarding hours and wages and the negotiations with the owners. He explained that they ultimately came to an arrangement on the basis of a straight seven-and-a-half-hour day:

In carrying out that change we had to give up part of our minimum standard rates of wages. That change was wrung from us. It was one to which we had to agree, realising that if we took the alternative of resisting, that course might result in worse conditions for the men. . . . I and my executive have no regrets at the advice we tendered to the men. (August 31, 1931.)

President Doonan's reference to the wages and hours agreement with the coal-owners is significant. This had come up for discussion during the month of July 1931. The Act of 1930, amending the Act of 1926 (permissive eight hours plus winding time), had set the hours at seven-and-a-half a day up to the spring of 1931. A further Act had now confirmed seven-and-a-half hours (plus winding time) as the legal maximum. The Scottish owners held that if this were set forth in an agreement there must be a reduction of wages. This was in strong contrast to the situation a dozen years earlier, when the Sankey reduction of working hours from eight to seven was accompanied by a successful demand for an increase in piece-work rates of wages.

WORKING IN A NARROW WET SEAM, CANDERIGG COLLIERY, LANARKSHIRE

MINER AT WORK, PRIORY PIT, LANARKSHIRE, 1953

By mid-July 1931 negotiations had reached the point where the owners' proposals for a seven-and-a-half-hour day (which were for a reduction down to 7s. a day) came before a Scottish Delegate Conference: eleven days later, after the proposals had been modified, a Delegate Conference with fifty-three present on July 24 recommended their acceptance as being what Doonan described as 'the best that could be attained under the circumstances'. A ballot had now to be taken. The ballot paper issued stated that the Executive and Scottish Conference unanimously recommended the terms offered, i.e. a reduction of 4¾d. a shift, a forty-eight-hour week on the surface, and uninterrupted winding of coal throughout the shift. At the same time the Scottish Executive issued a manifesto justifying their point of view, in which they stressed the economic crisis and especially the difficulties of the coal export trade. The Minister of Mines was quoted on the 'menace of foreign competition'. The Executive then went on to declare:

The alternative to, or refusal on the part of the men to accept above terms may result in a stoppage at all the collieries in Scotland. We are convinced that a stoppage of the collieries throughout Scotland at this time would be a huge blunder. It could not in the present economic circumstances help to get better terms than above. It would probably result in worse terms being offered and enforced, when you had exhausted anything you now have, causing misery and hardship which every right-thinking person desires to avoid.

By August 3 the Scottish Executive learned that the ballot vote had resulted in: For Acceptance—19,150; Against Acceptance—5757.

At that same Annual Conference, meeting just after the dismissal of the Labour Government by Ramsay MacDonald, James Brown, M.P., said he could not remember them meeting in all their long experience under circumstances which gave rise to so much industrial and political fear. He said:

The men are very restless. The surfacemen are working not only below the old rates but in many instances for a weekly sum below even what the parish councils would allow as relief benefits. Everywhere in all grades there is discontent. Indeed, there is a spirit of revolt in the hearts of the men the like of which we have not seen for a long time. (August 31, 1931.)

Scottish Miners   P

James Doonan fell ill in April 1932 and died after a short illness a few weeks after the death of a former president, Hugh Murnin, and three months after the death of James Hood of Ayrshire. Vice-President Andrew Clarke therefore delivered the presidential address at the Annual Conference held on June 27, 1932.[1] He set the habit, since followed, of a carefully prepared address. Referring to the unemployed workmen he said:

Those workmen through no fault of theirs, and due to causes over which they have no control, are compelled to go about seeking for that employment which is denied them and without which they are buffeted about and in many cases treated more harshly than those who have committed a crime against the community. In receipt of unemployment benefit for a temporary period their ultimate lot is to eke out a miserable existence dependent on transitional benefit or public assistance, the amount of which is determined by an inquisitionary system called the 'means test' that is more degrading in its operation than the Poor Law was 100 years ago. (June 27, 1932.)

There remained the further problem of the underpaid workman, whose earnings were no greater than those who were in receipt of unemployment benefit. On this he said:

No one can possibly defend the wages paid to the lower paid workers employed in or about the mines. The power to improve them may for the moment be beyond us, but at least all of us realise that the present standard cannot continue longer than by whatever means possible we may be able to effect some improvement. A standard of life that is frequently lower than the subsistence level authorised by the Public Assistance Authority is a reproach to all of us who are associated with the industry.

Following the Annual Conference, at which a very bare record tells us that 'after a general discussion' it was proposed 'that we accept the new wages agreement' and that this seven-word resolution was 'carried unanimously', the Scottish Executive prepared a manifesto, which was to be printed and issued to the six districts for ratification.

It stated that following the last Wages Agreement for the seven-and-a-half-hour day, reducing minimum wages to 8s. a day, the position of the industry had become worse, with a

---

[1] There were seventeen delegates from Lanarkshire, seven each from Fife and Ayrshire, eight from Mid and E. Lothian, four from Stirling, two from W. Lothian, or forty-five in all.

drop both in home demand and in exports. Many pits had been stopped, permanently or temporarily, thousands were unemployed and thousands more working only three or four days a week. Further, the Labour Government had been replaced by the National Government, 'which from the experience we, as workers, have already had of it has convinced us how much poorer we are by the change'.

In these circumstances the Scottish Executive had to negotiate a new agreement. The M.F.G.B. and miners' M.P.s had managed, through the Government representatives, to secure from the owners in each district a guarantee that existing minimum rates should continue till January 1933. The Scottish owners refused to go beyond this in any way, and the Executive recommended acceptance of their terms (to continue the existing agreement for another year)

as being the only course open to us under the circumstances. If the recommendations met with the approval of the Members, the Executive Committee were instructed to again endeavour to secure readjustments on the following points, viz.: Subsistence allowances, increased time for meals, reduction in charges for tool sharpening, house rents and costs of explosives; also security for workmen's wages who are employed by contractors.

At the Annual Conference on June 28, 1933, in Glasgow, there is hardly anything recorded about the wages agreement due to expire on July 7; and the forty-four delegates unanimously agreed to remit the whole question to the Scottish Executive. Nor was there any but the barest mention of it in Andrew Clarke's presidential address. His reference to wages was as follows:

There are in Scotland between 35,000 and 40,000 workers above and below ground whose wages for a full week of six days vary from 30s. to 38s. per week, from which falls to be deducted a formidable sum in off taxes. When, however, the working time amounts to only four or five days per week as it does in many instances, the amount earned is proportionately reduced. . . . Can it be wondered at that they are tempted at times to envy those of their fellows who are unemployed and in receipt of unemployment insurance benefit?

He stated that the wages of the surface and lower paid underground workers in Scotland were lower than any other coal-field; while excessive overtime was being worked at many collieries, with frequent 'gross violations of the Act of Parliament'. He said:

> Men are being compelled to work 8 and even 9 shifts in a week while scores of workmen at these same collieries are unemployed and unable to obtain even a single day's work.

It may be said here that the agreement was apparently continued by the Scottish Committee (the minutes are vague about what happened) while they negotiated about an increase for the lower paid men for several months. In the end it was the employers who insisted on a new agreement and one that would run for a longer period than twelve months. To this the Scottish Executive, after discussions and joint discussions throughout the winter of 1933-4, in the end gave their assent. Accordingly on April 13, 1934, there was signed an 'Agreement for the Regulation of the General Rate of Wages' which was to operate until March 31, 1936.

In his presidential address to the Annual Conference held at the County Hall, Ayr, on June 29 and 30, 1934, with fifty-three delegates present, Andrew Clarke admitted the fact that it was a bad agreement when he said 'No one for a single moment will contend that the present Wages Agreement is anything other than such as was dictated to us by the circumstances surrounding the industry'. Later he said:

> We have an average output of $25\frac{1}{2}$ cwt. per man per shift worked, compared with $22\frac{3}{4}$ cwt. over the whole of Great Britain and the lowest cost of production other than wages compared with any other district. Yet in spite of these advantages our average wage per shift worked is 8s. 9d. as against 9s. 2d. over the whole coal-field of Britain, and while it is stated that the number of shifts per week obtained by the mine workers of Scotland is greater than that of any other District and that in consequence the volume of wages is higher in proportion, this in no way alters the fact that increased output has *not* brought with it a commensurate increase in wages.
>
> Rationalisation has therefore only resulted in the lowering of prices to the consumer, *without* any compensating advantage to the workmen employed in the production of coal. (June 29, 1934.)

Rationalisation, however, was part of the programme of Mondism to which a majority of the trade union leaders, including the Scottish Executive, had committed themselves in 1927-8. The Dead Sea fruits of it were thus acknowledged after seven years. It was a belated recognition and the conditions of the mine-workers had for a long time before that been evidence enough of the meaning of rationalisation.

5. THE UNITED MINEWORKERS OF SCOTLAND

We have now to consider the activities of the U.M.S. which was set up in the spring of 1929 after a year of strife and schisms. This all-Scottish union, containing to begin with a goodly company from Lanarkshire and the great majority of the Fife colliers, especially those organised in the bigger pits, was not able to enrol in its ranks more than a minority of the miners in Ayr, Stirling and the Lothians. It was not affiliated to the M.F.G.B. which more than once came to the rescue of its rival, the old Scottish Executive. It was not 'recognised' by the associated coal-owners of Scotland, though in practice they had to take account of it and to negotiate locally. When the world economic crisis developed from 1930 onwards, the militants within the U.M.S. were amongst the first to be thrown out of employment: and to be known as a member of the United Mineworkers certainly made a collier's job more precarious.

In these circumstances the struggle carried on by the U.M.S. was sometimes far-reaching, involving great numbers of the old county unions and also non-unionists (as in the days of the 1894 strike), but often limited to a particular county, and a particular local issue. A pamphlet entitled *Scottish Miners in Battle* set forth aims of the U.M.S. as follows:

The U.M.S. is a militant trade union, catering for all Scottish mineworkers, irrespective of what their politics are. It was founded in 1929 as a result of the demands of the Scottish Miners for militant trade unionism and for democracy inside of the Union, which the old Union leaders had fought against for years, resulting in mass disorganisation in the Scottish coalfield.

The U.M.S. takes as its guide the fundamental principles of trade unionism, that a trade union exists to struggle for its members and against the masters, an idea that has been replaced in these days of 'Mondism', 'Rationalisation', etc. with the belief that the trade union exists to help the coalowners to make a profit out of their industry, i.e. to rob the miners, and to be the instrumental body that will carry through wage reductions. . . .

The record of the U.M.S. is one of struggle at the pits, in the Law Courts, successful leadership of strikes, introduction of intensified campaign for 'Safety' by election of Workmen's Inspectors, and a growing influence and strength throughout the coalfield, all proving that the U.M.S. is a real trade union—the only union, in fact, which fights for the Scottish Miners. (1933.)

But the best existing account of these activities in the period of the slump is given in an article[1] written in February 1934 by Abe Moffat who had been for nearly three years the General Secretary[2] of the United Mineworkers of Scotland. Looking back on the past five years period he stated:

In the last two years it is correct to state that the influence of the U.M.S. has greatly increased amongst the Scottish miners as a result of their concrete work in the daily struggles of the miners, linked up with the campaign for increased wages, shorter hours, greater safety precautions and against overtime.

When the Scottish miners struck against the spread-over in December 1930, the U.M.S. played a big part. When, six months later, as we have seen, the leaders of the N.U.S.M.W. signed an agreement permitting the illegal spread-over despite the decision against it of the M.F.G.B., it was the U.M.S. who led the men. In July 1931 the U.M.S. conducted a struggle of 15,000 miners for three weeks, including many members of the other unions, against the illegal eight-hour day, and against the coal-owners' demand at that time for a wage-cut of 1s. 4¾d. per day. At this time the N.U.S.M.W. leaders advised the miners to continue working the illegal eight-hour day. Despite difficulties this strike had its gains for the miners. The 15,000 miners were actually working on a seven-and-a-half-hour shift, while the other 65,000 miners continued to work the illegal eight-hour day at the instance of the N.U.S.M.W. leaders for a week after this strike was called off. The owners were forced to modify their demand for wage-cuts from 1s. 4¾d. per shift to one of 4¾d. per shift reduction.

Again in May 1932, the U.M.S. conducted a struggle for two weeks of 5000 miners against the coal-owners in the Fife

[1] See *Labour Monthly*, March 1934.
[2] William Allan, the first General Secretary, was succeeded late in 1930 by David Proudfoot, who in turn was succeeded by Abe Moffat towards the end of 1931. Frank Moore became the President.

coal-field, who were demanding wage-cuts ranging between 6d. and 1s. 6d. per shift. The N.U.S.M.W. leaders, as in 1931, opposed the strike, but eventually the miners succeeded in defeating the wage-cutting policy of the owners at that time.

A significant feature about each of these strikes was the unity displayed between the members of the U.M.S. and the N.U.S.M.W. unions (in spite of the latter's officials) and the way in which they formed their strike committees, succeeded in obtaining strike relief from the Local Authorities for women and children, and set up communal kitchens to feed the strikers. More important still, in each strike the miners got the guarantee from the coal-owners that no victimisation would take place on the resumption of work.

On this Abe Moffat commented at the time:

This is in striking contrast to the previous strikes under the control of the reformist leaders. In the big strikes of 1921 and 1926 scores of active and militant miners were victimised, and the reformist leaders did nothing to have them reinstated. Here we have a glaring contrast between the policy of the U.M.S. in concluding the strike of the miners especially in this period of acute crisis, as compared with the bankrupt policy of the reformist leaders who declare it is impossible to conduct successful strikes in this period of crisis.

Besides those greater strikes, many pit strikes took place in Scotland in 1932 and 1933. The conditions of the miners in those years were bound to call forth a kind of guerilla warfare of strikes. These could never be repressed, however much they might be disclaimed and discountenanced by local or county officials. Where, however, strikes of this kind were not only countenanced but led by a body which had a powerful influence in a pit, the colliers had a good chance of winning concessions.

The U.M.S. also made considerable progress in a campaign for better safety precautions. In most pits no inspections (by Workmen's Inspectors) had taken place for a period of fifteen or twenty years: while those carried out were incomplete, only part of the pit being inspected. Inspections, under U.M.S. auspices, were carried out regularly every month (in pits where Workmen's Inspectors were appointed by ballot vote of the men). Every part of the pit was inspected. In his 1932 Report H.M. Mines Inspector mentioned the value of these inspections carried out by the U.M.S. For the first time he had to report that twenty-nine full and detailed inspections had been carried out at four pits that year.

The campaign for Workmen's Inspectors met with bitter opposition from the coal-owners, and not infrequently at the early stages by leaders of the county unions. Sometimes police were brought in to intimidate the miners: and coal-owners seized opportunities to victimise miners who supported the inspectors, and the inspectors themselves. We have seen in Chapter VIII the case against the two Moffat brothers in 1929. Another instance took place at Klondyke, Lothians, where a three-day strike to prevent the eviction of a victimised unemployed miner and his family forced the withdrawal of the eviction notice. He was elected as a Workmen's Inspector. Particularly bitter feeling was aroused when Andrew Clarke and other leaders of the county union distributed leaflets urging them not to strike and describing the man as a danger to trade unionism, as 'a Communist and supporter of the U.M.S.' Two months later the coal-owners repeated their offensive, and the man was evicted at a time when he was actually carrying out an inspection of the pit. However, as time went on, the county union officials began to bestir themselves over pit inspections.

The method by which regular U.M.S. inspections were carried out each month and their reports made known was set forth (in a pamphlet published by the U.M.S.):

The report is not only submitted to the Government Mines Inspector and the management, but a verbatim report of the full inspection is submitted to every miner in the pit whether they be members of the reformist union or of the U.M.S. The benefits of these inspections are clearly grasped by the miners; they see improvements being made for the safety of the men arising from the reports of the U.M.S. Workmen's Inspectors and the wide exposure given to the unsafe conditions through the distribution of eight thousand copies of the pit inspectors' reports amongst the miners monthly. As a result of this concrete work for the safety of the miners, the company have been forced to spend thousands of pounds at these eight pits alone, where the U.M.S. is carrying out the inspections.

Moreover, the U.M.S. inspectors have been able to prove, arising from their inspections of serious and fatal accidents, that the fault was entirely due to the neglect of the company. Consequently the miners or their dependants have been able to obtain a larger sum of money for compensation under common law than they would have done under the ordinary Compensation Acts, which have their limitation in the amount that should be paid for Workmen's Compensation.

The U.M.S. sent detailed guidance and advice to all its branches about the right procedure to be adopted: they were in daily contact with the local representatives and Workmen's Inspectors.

Another issue which the U.M.S. took very seriously was the forced overtime then being worked which in itself added to the numbers of unemployed. When Members of Parliament raised this question, the answer from the Ministry was always that there was 'insufficient evidence' to prove illegal or excessive overtime. At two pits in Fife, Peeweep and No. 1 Lumphinnans, the U.M.S. held mass meetings: the men decided to refuse to work overtime and to strike if any man was dismissed on that ground. Thereupon the Mines Department finally investigated the charges. As a result overtime was reduced to one-sixth of what it had been, and thirty unemployed miners were started at those pits.

A persistent campaign was organised at the pits by meetings and pit papers to carry through a fight for a new Agreement. This included a demand for a 2s. a shift increase for all miners.

With the struggle under way and daily growing fiercer at the pits themselves, especially with the new Wages Agreement in the offing, to those in the leadership of the U.M.S. it appeared of the first importance that united action in support of the men should be taken at a higher level. Accordingly from the beginning of 1933 onward, the U.M.S. made approaches, on specific problems and in general, to the N.U.S.M.W. and to the county unions for co-ordinated action.

On January 9, 1934, the U.M.S. wrote as follows to the N.U.S.M.W.:

On April 4, 1933, we submitted a statement to your Executive Committee and the affiliated County Unions proposing a joint meeting of your Executive and our Executive, to discuss what steps could be taken to improve the scandalously low wages of the miners, as admitted by yourselves.

Further approaches were made to the affiliated County Unions of the N.U.S.M.W. on April 16 and August 22, 1933, on similar lines inviting a joint meeting to deal with the critical situation in the Scottish Coalfield, but no attempt has been made on your part to meet the request.

This is a most regrettable attitude taken up by your Executive in face of the distress of the miners, which calls for solid unity of all forces; especially when you take into consideration that it is now six months since the Agreement terminated in Scotland, and the attitude of the coal-owners is the same today as it was in July 1933. They even refuse to consider your limited demand of a wage increase for a section of the miners, namely, surface and lower-paid underground workers.

It must be obvious to your Executive that the situation calls for immediate unity of action, and that it is only by solid unity that the miners will secure their demands.

The letter went on to refer to the 'growing support of the U.M.S. policy of mass action', indicated in the recent ballot vote taken for the appointment of Workmen's Inspectors.[1] The letter concluded by outlining four proposals on which there might be a joint campaign: (1) Joint campaign in the coal-field for the termination of the present agreement. (2) A new agreement consisting of a 10 per cent wage increase for all miners, and the Seven-Hours' Day. (3) Appointment of Workmen's Inspectors at every pit as a means of diminishing the excessive rate of accidents and loss of life. (4) Abolition of all excessive and illegal overtime.

The Scottish executive recorded their attitude to this letter:

Letter from Mr. Moffat. A letter from Mr. Moffat of the U.M.S. was placed before the Executive. Decided that no action be taken. (Minute 552, January 15, 1934.)

The U.M.S. were not prepared to leave it at that.

They felt the need for joint action by the miners. They knew that weakness in Scotland would affect all British miners.

[1] Details and further arguments were given in the letter as follows:

6153 votes were cast in favour of the U.M.S. Workmen's Inspectors being appointed at the following collieries: Bowhill, Minto, Lochhead, Francis, Aitken, No. 1 Lumphinnans, Klondyke, and Priory. Some of these pits are the largest in the Scottish coalfield, and two U.M.S. Inspectors have been appointed at each, with the exception of Francis and Priory, one U.M.S. Inspector being elected at the latter. These achievements were obtained under the most difficult circumstances, where members of our organisation were victimised as a result of their participation in the appointments, coupled with police intimidation in some instances at the ballot boxes, of which you are already aware. In addition to the collieries mentioned above, we have U.M.S. Inspectors appointed at No. 11 Pit, Lumphinnans, and the Michael Colliery. With this increasing support for the U.M.S. policy, it proves conclusively that the situation calls for combined action of all our forces, and we sincerely hope that your Executive will agree to this proposed joint meeting, basing our discussion on the following demands.

They decided to call for the support of the miners' associations outside Scotland for their proposals. Moffat wrote:

By supporting these proposals we will strengthen the whole united front of the British miners, build confidence in the miners in their own united strength, in their own power of militant trade unionism, out of which we can go forward to compel the owners and the National Government to concede a National Agreement containing wage increases for all mineworkers; for a shorter working day; better safety precautions; against overtime; and to go forward rapidly to the period when the private ownership in the mining industry—which has brought ruin and starvation to the miners—will be completely abolished.[1]

Following up this purpose, the U.M.S., having circulated their statement to all county associations on March 15, 1934, wrote a letter to the M.F.G.B. in which letter they explained very fully the position in the Scottish coal-field, outlined various proposals for joint action in Scotland, and raised the question of their direct affiliation.

William Adamson, the inveterate opponent of these new forces in the U.M.S., was the representative from Scotland on the M.F.G.B. Executive Committee—which decided that 'your application could not be entertained'.

It might perhaps be thought that at this point the U.M.S. might have decided to 'gang its ain gait'. But the situation was worsening, and in the pits there was ever-mounting anxiety about the wages agreement. So the U.M.S. wrote to all the affiliated unions in the M.F.G.B. Nor was it without response: for South Wales wrote back to the M.F.G.B. urging them to use their good offices to make an effort to secure peace in Scotland. But on the M.F.G.B. Executive Committee, with Adamson sitting grimly in his place, each successive approach was rejected.

The U.M.S. sought other means to bring the facts to the attention of all affiliated sections of the M.F.G.B. The pamphlet, previously quoted, was written and circulars sent out:

To the miners in other parts of the British coalfield, we call for their strength and support to the proposals made by the U.M.S. to the M.F.G.B. for direct affiliation. On this basis, we can found

[1] *The Scottish Miners' Struggles*, by Abe Moffat. (*Labour Monthly*, March 1934.)

One National Miners' Union for the British miners under militant leadership, courageous enough and capable of leading the British miners to gain their demands against the combined enemy—the Coalowners and the National Government.

An immediate step towards this objective is for every trade union branch and lodge in the British coalfield to demand that the M.F.G.B. will reconsider the concrete proposals put forward by the U.M.S. for united action in Scotland.

Only by this policy of united action, not only in Scotland, but in the whole of Britain, can the miners be mobilised to fight for One National Agreement based on increased wages and shorter working hours, abolition of overtime, and increased safety in the pits.

At the end of the year the U.M.S. again wrote to the N.U.S.M.W. This appears in the Minute 569 of December 24, 1934:

Letter from Mr. Moffat, U.M.S.
Decided unanimously that the letter lie on the table.

That winter miners were still suffering unemployment and short time, and all the indignities of the Means Test, on which feeling in the coal-fields was growing. The U.M.S. wrote once more to the N.U.S.M.W. appealing for some concerted action on this and other problems: their overture was set aside. But while it was always possible for officials to dispose easily of letters received, problems in the pits themselves could not be voted out of existence: nor were the rank and file members so uninterested as their Executive. Throughout the year 1935 there was a growing sentiment for unity: but a motion disapproving the Executive's refusal to admit a deputation or hold joint discussions with the U.M.S. was defeated at a half-yearly delegate conference in August.

During the autumn the U.M.S. were extremely busy, more especially in Fife, in the campaign for 'The Miners' Two Bob'. The winter was to see mounting difficulties and a mood of greatly heightened militancy among the men. This was shown in a large number of disputes and bitterly fought strikes, notably in Stirlingshire and at Whitrigg Colliery and Kinniel Colliery at Bo'ness, West Lothian. But the storm centre once more was in Fife, where there was a strike at Blairhall and a prolonged and bitter struggle at Valleyfield. In this storm raging in the Fife pits the need for unity was more

keenly than ever appreciated by the U.M.S. They made yet
another offer to the Fife County Union: that their own
U.M.S. members should be recommended to join Fife. At the
same time the U.M.S. notified the M.F.G.B., who called on
the Scottish district for their comment, at the end of November 1935. But while they were considering their reply, the
mood of the whole Fife coal-field was affected by this fiercest
and most long drawn-out struggle against the Fife Coal Company at Valleyfield, against the imposition of a dirt scale
which would have worsened the miners' conditions. This
strike dragged on for thirteen weeks, amidst strife and division.
Bad feeling between the county union and the N.U.S.M.W.
increased, and Fife finally declined their assistance.

The moral was clear; greater unity was urgently needed.
Their relations with the Fife county union were brought to
the attention of the M.F.G.B., as was the attitude of the Fife
county union to members of the U.M.S. who were applying
for membership. Disturbed by the complaints, both of acts
of omission and commission, the M.F.G.B. instructed its
Secretary Ebby Edwards to ask for an explanation. The
Valleyfield dispute was at its height. The Scottish Executive
was in an equivocal position with regard to the county union.
Andrew Clarke wrote, in reply to the M.F.G.B.'s enquiry in
the first half of December 1935, a letter of explanation. He
impugned the motives of the U.M.S., which he alleged 'in all
seriousness' would not exist ' but for the unfortunate happenings in West Fife, brought about by the equally unfortunate
and regrettable dispute in Valleyfield'. Then he turned to the
Valleyfield dispute itself.

Our Scottish Executive, at the request of the Strike Committee,
immediately granted an interview to a deputation and, after hearing
each of the four representatives who came, at once agreed to offer the
service of our three officials with a view to assisting in any way possible in bringing about a *satisfactory and acceptable* settlement of the
dispute, and we at once asked the Fife Mineworkers' Executive to
authorise us to do so. Up till the time of writing this authority has not
been given us.

Meantime, the strikers' families were in bad straits and
were deprived of unemployment benefit. A vigorous campaign
by the U.M.S., assisted by William Gallacher, M.P., who

had just taken his seat for West Fife in the House of Commons, won a decision from the Umpire that unemployment benefit should be paid, except to the face-workers directly involved in the dispute. The back-money was paid out on Hogmanay 1935; the miners and their wives had a real Happy New Year as a result, indeed a better one than if they had been working, so low were wages at that time. Finally the strike was ended satisfactorily by the middle of January 1936. The need for unity and the successes which could be obtained by united action, even in the most adverse circumstances, were very clear. Nor was the lesson lost on the Fife county union officials, both in their difficulties with the Scottish Executive and in the mood of their members, who had learnt much in common struggle.

At this point the U.M.S., having tried so many ways of bringing the matter to an issue, finally took the unprecedented decision of dissolving its own organisation and advising its members to join the N.U.S.M.W. The letter applying for membership signed by Abe Moffat and Frank Moore came before the meeting of the old Scottish Executive of January 27, 1936. It was the last meeting William Adamson was to attend. Before the month was up he was dead; only two months before he had lost his parliamentary seat in West Fife to William Gallacher. The members of the U.M.S. were accepted; but the leaders of the U.M.S. were rejected, although they were all miners and active trade unionists.

CHAPTER X

THE MINERS AGAINST FASCISM AND WAR

1. THE COMING OF FASCISM

THE world economic crisis of 1929–33 plunged the miners into deeper poverty and misery. It had other consequences of a far-reaching nature. In each country there was an attempt to throw the burden of the crisis upon the shoulders of the working class and, outside Britain, upon the peasant tillers of the soil. The formation of the National Government in Britain, with its harsh economic measures and political repression, was paralleled in a whole series of countries, giving rise to widespread discontent and growing resistance. Where this discontent began to grow into revolutionary disaffection to the ruling class, the repression grew more and more severe and even ferocious. In Germany power was seized by a Fascist dictatorship, headed by Hitler, Goering, Goebbels and Himmler, and backed by such big business men as Krupp and Thyssen, masters of the rich coal and iron concerns of the Ruhr. This terrorist dictatorship, with adherents organised in a mass party which, for the deception of the unwary, they called the 'National Socialist Labour Party' (the Nazi party), abolished all other political parties, together with trade unions and co-operative societies, and swept away all that had been gained by the working class in a century of struggle. In their foreign policy the Fascists drove forward to war, with the object of subjugating other countries, and of redividing the colonies and mandated territories. Meanwhile in the Far East Fascist-imperialist Japan had begun earlier with its suppression of the working-class movement and had already begun a war of aggression. The upward trend of world trade after the crisis ended in 1933 did not reach pre-1929 level. Therefore the tensions at home and abroad did not diminish but grew. The aggressor States tried to make up for their difficulties and losses at home at the expense of other countries. In 1935 Fascist Italy made an unprovoked attack on Abyssinia, the only independent State left in Africa.

Meantime the Governments of Britain and France, while fearful of the consequences of further outbreaks of aggressive war, took no effective steps to maintain peace. Instead of establishing collective security in agreement with the Soviet Union, the Governments of Britain and France did nothing effective, while hugging the delusion that Hitler and his fellow Fascists would do what they so loudly said they would do, namely, attack the Soviet Union first of all. But Hitler, Mussolini and the Mikado were out for easier meat.

If this was the attitude in these fateful years of the British Government under MacDonald, Baldwin and Neville Chamberlain as successive prime ministers, an entirely different feeling was widespread in the British working class. They saw the danger of Fascism, which destroyed the trade unions but not the employers' associations: and behind Fascism they saw looming the danger of war. A whole series of events since the 1914–18 war had taught the miners that their livelihood, their wages and hours and other conditions, as well as their liberties and civil rights, were highly dependent upon the international situation. Hence a new and intenser meaning was given to international solidarity, to the belief in the common interests of the workers of every country. In the records of the Scottish miners' unions there is found a much greater preoccupation with events abroad than at any time earlier in their history. To these questions therefore we turn in the first place.

2. HELP TO THE SPANIARDS

As Fascism or something akin to Fascism got a grip on one country of Europe after another, there began to be a linking up of the scattered forces of the common people to resist it. In Spain and in France especially this resulted in the building up of what was called 'The People's Front' or 'The Popular Front' by which there was effected a combination for electoral and other purposes. In Spain the 'Frente Popular', made up

MINERS AT WORK IN A NEW PIT, COMRIE, FIFE, 1953

MINERS AT WORK IN OLD-TYPE PIT, PRIORY PIT, LANARKSHIRE, 1953

largely of trade unions and working-class parties, had a resounding victory in the General Election in February 1936. This was not to the taste of the Spanish militarists and Fascists (there called 'Phalangists') who promptly entered into a treasonable conspiracy with Hitler and Mussolini for the overthrow of Spanish democracy. When the conspiracy was ripe General Franco rose in rebellion, seized Seville and marched upon Madrid. Other columns of the regular army, led by other Fascist generals, were soon converging upon the capital. One of them, General Mola, announced that there were four columns outside Madrid but that inside he was relying upon 'a Fifth Column'.[1] As soon as General Franco began his approach to Madrid, Fascist Germany and Italy came to his aid—as arranged beforehand. Thus a rebellion, a civil war, was turned into a war of intervention. The British Government, whose obligation under international law was to enable arms to be supplied to the legitimate (and in this case duly elected) government and to prevent them being supplied to the rebels, took up the attitude of 'non-intervention'. This in practice meant that other countries were not to do anything *for*, while the Fascist powers continued to aid the rebels *against*, the democratically elected Government of Spain. The Fascist rebellion in Spain was hated in the British working-class movement, amongst whom there was widespread dismay when for a time the T.U.C. General Council said, in opposition to such leaders of the Labour Party as Clement Attlee, that they would support the Foreign Office policy of 'non-intervention'. So strong was the feeling in support of the Spaniards that a considerable number of young British workers volunteered to fight Fascism in Spain. There they formed part of the famous International Brigade. So much has to be said in preliminary explanation of the decisions of the Scottish miners on Spain.

The first item, however, comes even before the Franco rebellion. The governments of Spain immediately preceding the victory of the Popular Front at the General Election of 1936 had been increasingly reactionary ever since the

---

[1] He meant the rich reactionaries who had not accepted the verdict of the general election and who were ready to open the gates to the Fascist rebels. This is the origin of the well-known use of the phrase 'fifth columnist' to signify treacherous behaviour.

monarchy ended in 1931. They provoked a general strike and rising of the miners of the Asturias in the north-west of Spain, who appealed to the Scottish miners, and did not appeal in vain. A donation was sent in February 1935.

The question of action to aid the Spanish democrats was raised in the Scottish Executive almost immediately after the outbreak of the rebellion in July 1936, though no immediate action was taken. At the end of September appeals were read from Ebby Edwards, the United Socialist Party of Catalonia, and the Scottish Ambulance Unit for Spain, requesting financial support. It was agreed to donate £50 from Scottish federal funds and to ask the six county unions to supplement from their local funds. In February 1937 the National Council of Labour's circulars on the Spanish crisis, with suggestions for helping the civil population, were sent on to the districts; the next month it was reported that Lanarkshire had sent £25 for the Spanish Relief Fund.

The interest of the miners was reflected in the presidential address of Andrew Clarke at the Annual Conference of 1937:

We, as workers, cannot but be deeply concerned as to the ultimate fate of the Spanish Government when we realise the Sinister Forces that are behind the Insurgents, who are doing everything possible to discredit the *Democratically* elected Government of Spain. Every day brings forth fresh evidence of this and clearly reveals the issues involved in the fight that is being waged by the Spanish Workers. Theirs is a brave struggle indeed! One that has called forth the admiration of people in every country. While our members have already given financial assistance yet the need is still so urgent that I would again *appeal* to you for further generous assistance—*Not as a Charitable Donation*, but as a *Duty* to those who are fighting to preserve our present and future *Democratic Rights and Liberties*.

On the last day of the 1937 Conference an emergency resolution, moved by A. K. Davidson and seconded by James McKendrick, was carried unanimously:

This Conference of Scottish Mineworkers declares its whole-hearted sympathy with democracy in Spain, deplores the wanton destruction of human life, and emphatically condemns the attempt to establish Fascist dictatorship on the Spanish people.

Further, we call on all lovers of freedom to subscribe to the relief funds organised by the Labour and trade union movements. (June 26, 1937.)

The accounts show that up to May 1937 no less than £239 had been donated to the Spanish Relief Fund, of which £50 came from the National Union and the remainder from the districts.

In November 1937, a letter from William Pearson asked the Executive to pass a resolution calling on the National Government to arrange for the evacuation of the Asturian miners and their dependents. It was agreed to send this to the M.F.G.B.: and later it was unanimously agreed to send a donation of £50. At the 1938 Conference deep concern with the Spanish struggle was voiced in several resolutions, from Lanarkshire, Fife, Mid and East Lothian and Ayrshire, protesting at the policy of the National Government as aiding the warmakers and demanding an end of the so-called policy of non-intervention. A composite resolution was moved by Duncan Graham, M.P., seconded by Peter Henderson, based on these, and was carried unanimously by the conference. It declared:

This Conference strongly condemns the National Government for its betrayal of the League of Nations: its substitution of a balance of power policy, in place of a policy of collective security. This Conference also denounces the armed intervention by foreign Fascist Powers in Spain and deplores the action of the present Government in refusing to carry out International Law which gives the right to Constitutional Governments to purchase arms in their own defence.

Further, this Conference views with horror the continuous bombing of British merchant ships with the consequent sacrifice of the lives of innocent seamen.

Andrew B. Clarke in his presidential address of 1938 devoted considerable space to these questions and said:

The rigid application of the Powers invested in the so-called non-intervention Committee which has prevented the Spanish Government Forces from obtaining the necessary supplies of munitions and other war material, has undoubtedly been responsible for prolonging the struggle, and what is infinitely worse, they are equally responsible in no small measure for the appalling and unparalleled destruction of life among the civil and non-combatant people of that unfortunate country.

Despite this barbaric slaughter, our own Government—for reasons best known to themselves—have resisted every appeal made to them by people in every walk of life and every shade of political opinion to lift the ban which at present hinders the Spanish Government and prevents their Forces from giving that necessary protection to their women and children which every human instinct in us demands.

But on the question of practical steps, he was strongly against a British Popular Front and denounced any joint activity with Communists. That year a further £75 was donated to the Spanish fund. But in the summer of 1938 the M.F.G.B. Executive had taken a decision to raise £50,000 on behalf of the Spaniards, of which sum Scotland's share would be £6250. In February 1939, when the British Battalion of the International Brigade had already returned from Spain, the Scottish Executive decided to give £20 to the appeal for a National Memorial to the battalion.

At the Annual Conference, April 19–22, 1939, Andrew B. Clarke, J.P., in his presidential address said on 'that epic struggle':

They have been robbed of that victory which they so richly deserved, and once again might has, for the time being, triumphed over right, and victory has gone to the big battalions.

We, as workers, need be under no illusion as to what the suppression of democratic government in Spain means to us, as should the occasion warrant it, British capitalism will take similar action to preserve their power and domination at the expense of our liberties also.

3. HELP FOR THE CZECHOSLOVAK MINERS

The records show clearly that Scottish miners paid considerable attention to what was boiling up in Europe and Asia. There was every reason to do so. In 1935 Hitler had torn up the Treaty of Versailles by his decision for German conscription and armed occupation of the demilitarised Rhineland: and while the French Government hesitated, Baldwin's Cabinet without the agreement of the French negotiated an Anglo-German Naval Treaty by which Germany was once again allowed to build submarines and on a parity with the British navy.

At the beginning of 1938 the Fascists made a further leap forward in aggression. Hitler invaded Austria, and annexed it to Germany in the spring of 1938. He followed this by threats against the independence of Czechoslovakia. It was the

behaviour of Prime Minister Neville Chamberlain towards
these Fascist aggressions that led finally to the ignominy of
Munich. There at a meeting with Hitler and Mussolini the
British Prime Minister signed away the rights of Czechoslovakia. In the meantime the Japanese Fascists had seized
Peking in July 1937, occupied Shanghai and launched war on
the Chinese people.

On all these questions, raising vital issues of war or peace,
there was a lively interest taken at the time. Here we can
only select a very few examples, mainly from 1938.

On the Munich meeting itself the Executive Committee of
the Miners' Federation of Great Britain had passed resolutions. These were placed before the Scottish Executive which
took the somewhat unusual step of formally printing them in
their minutes, with unanimous endorsement, as follows:

The Executive Committee of the Mineworkers' Federation of
Great Britain, representing nearly 600,000 British miners, expresses
its deep disgust with the action of the British Government in sacrifi-
cing Czecho-Slovakia to the insatiable appetite of the dictators.

It regards the foreign policy of the National Government during
the last few years as being that of an accomplice to the murder of the
smaller democracies, and as a betrayal of all that is decent in international relations.

The dangerous war situation which prevailed last week was the
only possible outcome of this policy, a policy which has disorganised
the peace forces and given consistent support to the Fascist warmakers.

We call upon the whole Labour Movement to organise a most
vigorous struggle against the present Government and pledge the
full support of the Federation in that struggle.

Further, we request that facilities shall be given to the Trades
Union Movement to have its observers present in the disputed areas
of Czecho-Slovakia in order to afford some protection to the victims
of this act of aggression and to save them from the concentration
camp methods of the Nazis.

The Mineworkers' Federation is prepared to appoint representatives to a Commission of this nature that may be formed by the
International Trade Union Movement, and also agrees to donate a
sum of £1000 to assist the miner victims in the Czecho-Slovakian
coalfields. (Minute 686, October 10, 1938.)

The second resolution ran as follows:

The Executive Committee of the Mineworkers' Federation calls
upon its District Organisations to wage ceaseless educational propa-

ganda amongst their members in order that a proper perspective of the present position arising from the Crisis can be placed before them. (Minute 686, October 10, 1938.)

Some ten weeks later the M.F.G.B. Executive sent a letter dealing with the appeal of the Miners' International Federation for aid to miner-refugees who had to flee Czechoslovakia on the advent of the Hitler regime. It was agreed to give a donation of £25, and to ask the districts to augment this from their own resources; later, response from the districts made it possible to send £100. But the total of just under a thousand pounds received from all the coal-fields did not meet the needs of this fund and on March 21, 1939, Ebby Edwards sent out a circular which fixed a quota in proportion to the membership of each district of the M.F.G.B. Scotland's quota amounted to a further £186, which was remitted at once and made good by a levy on the districts.

4. AN UPWARD SWING

We have seen what were the sharp changes in the national and international background of the 'thirties after the world economic crisis, and the attitude taken by the Scottish miners to these events. Their problems in the industrial sphere ran parallel to this.

The latter part of the year 1935 marked the beginning of an upward swing both in the mounting awareness of the danger of Fascism and war and in the activities of the miners' unions. The M.F.G.B. Annual Conference at Rhyl in July 1935 had decided to launch a public campaign for an increase of 2s. a day or, as it came to be called, 'The Miners' Two Bob'—and for a national wages agreement. For the first time for ten years the county unions were called upon to engage in a nation-wide campaign of propaganda.[1] For this purpose a levy was called of 2d. a member. The campaign was to be carried on with the more energy, not only because the coal-owners had refused to meet the M.F.G.B., but because of the Government's blank refusal to take any step towards

[1] *The Miners' Two Bob*, edited by W. H. Williams (Labour Research Department), 1936, contains interesting material on this.

the setting up of a national wages machinery; and strike action was to be resorted to if it should prove necessary. There had been enough local struggles in the previous months to show that the miners were ready for action. In Scotland the claim for damages by the Fife Coal Company against five Dysart miners had been before the court on April 11: and during the spring the United Mineworkers of Scotland had been conducting a campaign for the withdrawal of the summons and were extending their effort to include a wage demand of 10s. 6d. for strippers, with corresponding increases for other workers.

Each of the six Scottish counties had allocated to them scores of posters to put up and tens of thousands of leaflets to distribute: nor were these to be limited to the mining areas. Thus fifty posters each were to be put up in Aberdeen, Dundee, Greenock and Paisley. The whole of Scotland and the whole of Britain were to be aroused to the condition of the mining population. Help was sought from a number of English and Welsh Members of Parliament for the bigger meetings (forty in all were held during the campaign in the first half of October). Help was also accepted from various quarters outside the miners' unions: but help was not accepted from the Communist Party [Minute 589] whose Scottish organiser, Mr. Finlay Hart, had written offering assistance in the fight for 2s. increase.[1] The Miners' Federation, however, sent supplies of its leaflets to be distributed in Fife by members of the U.M.S. and at this James Cook had sent a letter of protest.

When the M.F.G.B. Conference on October 17 and 18 heard the reports of the campaign from Scotland and other districts and also learned of the unyielding attitude of the coalowners (which was backed by the Government), the delegates decided to take a kind of strike ballot in November. The ballot paper was made ready immediately. It asked the

---

[1] There was an implied rebuke to the Scottish Executive some time later in the programme speech of Ebby Edwards, when he took occasion to say:

May I also say a word in regard to the Communist section and their service in delivering our literature? I am not speaking of the Communists going up and down the country delivering their literature, but the Communists going up and down with our literature, delivering it in Brighton, Hastings and seaside towns in the south. Whatever our opinion is—and the owners drew our attention to my message to Russia—I do that which I think I am entitled to do. I do pay tribute to the work they did on behalf of the campaign of the miners. (M.F.G.B. Special Conference, January 24, 1936.)

miners in every coal-field to answer 'Yes' or 'No' to the following question:

Are you in favour of authorising the Executive Committee to press for an advance of Wages of 2s. per shift for Adults over 18 years, and 1s. per shift for Youths and Boys under 18 years, even to the extent of tendering your notice to enforce the claim, if necessary? (Minute 592, October 28, 1935.)

Meantime the National Government, now since the early summer headed by Baldwin, decided on the dissolution of Parliament. Thus when the special N.U.S.M.W. Conference met on November 2 it was in the middle of a general election discussion and only twelve days from the polling day. Unanimously the delegates resolved:

In view of the attitude of the coal owners to our claims, this Conference unanimously agrees to recommend our members to ballot in favour of tendering notices to enforce the claim, if necessary, knowing as we do that the wages paid in the coal-field to-day are scandalously inadequate.

Further, realising that the consequence of a national stoppage of the industry would inevitably inflict serious loss and hardship on the whole country, we call upon the Government to exercise its authority to secure for the miners the satisfaction of their reasonable and just demands, and to this end we request all who are in sympathy with us only to support candidates who are pledged to secure fair terms for the miners. (Minute 593, November 2, 1935.)

In that general election of November 14 the Miners' Federation put up forty candidates and returned thirty-five of which ten were gains. In Scotland seven candidates were put up: four were successful.

This was an improvement on the rout of 1931. In Lanarkshire particularly there was success. In Fife Wm. Adamson again failed to win. But the victor this time was not a Conservative who would support the coal-owners, but a doughty champion of the miners, William Gallacher, the Communist. This was shown most clearly a month later by the scene in the House of Commons, when, contrary to all custom of never interrupting a maiden speech, the National Government benches shouted interruptions at Gallacher as follows:

On this side of the House we represent and speak for the workers of this country, the men who toil and sweat. (*Hon. Members:* 'So do we'.)

Oh! You do speak for the workers, do you? (*Hon. Members:* 'Yes'.)
All right. We shall see. The leader of the miners says that theirs is the
hardest, most dangerous and poorest paid job in the country. Is there
anybody who will deny it? The miners make a demand. They ballot
for it, and the ballot is a record, and we who speak for and on behalf
of the miners demand an increase of 2s. a day for the miners. That is
how we speak for the miners. Now it is your turn. Speak now. Speak,
you who claim to represent the workers. . . . (*Hansard*, 1935–6, Vol.
307, p. 205, December 4, 1935.)

A week after the general election the ballot vote was taken.
It showed an unprecedented majority of 93 per cent in
favour of strike action to enforce the demand for 2s. a day.
The 'Yes!' votes were 409,351 and the 'No!' votes 29,215, a
majority of 380,136. In Scotland the vote was in the same
proportion: 'Yes!'—39,858; 'No!'—3007; majority for 'Yes!'
36,851.

In spite of this the Mining Association maintained its
refusal to recognise the Miners' Federation. But the M.F.G.B.
Executive were informed of the views of the district coal-
owners' associations on the dispute. They were willing to concede an increase, varying from district to district. These
proposals were laid before the M.F.G.B. Conference in
London on December 18 and 19, 1935, which passed the
following resolution by a very large majority:

That this Conference regards the suggestions so far made as being
entirely unsatisfactory and as by no means reflecting the pronounced
opinion throughout the country in support of the Miners' wages
claim. It was resolved therefore:

That notices be tendered on January 13th and 20th respectively
unless wage proposals satisfactory to the Executive Committee are
obtained in the meantime.

Further meetings with representatives of district coal-
owners' associations were held on January 8, and on January
23 to see if they would improve their offers. Meantime the
M.F.G.B. Executive on January 11, 1936, postponed the strike
notices. An amended offer gave Yorkshire 1s. a day, while
in Scotland the offer of 9d. (and 4½d. for boys) was made to
apply to all rates instead of as previously only to able-bodied
persons. At the same time there was to be set up a national
joint consultative committee to discuss 'all questions of com-

mon interest and general application to the industry'. The M.F.G.B. Executive strongly recommended acceptance of these revised terms. The conference on January 24 voted: for, 360,000; against, 112,000; neutral, 34,000. Scotland was neutral. This was the outcome of the nation-wide agitation for 'The Miners' Two Bob'.

In March 1936 Lanarkshire, supported by Stirlingshire and West Lothian, requested the Scottish Executive to tender notice terminating the 1934 wages agreement. The Chairman of the Conciliation Board, Sir Adam Nimmo, suggested a joint sub-committee of five a side 'to explore the question of a new wages agreement'.

In December 1936 the miners were asked to ballot for acceptance or rejection of an agreed set of terms, which included an increase of 3d. a day in the minimum wage (to 9s. a day): cancellation of all accumulated 'debts' under the ascertainment system which prevented the miners sharing in any increase in the proceeds from coal; increase in meal-times to twenty minutes; and promises to consider a shorter working day on Saturday and a wage-for-age scale for boys. The Scottish Executive strongly recommended acceptance.

The ballot vote (which apparently resulted in an affirmative majority, though nothing is recorded in the minutes) did not settle everything, as certain questions such as boys' wages were very indefinitely worded. There was therefore much negotiation with the owners after the ballot. Finally, after the expiry of another twelve months, in the second week of January 1938, a special circular and ballot paper on Boys' and Youths' Wages was issued. Lanarkshire was against acceptance by seven to six, but the other five counties carried Scottish acceptance by 31,784 to 15,671.

For the first time a uniform minimum starting wage for every colliery and district in Scotland was included in the terms—the figure for underground workers being 4s. 1½d. at fifteen years and 5s. 7½d. at seventeen years, and that on the surface 3s. 1½d. at fourteen rising to 4s. 1½d. at seventeen. These proposals were estimated by the Executive to mean an increase for 50 to 70 per cent of the boys employed.

There had been for some years an attempt to organise fire-men and shot-firers separately. This was considered many times by the Executive Committee until in April 1937 it was agreed to take a decisive step to end the difficulty by the issue of a leaflet, explaining the reasons why the Scottish Executive had always opposed the request of the Scottish Firemen and Shot-Firers' Union for recognition. It pointed out that the N.U.S.M.W. had negotiated for these grades for many years, and had done much to improve their position; that the majority of firemen and shot-firers were members of the N.U.S.M.W. and wished to continue so; and that the opposition to this came basically from the owners who, for obvious reasons, did not want the firemen to be organised along with their fellow-workmen.

The relations with the craftsmen's union, on the other hand, continued to be cordial. On the Scottish Executive, William Pearson had repeatedly pressed for a campaign to end non-unionism in the pits. This led to the suggestion of joint working with the craftsmen, and eventually to a joint meeting of the two Executives on November 8, 1937. By March 1939 a joint meeting was held between the owners on the one side and representatives of the N.U.S.M.W. and the Scottish Enginemen, Boiler-Firemen and Tradesmen's Association on the other, to discuss the question of non-unionism. Thereafter the two unions worked together in a campaign to eliminate it in the pits.

5. REUNITED

For well-nigh ten years from the Great Lock-out of 1926 the miners of every British coal-field had passed through a difficult and trying period, with scores of thousands idle and those at work toiling for low wages. In Britain as a whole the Miners' Federation membership was halved, from a million to half-a-million. But in the old Scottish National Union the number of trade unionists had sunk by four-fifths from 111,500 in 1921 to 23,000 in 1932–3. This was the tragic result of the dissensions in the years immediately after 1926. But now there was an upward swing. Membership more than doubled in four years. By 1938 the total Scottish membership was 51,000. This was the result of unity in the ranks of the Scottish miners.

Meantime certain changes were taking place amongst officials and Executive members. Andrew B. Clarke, J.P., continued as President, James Barbour as Vice-President and Edward Hawke as Treasurer. But in February 1936 James Brown resigned the secretaryship to which Alexander Sloan of Ayrshire succeeded. In the next years new and younger elements began to appear on the Executive Committee, William Pearson in 1937, James McKendrick and William Sneddon in 1938, and Alexander Cameron of Midlothian in 1939. On the other hand, there was reluctance in parts, particularly in Fife, to accept into the union leading members of the former U.M.S. For example, complaints had been remitted from the M.F.G.B. to the Scottish Executive within a few weeks of the U.M.S. having recommended its members to join the old National Union. Gradually it became clear that this appeared to be a personal vendetta against the leaders of the U.M.S., and particularly against Abe and Alex. Moffat. This story and its long continuance make a curious historical footnote to the times; it reached far beyond Fife itself.

To the remonstrances from Ebby Edwards the Scottish Executive replied that

the Rules of the Union did not provide for persons who were not miners becoming members, and that as Mr. Moffat was not a miner it was not possible to accommodate him. (Minute 609, May 11, 1936.)

The Moffats and many thousand others were at the time unemployed miners. It should be noted that both of them had for a long time been working as Workmen's Inspectors elected on a ballot vote of the men. The Miners' Federation Executive Committee were dissatisfied. They sent up to Scotland, to meet the Scottish Executive, Will Lawther, Vice-President, and Ebby Edwards, Secretary of the M.F.G.B., who stated that

They were of opinion that under the arrangement when the reform union disbanded the National Union of Scottish Mineworkers were under obligation to accept all members of the disbanded organisation. The M.F.G.B. Executive were anxious that any pledges made in that direction should be honoured. (December 7, 1936.)

Clarke, speaking for those who allowed sour memories of

the past to determine their conduct, remained obdurate, and so nothing came of this or of a later discussion in midsummer 1937. Subsequently the matter was raised several times but the majority of the Scottish Executive refused to budge. Moreover, the Fife Coal Company and other mine-owners in Fife and Clackmannan were equally obstructive in blacklisting the Moffats and others so as to keep them out of employment in their pits. Late in 1939 the Moffats at last got into Brucefield pit, Clackmannanshire, which belonged to a company not at the time affiliated to the Scottish Coalmasters' Association. They then joined Lumphinnans branch of the Fife and Clackmannan Miners' Association, whose own constantly reiterated rule made it impossible to exclude the brothers. Within a twelvemonth Abe Moffat had been appointed by Fife, which had become entitled to an additional delegate, to the Scottish Executive.

CHAPTER XI

THE WAR YEARS 1939–1945

I. MAN-POWER AND THE WAR

In the Easter of 1939 Hitler's seizure of Czechoslovakia compelled Neville Chamberlain to repudiate publicly his previous policy of appeasement. Thereafter followed one of the most tortuous periods of British diplomacy, with elements in influential circles still striving to push through the appeasement policy. A system of alliances was announced, particularly with Poland which now began to be threatened by Fascist Germany. But over the working out with the Soviet Union of the detailed application of what was now proclaimed to be the policy of building collective security, there were seemingly inexplicable hesitations. Severe criticisms of this fumbling diplomacy were uttered at the time by Lloyd George and others, who were aware of the activities of the Anglo-German Fellowship. There were in fact very strong influences behind the scenes operating for appeasement with Hitler on the understanding that he would sooner or later attack the Soviet Union. This, as it turned out, came later. At the time the Soviet Government, also aware of all these moves, drew the conclusion that no trust could be placed in the Chamberlain Government, and that it was hoping to make a catspaw of the U.S.S.R. The Government of the U.S.S.R. therefore decided to draw out of these tortuous entanglements and made a pact of non-aggression with Germany in August 1939. Meantime Hitler's preparation for war upon Poland had been going on with growing intensity for over four months. By the end of August his war preparations were complete: German troops crossed the frontier and marched upon Warsaw. Britain and France had that spring as well as earlier given guarantees to Poland. Within a few days Britain and France declared war upon Germany. The war, thus begun, was to spread to nearly every country on the globe, to

involve the populations of entire continents and to last close
upon six years.

For the second time in twenty-five years war fell upon the
mining industry. But it was very different in 1939 from 1914.
Then the miners, united throughout for five years in the
Miners' Federation, and welded together by the first national
strike of 1912, were suddenly plunged into conditions unfore-
seen either by themselves or by the Government: soon after
the 1914–18 war they had won shorter hours, a rise in the
standard of living, and a promise of nationalisation of coal-
mines. By 1939 the miners had passed through the troubled
period between the wars, marked by unemployment, low
wages, longer hours, coal-field split from coal-field, while
their once powerful Miners' Federation was for the most
part unrecognised by the coal-owners and disdained by the
Ministers of the Crown. Compared with 1914 the miners
were in a very weak position in 1939. Yet by the end of the
second war they were stronger than ever before. Their wages
were higher; their conditions better; their separate county
associations fused into one national union; and they were
soon to see their age-long opponents, the coal-owners, driven
out of the industry.

It is clear there must have been some over-riding factor to
bring about such a transformation. In the zenith year of coal
production in Britain over 287 million tons were produced. By
1924 there was a fall to 267 million tons. The mine-owners had
always held out the prospect of better times if their policies
were accepted. Together the Goverment and the mine-owners
inflicted a heavy defeat on the miners, first in 1921 and then
in the lock-out of 1926. They imposed longer hours and lower
wages. They divided the ranks of the miners by insisting
upon separate agreements in competing coal-fields. Their
method of wages ascertainment kept the miners on a low level,
often 'owing' money to the owners who, despite frequent ascertainment 'losses', were able to reap large profits and to combine in a most profitable manner with iron and steel and
other industries.

Yet the victory of the coal-owners was not followed by an
expansion of output. Output per manshift was driven up, but
total production fell steadily, from 251 million tons in 1927

to 244 million tons in 1930; and then in the last complete year before the war, to 227 million tons in 1938. When, with the coming of war, there came need for greatly increased production, the main source of production was no longer there. The coal-owners were there ready to make their offer, but the miners were not. As the Conference President said a few years later, quoting Aneurin Bevan: 'You can get coal without coal-owners, but you cannot get coal without miners'. The number of miners which in 1924 had been 1,214,000, had fallen even more rapidly than the fall in output. By 1928 there were less than a million. By 1930 there were 931,000. By 1938 the figure had fallen to 781,000. But there was a further factor which affected output. This reduced labour force was to a greater extent than ever before composed of ageing men, bound soon to fall out of the industry. In 1939 the rate of wastage of the labour force in the mines was higher than it had ever been. There was, therefore, not only a shortage of miners, but there was bound to be an increasing shortage. As in Dante's great poem 'Hell is said to have nine circles, one below another', in the industrial inferno the British miners had been driven down to the ninth circle of wages. It was this shortage of miners that provided the lever that was to raise them towards the top circle.

In the second week of the war the Secretary for Mines wrote to the Miners' Federation and the Mining Association setting out the extreme need for coal. He put the needed annual output at between 260 and 270 million tons, or some forty million tons more than production in 1938. It might seem clear that to meet this extreme need extreme measures would have to be taken and the whole outlook of the Government radically revised. No such measures were taken: the Government maintained for many months its traditional attitude to the miners; and in consequence the situation went from bad to worse. For a time this was masked by the loss of the European markets in the spring and summer of 1940, when the Nazis overran Norway, Denmark, Holland, Belgium and France, and when Fascist Italy declared war. Miners were thrown idle specially in the exporting districts, unemployment stood at 56,000 in August 1940, and there was a loss of mining man-power to the armed forces and to the

VALLEYFIELD COLLIERY DISASTER, FIFE, OCTOBER 1939
Wives and children waiting for news

VALLEYFIELD COLLIERY DISASTER, OCTOBER 1939

Rescue squad bringing in one of the victims

new munitions industries. Later the Select Committee on Expenditure of the House of Commons criticised the Government for having conscripted miners and encouraged them to drift out of the industry in 1940 despite warnings given:

The consequent psychological effect on the miners of the absence of any measures to meet this sudden change in demand was deplorable, as at one moment they were urged to produce as much as possible and the next they found themselves without work. . . .

It was only in the late spring of 1941, when the war effort was then fully developing, that the situation was realised by the Government. From that time onwards the need for coal-miners was acknowledged to be one of the main problems of the war. But it was not till the middle of 1942 that the Government made efforts that were on a large scale to meet the magnitude of the problem: and even so these turned out to be insufficient. Exceptional measures such as the Essential Work Order, a guaranteed week, the setting up of controls, better conditions for young miners, and finally conscription for the pits, were tried one after another, but these measures never solved the problem. On the other hand, they brought home to the miners what scandalous treatment they had received for so long, at a time when their bargaining strength was transformed.

As only once or twice in their history, supply and demand could work in favour of the miners; the coal-owners had taken full advantage when supply of labour exceeded demand. Two factors, however, prevented the miners from fully exerting their strength. The first was the measure taken by the Government to prevent the rise of wages that would occur in a free market with a short supply of labour. The second, and more important, was the attitude of the miners themselves to the needs of the war; advantage was taken of their willingness not to press claims in their determination to ensure the defeat of the Fascist powers.

This political attitude was also shown in the development of a strong feeling of solidarity with the other sections of the working class engaged in the anti-Fascist struggle, both at home and abroad. It was shown, too, in the anti-Fascist initiative displayed in activities that would strengthen the

war effort, for example in the development of Joint Production Committees at the pits. When these activities were
hampered, the miners' unions proposed measures that would
have gone very far to solve the coal problem. These measures
were turned down by the Government, and the coal problem
remained unsolved to the end of the war. While the efforts of
the Miners' Federation to find a final solution for war purposes of the coal crisis were frustrated, the anti-Fascist
activity and the keenness in the struggle to win the war continued. But there was at the same time a growing determination to strengthen their organisation to safeguard the improvements reached and to maintain them when the war was
won. The question was never absent from their minds: is
it to be the same after this war as it was after the 1914-18
war? To remove the dread of such a future became a
firm purpose in their minds. As a result there were many
internal changes, above all in the leadership that was chosen
in the successive stages of the war. There was a closer unity
and a preparation for a mining industry after the war that
would be very different from anything in their past painful
experience.

2. VALLEYFIELD DISASTER

In the Scottish coal-fields the opening months of the war
were darkened by a serious disaster. On October 28, 1939,
the first raid over Britain took place, on warships lying in the
Forth. Several sailors were killed. That same day nearby
underground, there was an explosion in which thirty-five
men were killed. There were only two survivors, both very
seriously injured, among the men in the headings immediately
affected. It was early on a Saturday morning, in the No. 2
Section of the Diamond Seam of the Valleyfield Colliery,
Culross, Fife. A Court of Investigation, lasting three months,
opened on January 9, 1940, under R. P. Morison, K.C.
Among the fifty-five witnesses were: C. C. Reid, General
Manager of the Fife Coal Company; George Toal, one of the
two survivors; and Abe Moffat, who was Workmen's Inspector and a witness for the miners. The Fife, Clackmannan

and Kinross Miners' Union was legally represented. William Gallacher, M.P. for West Fife, also played an active and sympathetic part in the distressing circumstances which followed in the mining villages after the explosion.

Abe Moffat, who had been elected pit inspector by the men though as we have seen, he had been blacklisted, was largely responsible for discovering the cause of the explosion. It was he who charged the leading officials of the Fife Coal Company to their face with the major responsibility for the disaster. Together with his fellow-inspector Andrew Flynn, he submitted a series of statements gathered from seventeen witnesses, which made clear the circumstances of the explosion. To this was added on November 15, 1939, 'Observations by Workmen's Inspectors' which largely became the basis of the findings of the Court of Investigation.[1] After giving the cause of the explosion and after mention of illegal shot-firing and other breaches of the law (including the failure to apply stone dust), the Observations continue:

5. The management of this Colliery are mainly responsible for these Regulations being broken for the following reasons.

(a) Excessive explosives and detonators were being used in those narrow places due to number of holes being fired in the solid. If they plead ignorance to this fact then it brings out negligence on their part in failing to control explosives under the Regulations.

(b) Management have also a definite responsibility under Regulations to enforce the provisions for regulating usage and storage of explosives. This was not carried out otherwise Unsheathed Samsonite and its excessive use would not have been permitted in Dodd's Heading which was a coal place and not a stone mine.

(c) A proper check was not kept at the Colliery by the management for the supply of explosives. No indication was given in the Magazine Record as to the kind of explosive issued to workmen. Had a proper check been kept of explosives supplied and compared with the Fireman's record of shot firing, management would have investigated and stopped the storage of explosives in the Pit. This was not done, otherwise Workmen's Inspectors would not have discovered 20 lbs. of Samsonite on 6-11-39 stored in the pit which is not permissible under the Coal Mines Act.

The Observations went on to note other breaches of the law: such as the failure to appoint a competent person from the contractor's men to test for gas; an example of insufficient

[1] *Explosion at Valleyfield Colliery, Culross, Fife, Report.* Cmd. 6226, 1940, p. 15.

ventilation 'in view of the gassy nature of the coal'; the inadequate number of Ring Rose Detectors; and the fact that a
battery was in use capable of firing, contrary to regulations,
more than one shot at a time. The Observations conclude:

> On the basis of the above report and investigation and our own
> observations it is our opinion that the Owner, Agent or Manager
> should be held responsible for this disaster.
>
> (Signed) ABE MOFFAT ⎫ Workmen's Inspectors.
> ANDREW FLYNN ⎭   15 : 11 : 39.

The Commissioner of the Court of Investigation found
himself obliged in his general conclusions to note breaches of
regulations, and to criticise 'an absence of proper supervision'. Later the manager of Valleyfield Colliery and the
agent of the Fife Coal Company supervising the colliery were
both prosecuted and sentenced to pay fines.[1]

Within six months of the beginning of war there were big
changes in the office-bearers. Alexander Sloan, who had won
a parliamentary bye-election in South Ayrshire in April 1939,
found it necessary after six months to resign the secretaryship
but remained a member of the Executive Committee. James
Cook, from 1895 to 1917 Secretary of the Clackmannanshire
Miners' Association and then for some years Secretary of the
Fife, Clackmannan and Kinross Miners' Union, took his
place on October 9, 1939, as Interim Secretary and in May
1940 was elected Secretary. On February 1, 1940, President
Andrew B. Clarke died in hospital after a short illness. His
successor was James Barbour of Stirlingshire.

On February 16, 1940, Robert Smillie, who had been an
invalid for over ten years, died at the age of 83. At the Scottish
Delegate Conference of March 6, James Barbour paid a
tribute to Smillie, whom he described as

a pioneer to whom we were indebted for many of the reforms we now
enjoy. Few of us have the gifts he possessed, but he used those gifts

---

[1] The experience gained by Abe Moffat at Valleyfield stood him in good stead when,
eight years later, along with J. R. A. Machen and T. Stephenson, he represented the
National Union of Mineworkers at the enquiry into the August 1947 disaster at the
William Pit of Whitehaven in Cumberland, when only 14 men out of 118 survived the
explosion. At this enquiry, where the cause of the explosion bore certain similarities to the
cause of the earlier Valleyfield disaster, the union during the examination of witnesses was
able to establish that there had been breaches of the law. This was mentioned by H.M.
Chief Inspector of Mines (A. M. Bryan) who presided at the enquiry and who as a result
recommended a necessary amendment of the regulations.

exclusively in the interests of the mine-workers of Great Britain. Mr. Smillie never brought reproach upon the mining movement. The savour of his memory will long remain among us.

At the Annual Conference, held in Ayr in the first week of May 1940, Barbour was elected President by 35,000 votes against 16,200 for McKendrick; Armstrong Vice-President by 28,000 against 23,200 for D. Robertson; Cook Secretary by the same number against D. Sim; while Edward Hawke, who had held the post of Treasurer ever since he defeated Adamson in 1921, had again been nominated by all districts.

Within the next few months there were further changes in the Executive Committee. In the summer W. McLean came on to the Executive Committee for West Lothian. Of great significance for the future was the seating of Abe Moffat, who until the eve of the second World War had been kept out of the pits. But after he and his younger brother had obtained work at Brucefield, it was not long before the Fife miners chose them as their representatives, as we have seen.

3. WAGES AND WORKING CONDITIONS

The first impact of the war on the miners was a rapid rise in the cost of living. This, together with the requests of the Government for forty million tons additional production of coal, led to national discussions between owners and men. After several months they were able to reach an agreement, which was to last for the period of the war, on a regular relation between the rise in the cost of living and the amount of war-bonus to be granted.[1] The first provision of this agreement was:

[1] Under the agreement which was signed on March 20, 1940, the following cost-of-living increases took place:

1st November 1939	..	..	..	8d. per shift
1st January 1940	..	..	..	5d. per shift
1st April 1940	..	..	..	4d. per shift
1st October 1940	..	..	..	5d. per shift
1st January 1941	..	..	..	6d. per shift
1st July 1941	..	..	..	4d. per shift

In 1941 there was also arranged an 'attendance-bonus' on June 1, but the conditions attached to this, as interpreted by the managers, led to so much controversy and local dispute that after three months it was merged in the flat-rate advances.

The district wage arrangements shall continue to operate during the war, subject to mutually agreed alterations, but increases of wages necessary to take account of the special conditions arising out of the war, and particularly the increased cost of living, shall be dealt with on a national basis by means of uniform flat-rate additions.

This bore hard on some of the districts, for example in Scotland, where wages had been particularly low and where a levelling-up process might have been expected. This provision was to cause trouble in the future, and be the subject of considerable discussion some four years later. Meantime the N.U.S.M.W. had been endeavouring to negotiate terms of a new agreement to take the place of that which was due to expire in January 1940 but which the owners wished to continue in view of the war emergency conditions.

After some months of negotiation and even after the temper of the men had been made clear on April 1, 1940, by a twenty-five to one majority in a ballot on the question 'of forcing the employers to meet us under the auspices of the Conciliation Board to discuss a new wage agreement', the owners would not yield.

But now there was a rapid change in the international situation, with the overrunning of the Netherlands, the unconstitutional surrender by King Leopold of Belgium and the fall of the French Republic. Neville Chamberlain resigned. Winston Churchill then formed a Coalition Government (Conservative, Labour and Liberal) with Clement Attlee as deputy premier. Then came the evacuation of Dunkirk and within a few weeks Fascist Italy declared war. The new Coalition Government with Ernest Bevin as Minister of Labour and National Service passed a second Emergency Powers Act under which the right to strike was restricted, but which also made it possible to coerce employers. The Scots owners now offered terms. These the Delegate Conference accepted on July 1. By this Conciliation Board agreement there was set up a new basis of 8s. a day instead of the 1888 basis of 4s. and a 10s. minimum (8s. basis + 12½ per cent + 1s. flat rate), while boys' wages went up by 3d. a shift.

At this same conference a resolution moved by Wm. Pearson caused a significant division of opinion amongst the 110 delegates:

That this Executive calls for a special Emergency Conference of the Scottish T.U.C. to determine policy arising from the new War situation following the capitulation of France. We believe that policy should now demand the establishment of a Labour Government and complete removal of elements associated with the Chamberlain Government from important offices in this country. (July 1, 1940.)

The minutes record that:

Mr. Pearson argued that the collapse of France had been prepared for months in advance. Trade Unions had been suppressed, leaders put in jail, Fascists were negotiating with Hitler, and they did not belong to the working classes. Friends of Hitler are in the ranks of the Government. We ought to seize this opportunity to bring Socialism here.

Alexander Sloan, M.P., seconded the resolution and said

The working classes are fighting because they believe they are fighting for freedom. The possessing classes are fighting for their own interests. Ten per cent of the population possesses 90 per cent of the wealth. France was defeated because 200 families of France possess nearly the whole of the country.

It was opposed by A. K. Davidson of Stirling, and also by Duncan Graham, M.P., who argued strongly against it. But it was carried by 61 votes to 45.

That autumn of 1940 there began the day and night enemy bombing of towns and centres of industry, which continued with full intensity till the middle of May 1941. This brought problems connected with civil defence and air-raid precautions. There were also problems arising from rationing, taxation, the call-up of miners. All these things had to be dealt with by the unions. Finally, in the late spring of 1941 there came in under the Emergency Powers Acts the Essential Work Order[1] bristling with problems which had to be unravelled by the miners' agents and the union Executives.

As we have seen, the district wages, apart from the flat-rate war-bonus advances, were settled as they had been before the war. With the rise in pit costs of all things other than wages, the quarterly ascertainments began to yield less and less for earnings. The whole method which had served the mine-owners so well was found to be serving the national interests

[1] S. R. & O. 1941, No. 707. Emergency Powers (Defence) Essential Work (Coalmining Industry) Order, 1941, May 15.

very ill. But in addition to this the miners were now seeing a rapid rise in the earnings of those in the munition industries. Thus, for example, they could see men no longer fit to work in the pit immediately obtaining in a neighbouring munition factory a higher wage than a skilled miner. They could not leave the industry; tied to the pits as they were, miners were bitterly resentful at the wages they were being paid. They were working longer hours than before; they were working more shifts in the week; but apart from the advance to meet the increasing cost of living, they were tied to conditions from which workers in many other industries were free. This, taken together with all the other factors, worsened the crisis in the coal industry.

This strong feeling amongst the Scottish miners was expressed in their Annual Conference of April 1941, where no less than fifty motions had been put down. They resolved:

This Conference calls upon the Government to grant a subsidy to the mining industry that will be used solely to provide wage increases to miners, and instructs the M.F.G.B. to press for an immediate advance of 2s. per day. Further, we ask the M.F.G.B. to insist that a weekly wage system be established in place of the present shift system, guaranteeing a weekly minimum wage, and that a Special Conference be called to consider the result of these negotiations.

This was moved by Wm. Pearson, Lanarkshire, seconded by Wm. Drylie, Fife, Clackmannan and Kinross, supported by delegates from Mid and East Lothian, Ayrshire, Fife and Lanarkshire. It was contended that a guaranteed weekly wage on the present basis for a six-day week amounted only to £3 14s., as compared with the dockers' minimum of £4 : 2 : 6. A 2s. per shift increase meant a minimum wage of only 13s. 5d. per shift. The conference also demanded 'the operation of the seven hours' day to all workers in and about the mines'. Some men were leaving home at three and four o'clock in the morning and returning at four or five o'clock in the afternoon, a ten- or eleven-hour instead of a seven-and-a-half-hour day.

Despite these signals from Scotland as well as from other coal-fields, the Government still took no effective steps to deal with the deepening crisis in the winter of 1941–2. The tardy realisation of the depth of the crisis finally had its result in considerable strikes in Lancashire and South Wales in the latter part of May and in June of 1942. At last in the early summer of 1942 the Government took significant steps, though not sufficient to meet the problem. These steps were set forth in a White Paper, *Coal*, of June 3, 1942 (Cmd. 6364).

The man-power of the industry had to be prevented from shrinking any further. No one could leave the industry because of the Essential Work Order; 33,000 men had been brought back from other industries in 1941; over 10,000 men were being released from the armed forces in 1942. Yet there was a net wastage of 25,000 men per annum. Uncontrolled private ownership of the mines, despite all these special measures by the Government, had failed to deliver the needed coal, had failed to get the needed number of miners. The Government decisions were two-fold. First, the Government took full control of the operation of all coal-mines and the allocation of the coal raised: and for this purpose set up a National Coal Board, with Regional Controllers under it. Thus the Government would conduct mining operations, but financial control and ownership remained with the colliery companies. Second, wages and conditions were to be dealt with by a new national body, entirely separate from the National Coal Board.

The problem of man-power depended, it was at last realised, on better conditions in the coal-mines.

Two days after the White Paper the Government, in accordance with the separation of the National Coal Board from wages negotiation, appointed a Board of Investigation headed by Lord Greene and usually referred to as The Greene Board. The terms of reference were as follows:

1. To consider and to report in the first instance upon the immediate wages issue; and further,

2. To enquire into the present machinery and methods of determining wages and conditions of employment in the industry, and to submit recommendations for the establishment of a procedure and permanent machinery for dealing with questions of wages and conditions of employment in the industry.

The result of their first investigation was to accept the miners' claim for a national minimum wage, and at the same time to give 2s. 6d. per shift wage advance unconnected with the cost of living and unrestricted by any condition. This Greene Award, given on June 18, 1942, was of extreme importance.[1] By establishing a national minimum wage it not only for the first time gave to the miners an assured *weekly* standard, such as had been customary in other industries for over a generation, but it thrust into the background the ascertainments method which had brought and kept the wages of the miners so low. At the beginning of the war the miners had been eighty-first on the official list of industries. Following on the Greene Award, which took effect from June 1, 1942, they were twenty-third on the list.

In the whole long history of wages negotiations in mining, the Greene Award marks a goal attained. At last the miners had a weekly minimum wage. Moreover, the result of the Award was that in relation to the cost of living, the miners, in June 1942, stood higher than they had been for many years, and indeed higher than they have been in the last seven years.

That spring and summer of 1942 there was an almost complete turnover of the officers of the Scottish union. Hawke, Treasurer for twenty-one years, died at the beginning of March. The next month William Pearson was elected Treasurer at the Annual Conference. The voting was 40,700 (four counties) for Pearson and 10,500 (the Lothians) for John Rutherford.

William Pearson, born at Armadale on August 23, 1896, began work in Barbauchlaw mine on his fourteenth birthday, having lost his father (killed at Butress Colliery) when he was eight years of age. When he was fifteen the family removed to Coalburn in Lanarkshire and there he began work at Auchinbeg Colliery. In 1917 he was put on the Coalburn Miners' District Committee. He was elected as Delegate to the Lanarkshire Miners' Council in 1923, elected as Checkweigher at Canderigg Colliery in Stonehouse in 1931 and shortly after elected a member of the Lanarkshire Miners' Executive Committee. At the age of forty he took the place of Paul McKenna on the N.U.S.M.W. Executive Committee, on which he continued to sit for many years, first as member

[1] Continuing a long association with the M.F.G.B., the Labour Research Department once more prepared the miners' case; on this occasion it was at great speed, the work being done in the course of a single week-end.

and then as Treasurer and finally as Secretary and Treasurer. It was in 1940 that he became President of the Lanarkshire Miners' County Union.

By mid-July Vice-President John Armstrong resigned in order to take up a Government post in London. By mid-August President James Barbour had resigned, as he had accepted the position of Regional Director of Labour for Scotland. By September 1 there were left only the Secretary, James Cook, and Treasurer, William Pearson, who on that day became Interim President. Nominations for the two vacant posts were sent in during September 1942 and were sent out to the six district unions. As a result, at a Special Conference held November 9, 1942, and attended by 118 delegates, the following were declared elected,[1] namely: Abe Moffat, President; John Colthart, Vice-President. In the course of the following months two new members came on to

[1] There were several nominations and several ballots. The full results were recorded as follows (Minute 20, November 9, 1942):

For the PRESIDENT three had been nominated: James McKendrick, Lanarkshire; Abe Moffat, Fife, C. & K.; Robert Burnside, Mid and E. Lothian.

1st Ballot			2nd Ballot		
J. McKendrick	16,200	Lanarkshire	J. McKendrick	16,200	Lanarkshire
	3,500	Stirlingshire		3,500	Stirlingshire
	19,700			19,700	
A. Moffat	14,000	Fife, C. & K.			
	3,000	W. Lothian			
	17,000		A. Moffat	14,000	Fife, C. & K.
				7,000	Ayrshire
R. Burnside	8,500	Mid and E. Lothian		8,500	Mid and E. Lothian
	7,000	Ayrshire		3,000	W. Lothian
	15,500			32,500	

Mr. Abe Moffat was declared elected President.

For the VICE-PRESIDENT five had been nominated: Alex. Hunter, Lanarkshire; Peter Henderson, Fife, C. & K.; Robert Burnside, Mid and E. Lothian; Alex. Smith, Stirlingshire; John Colthart, Ayrshire.

The voting on the 4th ballot was as follows:

A. Hunter	..	..	..	16,200 Lanarkshire
				3,500 Stirlingshire
				19,700
J. Colthart	..	..	..	7,000 Ayrshire
				8,500 Mid and E. Lothian
				14,000 Fife, C. & K.
				3,000 W. Lothian
				32,500

the Executive Committee, Daniel Sim of Kilmaurs, Ayrshire, and John Wood of Kelty, Fife.

The new President had been for two years a member of the Scottish Executive; but his previous activities, some of which are already recorded in this narrative, had made him well known throughout the Scottish coal-field. Abe Moffat came from a family strong in the traditions of trade unionism. His grandfather, David Moffat, was one of the pioneers associated with Alexander McDonald; like other pioneers, he had suffered for his efforts on behalf of the miners. Forced to leave Midlothian, David Moffat crossed the Forth with his family and settled in Lumphinnans, a very important mining village situated in the heart of the Fife coal-field. There his grandson Abe was born on September 24, 1896. After leaving school he entered the pits at the age of 14 years, like his father Abe and his brother Alex and all the other male members of his family. In his early manhood, after the experience of the great lock-out of 1921, Abe Moffat became a member of the Communist Party; this was in January 1922. Two years later he became a Communist Councillor, and thereafter he was never defeated in any contest. In 1942 he resigned his position as a Fife County Councillor (for Valleyfield and Blairhall) to give his whole time to the job of President of the Scottish Mineworkers.

His political opinions had always been widely known; he gained the respect of those active in the broader trade union and labour movement. That he had strong support amongst the Scottish mining unions was shown at his election by the county ballot. That he had the full confidence of the over-whelming majority of the Scottish miners was to be shown in the members' ballot vote twenty months later, and in his continued return to the National Executive Committee of the N.U.M. without a break during his period of office.

4. DUAL CONTROL AND OUTPUT PROBLEMS

The Miners' Federation were concerned about the position of young workers. Before Lord Greene's Board of Investigation they claimed that the flat-rate addition to wages should be paid to all at the age of eighteen. The Greene Award restricted the flat-rate addition of 2s. 6d. per shift to those of eighteen only if they were working underground. Between the age of fourteen and fifteen the addition per shift was 1s. 3d. underground, which rose until at eighteen it was doubled. For the surface worker the addition was 9d. per shift and thereafter rose by 3d. each twelvemonth until he reached 2s. 6d. at the age of twenty-one. This increase, however, was not sufficient to make the mining industry attractive to young workers. The Minister of Labour and National Service a few months later endeavoured to meet this difficulty by allowing those who were called up for the Forces to 'opt' for underground mining work instead. But any hopes reposed in this solution were not borne out by the facts. Up to August 31, 1943, only 5000 men when called up had opted for underground mining work instead of the Forces. At the Annual Conference of the Miners' Federation in July 1943, Ernest Bevin, Minister of Labour and National Service, announced that in future there would be conscription for the mines as well as for the Forces: every tenth man of those called up would be allotted to the mines.

It was only at this particularly grave stage of the coal crisis that there was an attempt to settle a minimum for young workers. The Award was 12s. less than the M.F.G.B. had claimed for those at the age of fourteen, and 16s. less than it had claimed for those aged twenty. The claim itself was less than was actually being paid in such higher-rated areas as Nottingham, Derby, South Yorkshire and Lancashire. It can be understood, therefore, that this minimum of July 1943 gave no new encouragement to the young workers. This was not the way to bring man-power into the industry.

Not only on this issue of the young workers, but on behalf of other hardly treated sections of the industry, for example women and firemen, the Miners' Federation kept up a steady pressure, putting forward claim after claim.

The agreement on wages and conditions of March 1942, being for the duration of the war, precluded any general change. The Scottish Executive Committee, however, continued negotiations on women's wages. By April 15, 1943, in his presidential address Abe Moffat could report:

Finally we succeeded in obtaining uniformity in wages for the first time, for all women employed in the Scottish coalfield, providing increases from 4d. to 5½d. on basic rates, plus 2/3rds of the flat rate war wage, Greene Award and attendance bonus paid to boys of the same age group.

Your Executive endeavoured to get the overtime agreement changed to time and a third for overtime during the week and time and a half for week-end overtime, but the coalowners refused to depart from the agreement signed in March 1942. We did succeed, however, in obtaining for the first time in our history, the right of all miners to be paid time and a quarter for all shifts worked above a normal week of six shifts. Your Executive also carried out negotiations for a wage increase on behalf of all underground firemen and shotfirers employed in the Scottish coalfield. Finally we succeeded in establishing a minimum basic rate of 10s. plus 12½ per cent for all firemen and 9s. 4d. plus 12½ per cent for all shotfirers. This represents a substantial increase for practically all firemen and shotfirers, and puts the firemen in the most favourable position in the history of the Scottish mining industry.

The second task of Lord Greene's Board was, after enquiry, to submit recommendations for permanent machinery to deal with questions of wages and conditions. The Inquiry was protracted. It was not until its third Report, March 16, 1943, that the Greene Board put forward a scheme for conciliation between owners and workers. This comprehensive scheme, accepted in draft by the M.F.G.B. Conference of January 22, 1943, set up a National Conciliation Board. The main questions of wages and conditions in the U.K. henceforward were dealt with through this conciliation machinery.

Throughout 1943 conditions were worsening in the industry. A stage was reached in October 1943 when it might be said the last hope of getting an effective solution as recommended by the M.F.G.B. (Nationalisation or Requisition of the mines, etc.) was rejected by the Cabinet. Churchill in his speech on October 13 in Parliament made it clear that he was not in favour of nationalising the mines as a necessary step towards the winning of the war.

When the Scottish Executive met next week they discussed the matter at length, and regarded the Prime Minister's speech as 'most unfortunate and entirely incorrect and misleading': for he had tried to disprove the value or necessity of nationalisation, which was not then an issue. The miners' standpoint was simply that dual control had failed and that the Government should take 'financial as well as operational control of the industry'. (October 10, 1943.) Three months later a Scottish Special Conference unanimously adopted a resolution, moved by Treasurer Pearson, which ended with the request to the Executive Committee of the M.F.G.B. 'to pursue the policy of the Federation for unified financial and operational control as a means of solving coal production for the successful prosecution of the war'. (January 31, 1944.)

Meantime, during the month of October 1943, the miners had put in a claim for a minimum wage of £6 underground and £5 : 10s. on the surface, with corresponding adjustments to piece-work prices. The Award of the National Reference Tribunal on January 23, 1944 (usually known as the Porter Award), conceded a £5 minimum underground[1] and £4 : 10s. on the surface, but no change in piece-work prices, which it held would be 'inconsistent with the guaranteeing of what is merely a minimum wage'.

The Miners' Federation Conference (January 27, 1944) which accepted the Award warned the Government of the further problems and anomalies that would arise from it. To settle these anomalies the Miners' Federation began negotiations with the coal-owners in the various districts. They did this on the understanding that the cost of any settlement on anomalies caused by the Award would be met out of the Coal Charges Fund.

Suddenly, on February 11, 1944, the Government issued a statement refusing to meet the cost of adjusting anomalies. This immediately invalidated the settlements and created chaos in the coal-fields. The following unanimous resolution (together with a message to the M.F.G.B. and telegrams to the Scottish mining M.P.s) was sent to Major Lloyd George:

The Executive Committee of the National Union of Scottish Mine Workers having received a report of the negotiations between the Scottish coal-owners and the workmen's representatives at which a basis for removing the anomalies arising from the Porter Award was agreed to, express strong resentment at the attitude of the Govern-

---

[1] It was over eighteen months since Lord Greene's Board had settled the minimum at 83s. and 78s. There were corresponding minima for youth ranging from 38s. 6d. for a fourteen-year-old underground worker to 80s. for a twenty-year-old; and in the case of surface workers, 31s. 6d. for a fourteen-year-old and 70s. for a twenty-year-old.

ment in refusing to meet the cost of now removing the anomalies. This will cause serious repercussions in the coalfield, and we urge the Minister of Fuel and Power to reconsider the whole position immediately and request the Government to meet the cost of removing the anomalies as agreed upon in the Districts by both sides of the mining industry. (February 14, 1944.)

The Government refused to budge. Thereupon, although the Scottish Executive on February 21 appealed to all members 'to continue normal working, especially in view of the present military situation', unofficial strikes began. Some 15,000 men were out between March 8 and 20. There were similar big unofficial strikes in the main English and Welsh coalfields. By March 9 the Government began to realise its mistake and made concessions, including proposals to the two sides of the industry for an overhaul of wages structure with a stabilisation of wages till the end of 1947. The terms of the agreement then made between the M.F.G.B. and the Mining Association of Great Britain and signed on April 20, 1944, were highly important.

With the conclusion of this agreement, a further stage was reached in the improvement of the position of the mineworkers. They had now a national minimum rate which raised them from the twenty-third place reached by the Greene Award of June 1942 to what was for the time being the first place in industry. Secondly, it was a consolidated rate. Merged in it were the percentage additions under the ascertainment agreements, and also the flat-rate additions since 1936 (of which 21s. had been given since the war began): outside this consolidated rate was the cost-of-living advance of 16s. weekly. Thirdly, it was stabilised for four years, while the Government for its part had undertaken to maintain for these four years the national pool on which the minimum rate was based. Fourthly, the ascertainment system in its existing form was finally put into cold storage. Against these benefits, however, there had to be set the fact that no variations were to take place in district or pit rates, a provision which bore rather unfavourably on such districts as Scotland especially in the matter of pit price-lists.

On the first day of the same month of April the M.F.G.B. reached an agreement with the coal-owners on holidays with

VALLEYFIELD COLLIERY DISASTER, OCTOBER 1939
Waiting at the pithead for news

pay. Adults were to receive five guineas for a week's holiday, those between eighteen and twenty-one four guineas, and those under eighteen three guineas. It was seven years since the M.F.G.B. Conference had begun to fight for paid holidays.

At the 1943 Scottish Conference the four officials (Moffat, Colthart, Pearson, Cook) were re-nominated by all districts and were consequently re-elected without contest.

5. POLITICAL STANDPOINT ON WAR ISSUES

At the beginning of the war the M.F.G.B. had, in accord with the T.U.C., adopted an attitude of full support of the Government against Germany. In common with the other constituents of the M.F.G.B., the Scots also supported the war.[1]

There were, however, differences on questions arising out of the course of the war. One of these was on the attitude towards the Soviet Union, especially in 1940 and early 1941. At a time when there appeared to be a disposition in the Chamberlain Cabinet to attack the U.S.S.R., and when speeches were made by some trade union leaders against the U.S.S.R., the Scots took a very different attitude. The following resolution, moved by McKendrick, seconded by A. Cook, was carried on May 4 at the Annual Conference:

That the Scottish Miners send fraternal greetings to the Russian miners' trade unions and trust that the building of the Socialist state will continue and, despite provocation and threats, will emerge successful from the International struggle, and calls for the support of workers' organisations throughout the whole world. (May 4, 1940.)

Their friendliness to the U.S.S.R. was again displayed at their Annual Conference in the spring of 1941; a Lanarkshire resolution caused a division of opinion resulting in a card vote

---

[1] The following resolution, moved by McKendrick and seconded by Pearson, was brought forward from Lanarkshire and unanimously agreed to by the Scottish Executive Committee:

That this Council of the Lanarkshire Mine Workers' Union condemns the action of the German Government in invading Poland without an official declaration of war, and massacring the civilian population. Further, we pledge ourselves to support the policy adopted by the National Council of Labour in supporting the war against Fascist aggression, but reserve the right to retain our democratic liberties in this country, and we call on the National Labour Council to be extremely vigilant in safeguarding the interests of the working classes. (September 11, 1939.)

of 38,700 to 12,500 against—the opponents wishing merely to reaffirm the previous year's resolution:

> That this Conference of Scottish Mine Workers records its appreciation and approval of the socialist policy of the U.S.S.R., and commends its ability to maintain peace within its borders for the further advancement of international Socialism.

At the same conference, resolutions were carried unanimously in protest against the Cabinet's decision to ban the *Daily Worker*. Most comprehensive was one from Midlothian.[1] Thus they showed themselves watchful critics of the whole war policy of the Government, coalition though it was of their own Labour representatives together with Tories and Liberals.

Two months after this Scottish Annual Conference, when Fascist Germany, on June 22, 1941, launched a sudden and unprovoked war upon the Soviet Union, the Scottish miners, in common with the other mining unions, showed themselves willing to do their utmost to help their Soviet allies. At the Annual Conference of the M.F.G.B. held in Ayr, July 14 to 16, an emergency resolution on 'support to Russia' was moved by a Durham delegate and carried unanimously.

It was seconded by Abe Moffat for Scotland in these words:

> The central issue for us at present is to do everything possible to bring about a unification of the forces of this country with those of the Soviet Union for the defence of our peoples and a joint victory over the common enemy. I believe there is no other trade union in this country that could make such a call as can the Miners' Federation, because no trade union organisation in this country has had better relations with the Russian working class, particularly the Russian miners.
>
> For many years past, our relations with them have been very strong indeed. I think it is correct to say that we have sent there more delegations than any other trade union, and we do not forget the valuable assistance given us by the Russian miners some years ago.

[1] This Conference believing that democracy and freedom are real concrete facts condemns forthrightly the banning of 'The Daily Worker' by Mr. Herbert Morrison, Home Secretary. We believe that free speech and a free press are the essential corner stones of a free country without which it is impossible sincerely to believe we are fighting to maintain democracy and freedom, therefore we condemn the action of the Home Secretary as being undemocratic and repressive. We call for the lifting of the ban.

In mid-April 1942, the Annual Conference of the Scottish Miners unanimously welcomed the agreement arrived at between the representatives of the British T.U.C. and the Soviet Trade Unions in October 1941, and stated:

We pledge ourselves to exert our maximum efforts for increased efficiency in production, and urge an interchange of delegations between the British and Russian miners as a further step in strengthening the bonds of unity between the two countries. (April 17, 1942.)

Nearly eight months earlier when McKendrick and Barbour, representing the Scottish miners on the M.F.G.B. Executive, reported the August 11, 1941, decision on aid to the Russian miners with a grant of 2s. 6d. per affiliated member, the Scottish Executive pressed for an approach to the Government 'on the question of all aid to Russia, as there was a growing feeling in the country that much more could be and should be done, militarily and in other ways, to ease the pressure which the Nazis were exerting on the Russians'. In the Scottish accounts for the year up to the end of February 1942, there is shown a sum of £7616 for Aid to Russia.

The miners came to have a highly conscious outlook on the strategy of the war and the political implications behind that strategy. They showed a critical attitude from the autumn of 1941 onwards, when it appeared that the surest means of bringing the war to a speedy end and victory was through setting up a second front against the Nazi armies in the west. It had been revealed at the T.U.C. of 1941 that there were members of the Government who were content to sit back and watch the Nazis attack the people of the Soviet Union. Thus the miners came to believe that the second front was by no means a purely military question, but was bound up with the persistence of an attitude fundamentally hostile to the workers and to the Soviet Union. It seemed clear, too, that just as a victory of the Fascist powers presented a black prospect to the future of organised labour in Britain, so a victory of the Socialist Soviet Union would open up a bright prospect of advance not only for themselves but for the forces of organised labour in Britain. Throughout the years 1942 and 1943 until the Conference of Teheran in

December 1943 (and even after it), the call for the second front was heard in the ranks of the Scottish miners and resounded from every speech of their leaders.

Thus at the Annual Conference of April 1943 a composite resolution moved by M. Waugh of Lanarkshire and seconded by A. Edgar of West Lothian, was carried unanimously:

This Conference recognises that the offensive operations in North Africa together with the Red Army's great winter offensive represents the seizing of the initiative by the Allied powers in 1943. Conference pledges itself to support all offensive operations and calls upon the Government to fulfil its pledge by the opening of a Second Front in Europe now, recognising that Europe is the only place where Fascism can be defeated. . . . We pledge ourselves to support the Government in all measures for the carrying out of such a policy for speedy victory. (April 16, 1943.)

On the same day, on a motion moved by W. Small of Lanarkshire and seconded by John Wood of Fife, the conference unanimously sent its 'fraternal greetings to the people of the Soviet Union and to the Soviet miners', and declared full support for the joint victory of the allied nations over Fascism.

A month after the conference the Executive Minutes conclude with the following, under the heading *Resolutions by the President*:

The National Union of Scottish Mine Workers salute our comrades in the 1st and 8th Armies along with our American and French Allies who have been responsible in the smashing defeat of the enemy in North Africa. We also pay tribute to the Red Army in their new offensive in the Kuban area.

We are proud of the fact that the miners have also played an important part in bringing about these victories, recognising that victory is impossible without coal. We believe that this favourable turn in the war lays the basis for the final assault in Europe that will completely destroy the enemy, and we now call upon all miners to intensify their efforts to eliminate all unofficial stoppages and ensure maximum production of coal for speedy victory.

We also make a serious appeal to all coal-owners and managements to eliminate all friction in the coalfield so that a united effort can be carried out in every pit, realising that our main objective in the present stage of the war is maximum production of coal for the defeat of Fascism. (May 17, 1943).

Together with this keen attention to all the war issues the

miners became increasingly conscious of their own part in the war effort. This took the form of a fight for increased production both in each pit and in the coal-mining industry as a whole. In each pit it centred round the question of Joint Production Committees; in the industry as a whole it was the question of a more adequate control. These Joint Production Committees had been set up in early June 1940, except in Scotland where owing to local causes they were set up a few weeks later. The attempt to develop the Pit Production Committees was frequently frustrated by the attitude of the coal-owners and their managers, who tended to look on these bodies simply as a means of dealing with absenteeism. Hence by the summer of 1941 Pit Production Committees tended to have lost virtually all authority amongst the miners. Yet in spite of this, the Pit Production Committees were not freed from this incubus of absenteeism until the Government at last realised the need for entirely different machinery on this matter. Then the White Paper of June 1942 made the necessary alteration:

Pit Production Committees will continue as at present constituted, to assist pit managers to secure maximum output. They will be relieved of all responsibility for dealing with individual cases of absenteeism, and will thus be free to devote their full attention to matters associated with production.

Thereafter the miners' representatives, with the full backing of those who elected them, were able in each Production Committee to make a push for the necessary changes to maintain the fullest possible output. In this, as will be told in the next section, they often encountered difficulties on the side of the management.

On a national scale the biggest difficulty was the absence of effective control. It was a system of dual control that had been set up by the White Paper at the time of the Greene Award in June 1942. In Scotland Lord Traprain (afterwards Lord Balfour) had been made Coal Controller, with James Barbour and Carlow Reid of the Fife Coal Company as his deputies. Nevertheless, the coal-owners had retained their financial control. More than once acute differences arose between the union and the control. Similar difficulties were arising in other districts. The solution proposed was to take the pits out of the hands of the mine-owners and so do away with the insistent hampering effect of the profit-making motive. The influence of the mine-owners on sections of the Government, however, continued to be too strong for this, and it was Churchill who, in the last week of October, finally blocked the possibility of a single control.

The Minister of Fuel and Power was forced to take steps to bring about a reorganisation of the coal industry, arising out of the publication of the Reid Report shortly before the end of the war. This report, which stopped short of nationalisation, was accepted by the Coalition Government as a whole. But the two main parties in the coalition were divided on the question of nationalisation. When the coalition was broken up by Churchill once victory was in sight, in the late spring of 1945, the Labour Party went forward to the election with a platform based on the Miners' Federation proposals. The Conservative Party, on the other hand, adopted the proposals put forward by the coal-owners. With the end of the war and in preparation for the General Election the miners put an additional effort into the fight for the return of a Labour Government.

This fight was greatly strengthened by the internal reorganisation of the miners' unions. Once the method of ascertainment district by district had been practically abolished by the successive Awards after the Greene Award of June 1942, the obstacles to amalgamation were removed. In Scotland, however, hindrances of this kind had not existed. There had been since 1900 a single Conciliation Board for Scotland. The obstacles that prevented the formation of a single Scottish union had been of a different kind.

6. ONE UNION FOR SCOTLAND

When in autumn 1914 the eight federated county associations of Scotland agreed on a close-knit form of organisation—and in token thereof changed their name from Scottish Miners' Federation to National Union of Scottish Mine Workers—the general hope was that this new aim of a single union would soon be realised. But actually it took thirty years to accomplish. By the middle of the first World War, James Cook, the Clackmannanshire Secretary, had led his association into fusion with the miners of Fife and Kinross. But the others remained obdurately separate, though their delegates always cheered at Annual Scottish Conferences when the need for amalgamation was mentioned in a presidential address. It became a commonplace for each President in his annual address to refer to the need for one union and for the delegates to cheer him. Nothing came of it. Every now and then a scheme was tabled. Either these schemes never won approval; or, if approved, they somehow, like an Australian river, presently disappeared into the ground. Yet with each passing year the urgency became greater.

These were the circumstances in which the Annual Conference in 1942 passed a resolution in favour of speedy measures for bringing about One Union in Scotland. This decision was now to be handled by men who were not prepared to be put off by the difficulties and obstacles that had baffled their predecessors. Led by Abe Moffat, the Executive Committee in the winter of 1942 got down to the details of a scheme. A One Union Committee was set up. Draft followed draft, amendment followed amendment; more than once Executive Committees were specially summoned to deal with this question. By April 1943 it was possible for the Annual Conference to be told by its President:

So far as your Executive is concerned the day has come when we are on the eve of having one union for the Scottish miners. The next step will be to approach the Districts on the draft rules for one union. This is the real test for all of us, whether we give lip service to one union or if we are serious and recognise that progress can only be made on the basis of strong united trade union organisation.

Within three months draft rules had been discussed with the Board of each of the six counties, their eleven amendments had been accepted and the whole remitted to the counties to send in further amendments. The next step was a Special Conference of 103 delegates with nineteen Executive Committee members on October 11, 1943, where twenty further amendments to the rules were debated and settled. It now only remained to take a ballot vote of the entire membership of the six county unions. The result of the ballot vote taken on November 3 and 4, 1943, was an overwhelming majority for fusion.

	For	Against
Lanarkshire	15,074	758
Fife, Clackmannan and Kinross ..	14,807	440
Mid and East Lothian	6,104	356
Ayrshire	8,220	983
Stirlingshire	3,339	110
West Lothian	3,026	364
	50,570	3,011

Thus by March 1, 1944, the six county unions had come to an end, and the N.U.S.M.W. became not in name only but also in reality one union for Scotland. Its officials were elected[1] two months later.

At the Annual Conference Abe Moffat could say in his presidential address:

In the previous years we talked about the need for One Union, but we are now in the fortunate position to declare that One Union for the Scottish miners has been established. The ballot vote of 50,570 in favour and only 3,011 against showed how correctly the Executive had interpreted the strong desire of the miners to build unity within their own ranks. Having achieved this, it in no way means that our tasks are finished. (September 20, 1944.)

He hoped the path was clear for the advance to a single union for the British coal-fields. Within a short time the hope was

[1] In May 1944 for the first time elections of officials and of executive committee were by members' ballot. The result of the ballot for the officials (Minute 47, May 22, 1944) was:

President:

Abe Moffat	33,953
Hugh Brannan	10,064
Total vote	44,017
Majority	23,889

Vice-President:

John Colthart	14,396
Peter Henderson	7,549
John Wood	6,858
James Connelly	5,460
Hugh McLauchlan	4,788
Richard Scambler	1,908
Total vote	40,959

Treasurer:

William Pearson	25,220
John Rutherford	5,522
James McKendrick	5,449
William Pender	3,075
William McKibbon	2,389
Total vote	41,655
Majority	8,785

Secretary:

James Cook	26,938
Andrew Hamilton	11,533
John Milgrew	3,743
Total vote	42,214
Majority	11,662

fulfilled. Just a year after the Scottish amalgamation ballot, a ballot of all districts of the M.F.G.B. resulted in the formation on January 1, 1945, of the National Union of Mineworkers.

The miners began the second half-century of Scottish national trade union organisation under auspicious circumstances, of which the keynote was struck in the opening of the President's Address to the Annual Conference in Dunoon on June 13, 1945, of what was now officially called The National Union of Mineworkers (Scottish Area). He said:

... In spite of any attacks that have been made against us during the last five and a half years, we declare that victory would have been impossible without the coal-miners of this country. The victory of democratic forces over Fascism now places a special responsibility on the whole Labour and Trade Union movement to ensure the winning of a people's peace, so that the sacrifices made shall not be in vain, as we experienced following the last war.

Abe Moffat then went on to deal with the immediate question before all of them, the forthcoming General Election.

The main task before the whole Labour Movement is to bring about the defeat of the Tory Government. This is the first and immediate step to ensure the fruits of victory. We can never forget what a Tory Government meant to the people between the two wars—mass unemployment, low wages, social insecurity, bad housing. The Tory Government supported Franco and Mussolini; they carried out a policy of appeasement to Hitler, while opposing unity and a common understanding with the Soviet Union, which policy eventually led to war. Such a party can never be entrusted with the destiny of the people in peace or we shall go back to the days of pre-1939, with poverty, misery and future wars. To avoid this we must take all the necessary steps to ensure the defeat of the Tory Government at the forthcoming General Election.

He then stated that 'Your Executive Committee have considered it necessary to place on the agenda a resolution on electoral unity'. This resolution the conference of 179 delegates carried as follows, with only one dissentient:

That this Conference requests the National Executive Committee of the National Union of Mineworkers to take immediate steps to bring together all Labour and Progressive organisations including the Communist Party, to discuss the unity of all progressive forces to ensure the defeat of the present Tory Government and to establish a Labour and progressive majority as a means of winning the peace.

The general outlook of the conference was also shown by unanimous resolutions for liberation of all political prisoners in India and the setting up of a national Government there, and for welcoming the Crimea Conference (Yalta) of February 1945. ('In particular we welcome the decisions on measures to completely disarm Nazi Germany and to ensure that never again will Germany disturb the peace of the world.')

Treasurer William Pearson explained points in the first and last statement of accounts of the N.U.S.M.W. as a single united trade union. It may usefully be compared with earlier years in the Scottish coal-fields. The Balance Sheet as at April 30, 1945, showed that the General Fund, with balances thirteen months earlier of £125,000, had added to it £105,000; to set against this there had been payments out of £82,000, a transfer to the Political Fund of £2000 and the unique capitation fee of £50,000 to the N.U.M. This left the area with £96,000 to carry forward.[1] With the doubled contribution, from 6d. to 1s. a week (carried at the Special Conference of the N.U.S.M.W. of December 4, 1944, by 127 votes to 31), it was possible for the Scottish Area, after deductions weekly for the N.U.M. and for branches, to meet all its obligations.

In the year ending April 30, 1945, lump sum settlements totalling £81,750 were secured by the union in Scotland on behalf of members in compensation for accidents. This was apart from the ordinary weekly compensation payments dealt with by the union, and apart also from the claims made under the compensation scheme for pneumoconiosis which came into force in July 1943.

The delegates then dispersed to their localities, there to plunge into the parliamentary electoral campaign, on whose result so many of their hopes were reposed.

---

[1] Before the formation of the one union for Scotland, the total assets as shown in the Statement for the year ended February 28, 1943, were £20,920 7s. By December 31, 1950, the total funds were £402,484 1s.

CHAPTER XII

NATIONALISATION

I. THE LABOUR GOVERNMENT

THE General Election of July 1945 brought an overwhelming victory for Labour. To the vast mass who supported the programme 'Let Us Face the Future' it seemed that the future was now assured. A Socialist Europe within a few years (apart from Spain and other Fascist countries), together with a rapidly advancing standard of living for the mass of the people so soon as war devastation had been overcome, seemed to them a measurable goal.

The British miners faced this prospect with the liveliest anticipation of speedy fulfilment. Gone were the days when, as in the Labour Governments of 1924 or 1929–31, the aspirations of the miners were foiled on the ground that these governments existed on sufferance, each representing a minority of the House of Commons and therefore unable to pass legislation which would unite Tories and Liberals in opposition to them. But this third Labour Government had come into power with a sweeping majority such as had only been exceeded by the Liberal majority of 1906. The hopes of the electors of 1906, then mainly Liberal, had encountered many set-backs: and a series of disappointments had led the miners in particular to swing away from Liberalism and to place all their future hopes in Labour. Now, with a Government drawn from the Labour Party, itself mainly made up of affiliated trade unions and endowed with a programme for socialism, there appeared no strong reason why all their aspirations should not be fulfilled. Consequently they looked forward, both at home and abroad, to a Britain of prosperity and a world at peace. 'I think', said the Treasurer William Pearson, moving a resolution at the Special Conference in Glasgow on August 13, 1945, 'the miners can claim a great deal of credit that there is today for the first time in our history a Labour

Government with full power to carry out a Socialist policy in this country.' The resolution, carried unanimously, welcomed the new Labour Government and pledged 'full support in the carrying out of the election policy'. The Scots in their conference also undertook a series of measures 'to improve the output of coal'. For this purpose they carried through a campaign. Whilst Arthur Horner was British National Production Officer, the Scots appointed Vice-President Colthart as full-time Production Officer to co-ordinate the work of Pit Production Committees and to stimulate effort in the coal-field. Thus the union was undertaking the novel responsibility, through its Production Officer and elected bodies, for an emergency increase in production: while at Westminster the plan of nationalisation was going through Parliament. For the miners realised that the end of the war had left Britain in a critical economic situation.

It was at this time that the Scottish Area lost the services of Alexander Sloan, M.P., who died in November 1945. As an Executive member, more directly than other mining M.P.s from Scotland, he could express in Parliament the standpoint of the Scottish miners' union. His outlook had broadened during his six years in Parliament and it was as one of the most militant of the mining members that he was mourned by the Scottish miners. His successor in the union was Dan Sim, who was able to carry on in Ayrshire a similar work to that of Sandy Sloan. A month later, at the end of 1945, Secretary James Cook retired, to be succeeded by Treasurer Wm. Pearson, who in accordance with the new rules continued also as Treasurer. James Cook, Secretary of the Clackmannanshire Miners' Association from 1897, and then, after the fusion in 1917 with the Fife and Kinross Miners' Association, a leading official of the latter for twenty years and more, had been Secretary of the N.U.S.M.W. from the beginning of the war. In 1897 at an Annual Conference of the M.F.G.B. he had spoken defending nationalisation of mines against the old Lib.-Labs. Nigh fifty years later he witnessed the introduction into Parliament of a Bill to end private capitalist ownership of the mines. With all his vigour unabated, he was up in years (for he had reached a much greater age than was generally known) and the occasion seemed to him suitable for his retirement. It was pleasant for him that, as he often said, his relations with his latest and youngest colleagues (much as he differed from them in political outlook) were the best of all in his long experience.

2. THE MINERS' CHARTER

The Scottish miners welcomed nationalisation, for which their forefathers had fought for so long, and felt it to be their job to make it a success. But they knew it would not be an easy task, because of two legacies left by private enterprise. The first was the reduction of man-power: the second was the technically backward condition of the industry. The deep crisis in man-power had caused the Minister of Fuel and Power to ask for proposals from the National Executive Committee of the N.U.M., which in reply drew up a list of twelve requirements that would help to provide a solution, with the remark that the extent to which these changes were made would determine the rate of entry of new recruits to the industry. As adopted they came to be known as the Miners' Charter.

THE MINERS' CHARTER

(1) The modernisation of existing pits and the sinking of new ones as rapidly as possible whilst strictly observing as a minimum the standards laid down in the Reid Committee Report; the provision of adequate compensation for those who become redundant; and at the same time aiming at the general application of the day-wage system.

(2) The adequate and careful training of youth in the various phases of mining operations, and the establishment of a clearly defined scheme of promotion; the provision of further training and tuition required in cases where workers desire to enter for a colliery technician's career.

(3) The introduction of new safety laws to meet the conditions of modern mining and especially to suppress the development of industrial diseases.

(4) The payment of compensation rates to meet incapacity due to industrial injury or disease which shall guarantee the injured person from financial loss and the provision of an adequate income for the dependants of those killed as a result of injury or who die from an industrial disease. . . .

(5) The average wage standards shall not be permitted to fall below those of any other British industry.

(6) The restoration of the 7-hour day for underground workers; the introduction of the 40-hour week for surface workers; and the establishment of the 5-day week without loss of pay.

(7) The continuation of the principle of the guaranteed weekly wage. . . .

(8) Payment to be made for two consecutive weeks' holiday and six statutory holiday days in each year.

(9) The provision of pensions for mineworkers who cease to be able to follow their employment after 55 years of age and the payment of a subsidiary pension from the industry in addition to pensions provided from other legal enactments.

(10) The building of new towns and villages of a high standard and situate at places calculated to enable miners to have increased opportunities for social facilities and to break down the segregation of mineworkers and their families from the rest of the community, accompanied by the provision of adequate transport services at reasonable rates.

(11) The complete re-organisation of health and welfare services so as to put a brake upon the wastage of manpower due to ill-health.

(12) Compulsory medical examination with training arrangements at full wages pending employment as a skilled workman in another industry if withdrawn from the coal mining industry on medical grounds.

The Scots had played their part in working out this Charter, and they were to play a bigger part in the fight to put it into effect. It was and is a statement of very great importance. It represented the union's firmly held standpoint that, the war being over, man-power for the mines must be secured by a steady improvement of wages, living standards and working conditions and not by exceptional measures, such as conscription or tying the men to the industry. On June 12, 1946, the Scottish presidential address summed it up:

Your National Executive have also submitted a Twelve-Point Charter of demands which they believe, together with nationalisation, can revive the mining industry and provide wages and conditions which will be a credit to it.

Your National Executive places the greatest importance on the five-day week being introduced at an early date. This is the key to solving the manpower crisis, which must be cleared up immediately if coal has to be produced in sufficient quantities to meet the requirements of the country.

I am confident that the introduction of the five-day week without loss of earnings would ensure greater regularity of work, continuity in production, adequate attention to repairs of roads and machinery, reduction of absenteeism, and the elimination of early lousing and unofficial stoppages, all of which would play an important part in coal production. It would enable the powerful Miners' trade union movement to make a call for manpower from all sections and from all parts of the country. Above all, it would win the confidence of both miners and management, which is so vitally necessary for the future development of the industry under nationalisation.

The demand for the Government to fulfil this charter 'in accordance with a time-table and a progressive plan', to quote the N.U.M.'s memorandum accompanying the Charter, was the central demand made by the miners for a progressive policy in a nationalised industry. Assent was given to this: and, in practice, the Government started putting portions of the Charter into effect. Later, however, there began a search for cheaper alternatives. There was the insistence on Saturday working and extra stints in the work. There was the importation and use of Polish and Italian labour instead of the drastic improvements needed to attract British labour into the mines. The demand for the fulfilment of the Miners' Charter thus became controversial and the fight to obtain it in full was still going on, a decade after nationalisation.

3. THE NATIONALISATION ACT

The Nationalisation Bill brought a new situation for the miners. There came the first reading in the House of Commons on December 19, 1945; animated parliamentary debates on it during the spring and summer; and the royal assent on July 12 to the Coal Industry Nationalisation Act, 1946. The settled policy for over two generations of the miners' associations was now at last to be put into effect. It was, they felt, none too soon. Many of them could remember how a British Government had pledged its word in 1919 that the decisions of the Sankey Commission would be carried out 'in letter and in spirit' and how that pledge had been broken, with disastrous consequences for the mining community. They looked back on the quarter-century in which the coal industry had been ripe, and rotten ripe, for nationalisation, and in which the coal-owners, aided by the press lords, had put every obstacle in the way of this most desirable reform. In fact, as they knew well, the existing system of private ownership in the coal-mines had in that quarter-century ceased to serve even the purpose of a capitalist economy in Britain. The series of Acts of Parliament, the series of Royal Commissions and official Inquiries, the series of special statutory bodies had none of them accomplished very much; some of them had accomplished nothing at all. Always the interests of the hundreds of separate colliery companies had blocked the path to any kind of real advance. Always temporary solutions of the increasingly acute problems of this industry with its obsolete form of capitalist structure, had been found—at the expense of the miners. The twenty-five years since a coalition British Government made up of Liberals and Tories had broken its pledged word had been, until the war years brought some alleviation, a painful record of exploitation, poverty and beggary with hundreds of thousands of miners out of work and the total man-power falling from nearly a million and a quarter in 1920 to under three-quarters of a million in 1945. With these recollections burnt into the memories of the older miners, there was certainly no regret for the passing of the coal-owners: and while there was relief at the change of ownership, enthusiasm was tempered by the inordinate delay of twenty-five years. The Bill before Parliament was not the same kind of measure as the M.F.G.B. had put forward in 1919, when 'workers' control' had featured so largely in the scheme for socialised mines. It could not, therefore, have quite the same appeal. But, whatever reservations some of the older colliers might have, the miners gave a welcome to the new dispensation and were thoroughly willing to work it.

The Coal Industry Nationalisation Act, 1946 was described as 'an act to establish public ownership and control of the coal-mining industry and certain allied activities; and for purposes connected therewith'. It transferred the assets of the coal-owners, with compensation, to a National Coal Board, made up originally of a Chairman and eight other members,[1]

[1] This maximum number was raised from eight to eleven by the Coal Industry Act, 1949, which made a number of amendments to the principal Act of 1946 and also to the Coal Mines Act, 1911.

FIRST SCOTTISH MINING SCHOOL AT DUNOON IN MAY 1947

ANDREW McANULTY (*3rd from left*) AT THE 1947 GALA

which had the duties to work and get coal in Great Britain as a monopoly; to develop the industry; and to make supplies of coal available. The coal in its varying qualities and quantities was to be supplied 'at such prices as may seem to them best calculated to further the public interest in all respects, including the avoidance of any undue or unreasonable preference or advantage'. The N.C.B. in carrying out these duties was to be subject only to general directives issued by the Minister of Fuel and Power and to parliamentary discussion once a year on the issue of its annual report.

This kind of nationalisation differed from the earlier policy of the Labour Party and the Miners' Federation in a number of ways. It followed the general policy on publicly-owned industry laid down by the T.U.C. in 1944 and 1945, which in turn had been largely inspired by the writings of Herbert Morrison, deputy leader of the Labour Party. Instead of nationalisation regarded as one step toward socialism, the new conception was put forward of taking into public ownership 'inefficient' industries (of which the coal-mining industry, as Lord McGowan, the Chairman of Imperial Chemical Industries, had pointed out, was certainly an example, even from the capitalist viewpoint), in order that they might give better service to a 'mixed economy', envisaged as continuing for many years. That nationalisation of this kind was not socialism was quite clearly understood by some of the miners' leaders. While the Bill was being debated in Parliament, Arthur Horner wrote:

State ownership of industry in class society is, however, not Socialism. The purchase of various industries will not terminate the kind of society in which we live. The system in which one class lives by the purchase and exploitation of the labour power of the other is not brought to an end. . . .

The change from private to state ownership in class society is not fundamental; that is to say, it does not produce a change in the character of our existing society, which will remain capitalist society. . . . While the nationalisation of a single industry or even of more than one industry is to be distinguished carefully from the fundamental change into a socialist society, it is nevertheless of very great importance. The nationalisation of the coal industry is a democratic measure, absolutely necessary at the present time and a great step forward in the right direction. (*Labour Monthly*, February 1946, pp. 45–6.)

This difference from the earlier aim had indeed been clear enough in 'Let Us Face the Future', which did not speak of socialism or workers' control in the coal-mining industry, but put its emphasis on the technical ground that 'Amalgamation under public ownership will bring great economies in operation and make it possible to modernise production methods and to raise safety standards in every colliery in the country'.

Another difference was that instead of the earlier policy of workers' control of industry or close parliamentary control, the Act of 1946 created a 'public corporation' deliberately removed from either kind of control, in order that it could operate in a more 'business-like' way, secure from 'interference' by amateurs. This was of course the model established by Mr. Herbert Morrison as Minister of Transport in the MacDonald administration of 1929–31, when he set up the London Transport monopoly as a 'public corporation' under Lord Ashfield, the previous head of the privately-owned combine. This had become the T.U.C. policy. While insisting strongly on 'consultative machinery' from top to bottom based on the unions, the 1944 T.U.C. Interim Report on Post-War Reconstruction was against this machinery having any executive authority. Neither T.U.C. nor M.F.G.B.[1] favoured workers' representation on the controlling bodies.

As far as the miners were concerned, they put their proposals for the future of the industry in the form of the 'Miners' Charter' (already given above) rather than, as twenty-five years before, in demands and agitation on the form of State ownership. They felt that they were in a strong bargaining position to obtain these demands and at the same time to solve the man-power problem. Yet they did not take advantage of their strength. Indeed the odd feature is that one main

[1] In this change of attitude on 'workers' control' from the previous effort to achieve nationalisation twenty-five years before there coincided two separate standpoints. On the one hand there had always been within the Labour Party a strong objection to 'workers' control', voiced in earlier days by Philip Snowden and Ramsay MacDonald, whose tradition in this matter was continued in the utterances of Herbert Morrison. For this school of thought 'workers' control' savoured of 'syndicalism': and 'syndicalism' before the first World War had been the bogy not only of the Liberal and Conservative but also of the parliamentary Labour leaders. For a third of a century it had been their endeavour to wean the trade unions and the leading trade unionists away from it. By 1944 they had succeeded, at any rate as regards the Miners' Federation. On the other hand there were not a few within the Miners' Federation who agreed but on entirely different grounds. They held that since nationalisation under capitalism was not socialism the union should keep its hands free and not be embarrassed by being represented as such on the nationalised boards.

effect of nationalisation was to prevent their position of strength being used to the full, lest it should upset public confidence in nationalisation.

4. CONFISCATION OR COMPENSATION?

The doctrine of socialism towards private capitalist ownership of the means of production, distribution and exchange had always been explicit. It stood for confiscation. There could be no question of compensation for the capitalists, those whom William Morris had succinctly described as 'damned thieves'. Consequently even the most reformist of the British organisations, the Fabian Society, had maintained in its basic statement of principles that nationalisation should be carried through 'without compensation'. But as soon as the demand for nationalisation of mines began to be put forward in detailed form such as a draft parliamentary Bill, allowance was made for compensation of the capitalist owners. The demand for the mines to be nationalised was put forward under Conservative and Liberal Governments before the Labour Party were more than a handful, or even before there was any Labour Representation Committee. A Liberal Government had carried through measures of nationalisation such as the transfer of telephone companies to the Postmaster General with full compensation for the previous owners. It was this kind of State purchase which alone seemed possible to the miners in the opening years of this century, and the minority of leaders with socialist views concurred in this. This was still their view after the war of 1914–18; and when the Cabinet of the Lloyd George Coalition pledged itself to nationalise, it became their settled outlook on the matter in the years that followed. When during the war of 1939–45 the Miners' Federation urged that the mines be taken out of the hands of the private capitalist owners, the assumption was that these would be compensated. The sweeping victory of the Labour Party in the General Election of summer 1945 and its overwhelming majority in the House of Commons raised in some minds the question as to whether there was now any need to stick to the policy of compensation adopted so many years before and under such different circumstances. But the question was raised only to be dismissed. If, however, it was thus agreed by the great majority in the Labour movement that the coal-owners should be compensated, there remained the amount and form of the compensation to be considered. How much money? This was the question. The T.U.C. in September 1945 had endorsed a memorandum laying down general principles about the nationalisation of an industry. Amongst these general principles were:

(1) 'Fair compensation' should be paid, based on reasonable net maintainable revenue multiplied by a number of years to be agreed. This formula, however, should exclude high war-time profits, and should 'permit special consideration of that part of past earnings which has been due to monopoly or semi-monopoly activities, or to any direct or indirect subsidy previously granted by the State'.

(2) The capitalisation of the new undertaking should be computed apart from what was to be paid in compensation, and should be fixed at a reasonable figure, bearing in mind that it would be operated as a public service and not, as in the past, for maximum profit. Over-capitalisation might make it difficult to give good wages and conditions, or to show successful financial results, and might thus hinder the extension of nationalisation.

(3) Compensation should be paid in Government stock divorced entirely from the industry and carrying a fixed rate of interest. The security having been increased, the rate of interest should be lower than that on the stocks of the private undertakings replaced, and 'attempts to balance past dividends with future receipts are out of place'.

These were general principles: but it was widely expected that in the coal-mining industry the compensation would be lower than in others, and that for two reasons. First, the security of the Government stock would be very much greater than shares in colliery companies, given the stormy history of the industry after the first World War; and second, much of the assets that were to be taken over were derelict. Consequently when the actual figure was announced it came as something of a shock—which was not diminished by the considerable complacency of many of the owners. The Scots miners raised objections to the amount, no less than £164,660,000. Again, the burden of this vast sum was placed on the industry, and during the protracted accountancy that was to settle how this global sum was to be shared, interim payments of interest were to be made to the colliery company shareholders, also out of the proceeds of the labour of the miners. In short, the criticism was that too much was being paid[1] and that this 'too much', instead of coming out of national revenue, was made a burden on the industry; indeed, a first charge upon it.

5. THE END OF PRIVATE OWNERSHIP

The last months of 1946 were devoted partly to discussions on lesser matters with the private owners whose days were numbered and partly to plans for the future and negotiations thereon. The repeal earlier that year of the Trade Disputes and Trade Unions Act of 1927, imposed as a measure of repression by the Baldwin-Churchill Government after the struggle of 1926, made it necessary to redraft the political rules of the union.

Meantime within the union the amalgamation of smaller branches, decided upon by conference, was being carried through by the Executive Committee. Friendly relations were built up with craft unions such as the Electrical Trades Union, following upon similar relations built with the Amalgamated Engineering Union and others, while an agreement on August 27, 1946, was made with the Scottish Colliery Deputies and Shotfirers' Association, with whom there had for some time been a quarrel over the right to organise and represent these grades. As for the Colliery Enginemen, Boilermen and Tradesmen's Association, the link was now so close that in the Conciliation Board[2] with the coal-owners the President of the Scottish Miners was the spokesman also for remedy of

[1] 'While accepting the principle of Compensation as decided by the movement, we deplore the idea of huge sums of money being paid out in Compensation to the owners who brought the industry to the verge of ruin.' (Moffat, presidential address, June 12, 1946.)
[2] Notice to end the old Board had been given in 1944 and a new Board constituted in the end of 1945.

grievances of members of the 'Engine-keepers' Association', as the craft union continued to be called.

Lastly there was the Miners' Charter of demands, as well as the demand to raise Scottish piece-rates more nearly to a level with those paid for comparable work in other parts of Britain. There was also the Scottish proposal for an entirely new wage-structure to be elaborated for the British coal-fields as a whole. Preparatory discussions on these matters were taking place in the last months of 1946 with the N.C.B., which, appointed in the summer, would not have full legal responsibility for the coal-mines until the date of 'vesting day' had been fixed by the Ministry. But in November 1946 the Minister, after some pressure from the union, fixed the date of 'vesting day' for January 1, 1947. This caused much pleasure to the miners; the Scottish Executive Committee at its meeting on November 25, 1946, welcomed the decision, pledged themselves 'to co-operate with the new Divisional Coal Board to overcome any obstacles which may arise' and also called upon all mine-workers similarly to co-operate so as 'to establish good relations between management and workmen'. At the Scottish Area Conference a week later this was fully endorsed. The Divisional Coal Board, when it took over, did so with the utmost goodwill from the mine-workers.

6. CONTROL AND DEMOCRACY

After Vesting Day on January 1, 1947, it was not long before the initial goodwill of the miners came up against an obstacle that was really inherent in the origin and composition of the National and Divisional Boards and their subordinate authorities. The demand for a measure of workers' control had not been put forward, nor was the Act constructed on this principle, though it had been stipulated that 'experience in labour relations' was to be one of the qualifications of membership of the Boards. But in practice when it came to setting up the Boards in July 1946 and subsequent months, it was found that the majority of the Boards came from the side of the old private owners. Trade unionists were given nothing but a minor part to play; they were not put in a position where they could control high policy: yet high policy was bound to determine the scope of their important but subordinate functions. A realisation of this led some of the key leading figures to refuse to take posts (and very lucrative posts) where they would find themselves in a permanent minority on the Board. Abe Moffat, for example, was pressed to take over a highly responsible position. But this he declined on the ground that the post of union President was just as essential for the success of public ownership as for the well-being of the miners.

For some appointments, particularly those of Labour Director or Labour Relations Officer, the union was asked to submit a panel of names, the final choice resting with the Ministry of Fuel and Power. The Scots early protested against the overwhelming weight of former owners or officials on the Boards. They had an inkling that with all the goodwill in the world trouble was bound to result. At the Annual Conference in June 1946, to the protest against the high level of compensation to former owners there was added the remark: 'Neither do we agree that National, Regional and Sub-Area Boards in the new machinery under nationalisation should be controlled by the same people who controlled the industry under private enterprise'.

As in the last half of 1946 the new machinery of control was built up and the personnel of that machinery announced, there was frequent disappointment amongst the working miners vocally expressed in forceful variations on the phrase 'The same old faces'. This had a chilling effect on the new-found enthusiasm. These forebodings were borne out first of all on the National Board where even in the honeymoon period some of the old employers continued to think as such and objected to the Board's policy as too liberal. As this factor, in the Scots' opinion, was to bedevil relations between employer and employed on many issues that arose, it is necessary to deal with it in some little detail and to give a particular example.

The incident to be related shortly here first raised the question: Whether the Coal Mines Act and Regulations could be used to put in jeopardy a local trade union official carrying out normal functions. But in the course of it a more far-reaching question arose: Whether the Coal Board would permit the actions of a manager or his association to render nugatory decisions reached between the Board and the union. Before this was finally thrashed out, all relations between Board and union were broken off, and a stoppage throughout the entire coal-field seemed to be inevitable.

At Thinacres, near Hamilton, Thomas Whitelaw was dismissed on April 10, 1950, when, in his capacity of branch Chairman, he was called from his place to another part of the mine where men were threatening to stop work. The reason given was that he had committed a breach of Regulation 4 of the Coal Mines Act which requires that,

Subject to any direction which may be given by any official of the mine, no workman . . . shall go into any part of the mine other than that part in which he works.

An unofficial strike immediately took place and the manager claimed that the Divisional Disputes Committee had no jurisdiction because dismissal for a breach of the Coal Mines Act was outside conciliation machinery. A joint meeting of the Coal Board and the union decided that Whitelaw should go to the manager and 'make his peace', promising to observe pit rules and conciliation machinery, whereupon he should be reinstated. But the manager, under the guidance of the British Association of Colliery Management, repudiated the decision arrived at between Board and union. The Thinacres men were then authorised by the union to tender notices, whereupon the Board proposed arbitration with a remit to investigate the circumstances of Whitelaw's dismissal 'and to make a recommendation as to whether he should be re-employed in the mining industry'; and if so, whether at Thinacres or elsewhere. Thus the dispute had now become one between the union and the Board for not operating the joint decision. Yet meantime, as delegates were reporting back to their branches, the Board issued a press statement attempting to throw the blame on the union, and laying stress on the view put forward by the manager, and that 'it would be a most serious step to order him to take any action which he felt would be prejudicial to safety'.

A vital trade union principle was now at stake; for, as Abe Moffat put it at the executive meeting, 'if this case were not fought strenuously by the union it was obvious that managers and their Association, B.A.C.M., could determine policy and make any agreement between the union and the Board null and void'. (Minute 1, June 5, 1950.) The executive unanimously decided to break off relations with the Coal Board and to call a Special Coal-field Conference.

There were immediate results. Meetings took place in London, and after tense negotiations the union officials finally succeeded in forcing an enquiry, with Whitelaw reinstated pending the result, on a satisfactory remit: that if he were found guilty of a breach of the Regulations the union would not resist his removal from Thinacres mine, and that if he were found not guilty the manager would not be retained there. At the Special Area Conference, the President

asked those delegates to be upstanding who had recently left their working places to deal with any kind of dispute without the authority of the manager or other official. The majority of the delegates immediately rose and the President asked these men to assist him in his task at the enquiry by submitting to him in writing at once details of the instances. (Minute 3, June 12, 1950.)

The Arbiter was Mr. John Cameron, D.S.O., K.C., and Abe Moffat and James McKendrick represented the union. A feature of the enquiry was the able presentation of the case on Whitelaw's behalf, in the course of which Abe Moffat pointed out that if the case went against him, the union would have no alternative but to

instruct all our representatives that in future, either with or without authority on the part of the management, they shall not interfere with a trade dispute underground under any circumstances . . . as the delegate from Wellsgreen submitted here—and I am quite sure he was speaking of similar experiences that have taken place at all the pits in Scotland—that had it not been for their action there would have been thousands of tons of coal lost in this country, if these lads had sat back and done nothing in order to prevent men from going home.

When the 120-page *Report of Proceedings at Hearing re Thinacres Mine* was published three weeks later, on July 18, 1950, it was found that the Arbiter had decided that Whitelaw had not breached the Regulations.

The manager was removed from the Thinacres mine.

7. PRICE POLICY

One feature of increasing importance during the first seven years of State ownership was the Coal Board's price policy which came to be recognised as having an effect on the living standards of the miners. In the old days before the Miners' Federation wages had actually been regulated by the price of coal under the sliding scale: and even later there was an element of sliding scale in the agreements under the Scottish Conciliation Board. It seemed, however, that all this had been done away with when the quarterly ascertainments had been instituted in 1921: and that nationalisation would make it even more remote. In practice coal prices came to have an effect on wages, though in an indirect manner, by the policy of cheap coal for the industrial consumer. At the same time the domestic consumer had to pay a high price for household coal out of which various merchant firms (some of them owned by former colliery companies) did very well for themselves.

The National Coal Board, however, was to make no change in this price policy. When the miners put in a wages claim they were told that there was 'nothing in the kitty' and warned that 'they must not make the industry a milch cow'; but it seemed to the miners, viewing this policy and its results, that the big capitalist owners of iron and steel, etc., had been making the industry a milch cow for several years—if indeed with a system of interlocking directorates and overlapping ownerships it had not been made a milch cow during the whole of the previous twenty-five years. The question naturally arose as to why the Board of the nationalised industry did not charge more for the product. There is no question that if private owners had the control they would certainly have charged more. The answer to the question could be surmised. But finally, in the Ridley Report of 1952 on the use of fuel and power, it was given openly. There it was frankly stated that one reason for not charging more for coal was that the miners in such a case would demand more wages.

The Scottish miners began to be more and more disturbed

about the price policy of the Coal Board and its effects, and at the Annual Conference in Aberdeen on June 3, 1953, it was stressed in the President's address about the price of coal:

The price of coal is certainly too high for ordinary householders, but they consume only about 40 to 50 million tons of coal per year. What about the remaining 180 million tons used by the big industrialists and private enterprise in general? They are making huge profits now and they want to make still greater profits on the basis of cheap coal. Coal prices since 1947 have not increased to the same extent as the prices of other commodities. (June 3, 1953.)

Again he said:

The ordinary consumer now pays up to £6 for a ton of coal, but the average selling price at the pithead is just over £3 per ton, and it is this latter figure which determines miners' wages and profit and loss in the mining industry. It is not high wages but Government policy which is responsible for the high price of coal. No objection is ever raised by the Tories to the high rate of compensation paid to the former coal-owners, who have received almost £100 million since nationalisation. Let us get rid of this burden on the industry and then cheaper coal can be provided for the ordinary consumer. Let us have less Tory control and more workers' control and the industry can be improved to the advantage of both the consumers and the miners.

At a later stage in the conference the statement was made with regard to the price of coal itself:

With regard to the price of coal itself, about which the Tories were making such an outcry, it was necessary that the general public should understand the true position. If you examined wholesale prices in this country since 1949 you found that they had increased by 42 per cent while coal prices had only been allowed to go up by 22 per cent. The President used the term 'allowed' because it was the Government which decided whether or not coal prices should be increased and there had been instances where they had scaled down price increases recommended by the Board. If the industry were really showing a loss it was the responsibility of the Government and the Board because they controlled the prices. The miners had every sympathy with the household consumer who had to pay 5s. or 6s. for his bag of coal, but household consumers represented only 20 per cent of the total consumption of coal in this country.

No newspaper told what the big industrialists were paying for coal, and there was a conviction among the miners that if an investigation were made it would show that they were securing it below actual cost. In particular it was believed that coking coal was being sold to the iron and steel industry at a price which involved a substantial loss to the coal industry. This meant that the coal industry was being used to subsidise the profits of other big industries. Naturally the conclusion was reached:

The miners could not, therefore, be content with present wages knowing that such a manipulation of figures was going on and that huge profits were being made by big industrialists at the expense of the miners. (Minute 35, p. 682.)

The Scots were not content with denouncing the system; they called for an enquiry into prices and into middle-men's profits. They asked the Labour Research Department to undertake an investigation, and in 1953 they were strongly in support of a demand for an investigation of the matter by the N.U.M.

8. TECHNICAL DEVELOPMENT

When the coal industry was nationalised, there was general agreement that technical development must be undertaken with the utmost speed. The need for this had been shown in the Report of the Technical Advisory Committee, published in March 1945 and commonly known as the Reid Report, wherein seven experts (most of them also managing directors of colliery companies) had made a devastating criticism of the backwardness of the industry. The Miners' Charter had put forward as its first demand 'the modernisation of the existing pits and the sinking of new ones as rapidly as possible whilst strictly observing as a minimum the standards laid down in the Reid Committee Report'; and had added to this the demand for 'the provision of adequate compensation for those who become redundant; and at the same time aiming at the general application of the day-wage system'. Immediate investments, amounting to £72 million in the first three years, were made in large or small projects of which a considerable number had been begun before Vesting Day. But it was not till October 1950 that the N.C.B. published its *Plan for Coal*, with a proposed investment of £635 million in the fifteen years up to 1965. These proposals were published as open to criticism: and criticism was immediately forthcoming. The Scottish Area commented that the plan was inadequate and foresaw no substantial benefit for the miners. For example, it was pointed out that 'scientific utilisation of coal' was not mentioned:

In spite of all previous declarations, we are being asked to continue producing coal to be burned in its raw state and wasted at a time when it is becoming more and more precious and valuable. (December 18, 1950.)

More severe was the comment that 'the Board is assuming that the miners will still be working $7\frac{1}{2}$ hours plus one winding time' for fifteen years ahead, a proposition that as a trade union they could not accept. For 'unless we secure a reduction in hours for the miners, we shall never succeed in getting sufficient recruits into the mining industry'. As it happened, however, throughout the whole period from Vesting Day, technical development fell far below even the planned level which the Scottish Executive had considered inadequate. Rearmament took the lion's share of available finance and materials: while priority was given to more profitable investments. In the *Plan for Coal*, unhappily published at the time when arms expenditure was leaping upwards (in December 1950 it was proposed £4700 million be expended in three years), the investment in collieries was to average £38 million over the five years 1951 to 1955. But then prices rose steeply and by the autumn of 1953 the revalued investment figure stood at £53 million. When the House of Commons debated the situation on October 26, 1953, the Minister of Fuel and Power, Mr. Geoffrey Lloyd, had this to say:

In 1951, against that figure of £53 million, the actual expenditure on colliery investment was only £27 million, which gives an arithmetical deficit of £26 million. In terms of the real investment itself, probably that deficit at present-day prices is between £20 million and £25 million. In 1952 the Board were able to increase the rate of investment by £10 million over the year before, bringing it up to £38 million. This year the rate of investment has been increased by another £10 million, bringing it up to about £48 million. I am informed that next year it will almost certainly go up by another £10 million to reach a figure of £58 million which, for the first time, will carry the actual investment in collieries above the figure in the *Plan for Coal*.

Thus the general agreement in 1946 that there must be the most speedy technical development and re-equipment of a decadent and backward industry was frustrated by governmental economic policy, itself determined by a foreign policy on which both Labour Government and Conservative Opposition were in full accord. The mines, and the miners, suffered by it. There were, however, some technical developments carried out, before the *Plan for Coal*. These brought new problems for the union. In the case of certain kinds of mechanisation, where new machinery meant new dangers and the need of new agreements, the problem for Scotland arose before the war ended. It was the foremost coal-field in Britain to introduce coal-cutting machinery, even before the first World War of 1914–18. But when the several new power-loading machines were introduced during the last war, wages paid in Scotland for the new method of mining were lower than anywhere else in the United Kingdom. It took a prolonged and determined fight to get this put right. Throughout 1944 they used all the conciliation machinery; in May 1945 the question was taken by the N.U.M. at their instance, to the National Tribunal to establish a national agreement for men working on power-loading. But this body referred them back to the Scottish coal-owners, who refused a district agreement; an appeal to the neutral Chairman in Scotland was unsuccessful; negotiations had to be opened at each separate colliery. It was impossible to achieve satisfactory pit agreements; and in case after case appeals to the same neutral Chairman were made, and refused by him. In other districts satisfactory district agreements were reached; but in Scotland wages continued to be lower than anywhere else.

Finally, in October 1946 a highly unusual incident took place. Correspondence was exchanged between the Scottish President and Mr. J. R. Blair, the neutral Chairman, who in an Award had attributed statements to Abe Moffat and John McArthur which had not in fact been made by them. Moffat's letter began:

I have never in all my experience as a trade union official raised objection to an Independent Chairman's decision, but I must take exception to certain statements in your Award, and at the same time claim that your Award is inconsistent with Clause 4 of the National Agreement. (October 18, 1946.)

In his reply Mr. Blair admitted the correctness of Abe Moffat's objection to the statements attributed to him and to McArthur; and while adhering to his Award, he announced that he would resign his office. When the Joint Negotiating Committee met on November 5, 1946, the coal-owners' side objected that it should have been remitted there in the first instance. To this Abe Moffat replied that 'in all cases where false statements were attributed to a representative of this union, the right was maintained for that individual to make a personal protest on that issue'. The resignation of the neutral Chairman was accepted.

After the mines had been taken over and the Scottish Division established, the effort to get the Scottish miners satisfactory wages for power-loading continued. Finally, the Scottish Area decided that no miners in Scotland would handle power-loading machines until an agreement had been reached covering the whole of Scotland. Then a satisfactory Area Agreement[1] on wages to be paid for power-loading was at last signed.

9. CONCENTRATION, DE-WATERING, DISTILLATION

Besides this one example of power-loading, there were many others of a similar nature. But the main form in which the Scottish Area had to face the problems created by technical development was the closing down of old pits and the transfer of men to new districts. This problem came up very sharply indeed with the closures in the Shotts area of North Lanarkshire and the transfer of miners to Fife.

The policy of the union was that while it would be wrong to insist that men should continue to work in obsolete and often dangerous conditions, yet closure brought with it grave social problems for which the N.C.B. must assume full responsibility. No pit should be closed, they held, on economic grounds alone—which, given the N.C.B. price policy, were in

---

[1] For its full terms, see Appendix to this chapter.

any case rather arbitrary. If a pit were to be closed, then the men and their families had to be looked after. Those who could transfer to another district must have suitable conditions provided. Those who could not transfer must have alternative work provided or be given redundancy pay.

An example of difficult relations with the Divisional Coal Board, of an entirely different kind from those that might emerge in the Disputes Committee, arose in 1949 in connection with a new problem. Concentration (on the more remunerative pits) was the name given to the closing down of pits that were either nearly worked out or had ceased to be remunerative. This was a policy that the N.U.M. did not feel could be opposed in general, while the closing down of any particular pit or pits would be, it was understood, a matter to be fully discussed between all parties concerned before final decision was reached. It was on this that difficulties arose.

The process was not new in the British coal-fields; least of all was it new in Lanarkshire, which had come to be spoken of by experts, in its northern part, as 'a dying coal-field'. As seams became exhausted or difficult to work, pits in north Lanarkshire had been closing down ever since the end of the first World War. From then for nearly thirty years the closing down of a pit under private ownership would take place: and nothing could be done about it. The pit just closed down: the colliers were thrown on the street: and they had simply to make the best of it. There was no one who had the right to interfere.

In addition this dreadful process had been accelerated, especially during the world economic crisis of 1929 to 1933, by pits in the lower Clyde valley becoming water-logged. In a particular area one pit would be closed down: the great wheels would cease to move: and the continuous action of the pumps would come to an end. Water rose in the abandoned workings. Presently the water found its way into neighbouring collieries still at work and in such quantities that they, too, after a vain struggle, were abandoned by their owners, leaving millions of tons of valuable coal. This drowning of the pits could have been avoided by a combined pumping installation for the whole area. But who was to set up and keep going

SCOTTISH MINERS' GALA DAY, 1950

SCOTTISH MINERS' GALA DAY, 1950

(1) One of the processions
(2) Competitors in the pipe band competition

such equipment, however necessary it might be? The answer was 'Nobody'. For under private ownership it was nobody's business. But under public ownership it was different, or should have been different. And it was the contention of the union that, late though it was, the necessary steps should be set afoot for de-watering some drowned pits, for pumping them dry and enabling the abandoned seams to be worked again.

Again there was the possibility of introducing in Lanarkshire projects for distillation of coal, by which employment could be given to some at least of the miners displaced by concentration, while in any given locality substituting a remunerative industry for the moribund industry of coal extraction. On this, too, the Scottish miners' union was to the fore in bringing these possibilities to the notice of the Coal Board, the Ministry of Fuel and Power, the local authorities and the local trade union movement; and in pressing for their speedy examination with a view to action. In this they had to encounter a very equivocal attitude on the part of some members of the Lanarkshire County Council—and of some Members of Parliament also. The union, however, persevered and on October 29, 1950, held in Hamilton a widely representative conference about a Coal Distillation Plan for Lanarkshire, attended by 129 delegates. Of these, seven came from the Scottish Executive and forty-four from twenty-five branches of the N.U.M. Other trade union branches sent twenty-nine delegates, trades councils fourteen, co-operators and women's guilds sixteen, the Scottish T.U.C. two, the town councils of Airdrie, Motherwell, Hamilton and Rutherglen nine in all, together with three Members of Parliament, three representatives of the N.C.B., and two others.

But the main question of concentration was that in each particular case there should be full consultation, and understanding reached with all the parties concerned. Given this in a full and frank way, the union was prepared to do its part. But in 1949 there occurred a very awkward incident, which very gravely embittered relations with the N.C.B. The matter arose in connection with the closure of Hillhouserigg, Fortissat and Hartwoodhill Collieries. In the case of the first of these, members of the Divisional Coal Board had stated their intention to open up a surface mine which would have

kept a good number of colliers employed. The argument in
the winter of 1948–9 largely turned on how soon this would be
done, the Coal Board saying 1950, and the union pressing for
an earlier date. On the understanding that this mine would
be opened up, the President of the Scottish Area went to a
meeting of the Shotts men. He put the case to them, explaining why, subject to further consultation, the closure of Hillhouserigg was considered inevitable; but stating that there
would be compensating employment in the mine that would
be opened up. Meanwhile, and without telling him anything,
the Divisional Coal Board experts had reported that the mine
from the surface was not a satisfactory project and should not
be proceeded with. This the Divisional Coal Board withheld
from the Scottish Area until after Abe Moffat had been to
Shotts.

Then came the announcement that the closure of the
colliery would take place right away and there would be no
new mine as an alternative. This immediately caused an up-
roar: and there was great trouble in the Shotts district, the
repercussions of which fell on the Scottish Executive. The
Executive bitterly criticised the Scottish Coal Board for their
behaviour and called a Special Delegate Conference in Edinburgh on April 21, 1949, 'to consider the question of Closure
of Hillhouserigg and Fortissat Collieries' at which Abe Moffat
gave a clear survey of the question and report on all that had
happened. The Executive then questioned each argument for
closure: and told the Coal Board they could 'do their own
stuff' on concentration in that area in the future. They took
the further decision to publish the speech of Abe Moffat at the
aforesaid Delegate Conference, and also the verbatim 'Reports
of Meetings between Divisional Coal Board and N.U.M.
(Scottish Area)' on the closure. This last made up a book of
104 pages, in which the miners could read in detail the stand
which their representatives had taken and the bitter complaint about the behaviour of the Coal Board toward the
Scottish Area. It was taken to London, where after prolonged
discussion, the policy decision on closure was maintained by
the National Coal Board; but at the same time Lord Hyndley
expressed apologies to Abe Moffat for what had taken place.
The form of the apology was not as ample as the Scots con-

sidered necessary: and Abe Moffat informed the N.C.B. that he would not address any further meetings on concentration in the Shotts area. In this standpoint the President had the full and unanimous backing of the Executive Committee.

The policy of the union remained clear and unequivocal and was voiced by Abe Moffat a few weeks later at the Annual Conference in his presidential address, as follows:

Let me say a word about the policy of concentration. As a Trade Union we have made our position perfectly clear on this matter from the very beginning. I do not want to repeat what has already been decided by our branches and Area Conferences, but I do want to emphasise that we, as a Trade Union, will not stand aside and allow the Lanarkshire coal-field to die out. We have put forward a positive policy on this important question and one which, in my opinion, is the only policy to save Lanarkshire. We must get the new sinkings laid down in the Scottish Coal-fields Report, along with the new developments for the Douglas area. We must fight to get consideration of the de-watering problem which can only be carried out with financial assistance from the Government. Lastly, the most important question of all is the need to install a coal distillation plant to conserve the limited resources of coal in this area. All those who are really interested in saving Lanarkshire will therefore support this policy in the interests not only of the miners but of the whole future economy of Lanarkshire. (Minute No. 35, May 31, 1949, p. 645.)

In the five years that followed the policy of the union remained unchanged. But they had to keep up a steady pressure on each issue to get any advance.

APPENDIX TO CHAPTER XII

AGREEMENT

Between the National Coal Board (Scottish Division) and the National Union of Mineworkers (Scottish Area) for Longwall Power-Loading (Meco-Moore and Logan Slab Cutter) at any Colliery in Scotland.

1. *Scope of Agreement.* This Agreement refers only to the Power-Loading Team as designated in Clause 2 hereof and will apply to future installations, in Scottish Collieries, of Longwall Power-Loading with the Meco-Moore or Logan Slab cutter.

2. *Power-Loading Team.* The following persons will constitute a Longwall Power-Loading Team:

(a) *Meco-Moore Cutter Loader.*

Grade 1—1 Operator (Chargeman).
Grade 2—1 Assistant Operator (2nd Chargeman).
Grade 3—1 Cable Man.
   1 Temporary Supports and cleaning up.
   2 Permanent Supports.
   1 Passing Supports from Waste Side.

TOTAL 7

(b) *Logan Slab Cutter Loader.*

Grade 1—1 Operator (Chargeman).
Grade 2—1 Assistant Operator (2nd Chargeman).
Grade 3—4 Conveyer Shifting and Propping.

TOTAL 6

3. *Wage Rates.* All members of the Team will be paid on a Day Wage Basis at the rate of the Average Earnings per shift of Piece-workers in the Colliery, or in Scotland, whichever may be the higher, with the following additions: (i) Grade 1 (Operator) (extra rate)—3/- per shift. (ii) Grade 2 (Asst. Operator) (extra rate)—2/- per shift.

The average piece rate earnings per shift at the face for Scotland, excluding overtime, week-end time and the bonus shift in terms of the Five-Day Week Agreement but including the War Wage addition, shall be taken as 31/- at the commencement of this Agreement. The average piece rate earnings per shift at the face, excluding overtime, week-end time and the bonus shift in terms of the Five-Day Week Agreement but including the War Wage addition, shall be calculated at each Colliery concerned for the period of 8 weeks following 19th January 1948. Whichever is the higher figure shall be taken as the wage applicable under this Agreement until

30th September 1948, and thereafter shall be subject to revision on one month's notice given in writing by either side. It shall be open to both parties after an experimental period has elapsed to negotiate for piece work rates for those to whom this Agreement applies.

4. *Alternative Work.* If, for any reason, the work of any/all members of the team is not available he/they will be paid the recognised shift and guaranteed wage paid to Strippers employed at the Colliery under similar circumstances. In the event of any of the men being employed on any other productive work they will be paid the prevailing rate for the alternative work on which they are employed.

5. *Additions to Team.* Should the Management consider that any additions to the team are necessary such additional persons will be considered as members of the team and will be paid in accordance with Clause 3 of this Agreement, on the same basis as Grade 3. Where with the Meco-Moore it is necessary to add two persons for the purpose of flitting or turning the machine such men shall be paid in accordance with the Grade II scale except that one man shall receive 6d. per shift extra for seniority.

6. *Chargeman.* It is agreed that the 1st Operator will be in full charge of the team and that the others will work under him as a team.

7. *Unsatisfactory Work.* It is a condition of this Agreement that all workers in the team will pull their full weight and work in the team spirit during each working shift.

In individual cases where the Management is satisfied that any member of the team is unsatisfactory by reason of the standard of work or attendance thereat, he will be replaced by another, but the Manager, before giving the appropriate notice of termination of contract, shall confer with the Trade Union Representative. The normal notice will be given and the unsatisfactory worker placed on a lower grade, or on other work in keeping with his capabilities. This does not preclude the possibility of dismissal for serious misconduct.

8. *Tools.* Special tools will be supplied by the National Coal Board. With regard to ordinary working tools such as Pick, Shovel, Axe, Mash, Saw and Pinch, the Board will supply these to the team initially and at the expiry of each six months period a payment of £5 (five pounds) will be made to the Chargeman for maintenance and renewal. Such payment will be made only if the contract is continued on day wages.

9. *Co-operation.* It is clearly understood that this Agreement is to be fairly carried out by both parties and will only continue in operation accordingly.

10. *District and National Agreements.* Nothing in this Agreement will affect District or National Agreements or the conditions of employment.

11. *Continuance.* This Agreement will not be altered in detail

without prior consultation with the signatories to this Agreement or their successors in office.[1]

Signed for and on behalf of the NATIONAL COAL BOARD (SCOTTISH DIVISION)   BALFOUR

Signed for and on behalf of the NATIONAL UNION OF MINEWORKERS (SCOTTISH AREA)   ABE MOFFAT

16th April 1948.

---

[1] Nearly seven years after the Scottish Area had negotiated this wage of 31s. a shift, in the winter of 1954-5 negotiations were carried on with the Divisional Coal Board and an agreement was reached in mid-January 1955. By this the wage was fixed at 46s. plus a bonus of 5s. per shift for completion of an agreed task representing a reasonable shift's work, with an addition of 3s. per shift to the leading man and 2s. per shift where a second man was appointed. This wage was also to apply, without any task being laid down, to all experimental power-loading machines. This was indeed a substantial increase since 1948.

CHAPTER XIII

WAGES AND HOURS UNDER STATE
OWNERSHIP

I. EARLY GAINS

THE kernel of the relations between the miners and their employers always lay in economic issues. Hours of labour, rates of wages and other conditions ranged the industry into two sides. There was give and take, especially at the beginning; but there were also matters of prolonged and sometimes bitter controversy. The first seven years of the nationalised coal-mining industry began in a mood of co-operation—which was temporarily strengthened in the opening months of 1947 by the attack made upon the Ministry, the Coal Board and the miners as though these had been responsible for the coal crisis caused by the blizzard of February and March 1947. During these initial months of the new dispensation, many benefits were gained by the miners and given with good grace by the new Coal Board, some having already been promised by the Ministry. Six statutory holidays with pay had been granted unconditionally. Short-time was abolished. Free pit-head baths, a long-standing aim of the miners, were established; and a guarantee was given of priority for the provision of these baths at all collieries. The welfare levy of a penny a ton was to be doubled. The need for priority housing for miners, raised by the Scottish Area, had been recognised. On another point raised by the Scots, the provision of household coal where men were transferred to England or another district, concessions had been made. These were halcyon days. It took a good many months of negotiation to deal with the major questions of hours and wages. The first of these had been settled in principle before the Coal Board was set up. To this change in the work-days we must now turn.

The number of days worked in a week or a fortnight had varied in different coal-fields. In Scotland the practice in the later nineteenth century had been eleven days a fortnight, succeeding to an earlier practice when the second Monday was the pay day, the day off, and the day of delegate meetings. In the early years of the twentieth century there grew up a demand in some coal-fields for a five-day week. After the 1912 Minimum Wage Strike this was much discussed, and, when the employers refused to entertain it, a ballot vote of the British miners was taken on whether they would come out on strike for a five-day week. The ballot, taken in February 1913, was for a strike, but by such a small majority that the decision was there and then made and incorporated in a new M.F.G.B. Rule, that a two-thirds majority was necessary on the issue of a national strike. In the 1913 ballot several coal-fields were opposed to the five-day week; others were strongly in favour; but none were so strong as the Scots, who voted by a four to one majority to get rid of their customary eleven-day fortnight. At the end of the second World War the agitation for the five-day week began once again. It was embodied in the Miners' Charter and in the latter months of 1946 became the subject of negotiations between the N.U.M. and the newly appointed N.C.B., with the Ministry of Fuel and Power and the Cabinet also closely concerned.

After Vesting Day negotiations continued and by March 27, 1947, a Special Conference of the Scottish Area had before it a National Agreement which settled the normal working week. For underground workers it was to be in future a week of five consecutive shifts of $7\frac{1}{2}$ hours plus one winding time; while for surface workers it was to be $42\frac{1}{2}$ hours (exclusive of meal times) to be worked in five consecutive shifts of $8\frac{1}{2}$ hours. Whoever worked these five full qualifying shifts was to receive a bonus of his average day wage-rate; or in the case of a piece-worker '16 per cent of his aggregate earnings (excluding overtime)' with a minimum of £1. Overtime was to be reckoned at one-and-a-half times the normal rate; and week-end work (from Saturday backshift to Sunday backshift inclusive) at double. The Agreement also contained a section headed 'Co-operation in the Interests of Production' of which the opening words were:

It is the joint determination of the Board and the Union to establish throughout the industry a relation of mutual confidence and respect between workers and managerial personnel at all levels, and a spirit of mutual co-operation based on the recognition of their joint responsibility for a national service.

There were many questions raised at the Conference: and then the Secretary, William Pearson, on behalf of the Executive Committee moved the following resolution:

That this Conference, having discussed the terms of agreement on the five-day week, agrees to accept these terms. We pledge ourselves to take every step possible to maintain output at the highest level.

Conference calls on the Scottish miners to ensure the success of the five-day week and nationalisation by working every available shift, preventing unofficial stoppages, and by making the utmost use of the pit machinery to obtain maximum output. (March 27, 1947.)

After a discussion, the Secretary said that 'the delegates would be able to go back proudly to their branches to report that, after long years of struggle, they had achieved something which the pioneers in the movement had seen only as a dream'. The resolution was unanimously accepted.

The N.C.B. had conceded that it would not hold the miners to the 1944 Agreement with the previous employers by which no changes in conditions of employment, including wages, could have been made before midsummer 1948. The National Executive Committee, having been instructed by the 1947 Annual Conference of the N.U.M. 'to endeavour to obtain a substantial increase in the minimum rates and to press for such rates for adults to apply to all workmen of 18 years of age and over', took the matter up on September 18. The next day the officials of the Scottish Area, in which there had been some restiveness, sent out a letter to their branches. After pointing out that 'the proposal for an increase of £2 per week, raising the present minimum from £5 to £7 (reported in the press that day), was a suggestion put by the Scottish representatives', they gave a warning to avoid 'any irresponsible action' and 'against any disrupters in our ranks who may attempt to undermine these negotiations by unofficial stoppages'. The Scottish miners' leaders went on to draw the attention of the general public to the facts:

Manpower is again going down, both in the Scottish and the

British coal-fields, and this is due to the fact that conditions are not sufficiently attractive to persuade people to come into the mining industry. It should be understood that approximately two-thirds of our men are receiving the low minimum of £5 per week, providing they work the full week. After deductions this amount is quite inadequate to provide a decent standard of living, apart from the arduous and dangerous nature of the miners' occupation.

The concluding sentences of the letter ran:

To solve the crisis in Britain we must get more coal. To get coal we require more manpower. To retain our present manpower and secure more manpower we must be prepared to give wages and conditions. More coal is going to cost more money, but let it also be understood that coal and more coal costs more blood and sacrifice on the part of the miners. (September 19, 1947.)

On October 3 the N.U.M. National Executive Committee limited their claim to £1, making £6 per week for underground workers and £5 10s. for surface workers. By November 24, 1947, a Draft Agreement giving as weekly minimum £5 15s. and £5 for surface workers was submitted to a Scottish Area Conference and accepted by an overwhelming majority of the 156 delegates, only eight voting against. Other Areas having voted similarly, the N.E.C. was able to accept. There was an increase in day rates of 2s. 6d. for underground and 1s. 8d. for surface adults. In Scotland the consolidated daily minimum rate had been 13s. 6d. plus 2s. 8d. war wage, giving a total of 16s. 2d.: this now became 18s. 8d. a shift. Surface workers' minimum rose from 13s. 10½d. to 15s. 6½d. Corresponding increases were given for youths and women. There was a 'ceiling', however, to this increase, which was not given to underground workers already getting 23s. 6d. a shift or surface workers getting 21s. 10d. But no surface worker in Scotland was getting such a high rate and therefore all of them got the increase. A detailed explanation of these changes was given to the Scots in a pamphlet,[1] which put the matter very clearly.

A series of other Agreements consequent on the new Wages Agreement of December 1947 was negotiated for various grades of staff. In the Scottish Division the union put forward

[1] 'Questions and Answers on New Wages Agreement' by Abe Moffat, President (November 1947).

a claim on the wages of weekly paid industrial staff which the Scottish Divisional Coal Board was not willing to concede. Finally this claim came up before the first meeting of the Conciliation Board under the Scottish District Conciliation Agreement, held on September 27, 1948. Mr. Abe Moffat put forward the case on behalf of the N.U.M. Scottish Area and of the Scottish Colliery Enginemen, Boilermen and Tradesmen's Association, whose Secretary, Mr. R. Smillie, was present together with Mr. J. Shearer, the General Secretary of Group 3 of the N.U.M. (later the Colliery Officials and Staffs Association). The Earl of Balfour argued the case for the Scottish Division of the Coal Board. The interest of this case, whose printed proceedings extended to ninety-one pages, lies in the skill with which facts and arguments were marshalled in support of the claim. The result of this lucid presentation before the independent Chairman was the decision for a big increase (dating, by agreement between the parties, back to July 1, 1947) to each of the grades concerned.

Wherever in the mine-fields of Britain the contractor system has existed it has been a source of friction and discontent. As far back as the conditions of Chartist days, described by Disraeli in his famous novel *Sybil or the Two Nations*, the evils of contracting were an obvious source of misery and trouble. This contracting had survived in Scotland in a number of places and was particularly bad at certain pits. Immediately after the war a statement was submitted to the Ministry on this complaint in the Scottish coal-field, in which the system, which the owners had refused to abolish, was described:

It is the system where one man has a contract with the company and has a few or several men working under him. He draws all the wages from the company and pays the men who are working with him individually. The workmen never know what the contractor has earned or the rates paid by the company. The system itself creates suspicion as some of these contractors have made huge sums of money at the expense of their fellow workers, and in most cases have done very little work for it. We can say that many contractors are detested even more than some coal owners.

When the matter was taken up some months later with the new Coal Board, there was to begin with a very different attitude from that of the old Conciliation Board machinery with the private owners or the neutral Chairman. After some twelve months' effective working of the Scottish Division, it was possible for Abe Moffat to comment: 'Your fathers before you passed many resolutions on this question. We passed them in our time.' Now, 'after all these years of resolutions', the problem had been tackled. The contractor system was abolished.

On November 6, 1948, there was a second meeting of the Conciliation Board for Scotland. The subject of this was the interpretation of the Seven Days' Notice Agreement which had been entered into on April 5, 1948. The independent Chairman, John Cameron, K.C., had the task of settling the exact meaning of the Agreement. The Divisional Coal Board had claimed that they had a right to stop payment or reduce payment to a workman with whom they had a contract if they or their manager believed that the terms of the contract were not being fulfilled. The union claimed that the Board had no such right under the April Agreement but must give seven days' notice to end the contract, and if they still felt aggrieved, must then take the usual action in the Civil Courts to find a remedy for their grievance. This, of course, would equally apply if the worker felt aggrieved and believed that the terms of a particular contract were not being performed by the other party to the contract. The Coal Board seemed to be a victim of a delusion found amongst many litigants that they may eat their cake and have it; in other words, that they may enter into a contract which will be binding on the other side but not on their side. Judgment was given in favour of the unions.

In the past when an individual dispute of this kind had arisen it had been customary for the workman, if he felt aggrieved, forthwith to leave his work, sometimes accompanied by others and on occasions by the whole pit. It was to find a way out of this that a strict agreement for seven days' notice on either side as to terms of contract had been entered into in April 1948. Had the Coal Board won its contention of being able, notwithstanding the above, to alter the terms of the contract, it would in the end have reproduced the same results as they had sought to avoid. From the point of view of the Coal Board, therefore, it may be considered that they were lucky to have lost the case.

2. COLD WAR AND WAGE-FREEZE

The years after 1945 disappointed high hopes of peaceful and friendly collaboration among the Great Powers. Instead of the 'one world' prospects of 1945 there came a division into two camps; and Britain was found in the same camp as the United States, but in a subordinate position. Economic difficulties were met by recourse to American aid, given with increasingly onerous political and economic conditions. Following 'Marshall Aid' American forces were stationed in Britain, and to the previous economic strain on the country there was added the burden of massive rearmament and a two-year conscription, as well as heavy overseas military expenditure.

In the crisis of the summer of 1947 almost the first step taken by the Government was to press for more hours to be worked by the miners. At meetings with the Prime Minister and his colleagues on July 30 and subsequently, the miners' representatives were asked by Mr. Morrison and Mr. Bevin to go back to the eight-hour day. This was felt to be an astonishing proposal, in view of the hundred years' struggle for a shorter working-day. In addition, the union was able to show that this would not produce the extra coal required. The union, however, was willing to do anything possible and offered extra shifts on Saturdays. The Government's conditions for this would have deprived the miners of overtime payment, as laid down in the five-day week agreement signed only three months before. For a time it was deadlock. The negotiations continued and eventually agreement was reached to extend working hours for a six months period from November 1, 1947. Following the N.U.M. Conference on October 10 accepting the agreement, a Scottish Miners' Conference on October 20 heard a report from Vice-President[1] John Wood and took the following decision, with only four votes against:

[1] On the sudden death of Alexander Cameron in May 1947, John Wood succeeded him as Vice-President, having been elected with a branch vote of £9873 : 11 : 2, the runners-up being A. K. Davidson with a vote of £5676 : 9 : 7, and D. Sim with a vote of £4537 : 1 : 9. In June 1948 Wood was re-elected with a vote of £19,026 : 6 : 2, the runner-up being E. McGhee with a vote of £5991 : 13 : 7. Traditionally branch votes in the Scottish Area are returned in terms of £ s. d.

That this Conference, having considered the report of the National Executive Committee on the negotiations which have taken place at the request of the Government on the question of increased hours, recommend all branches in the Scottish Area to work a minimum of eleven days per fortnight. This will mean the working of two Saturdays per month, with a 6½ hour shift, and payment shall be in accordance with the National Agreement, i.e. time-and-a-half for time actually worked. (October 20, 1947.)

The policy pursued by the Foreign Office had its effect on Government economic policy. Sir Stafford Cripps, in charge of economic affairs, laid stress on harder work, more exports to enable the country 'to pay its way'. On the grounds that it was necessary to prevent inflation, Cripps concentrated on the prevention of wage increases. This was called freezing of wages, or wage-restraint. The Southport T.U.C. (September 1 to 5, 1947) was overshadowed by the general economic crisis. A report pledging full co-operation to the Government, and in particular opposing the reintroduction of a Control of Engagement Order, was carried: and in place of a resolution to endorse the Miners' Charter a declaration on 'The Miners and the Nation', which pledged support to the miners in efforts they would make to overcome the economic crisis, was approved by Congress. The T.U.C. General Council agreed to give their support to the targets set. By December 1947 the General Council, in a circular to trade unions, requested the executives to exercise 'even more restraint' in wage-claims, but also asked that the Government should drop its plan to interfere in wage negotiations. By the beginning of February 1948 the Government's proposals were made known in detail in a White Paper.[1] The General Council's policy statement was to be tabled before a meeting of trade union executives called for March 24.

Meanwhile in Scotland the proposal for the freezing of wages had given rise to animated discussion in the branches. This was carried into the Delegate Conference (February 9, 1948) which showed itself opposed to the wage-freeze by a two to one majority. The matter had arisen from a Scottish Executive minute, containing a December resolution from one of the branches, to pledge full support to the Labour Govern-

[1] Statement on Personal Incomes, Costs and Prices (February 4, 1948, Cmd. 7321).

ment, as 'the best Government in the history of our country, in its activities nationally and internationally'. This resolution, moved by Mr. Cowan of Kelty, met with immediate opposition from Mr. Stewart of Glencraig. He was seconded by Mr. Kerr of Elphinstone who pointed out that the official cost-of-living index (June 1947 = 100) by November 1947 had risen to 103. He said:

To meet this it would have been necessary to raise an average wage of £5 to £5 3s. in this period, in order to purchase the same amount of goods. Between January and November 1947, prices of 48 different food commodities have been increased while the price of only six has been reduced. Government spokesmen, supported by the Tories, are saying that there is too much money chasing too few goods, but it can be proved that the increase in capitalist profits far outstrips any increase in wages. (February 9, 1948.)

A keen debate followed. The freezing of wages ran like a blue thread through the discussion. In the course of it Mr. Moffat intervened as follows:

On the question of the pegging of wages, the Trade Union movement in this country had not committed itself to such a policy and if it did so it would be abdicating so far as representing the interests of its members was concerned. No delegate in the Conference stating that he supported the policy of freezing wages could justify that to the members whom he represents. Even in the days of Tory Government Sir Walter Citrine, as Secretary of the T.U.C., forced that Government to consult the Trade Unions before taking any action, and the Trade Unions could not be expected now to abandon that principle when we have a Labour Government. The policy of freezing wages had been announced by the Government without consultation with the Unions. Did the delegates support that national policy 100 per cent?

Our conditions as Trade Unionists under this policy would be worse in two ways: (1) By a direct attack on wages, reducing the standard of living; and (2) by freezing wages and allowing prices to rise, as they were doing. No later than 31st December 1947, the General Council of the British T.U.C. had asked the Government not to freeze wages, but to freeze profits and prices as a means of preventing inflation in this country. Never in the history of the country had such high profits been made by the capitalist class. To show that this policy being pursued was one which might have been adopted by a Government of the enemies of the workers was not an attempt to undermine the Government, but an attempt to show that the continuation of this policy would be playing into the hands of the

Tories. . . . To accept the motion would be to tie ourselves to a policy of reducing the standard of living not only of the miners but of the whole working class.

Here Mr. McCann, Gartshore 3 and 12, interrupted to point out that the Government left a loophole with regard to the wages in the under-manned industries, of which the mining industry was one.

The President replied that it seemed that Mr. McCann was in favour of freezing the wages of other workers, provided there was a loophole by which this would not apply to his own industry. But last year, as the members knew, the Union had had a very stiff struggle to get the Coal Board to grant the 10s. per week increase in the minimum rates. That was before any Government pronouncement on this issue. The delegates had to bear in mind that negotiations for a national wages structure were on foot. If, in the previous circumstances, it had been difficult to obtain the increase of 10s., obviously they would get even less with this Government policy in operation. (Minute 19, February 9, 1948, pp. 314–15.)

After Mr. Cowan had again spoken in favour of the motion a vote was taken. The motion was rejected by 68 votes to 30.

A week later the Scottish Executive Committee meeting on February 16 had to discuss and decide on a branch motion:

We, the members of Elphinstone Branch of the N.U.M., deplore the attitude of the Government in deserting their 1945 election pledges. We protest very strongly against the peg-wages policy announced by the Prime Minister in Parliament. We resent most strongly the imposition of this policy on the working class of our country, while there is no serious attempt to control rents, interest and profits. (February 16, 1948.)

This, after a very prolonged discussion, was endorsed unanimously. All the Scottish Executive, whether or not they were strong supporters of the Labour Government's general policy, were affected by the report of the House of Commons debate (February 12) and by the description of 'how Tory Member after Tory Member had reason to congratulate the Government on its courageous step in freezing wages'.

When the N.U.M. National Executive came to consider the T.U.C.'s policy of conditional support for wage-freezing (March 11, 1948) the Scottish members strongly opposed the General Council's attitude, which declared for wage-stabilisa-

MINERS' ROWS, COWDENBEATH, FIFE, 1953

OLD SCOTTISH HOUSES, SHOTTS, 1953

tion provided there were safeguards for the under-manned industries; for workers 'below a reasonable standard of subsistence'; for wage-differentials; and for increases based on higher output. There was a further proviso that the Government should pursue a vigorous policy of reducing prices and profits. When it was moved that the miners should support the General Council at the Conference of Trade Union Executives, Moffat for Scotland proposed that the matter should go back to the districts for decision, since the rank and file were entitled to express their views. A vote was taken on this and by 17 votes to 8 it was decided to support the General Council. Reporting to the Scottish Executive, the President stated that while they had to accept the implied refusal to negotiate for further general increases, 'he personally was not prepared to accept the situation that miners in Scotland should continue to work for an average day wage of 3s. to 4s. less than miners in England, or for average piece rates 7s. to 10s. a shift less than in other districts in England'. (March 15, 1948.)

There was animated discussion in the Scottish Executive. Mr. Miller and Mr. McArthur both felt there should have been a Special National Conference of the N.U.M. and Mr. Sim predicted 'that no real action was going to be taken in regard to reduction in prices and profits'. It was agreed unanimously to record a protest against the action taken. When the ensuing letter embodying this resolution (together with one from Kent) came up before the N.U.M. Executive on April 1, it was decided 'that the letters be received'. From time to time branches protested against the wage-freeze policy, to which the Scottish Executive Committee could but reply that they, too, had sent their protest in the spring of 1948 and that it was impossible on this matter to take action separately from the rest of the coal-fields.

But though the T.U.C. General Council got the support of the N.U.M. (through the majority vote of its N.E.C.) at the Conference of Executives on March 24, 1948, its standpoint was not carried unanimously. The wage-freeze was adopted on a card vote by 5,421,000 to 2,032,000: and the minority included many unions in engineering, distributive trades and civil service. Events proved that the saving clauses in the

T.U.C. General Council's document were not very solid supports at an arbitration tribunal. Once the General Council had endorsed 'the principles which it was proposed should be applied to wage-claims', the ground had been yielded. The agreement in principle stood out: the qualifications were ignored.

Six months later at the 1948 T.U.C. a resolution[1] to end the wage-freeze was defeated by a similar but slightly smaller majority (5,207,000 to 2,184,000). By the time another twelve months were passed, there was another autumnal crisis (when the U.S.A. insisted on devaluation of sterling to $2.80 to the £) and the General Council got a larger majority for its policy. Within the trade unions, however, there was a lot of disagreement. This increased as the months went past. It was nowhere shown more than among the Scottish miners, who played a considerable part in the reversal of this policy.

3. THE SCOTS FIGHT THE WAGE-FREEZE

The wage-freeze, in the form accepted by the Conference of Trade Union Executives in March 1948, had allowed for advances to lower-paid workers generally and for those industries where man-power was short (as in mining) and for the need to maintain wage differentials. But it soon became clear that employers were not bound by these stipulations. By autumn 1948, when the T.U.C. had confirmed the wage-freeze, those who were opposed to it, like the Scots, found a cold climate both within their own British union and in relations with the Coal Board and the Government. The Government standpoint was made very clear. It coincided with a statement of the Board's policy by Sir Eric Young that 'the honeymoon period is now over'. The policy of the N.C.B. was, Lord Hyndley said, 'that there must

---

[1] 'Whilst appreciating the efforts of the General Council to formulate a policy for real wages and to combat inflation, Congress considers that the measures so far adopted by the Government have not prevented a decline of wages in relation to prices and profits which are still rising, and therefore calls on the Government to introduce statutory control of profits and dividends.

'Congress further declares that the present level of wages is insufficient to maintain a reasonable or adequate standard of living, and cannot therefore support a policy designed to stabilise wages at their present levels.' This was moved by the late W. C. Stevens for the Electrical Trades Union.

be no further increases in wages and other costs'. The course of this argument, which finally led to the Scottish Area putting forward to the N.U.M. its demand for an increase for the lower-paid workers, came from the post-war rise in the cost of living. Since summer 1947, when a new index of retail prices was instituted, the cost of living had been rising. Under the War Additions Agreement of 1940 this gave the miners a right, or at any rate a substantial claim, to have their wages increased correspondingly. When, however, this question was raised in the early autumn of 1948, based on the 1940 Agreement, it was met by the Coal Board in no favourable way. Lord Hyndley raised other questions of production, absenteeism, reducing costs, etc., and the statements of Mr. Gaitskell, the new Minister of Fuel and Power,[1] were felt to be very frigid towards any improvement in miners' conditions.

What was the main consideration the miners' side had in mind? It was the question of the lower-paid workers who were being reduced to a more and more difficult plight by the rise in the cost of living. Nowhere was there more difficulty experienced than in the Scottish coal-fields. Consequently, the Scottish Area put forward a resolution to the Annual Conference of the N.U.M. which was passed in the following form:

This Conference of the National Union of Mineworkers instructs the National Executive Committee to endeavour to secure a substantial increase in the minimum rates for all lower-paid workers. (July 7, 1949.)

William Pearson, moving the resolution, said that it dealt 'with the conditions of the vast majority of the men'. The real wages of the miners had fallen by 3 per cent in the past eighteen months because of the increased price of foodstuffs.

I remember attending the special Trades Union Congress in March, 1948, and I listened to Vincent Tewson, the General Secretary of the T.U.C., and he stated, 'I give you my word, prices will come down'. I have heard from this rostrum this week that prices will come down. But up to the present time the tendency has been for prices to go up. If we take Sir Stafford Cripps' statement yesterday, we are even going to get less food than we have been getting during the course of the war and since the war.

[1] The previous Minister, E. Shinwell, who had worked well with the union and had given promises on the carrying out of the Miners' Charter, had been transferred by the Prime Minister to the War Office in summer 1947.

I want to warn the National Coal Board that if they are tough with the miners, never forget that the miners can also be tough, and very tough, and the sooner they understand that the better it will be for everyone within this industry. The N.C.B. will also argue, as Lord Hyndley stated from this very rostrum, that they must close their ears to any claim until the deficiency of 1947 is wiped out; and in my calculation if we stick to that policy, then lower-paid workers will not get an increase for a further 13 years. That is what their policy will mean, and we cannot accept such a policy as that. Further, they will argue that they cannot consider a wage increase until production is increased. But I want to point out that every year since 1947 output has increased, and not a penny—not one penny piece—has gone to the lower-paid workers since November, 1947. Therefore if there is talk that the wages of the lower-paid workers will depend on increased output, there is the answer, and I want you to study that. I extend a very hearty invitation to anyone to come to the Scottish coal-field to speak to the miners there and try to convince these £5 or £5 : 15s. a week men that they are getting a square deal. That invitation stands to anyone who cares to take advantage of it. I also want to ask this: How many leaders in this trade union, or how many within the N.C.B., are prepared to send their own sons down the pit for such a miserable wage? And if it is not good enough for our own sons or for the sons of those within the N.C.B., then it is not good enough for the ordinary miner, and the quicker we understand that the better it will be for everyone.

My last point is this: If we do not lead this fight for an increased wage for the lower-paid workers, the lower-paid workers will lead it themselves. (N.U.M. Annual Conference, 1949.)

Other speakers had supported Pearson, when there came an intervention from the President, Sir William Lawther, who said:

Is it not far better for the Minister, who is invited here, to tell you the stark naked truth rather than to teem a lot of oil down your backs and create the impression that things are simple and easy, speaking as if there were not a crisis? All I can say is that we should be living in a fool's paradise if we believe we are going to surmount this crisis in the way suggested....

I am against allowing anything to go forward when we do not know where it is likely to lead us, and therefore I am asking that this resolution should be remitted to the Executive Committee in order that they may discuss the matter and face up to the harsh realities.

This statement created a tense atmosphere in the conference: but in his brief reply to the discussion Pearson contented himself with reminding the Chairman of his own previous decisions and saying 'he has no right abusing his position as Chairman of this Conference to try and say something that was contrary to the decision of his Executive Committee'.

The resolution was carried unanimously but the incident just related made a deep impression on the Scots, who felt that the fight against the wage-freeze was by no means over.

It was felt in the Scottish Executive that when the N.U.M. opened up negotiations with the Coal Board for an increase in wages for the lower-paid workers, one of the arguments which would be used against them, and used effectively, would be the statement made by Sir William Lawther: and that the only way to combat this would be to invite him to speak at meetings in the Scottish coal-field. From the prevailing mood of the miners which he would find at these meetings, it was hoped he would publicly withdraw his statement in view of the information he obtained. Accordingly a letter went to Sir William Lawther, who replied that he would be pleased to come to Scotland 'to outline Union policy'.

Meanwhile temper was rising in the Scottish coal-fields. By the middle of September 1949 unofficial stoppages had begun to take place. A week later there were seventeen pits affected and 5161 men idle. By September 20 the Secretary reported telegrams and letters from branches with resolutions for speed-up of the wages-structure negotiations to begin with: and ending with protests against the Government's wage-freezing policy, calling for 'a ballot vote of the British coalfield on the question'. (Minute No. 6, September 20, 1949.)

It was just at this time that Sir Stafford Cripps had announced the devaluation of sterling. When in the last week of September 1949 the N.U.M. Executive discussed the wages of lower-paid workers, the Scottish representatives pointed out the serious nature of the situation in their coal-field and urged speeding-up negotiations. But the matter was referred to the workers' side of the Joint National Negotiating Committee. The next meeting of the Scottish Executive, on October 10, had before it a further whole series of protesting letters and resolutions from branches. The resolutions, some of them in very vehement wording, all demanded a speed-up in negotiations on behalf of the lower-paid mine-workers. Some pits had sent resolutions direct to London. One of these, from a pit on strike, stated that in case of 'failure to get immediate redress, we demand a ballot vote of the British coal-field for strike action'. All condemned the wage-freeze policy, to which in some cases there were put forward positive alternatives. For example, from Manor Powis:

... pressure should be brought to bear upon the Government to secure stricter control, cuts in prices, heavier taxation on the high profits of the capitalists and a reconsideration of the over-generous compensation to the former coal-owners in order to greatly reduce the amount now paid in interest which is proving to be a crippling burden on the coal mining industry.

With particular vehemence branch after branch criticised Sir William Lawther. A comparatively mild example gives the tone of these criticisms:

We deeply deplore and roundly condemn the statements of our National President, Sir Wm. Lawther, at the Porthcawl Conference and at the T.U.C., when he called all workers 'criminals' who dared to ask for increased wages to meet the rising cost of living.

These statements are a betrayal of the interests of miners and all workers alike who are suffering under the burden of rising living costs, soaring profits and extortionate compensation payments to former bosses.

The Scottish Executive decided to forward copies of the letters dealing with lower-paid workers' wages to the N.U.M. in London so 'that the tension existing in the Scottish coalfield would be made known to them'.

4. SIR WILLIAM LAWTHER IN SCOTLAND

It was mid-October 1949 before meetings could be arranged at which the National President, Sir William Lawther, could address the Scottish miners. He spoke at several meetings, but the most important was his address to the Scottish Area Conference in Edinburgh. The purpose of this Conference was 'to discuss the decisions of the Annual N.U.M. Conference and particularly those in regard to wages submitted by Scotland and a number of other districts and the attitude of the National President, Sir William Lawther, at Conference on that discussion'.

Sir William Lawther began by reading the N.U.M. Conference unanimous resolution (July 7) on lower-paid workers' wages, and told how a memorandum had been prepared setting out various proposals for amendment of the War Additions Agreement of 1940 to meet the requirements of the National Conference decision, in the hope that thereby the Coal Board, or, failing agreement, the National Tribunal, could be persuaded to concede the claim. He added that the next meeting of the National Executive would decide whether or not the case should be placed before the Board:

He went on to deal with the changes which had taken place since the Annual Conference, saying that the Union could not separate itself from the outside world. Discussions had taken place in Parliament as a result of devaluation and regard must be paid to this situation. Within a few months we would be faced again with the responsibility of deciding whether to pursue the pathway taken over the past four years or to go back to a period of reaction. Whatever steps the Union might take with regard to the wages application must therefore be considered in the light of all the circumstances. At the International Miners' Conference this month a statement had been made regarding progress since the last meeting in 1938, and in no country, having regard to the standard of living operating, had there been changes so vital and fundamental as in our own country. In arguing a case before either the Coal Board or the Tribunal, we had to give due cognisance to the benefits received with regard to welfare, etc.

In relation to anomalies existing between different areas in wages, it was natural that everyone should wish to hold on to what advantage he had, and the changes demanded by the new wages structure called for a change in the whole policy and outlook of the organisation. At the beginning of the war the miners had been 82nd in the wages scale, while to-day they were at the top, and the average wage in the British coal-field in relation to the cost of living was higher than ever before. It was remarkable how, for the last few years, there had grown up a recognition of the fact that as well as rights Trade Unions had duties and responsibilities. . . .

In relation to our membership we had a two-fold task—to seek to reach that improvement of status which we believed vital, and at the same time to pay regard to the general situation. If we failed to do so before presenting our case, then we would have to face these things when the case was presented. He did not want to see any action the miners might take wrecking the structure which was giving to the common people a higher standard and a bigger share than ever before. Within the next few weeks the members would be faced with the steps taken by the National Consultative Council to bring home to the miners an appreciation of what was required in these, the most dire circumstances that we as a nation ever faced. (Minute 9, October 15, 1949, pp. 173–4.)

At the conclusion of his address, questions were showered on Sir William Lawther, whose replies were duly minuted. In the discussion that followed each speaker expressed criticism of Sir William Lawther's address. Here are given the first four speakers in the debate as they are set down in the minutes:

In the discussion following questions, Mr. Peaston, Ormiston, said that in the opinion of his branch, if devaluation was going to have any effect on wage claims it should be that of strengthening the claim for an increase for lower-paid workers. His branch, he said, was very attentive to the role played by the President and if he was to retain their support he would have to come closer to their aspirations and desires. No section of the British workers was more aware of the economic situation of the country than were the Scottish miners, but when Sir William asked them to take this situation into account he did not go into details about the effect that this economic situation and the devaluation of the pound was bound to have upon the standard of living of the lower-paid workers. Nobody could deny that there would be a considerable increase in the cost of living and therefore there would be an even stronger demand from the miners for an increase to meet this. The suggestion might be made that the needs of the lower-paid workers could be met by the sacrifice of the workers in the more highly paid districts, but the Scottish miners would strongly oppose such a policy.

Mr. Murray, Kames Branch, said that he had been instructed by his branch that, if the President had nothing constructive to put forward, he should ask that consideration be given to the resolution recently submitted by Kames Branch for a ballot vote in the coalfield for strike action. It was fifteen months since he had attended the N.U.M. Conference at which Mr. Abe Moffat had moved a resolution calling for a national wages structure and although this had been accepted nothing appeared to have been done about it. At the same Conference the Scottish Area had tried to have remitted back that part of the report dealing with wage freezing, in order to get the mind of the membership, but Sir William had refused to permit discussion, although it was obvious that it had a bearing on a national wages structure, which would cost a lot of money.

Mr. Alex. Moffat, E.C., said that the Conference was intended to deal with the wages demands of the miners, particularly with regard to the lower-paid workers, but the President's speech had given no encouragement regarding their position. Very strong feeling existed throughout the Scottish coalfield on this wage demand, and in his opinion a much more forceful presentation of the case could have been put forward by the President. Sir William had said that in other countries they were being told that payment must be based on merit, but to suggest that that did not exist here was to contradict the recent History of *The Miners* endorsed by him, which showed that the wages of British miners had always been based on production; but now we were being asked to increase production in a situation where increased production brought more money to the face workers, but harder work and no more pay to the oncost. In these circumstances we were being asked to exercise restraint in wage claims, but the President's acceptance of a spare-time paid post with the Miners' International, on top of his Union salary, did not indicate restraint. With regard to the drive for increased production, the position of the lower-paid workers was going to create a bottle-neck in the industry which would require stronger action than just examining it. If the claim for railway workers of £4 12s. 6d. per week was turned down because it was an uneconomic proposition, what were the chances for the miners? Did it mean that this examination of the position was going to involve a lot of talk but no gains for the miners? While it was true that it was only in July of this year that the resolution on the wages of lower-paid workers had been passed, this was not the case with regard to the new wages structure. In these circumstances, when Sir Stafford had said that the £ was now worth only 9s., a demand should be made from this Conference for the immediate tabulation of the new wages structure and for a setting forth of the Union's proposals on this question, and also for immediate action regarding the wages of lower-paid workers.

Mr. Comerford, Comrie Branch, expressed surprise at the attitude of the National President in relation to compensation to the former owners of nationalised industries. In his opinion the people who elected the Labour Government would not object to the suspension of these payments. It was true that certain people such as shareholders, etc., would object, but these people would be unlikely to vote Labour whether or not this policy continued. This was the best possible time for the suspension of these payments and it would rally the people in support of the Labour Government.

These four speakers were followed by Mr. McCann, of Gartshore 3/12, and by Mr. Brannan, of Kingshill No. 2, who in conclusion suggested

that unless something very concrete emerged from the negotiations pending, no power on earth would stop the Scottish miners from coming out on strike. In the recent series of strikes he had only been able to control his men by the promise that in the future something would be gained from the impending negotiations.

These were followed by Mr. Fullerton of Bardykes, and by the Secretary, Mr. William Pearson, who remarked:

In some quarters the view was being expressed that higher wages meant higher absenteeism, but he did not accept this. Absenteeism among face-workers was higher than among oncost, but it must be recognised that the face-worker was subject to more illness, accidents and greater fatigue than any other section in the industry. With regard to the statement on merit, in his opinion the trouble was that payment was not made on merit, because if it were, with increased production oncost wages would be higher now. As far as the present economic position was concerned, nobody with a sense of responsibility could be unmindful of it, but he was concerned about the fact that while the standard of living of the lower-paid workers in particular went down, the profits accruing from industry were continually rising. No one could accept restraint with regard to wages in such a situation.

Then Mr. Steele, of Harthill East, said that the National President

had made no real mention of the need for an increase in wages, and he had got the impression that he was paving the way for an announcement later that the resolution would be abandoned. Mr. Steele, with reference to the appeal for restraint, instanced recent statements quoting directors' fees, dividends declared, etc., to show that no restraint was being exercised among capitalist circles. He said that he had been mandated to tell Sir William, on behalf of 650 miners, more than one third of whom were piece-rate workers, that they demanded an increased wage for lower-paid workers. They wished to operate inside the constitution, but were prepared to overstep it if it did not prove effective. As long as compensation was paid to the former coalowners, so long would the miners press their demands.

Finally, Mr. McDonagh, of Dewshill, 'agreed that the economic situation was serious and in order to meet it called for a survey of the country's finances to provide the basis for the reimposition of a capital levy'. He urged the need for international trade and co-operation and denounced with vehemence the action of Sir Wm. Lawther in opposing the decision of the Scottish miners to support their French mining comrades.

Following the discussion the National President, Sir William Lawther, after some general remarks on devaluation, replying to criticism that he had said nothing as to whether or not the wage claim should go forward, said that there

was no argument at all in relation to whether or not a case could be made out. It was purely a question of the time and the circumstances in relation to it. . . . His salary, Sir William said, had been mentioned, and he explained that it had been shown in the annual balance sheets. It was £994 per annum, together with free house and coal. Annual Conference decided this. As far as the Miners' International was concerned, this had not been fixed by the Miners' E.C., but the amount paid for the last two years was £150 per annum. On the charge that he was preparing the Conference for a withdrawal of the wages claim, he said that that, if it were intended, was not his job but that of the National E.C. It might well be that there would be a National Conference upon this question. Referring to the protests from Scottish branches, copies of which had been forwarded to him, he pointed out that other areas receiving the same wages had decided that the best way to help the Union, the nation and the Government was to do their utmost by withholding any demands.

Here Mr. Stobbs, E.C., indicated that this was not a statement of fact, since seven districts of the N.U.M. and three of its groups had submitted resolutions to Annual Conference on this issue. Sir William Lawther accepted the correction, but pointed to the efforts

being made by the Durham miners, who were holding meetings urging greater production without a word about wages. When he thought of the efforts made by men who preceded him to bring about changes, and when he saw these changes operated, he thought that it would be criminal on his part to let things happen the end of which would be worse than where we began. We had a constitution in which we had accepted arbitration machinery. Whatever the case presented, we were in honour bound to accept the decision given through that machinery. It was necessary to realise that so much was at stake and so serious was the position, that it was the duty of those who had been in the movement all their lives to see that nothing was done which would impede this forward progress.

Abe Moffat, the Scottish President, speaking from the chair, then emphasised the importance of meetings of that kind. He said that there must be no misunderstanding on the

question that the Scottish Area had no desire to break away from national agreements. This area would never be a party to that, nor would it be a party to demanding that miners in any other part of the coalfield should suffer reduction in wages in order to raise wages in Scotland. That would never prevent them from demanding justice for the Scottish miners, however, and when reference was made to meetings about production it was important to draw attention to what had been done in Scotland. On the 1947 Extended Hours Agreement, for instance, the President recently said that we were now getting 104,000 tons from the working of the extra Saturday. Of that one third was being produced from the Scottish coal-field, which had less manpower than many other districts. He quoted this in order to support the claim that Scottish miners were second to none as far as this aspect was concerned.

He wished to make plain with regard to compensation to former owners that the policy of the N.U.M., as adopted unanimously at the last Annual Conference, was contained in the following resolution:

> In view of the many appeals by the Government and the National Coal Board for reduction of costs in the mining industry, this Conference of the National Union of Mineworkers instructs the National Executive Committee, in conjunction with the Trades Union Congress and Executive Committee of the Labour Party, to consider the effect of the present policy whereby the entire burden of compensation payments to ex-colliery owners is placed on the individual industry concerned and to examine the possibilities of a review of this policy.

This was a recognition that there was something wrong, if not with the amount of compensation then with the method of payment, and a recognition that as an industry we could not go on meeting this huge commitment.

Whatever might be the disagreement on the economic problems confronting the industry, however, there was no disagreement as to the fight against the Tories, the enemies of the working class.

Thus ended the mid-October Conference of the Scottish miners. A year was to pass before decision could be reached on the claim of the lower-paid workers; and it was not such as to satisfy the Scots, as we shall see.

5. THE WAGE-FREEZE AND THE T.U.C.

Despite the decisions of the N.U.M. Annual Conference at Porthcawl in July 1949 and the confrontation of the Scottish delegates with Sir William Lawther in the autumn, the struggle within the union against the wage-freeze and on behalf of the lower-paid workers was by no means ended. In the autumn the N.U.M. National Executive Committee, by a majority, decided to ask the N.C.B. for an increase under the cost-of-living Agreement—the whole of which would go to help the lower-paid workers. Scarcely had this decision been taken when a new factor against the prosecution of this wage-claim came into play. This was the influence cast by the

T.U.C. General Council, and behind it the Government, for an intensification of the wage-freeze. The devaluation crisis was followed by a stiffening of T.U.C. policy expressed as 'a rigorous restraint on all increases in wages, salaries and dividends'. Further, it was proposed that wages affected by cost-of-living sliding scales should be stabilised at their existing figure. This proposition, which would immediately affect the claim for lower-paid workers on the basis of the cost of living, was argued strongly within the N.E.C. by the two members who sat on the General Council. Furthermore it was proposed that when this and other propositions put forward by the T.U.C. General Council came to be discussed at a further Conference of the Trade Union Executives, the N.U.M. should, as before, continue to support wage-restraint. Within the N.U.M. delegation at the September 1949 T.U.C. the Scottish representatives with others had argued strongly for the ending of the wage-freeze, but found themselves in a minority. They were still in a minority in the later autumn on the question of the intensification of the wage-freeze which would in addition hold up the claim for the lower-paid mine-workers.

But when the next month came and the T.U.C. General Council's statement was made available, the Scots held a Delegate Conference (December 12) where it was all thrashed out. Abe Moffat, the President, made a statement of great importance. After referring to the T.U.C. new proposals and to the 'policy of wage-restraint or wage-freeze or wage stabilisation (the General Council called it wage-restraint)' which they had been told to accept (in March 1948) 'on the distinct understanding and condition that the Government would pursue a policy not just of stabilising but of substantially reducing prices and profits', he went on:

Unfortunately for us, while wage-restraint was put into operation, prices and profits have increased substantially since 1948. Later on we were told by the T.U.C. to continue that policy on the understanding that it would not apply to lower-paid workers, and some of us even amongst the rank-and-file were inclined to agree with that policy on the understanding that we would be free to negotiate for lower-paid workers.

To-day, however, an entirely different policy is put forward to us.

The question of reduction in prices and profits has gone by the board; because they are increasing. The question of leaving the door open for lower-paid workers is also finished; because according to the T.U.C. document your cost of living can rise six points and you have still to accept your existing wages as being satisfactory.

After referring to the increased coal got in 1949 with less man-power than in 1948, he pointed out that for industrial workers generally the cost of living since 1947 'had gone up by 12 points and wages by 8 points, making a reduction in real wages of 4 points', and went on:

But if you consider the mining industry, which has received no increase from 1947, and then relate it to the 12 points increase in the cost of living, it is quite evident that speaking relatively the miners' position is worse than the general position.

It would be correct to say that on that basis itself, while we had £5 : 15s. for underground workers in 1947, if you take into account the increase of 12 points in the cost of living, that £5 : 15s. is only worth £5 : 3s. to-day. On the same calculation, if a surface-worker had £5 in 1947, then in actual value his wage is not worth more than £4 : 9s. to-day. Then we have to consider that you are still being asked to forego your claim for the cost of living agreement until the cost of living goes up another six points. There is no doubt about the fact that the cost of living is going up and will go up, then on the T.U.C. estimate itself of a rise of six points your £5 : 15s. in 1947 will only be worth £4 : 15 : 6, and the £5 of the man on the surface will only be worth £4 : 5s. That, therefore, is the position we have to discuss: that is what we are being asked to consider by the T.U.C.

Now at the last National Executive meeting another attempt was made to get us to postpone our claim. It was put forward by the Vice-President, who happens to be a member of the General Council of the T.U.C. In supporting the policy of the T.U.C. he proposed that without prejudice to our claim we should suspend the claim for the lower-paid workers until the full document of the T.U.C. had been published.

An amendment was moved to that, suggesting that it was a wrong policy to ask to suspend our claim on the strength of a document which had not been submitted, and that therefore we should adhere to our previous decision until such time as the full document was submitted. That amendment was carried by a very narrow majority —14 votes to 12—and that places us in the same position as we were in on the previous occasion, when I reported to this Conference that as far as the policy of the Executive was concerned they were still proceeding with the claim on behalf of the lower-paid workers.

It was made clear to the delegates that they were at a

critical stage in their union's history. There was no need for them to deceive themselves or to believe that, if they agreed to suspend the claim for lower-paid workers, they could still press other demands to which they had already committed themselves and which would cost more than this claim for the lower-paid workers. As Moffat said:

If you agree to the suspension of the cost of living agreement and a rigorous restraint on incomes, salaries and wages, it means also in the same breath the suspension of your claim for holidays with pay, the claim for pensions for the miners, and the claim which the miners in this coal-field have been demanding for the last two and a half years, namely, a wages structure for the British mining industry. (Minute 15, December 12, 1949, Area Conference, pp. 307–11.)

Having thus reviewed the situation and conveyed to the delegates what this policy would mean, the President concluded his statement as follows:

If anyone came along and made a clear-cut proposal that miners' wages should be reduced from £5 : 15s. to £4 : 15 : 6 for underground and from £5 to £4 : 5s. for surface workers, what would happen? Not one of us here could say truthfully that such a policy could ever be condoned by a miners' trade union, but there is no difference between that and the other policy which increases the cost of living and reduces the value of real wages to the same extent as a straight reduction in wages. To operate such a policy would be a condemnation of all the traditions and fighting spirit of the miners in the days gone by, and would be gross betrayal of the lower-paid workers in this industry.

That your Executive Committee has discussed and discussed from every angle; and your Scottish Executive has taken a unanimous decision to oppose this policy of suspending our claim. We had no alternative, because every time we discussed this question either at Annual Conference or Area Conference your delegates (and I presume on the instructions and mandates of your own membership) have demanded, and rightly demanded, a substantial increase in the wages of the lower-paid workers in this industry. We also adhere to that policy, because at the N.U.M. Annual Conference this year, in spite of efforts to put it back and postpone it, as a result of a resolution from this coal-field it was eventually agreed unanimously that the N.U.M. should proceed for a substantial increase in the minimum rates. We see nothing even in this T.U.C. document which should change our attitude.

There was no dubiety about the delegates' views. Unanimously they decided:

That this Conference of Scottish Miners, having discussed the

T.U.C. report calling for a rigorous restraint on all wages and suspension of claims under cost of living agreements, emphatically
declares its strongest opposition to such a policy. Any attempt to
suspend negotiations on the present claim for lower-paid workers in
the mining industry, as decided at Annual Conference, will have
serious repercussions in the coal-field. We instruct our delegates
attending the Special Conference on 11th January 1950, to press for
the claim on behalf of the lower-paid workers; to call upon the
National Executive Committee to speed up the negotiations; and to
call for a ballot vote of the whole coal-field to determine the attitude
of the members. (December 12, 1949.)

Thus mandated the President and Secretary went to the meeting in London. There they were successful in getting a decision that an N.U.M. Conference on December 29, 1949, should
be followed by a vote of the men in the coal-fields. When the
N.U.M. Conference was held the policy of supporting the
intensification of the wage-freeze, as carried by a majority of
the N.U.M. Executive, was endorsed. But this decision was
reversed when it came to the vote in the coal-fields. By the
second week in January 1950 the miners' coal-field vote
showed 518,000 voting against and only 147,000 voting for
acceptance of the T.U.C. policy of wage-restraint. In Scotland the vote was unprecedented, not a single branch having
voted in favour of the N.E.C.'s recommendation to approve
the T.U.C. document on wages policy.

Further, when the Conference of Trade Union Executives
was held on January 12, 1950, the N.U.M. vote was cast
against the continuance of wage-freeze. The Scots' demand
for a coal-field vote had reaped a rich harvest.

The report to the Scottish Executive says: 'At the conference a vicious attack had been made on the miners by Mr.
Arthur Deakin and Mr. Tom Williamson, with references to
the high wages being paid in the mining industry. Their attention had been drawn, however, to the fact that there was still
no rush of new entrants to the industry.'[1]

The T.U.C. General Council, who had secured a seven to
one majority at their September Congress, now found that
majority had been narrowed down until it was only seven to
six. The actual figures were 4,243,000 for wage-restraint and
3,606,000 against.

[1] The industry was losing man-power at the rate of 1000 a week.

SCOTTISH MINERS' GALA DAY, 1953
Aneurin Bevan with miners' leaders at the head of the procession

SCOTTISH MINERS' GALA DAY, 1953
Section of the huge assembly

When this happened the Scots immediately took the initiative in asking for a Special N.U.M. Executive meeting to get a decision to proceed with the wage-claim.

Several other industries were also proceeding with their wage-claims. During the spring and summer of 1950 it became clear that it would be hard for the General Council, acting in accord with the Government, to secure the effective operation of the intensified wage-freeze. Accordingly at the September 1950 Congress the General Council put forward a resolution for a modified form of wage-restraint; but by this time the rise in the cost of living, coupled with the failure to effect the restriction of profits, had caused a revulsion of feeling against the continuance of the wage-freeze. Consequently their new proposal was defeated, and a resolution calling on the General Council 'to abandon any further policy of wage restraint' was carried by 3,949,000 votes to 3,727,000.

6. THE CLAIM FOR THE LOWER-PAID WORKERS

The agitation against the freezing of wages and on behalf of the lower-paid workers had begun in 1948; but, as we have seen, though decided at the Porthcawl N.U.M. Conference, July 1949, the claim had by one means or another been postponed from month to month. It was not until February 1950 that the claim was put in. The N.C.B., which all this while had been standing aloof, now at last considered the claim. Its reply was in effect a rejection. The claim was that by the War Additions Agreement of 1940 the miners had a right to a cost-of-living increase, which would yield a sum of money enough to raise the wage of the lower-paid workers. The Board disputed this right. Further negotiations brought no settlement. The Scottish Annual Conference in June 1950 and the N.U.M. Annual Conference at Llandudno in July each passed a strongly-worded resolution for steps to be taken 'without further delay' on behalf of those whose earnings were described as 'insufficient to maintain a reasonable standard of life'. Meantime in Scotland discontent with the delays had led in July to unofficial strikes, mostly in Lanarkshire. A Special Scottish Conference was convened because of this and of the

Llandudno decisions. It heard and approved a report in which it was mentioned that a press statement of Sir William Lawther 'had precipitated the Scottish strike'; and that this was also 'aggravated by the Report of the National Coal Board', which showed 'a gross profit of £31,000,000'. A resolution was passed:

We express our profound disagreement with the attitude of the National Coal Board in rejecting the claim of the lower-paid workers within the mining industry.

We call upon the National Executive Committee to proceed immediately with the new claim as decided at the Annual Conference. In the event of the Coal Board rejecting this claim, we demand that the claim be submitted to the National Tribunal without further delay. In view of the Annual Conference decision, we call upon all Scottish mine-workers to return to work and to present a united front within the Union in support of the claim for the lower-paid workers.

Should there be any unnecessary delay in these negotiations we instruct the Executive Committee of the Scottish Area to convene a recall Conference of all Scottish branches to discuss what further action should be taken to secure an immediate increase in wages for all lower-paid mine-workers. (July 10, 1950.)

An animated discussion followed. It should be realised that while this discussion was taking place fifty-seven pits in Scotland were still out on strike, while seventeen had resumed or partially resumed work. Bitter criticisms were made of the National President, Sir William Lawther.

When the Coal Board on July 25 made an offer, which the union thought utterly inadequate, negotiation ended: when the matter went to arbitration, it was found that the abandonment by the T.U.C. of 'wage-restraint' had no effect on the National Reference Tribunal whose decisions were still conditioned by Government policy. Their Award on October 7 increased the Coal Board's July offer of £2¼ million by another £1¼ million, rescinded the War Additions Agreement of 1940 and referred the distribution of the increases back to the parties to the dispute. This did not please the Scottish miners, as may be seen from the resolution passed three weeks later:

That this Conference expresses profound dissatisfaction with the recent Award of the National Tribunal on the N.U.M. claim for increased wages for lower-paid workers in the mining industry.

While the decision of the Tribunal according to the Conciliation machinery is binding on both sides, it must be clearly understood that the global sum of £3½ million will in no way provide an adequate wage for lower-paid workers and, despite the greatest decline in man-power in living memory, will tend to drive many more miners away from the industry.

In view of the dissatisfaction in the coal-field, we call upon the National Executive Committee to give serious consideration to a new wages claim and to the advisability of changing the National Con-ciliation Machinery, which makes it compulsory to refer all national disputes to the National Tribunal. (October 30, 1950.)

Despite a Scottish effort to refer it back to the areas, which was over-ruled, the York Conference of the N.U.M. on November 2 accepted the Award. The new Agreement, signed on November 28, increased the national weekly minimum wage underground from £5 15s. to £6 (surface from £5 to £5 5s.) and consolidated the War Addition of 2s. 8d. a shift into the existing shift-rates.

A final comment on all these negotiations and on the struggle against the wage-freeze may be taken from the Minute of the Second Annual Youth Conference of the Scottish Area held on November 27, 1950. In Abe Moffat's address to Scotland's young miners, there was a short but telling section on wages, which ran as follows:

If the gentlemen who express grave alarm at the coal situation are really concerned about it, let them condemn the insulting wage award of the National Tribunal, and support the claim of the lower-paid miners for a rise of at least 12s. per week. Scotland can be proud of its performance in the battle for higher wages. It was on the initiative of the Scottish leaders that the N.U.M. 1949 National Con-ference accepted a resolution for a substantial increase in wages for the lower-paid workers, in spite of the opposition of some national leaders, whose salaries are several times larger than the annual in-come of the average lower-paid worker. It was on Scotland's initiative that the British miners were given the opportunity to vote on the policy of wage restraint. The overwhelming rejection of wage re-straint by the miners on that occasion was a major blow against those individuals, inside and outside our organisation, who were retarding the claims of the lower-paid miner.

It is on the initiative of the Scottish leaders that a strong fight is being conducted for an immediate new wage claim, and for a change in the conciliation machinery that will give the miners the right in future to decide whether or not they will use their immense power to ensure the acceptance of justifiable wage demands.

What the Scottish miners thought was made very clear by a unanimous resolution of the Delegate Conference on December 11, 1950, in which, after dealing with the Extended Hours Agreement, the final sentence ran:

Conference demands that all reforms included in the Miners' Charter, and a substantial increase in wages for lower-paid workers, is the only way to solve the manpower crisis in the mining industry. (December 11, 1950.)

7. THE EXTENSION OF HOURS CONTINUES

The Governmental and T.U.C. policy for greater exports and fewer imports comprised much more than the freezing of wages in its scope. It covered also the need for greater output of coal and more exports of coal. The concession required of the miners therefore was not only on wages but on hours of labour: and the request of the Government in summer 1947 had been granted and embodied in the Extended Hours Agreement. This was to last over the six winter months of 1947–8. Before the six months ended, the request to the miners had been renewed: and at the beginning of April 1948 it had been agreed for a further twelve months by the N.U.M. National Conference. This, in the shape of the eleven-day fortnight policy, was unanimously endorsed by the Scottish Area Conference on April 5, 1948. The policy was put to the branches, which carried it by a thirteen to one majority. During the spring of 1949, the extended hours were again continued. The Government in summer 1947 had estimated that the critical situation would last for two years but Mr. Herbert Morrison at that time had been confident that the man-power aim of 720,000 miners by the end of 1947 would be achieved. In fact, this aim was not reached. When in the late autumn of 1948 the new Minister of Fuel and Power, Mr. Hugh Gaitskell, had intimated that progressive amelioration of the miners' conditions of life could not go forward, the effect of this upon the supply of man-power was soon to be seen. The result was inevitable. The existing body of miners were asked to do what should have been the task of a greater total number.

Another year elapsed. Then at the beginning of April 1950 the National Executive of the N.U.M. decided on 'a continuation of the extension of hours agreement for a further period of twelve months'. The Scottish Committee accepted by a majority a motion moved by Alex. Moffat and seconded by John McArthur, that the decision be accepted and put into operation on the understanding that it would not again be decided before districts and branches had given their voice on the matter. A branch financial vote of the Scottish Area afterwards accepted the Agreement, but by a smaller majority than two years earlier. The dissatisfaction increased in the next twelve months and it became clear that what seemed to be tending to become automatic renewal of extended hours would not take place in the spring of 1951.

The dissatisfaction arose both on hours and wages. The cost of living had been rising since Vesting Day of January 1947. In these circumstances extended hours began to be seen as a menace to the miners' standard of living. For, it was argued, not only was the seven-and-a-half-hour day plus one winding time[1] coming to be only a formal right and a basis for overtime calculations; not only were the total hours and winding times extended to forty-seven hours in every week (when there was Saturday working). In practice this meant many more hours worked in the year than under the old nominal eleven-day fortnight in Scotland, when the pits were on the average more often idle than in 1947. But it meant also that the larger weekly earnings brought by this systematic overtime masked the inroads made by higher cost of living upon the miners' standard of life. In so far as the extra coal was produced, it masked also the failure of the authorities to make the industry sufficiently attractive in a five-day week to new entrants. In brief, the man-power problem was not solved. By the beginning of January 1951 the man-power problem was more serious than it had been at Vesting Day four years earlier. All these circumstances had contributed to the mounting dissatisfaction with any automatic renewal of the Extended Hours Agreement. Consequently, when the matter came to be discussed in the spring of 1951, the N.U.M. Conference decided to meet the Government's need for more coal

[1] Equivalent roughly for five days, to an over-all forty-hour week.

by reverting to ordinary shifts in June, July and August and thereafter to continue the working of extended hours as before.

8. WAGES AND REARMAMENT

Earlier, on January 3, 1951, the miners' N.E.C. had been invited to No. 10 Downing Street to meet the Prime Minister, the Foreign Secretary, the Chancellor of the Exchequer and other Ministers. Mr. Attlee explained that, with stocks low and falling man-power, there was the danger of a coal crisis (so much so that the Government had decided to import coal from the U.S.A.) and asked the miners to do what they could to avert it by getting more coal produced. The miners were willing to do everything possible: but when they pointed out some of the difficulties, including the recent wages award, they were told that another approach to the Coal Board would be received 'in a sympathetic spirit'.

This was indeed a reversal of previous attitudes. The reason, however, was not far to seek. Some weeks before it had been realised by the Government (the union had been telling them for a year or more) that in the absence of sufficient inducement for men to enter upon the arduous and dangerous work of this industry, man-power was falling rapidly. Moreover it had been announced in December 1950 that the amount to be expended in three years on rearmament at the request of the United States had been raised from the £3,600,000,000 decided upon (without parliamentary sanction) in August to the figure of £4,700,000,000. This was bound to affect the demand for coal.

Within a week the negotiations with the Coal Board had been carried through and the miners had been given a substantial increase, though less than they considered necessary. They asked for a 12s. increase in the minimum. They were offered 5s. at first. A day later agreement was reached on 7s. The national weekly minimum wage rose from £6 to £6 7s. underground (surface from £5 5s. to £5 10s.). It was unprecedented that within six weeks of the signing of the 5s. agreement based on the Award there should be a further increase of 7s. without any difficulty raised. It was not, however, all that had been asked for, and at their Conference the Scots resolution ran:

That this Conference of the Scottish Area of the N.U.M. accepts the report of the National Conference held in York, including the new wage increase.

We regret, however, that the full demands of the miners were not conceded by the National Coal Board, and we call upon the National Executive Committee to press for two weeks' holidays with pay, supplementary pensions to include our old miners, and a new wages structure.

Conference is of the opinion that we cannot maintain and increase the manpower so essential in this great basic industry unless these reforms are introduced without further delay. (Minute 27, Special Area Conference, January 23, 1951, pp. 435, 436.)

From January 1951 onwards the cost of living rose rapidly. The Scots had already decided on March 19 to press for an increase, this time for all grades and starting with a £7 10s. minimum. By summer 1951 the index was twenty-one points over 1947, and at the Scottish Annual Conference in June it could be stated that '£6 7s. was only worth £5 8s' and that 'in real wages the miners today are worse off than in 1947'. The Scottish resolution was not opposed in principle by the N.E.C. which, however, wanted a free hand to negotiate for an increase. But at the N.U.M. Annual Conference the Scottish resolution,[1] moved in a brilliant and convincing speech by Alex. Moffat, was carried unanimously. Though the Scots, continuing their pressure, urged immediate action, the negotiations on the claim did not begin until October 1951.

The Labour Cabinet, which had been in office since July 1945, had won through the General Election of February 1950 with a small majority; and, within another twenty months, had decided on the dissolution of Parliament. The General Election of November 1951 resulted in a small majority for the Conservative Party. Churchill was now in his seventy-seventh

[1] That this Conference calls upon the National Executive Committee to press for a £7 10s. minimum weekly wage for all underground workers, with corresponding adjustments in the wages and rates of all other grades employed in the mining industry. (July 1951.)

year: he had built a reputation on actions, in and out of office, some of which miners were not likely to forget. The Prime Minister, however, was pretty well aware of this. He too had his memories of the miners' unions: and he was not anxious to provoke any trouble in the opening weeks of his administration. Consequently the negotiations with the N.C.B. for a wage-increase which had already begun went forward without a hitch.

By December 7 an N.U.M. Special Conference recommended acceptance by 625,000 votes to 75,000. Scotland voted with the majority. The Scottish delegation then demanded a further card vote on their amendment (previously rejected within the N.E.C.) that the recommendation be sent to the Areas for ratification. The conference carried this by a small majority. Within eleven days the Areas accepted the Agreement by an overwhelming majority. The Agreement, signed December 31, 1951, but operative from five weeks earlier, raised the national minimum weekly wage of adult underground workers from £6 7s. to £7 : 0 : 6 (surface from £5 10s. to £6 : 1 : 6), and made some corresponding improvements for higher grades. Piece-workers underground were given 2s. 3d. a shift (to be called the '1951 Flat Rates') and those on the surface 1s. 11d.

This Agreement gave the biggest wage-increase since 1947. But as the Scottish Conference resolution pointed out, the £1 was only worth 14s. 3d. compared with 1945, and 'the new minimum wage of £7 : 0 : 6 for underground workers is therefore only valued at £5 according to the Treasury statement, which means that the miners are in the same position as they were in 1945'. (December 11, 1951.)

Early in 1952 the union was asked to continue the extended hours. Thereupon the Scottish Executive recommended opposition in principle to continuation, several branches having demanded this, on the following grounds (as put to the Scottish Conference of March 17, 1952, which endorsed the recommendation by 120 votes to 10):

In 1947 we had accepted the Extended Hours Agreement on the grounds that it was a temporary arrangement to tide the country over its economic difficulties. In 1952, however, it was obvious that our economic difficulties rather than improving were becoming more and more serious, so that obviously Saturday working had brought no solution. The Scottish Executive was of the opinion, therefore, that while in practice we had fought as a Union to establish the five-day week, that agreement would be made null and void if the working of extended hours continued indefinitely. They further felt that no matter how much coal was produced from Saturday work there was no guarantee that it would mean an improvement in our living conditions.

When discussing general conditions it was impossible not to take into account the particular position of Scotland itself. Having produced more output from Saturday work than any other district since the commencement of the Extended Hours Agreement, average piece rates in Scotland were 4s. 10d. per shift less than the average for Britain.

The majority vote, however, of the whole of the British coalfields had been in favour of the recommendation of the National Delegate Conference of March 14. Accordingly the Scottish Area decided to adhere to the continuation of the eleven-day fortnight from May 3, 1952 to April 30, 1953. The same procedure in the next year had the same result: and the extended hours were to be worked up to the spring of 1954. By then the miners as a whole had been for seven years working longer hours a week and producing more than at any time before.

9. NATIONAL COAL BOARD SAYS 'NO!'

The reduction in food subsidies by the Conservative Chancellor of the Exchequer had led an N.U.M. Conference (March 17, 1952) to declare its intention 'of insisting upon increases in wages and in payments to injured workmen to offset the effects of this Budget upon our members' living standards'. On this basis the delegates to the Scottish Annual Conference, held in Ayr on June 18 to 20, unanimously resolved 'for an increase in wages of 30s. per week for all mineworkers'. The N.U.M. Executive had already been preparing a claim and on this were congratulated in July by the Scarborough Annual Conference which confirmed the demand for 30s. The same month there was a meeting with those who employed the mine-workers. The N.C.B. completely rejected the claim. It was a blank refusal.

This caused widespread dissatisfaction in the coal-fields. There were big demonstrations of miners in Scotland. An Area Conference declared:

The refusal by the Coal Board of the miners' demand cannot be separated from the Government's anti-working class policy of wage-restraint. We pledge ourselves to support the campaign for 30s. wage increase and warn the Government that rejection of this claim will have very serious repercussions in the mining industry. (September 8, 1952.)

By the machinery of coal conciliation (which the Scottish miners two years earlier had urged should be amended) the national union was obliged as its next step to go before the Tribunal. Here the claim for 30s. met with the same fate. To the Scottish delegates, meeting on November 10, it seemed clear that it would be ridiculous to continue working organised overtime under the Extended Hours Agreement if earnings from this overtime were to be used against them in negotiations as an argument to buttress a refusal to increase rates of wages. For the rest their opinion of the conciliation machinery was sourly confirmed by the Award. Not only did they record their 'strong dissatisfaction' with the Tribunal's rejection of the claim for 30s. increase in weekly rates, but went on:

We also express strong resentment against the action of the Coal Board and the Tribunal in quoting the earnings derived from Saturday working as one of the reasons for rejecting the miners' claim, when it is understood that the miners have worked on Saturdays at the request of the Government and the Coal Board in order to assist the country in its economic difficulties. (November 10, 1952.)

The concluding passage of this same unanimous resolution ran as follows:

In addition we call upon the National Executive Committee to ascertain the opinion of the Areas on the need to terminate the Extended Hours Agreement in April 1953, and to reconsider the conciliation machinery with a view to a change to permit of consultation with the membership in the event of deadlock in negotiations between the Coal Board and the Union.
Having considered this new position, the Scottish Conference calls upon all mine-workers to return to work and to maintain unity

within our ranks in the fight which lies ahead for improved wages and conditions.

A remarkable campaign had been conducted on the 30s. in the Scottish coal-field, including meetings, demonstrations and rallies; while the miners at a number of pits had ceased the voluntary Saturday overtime shift and others had come out on strike. Something of the state of feeling was conveyed by the delegates' speeches. Andrew Hamilton of the Wellesley Pit (at Buckhaven and Methil on the Firth of Forth) said: 'It was the campaign conducted by the miners which had forced the Coal Board (in the negotiations subsequent to the Tribunal) to make some concessions', and went on to tell what had happened in his own area:

They had organised a rally which had made necessary the stopping of Saturday work that weekend and the feeling of loyalty demonstrated by the miners, who had stood and listened in a downpour of rain, had been most remarkable. Last week they had sent a bus load of miners, led by himself, on a deputation to the National Conference. . . .

He contrasted the reception given to the deputation to the Scottish Conference that morning with that given to the deputation to the National Conference which was not allowed even to send representatives to meet the National officials. Fellow trade unionists of the Clerical and Administrative Workers' Union, however, members of the staff in the N.C.B. Head Office, had given them a real welcome and even invited them to dinner in their canteen, showing real trade union solidarity.

In the delegation of twenty-nine from Fife only five were members of the Communist Party and three were Labour County Councillors. They had also met a deputation from Midlands and Nottingham,[1] sincere trade unionists who were not members of the Communist Party or any party but out in defence of the members they represented. The Communists, however, were playing an important role and 'witch-hunting' was merely an attempt to create a split within our ranks. As a true socialist he had always believed in the policy of the Labour Party, but it was not the stronghold it had once been and until we moved forward united we would never remove this Tory Government. It was necessary to unite all the forces of the industrial workers to fight this Tory Government and have it replaced by a strong Labour Government which would pursue a real socialist policy and not the policy operated between 1945 and 1951.

[1] The N.E.C. of the N.U.M. at its meeting of December 4, 1953, took very strong exception to these deputations.

A Conference of the N.U.M. on November 7 had mean-time decided on a modified claim for wage-increases along with a number of other demands. The Coal Board put forward counter-proposals. The negotiations went on for some ten weeks. At each stage the Scottish miners protested vigorously not only against the N.C.B. proposals but also about the policy pursued by their N.E.C., as 'in their opinion it does not go far enough'. For example, the Board were willing to make a meagre concession if Extended Hours were continued. The Scots would have used Extended Hours as a lever to move the Government. The N.E.C. majority wanted, while keeping negotiations on hours formally separate, to indicate willingness as 'a sweetener' to the Coal Board. The attitude of the Scottish Executive was confirmed by the Area Conference unanimously and by the vote of every branch in Scotland. But the majority were against them, and in February 1953 a settlement was made with the Board on a small advance. The minimum went up by 6s. both for underground and surface workers. It amounted to one-fifth of what had been claimed nine months earlier, and during that nine months the cost of living had moved several points upwards.[1]

10. A NEW WAGES-STRUCTURE

It had long been recognised that the wages-structure of the industry was not only confusing and complicated but chaotic. At last in 1944 the private owners agreed that the problem, for which they had been responsible, must be tackled: and this obligation was transferred to the Coal Board. In 1946 the union reaffirmed its demand for this in a resolution moved by Abe Moffat who said: 'Unification of the wages system is in the interests of every miner in the British coalfields' (June 25, 1946). But the path to achievement of this demand was beset with obstacles, some of them within the ranks of the miners, where one area or one pit appeared to benefit from the existing chaos. Progress was bound to be slow. The Scots, however, kept up a steady pressure within the union, and the purpose

[1] The subsequent wages demand put forward by the Scots and adopted by the N.U.M. is set out in the Appendix to this chapter.

and meaning of a new wages-structure was convincingly set forth in pamphlets[1] and proposals by their President Moffat. 'You can take any pit in Scotland and you will find at least thirty or thirty-six different grades and different rates of wages', wrote Moffat, whose first proposal was to reduce these to six or seven grades.

It was not by chance that the initiative came from Scotland. The Scottish miners suffered most from a disparity that had grown up under the old system. For years production and financial results from Scotland were amongst the highest in the twenty British coal-fields while adult wages were amongst the lowest. For example, in the third quarter of 1945, of the six largest districts Scotland was yielding thrice the British average per ton to the central financial pool, its profit per ton was the highest, while its earnings per man-shift were second lowest. Under State ownership the position was worsened. In 1938 the Scottish all-in wage was 10s. 11d., the British 11s. 8d.—a difference of 9d. a shift. In 1947 the difference was nearly 2s. 4d., or thrice as much. Each year the gap grew wider, notably in piece-work. In July 1948 the Scottish average (all persons) was 1s. 8¼d. less than the British, and the coal face average 3s. 3d. less; and in July 1951, 3s. 2¼d. and 5s. 7d. On this, as early as September 1946, the three officials in their Memorandum[2] to the Ministry gave a telling array of low wage figures from over forty Scottish collieries.

What was the reason for this relative worsening? It was not the youth rate, which was slightly above the British average. It was a question not so much of men at the face on day-rates

[1] *Notes of Lecture on Wages Structure* by Abe Moffat. (May 20, 1948.)
'We not only submitted a resolution to the British Conference but, I think for the first time in the history of the Scottish miners, we issued a memorandum on the question, raising some very important questions and dealing in detail with the wages system existing at particular pits in the Scottish coal-field. We issued that memorandum publicly to our membership, but in fact it was a copy of a memorandum which we had submitted to the Minister of Fuel and Power prior to nationalisation, in order to bring out the inequalities which exist in the present wages system.

'There was no difficulty in getting the British miners' conference to accept unanimously the case put by the Scottish miners' representatives that there was need for a new wages-structure in this industry. We cannot continue on its present basis of the inequalities and anomalies which exist in the wages system. We cannot continue in a nationalised industry with the variations which exist in one pit in Scotland compared with another pit in Scotland. This is a relic of the past which must be changed. This, therefore, was the first attempt in our history as British miners to get a new conception within our own ranks of what a wages-structure means and how it is so vitally necessary that it should be supported by the N.U.M. itself.'

[2] *Memorandum re Wages Paid to Face-workers in the Scottish Coal-field.*

as of the low piece-rates. Again and again this matter was brought up by the Scottish Executive through the conciliation machinery; but while anomalies were progressively removed and a favourable decision gained at one pit could be treated as a precedent for others, a basic improvement was denied them. The position with the great and indeed growing disparity between the Scottish and British averages continued to be profoundly unsatisfactory. It was a factor in the consistently militant attitude of the Scottish delegates on a whole range of questions.

In the late autumn of 1951 it appeared as though the situation would be further worsened when the N.C.B. wanted a stabilisation of rates. Eventually the December 1951 Agreement set a standstill in district rates and piece-rates for a twelvemonth, or until a joint working-party reported on a new wages-structure with particular reference to piece-workers. The first task of this working-party was to provide a glossary of the multitudinous terms that varied from district to district. An interim report reduced 6000 different local names for occupations to 300 job descriptions, and thereby gave a basis on which arguments could proceed for establishing a proper system of grading.

When in November 1952 the arbitration award was given against the miners' claim, reference was made in it to the importance of the new wages-structure. For some weeks thereafter this was discussed with the Board, but it soon became clear that this was a long-term question and that the urgent need for a wages-increase was not met by such discussions. Therefore the February 1953 Wages Agreement, giving 6s., repeated the standstill clause, and the working-party on wage-structure continued at what was necessarily a slow pace. For the Board realised that a new wages-structure would cost them money: and the Scots, bound by a national agreement, had to endure this slow pace.

II. COMPULSORY ARBITRATION

Throughout the whole of this first seven years of State ownership of the mines the Scottish miners went through experience of considerable disillusionment. Some of the reasons for this have already been given in Chapter XII on Nationalisation. But the most potent factor in this growing disillusion was the treatment they received on questions of their livelihood at a time when they were willing to give of their best. In the past dissatisfaction with such treatment would soon enough have led to disputes, to withdrawal of labour. For this was their ultimate means of bringing pressure to bear on their employers. None of them wanted strikes if conditions were tolerable. But generations of miners had learned that without the possibility of recourse to this weapon, they were helpless in face of their employers. It was for this reason that the county associations in the M.F.G.B. had always set their face like flint against compulsory arbitration: and within the T.U.C., when this topic came up, it was always the miners' delegates who had been its uncompromising opponents.

During the war period, from the summer of 1940 onward, strikes or lock-outs had been made illegal and what was in effect compulsory arbitration instituted under Order 1305,[1] which corresponded to similar provisions in the first World War. But whereas in 1918 the signing of an armistice was immediately followed by the withdrawal of any such restrictions on the trade unions, this Order 1305 continued in force in peace-time year after year until, as the result of strong agitation, it was withdrawn in the summer of 1951. Quite apart from Order 1305, however, the miners had bound themselves: with the prospect that all they hoped would be won for themselves and for the community by State ownership, they had consented to a machinery of negotiation with their new employers, with the proviso of compulsory arbitration (the National Tribunal) in case of a deadlock. Some had even hoped that with State ownership there need hardly ever arise the question of referring a dispute to compulsory arbitration.

What no one had imagined, when they set up the special conciliation machinery with their new employers, was a situation where the N.C.B., with the Minister of Fuel and Power to back them, would begin and end negotiations with a flat statement that their policy was not to grant an increase. Still

[1] *Conditions of Employment and National Arbitration Order*, S. R. & O. 1940, No. 1305 (July 18, 1940).

less had anyone imagined, when they gave up their rooted objection to compulsory arbitration, that a time would come (as it did for them in 1950) when a British Government would dare to think of issuing warnings or instructions to boards of arbitration as to how they should operate. From a standpoint of legal history it might almost seem to recall the long-vanished days of the Stuarts, when King James I issued instructions to judges. They were met by employers who would not budge and their case was then handed over to a biassed tribunal, biassed officially and for reasons of State.

This had two consequences. In the first place, as might have been expected, the lower-paid workers, denied the kind of hearing they had been taught to expect under the new conciliation machinery, went outside the authority of their union and themselves took action. A strong sense of having been unjustly treated was the mainspring of the workers in one or another pit coming out on strike. The warping of the conciliation machinery by 'reasons of state policy' was the main cause of 'unofficial strikes'. As the freezing of wages bore very heavily indeed on the lower-paid workers of the Scottish coal-field, it was in Scotland that very many of these 'unofficial strikes' took place, both in 1949 and in 1950. The Scottish Executive and officials, faithful to their engagements, did what they could to prevent and stop these unauthorised strikes: and usually were able to prevent them spreading. But on the other hand these 'unofficial strikes' made the Scottish leaders acutely aware, to a greater extent than the leaders in some of the other coal-fields, of defects in the machinery of negotiations. They determined therefore to press for a reconstruction, or at any rate an amendment, of the machinery. The Scottish Area put forward its proposal to the 1951 Blackpool Annual Conference of the N.U.M. in the following resolution:

In view of the dissatisfaction in the coalfields regarding decisions of the National Reference Tribunal, this Conference of the National Union of Mineworkers calls upon the National Executive Committee to consider the need for an alteration in Clause 9 of the conciliation machinery, which will provide that, prior to a matter being referred to the National Reference Tribunal under Clause 9, Subsection 2, the Board or the Union shall have the right to consider separately what further action they deem necessary in furtherance of their respective claims.

VETERANS OF THE INDUSTRY
William Easton, Fife, 1953

MINERS' DWELLINGS, COWDENBEATH, FIFE, 1953

After a brief debate the resolution was defeated on a show of hands. But the problem of the machinery of negotiations being subjected to such a severe strain as had been the case in these last years still remained. The Scottish Area put forward the solution, believing that the time would come when the pressure of the whole British coal-field would become effective.

APPENDIX TO CHAPTER XIII

THE WAGES ADVANCE OF JANUARY 1954

It is again a great pleasure for me to report to this Annual Conference that the resolution which you passed last year demanding an increase in wages for day-wage workers to offset the increase in the cost of living and to improve the living standard of the miners became the accepted policy of the British miners at the N.U.M. Annual Conference held in July 1953. Had it not been for that resolution there would have been no claim for an increase in wages for the British miners in 1954.

You are aware that, following the National Conference, the National Executive Committee demanded a minimum weekly wage of £8 underground and £7 on the surface, and eventually succeeded in obtaining an increase of 8s. 6d. per week for underground and 7s. 6d. per week for surface workers, to cover all day-wage workers without any ceiling, and establishing the guaranteed minimum weekly wage of £7 15s. for underground and £6 15s. for surface workers.

While the agreement was finally accepted by the Areas by a majority vote, it is to the credit of the Scottish miners, who had led the fight, that by a majority of eleven to one in a financial vote they declared against the acceptance of the terms of the agreement, on the grounds that the offer was inadequate and that the conditions attached constituted a dangerous principle in wages negotiations. Even among the Areas voting for acceptance and in the report submitted to the Special Conference on January 27, 1954, there was a wide recognition that the new wages settlement placed the miners on minimum wages in a worse position than in 1947 so far as purchasing power was concerned.

As in every other wage negotiation we had many flat refusals on the part of the Board between September 1953 and January 1954. During this period many other trade unions were demanding wage increases. The Electrical Trades Union was conducting official guerilla strikes, the engineers called out three million workers for a twenty-four hour stoppage on December 2, and the railwaymen threatened strike action on the eve of Christmas against the miserable award of 4s. per week increase. It is significant that every employer, including the Coal Board, said 'No!' to the workers' demands, and that only after this trade union action demonstrating the power and determination of the organised workers did the Government and the employers change their minds. Everyone of us, therefore, owes a deep debt of gratitude to the action of those trade unions which revived the militant spirit of trade unionism to defend the workers of Britain. The Government and the employers know the force of united trade union activity and that is why in January they made haste to consider the miners' wage demands.

The lesson from this wages struggle is clear to all trade unionists—that when we stand together united in our determination to secure our demands, we can defeat the policy of the Government and the employers. (Presidential Address, Annual Conference of the Scottish Area, Minute 32, June 2, 1954, pp. 583–4.)

CHAPTER XIV

INTERNATIONAL RELATIONS

1. WAR OR PEACE?

It was in the spring of 1948, a year after the proclamation of the Truman Doctrine, whose sequel was Marshall Aid, that there was initiated the North Atlantic Treaty Pact. When the Scottish Miners' Annual Conference opened at Dunoon on June 8, 1948, there was already a tense atmosphere. In his presidential address Abe Moffat said:

It is no source of satisfaction to any of us, only three years after the conclusion of the war against Fascism, to hear so much talk about a third world war. War and preparations for war are a profitable business for those who exploit the production of armaments and the blood and sacrifice of the people. For the common people it is quite the opposite and the developments in connection with the atomic bomb spell the destruction of civilisation and particularly the people of Britain. In preparation for this third world war we are again subjected to the lies and slanders against those who have taken steps to remove the landlords and capitalists of their countries.

Some of us do not forget the campaign of falsehood against the Soviet Union following World War No. 1. The same vicious attacks are now being launched against the people of the countries in Eastern Europe. As miners we do not forget how we were slandered by our own capitalist class and how they tried to poison the minds of the public when the miners were fighting for a bare existence.

I am sure that the common people of Britain and America do not want war. I am sure that the people of the Soviet Union and the Eastern European countries who suffered so much in the war against Fascism have no interest in war, but are desirous of establishing peace in which to build a happy and prosperous life. I would say from this platform that it is the duty of each of us to fight against the warmongers and to establish peaceful relations with the people of the Soviet Union and the peace-loving folk of all countries.

The address was received with acclamation and, in the course of the conference, the delegates adopted unanimously a series of resolutions which were in accord with it. Thus on

June 9 the delegates urged 'the British Labour Government to intervene' in Greece, (1) in order to 'put an end to the Fascist activities' and (2) to stop the 'judicial murder of democrats in Greece'. Next, the conference called on the Government to take measures immediately at home to ban 'fascist activities, which are beginning to infest our country with their hated Nazi doctrines'. Next day, by an overwhelming majority, they passed the following resolution:

That Conference asks that the utmost pressure be brought to bear upon the Government to divert our trade from dollar countries, which are holding us up to ransom, towards the Soviet Union and the European democracies, which will trade without conditions or extortion. Conference also asks that members of the Trade Union movement should support a 'Hands off Czechoslovakia' movement, since in our opinion the events in Czechoslovakia recently were the result of a democratic decision of the people. (June 10, 1948.)

Early in 1949 the representatives of the British T.U.C., the United States Congress of Industrial Organisations and a few others seceded from the World Federation of Trade Unions, which had been called together as a result of a T.U.C. resolution in 1943 and set up at its London meeting early in 1945. This, referred to by the President in his address to the 1949 Annual Conference, was dealt with in the composite resolution put forward by eight branches:

That this Conference of Scottish miners protests at the action of the British delegates who withdrew from the Executive Bureau of the World Federation of Trade Unions. We also condemn their proposal that the W.F.T.U. should suspend all activities or dissolve, such a proposal being contrary to the interests of all trade unionists. We demand that they resume their place on the Executive of the W.F.T.U. forthwith and work for world Trade Union unity. We feel certain that such a task honestly pursued could brighten the lives of workers everywhere, by pushing forward their demands for better working and living conditions, and would assist in banishing the spectre of a third world war now gloomily confronting us. (May 31, 1949.)

There was a sharp discussion. An amendment in a contrary sense was moved. Eventually the motion was carried by 66 votes to 39: and later confirmed in roughly the same proportion by a branch financial vote.

The chief world event of 1949 was the overwhelming victory of the People's Liberation Army in China over the forces of

Chiang Kai-shek, who was supported by U.S. arms, and the establishment on October 1 of the (coalition) Government of the Chinese People's Republic, comprising a quarter of mankind. For a time it seemed as though United States policy would forsake its support of Chiang Kai-shek, even if it was unwilling to enter into friendly relations with China. But by the early months of 1950 the announcement that the U.S. Government was preparing a deadlier form of atomic weapon in the hydrogen bomb brought an increase in the war danger. The following is recorded in the Conference minutes:

That Conference calls upon the Government to support the immediate banning of the atomic bomb and all other weapons of mass destruction, as a first step towards the establishment of peaceful and friendly relations between the great powers through the United Nations Organisation. (May 31, 1950.)

After Vice-President Wood had moved this resolution on behalf of the Executive, it was seconded by Mr. Elliot of Roslin, supported by Mr. Steele of Harthill East and Mr. Penman of Bowhill Branch, and accepted unanimously.

This was followed by a unanimous decision 'that Conference urges the return of the British T.U.C. to the World Federation of Trade Unions'. The last resolution of the Conference, 'carried by an overwhelming majority', ran as follows:

That this Conference urges the British Government to order the withdrawal of all land, sea and air forces of the United States of America from British territory and territorial waters. (June 2, 1950.)

That same year William Pearson, as president of the Scottish Trades Union Congress, delivered his address at Rothesay in the county of Bute. This address[1] represented very fully the opinion of the Scottish miners, on a range of issues, as shown in the minutes of delegate conferences and executive meetings. Certain elements within the Scottish T.U.C. decided to indicate their disapproval of the Scottish miners, and marked it by rejecting their representative, William Pearson, from the S.T.U.C. Executive. The Scottish miners, however, did not secede; the folly of this exclusion was soon realised and the next year they were once more represented, on this occasion by Vice-President John Wood, who had previously been their representative, together with William Pearson.

[1] See the Appendix to this chapter.

2. THE WAR IN KOREA

The outbreak of war in Korea in the last week of June 1950, some three weeks after the Annual Conference, caused widespread anxiety. During the summer months of 1950 there was considerable discussion in the trade union movement and amongst the British people on the origins of the war, on the validity or otherwise of the decisions taken at the headquarters of the United Nations (with the U.S.S.R. and the Chinese People's Republic not represented), and on the nature of the Syngman Rhee Government in the south of Korea. At its meeting of July 24, 1950, the proposals before the Executive Committee and its decision are minuted as follows:

A letter was read from Crosshouse/Dreghorn Branch expressing disgust at the decision of the British Government to place armed forces at the disposal of the Americans in the war against the Korean people. It was felt that the danger of a third world war had been brought nearer as a result of this military intervention and they demanded the withdrawal of the forces. They felt that the necessary steps should be taken by the United Nations to gain the admission of the representative of the People's Government of China to their rightful seat in the Security Council.

Following full discussion on this very important question, it was unanimously agreed that the following resolution should be accepted:

The National Union of Mineworkers (Scottish Area) demands the withdrawal of all foreign troops and material from Korea and also that a full meeting of the Security Council should be held at which the representative of the People's Government of China would be present, as proposed by Mr. Nehru.

At this moment American troops which had been hurried to Korea were in full flight and were being pursued southwards by the North Korean army. When this decision came up for review nearly eleven weeks later at the Area Delegate Conference of October 9, 1950, there had been a change in the military position in the latter part of September. On the one hand General Douglas MacArthur, the United States Commander-in-Chief of all the foreign forces in Korea, was intent on crossing the 38th Parallel. On the other hand the Chinese Foreign Secretary, on September 30, 1950, had given public warning that China would not tolerate the crossing of the 38th Parallel and the approach of hostile armies to the Chinese frontiers, which, he said, had been repeatedly violated by United States bombers. The delegates from several branches were against the Executive Committee's decision, which was strongly supported by delegates from other branches. There was a keen debate.

Mr. Kellachan, Priory Branch, moved the remit back of the resolution, which he did not consider expressed the views of the Scottish miners, since it gave the impression that responsibility for the war in Korea lay on both sides, while his branch felt it lay on those it held guilty of aggression—the North Koreans. The course of the war proved the North was prepared and the South was not. Every potential aggressor must be met with the full armed forces of the world. He therefore asked conference to indicate support for the Government and for the United Nations policy in Korea, and stressed that support of the resolution would mean opposition to Labour Government policy. Other supporters of the remit back (including McCann of Gartshore 3/12, McGilvray of Bedlay, Hamilton of Wellesley, McLean of Broomfield) took in general a similar line. No one defended Syngman Rhee, but McCann and Hamilton thought the Koreans could get rid of him by democratic elections and not by force. One delegate (McLean) argued that since the N.U.M. Annual Conference had reaffirmed support for Labour Government policy and for the Labour Government in any future election, this must mean support of Labour's foreign policy and hence opposition to the resolution.

Supporters of the resolution included Innes (Newton), McQuade (Lingerwood), Comerford (Comrie), McLean (Harthill), Johnstone (Ponfeigh) from the floor, as well as the Secretary. Stress was laid on the corrupt regime of Syngman Rhee and also the fact that the evidence of aggression by the North rested on Rhee's allegations, the North having been refused a hearing at UNO.

Replying to the discussion on behalf of the Executive, which had unanimously adopted the resolution, the President pointed out that it did not refer to American, British or Russian troops, but to withdrawal of *all* foreign troops: to oppose that, whoever started the war, meant supporting the continuation of mass slaughter. Delegates who said the resolution was against official Labour Government policy had themselves on occasions opposed official Labour Government policy—over the wage-freeze, for example—and 'it was nothing new and no crime for this Conference to discuss a policy in opposition to the Government, the union, or even to the leadership of the Scottish E.C.' On aggression, surely the case of both sides should be heard. He quoted evidence from American sources to show that South Korea was a corrupt anti-working-class police State. To support this was not worth the life of one British soldier, nor would the fight of the Korean people for independence from colonial rule ever be defeated by armed force.

The resolution was accepted by 73 votes to 48 and confirmed by a financial vote. The Executive Committee standpoint on Korea thus became the settled policy of the Scottish miners.

Meantime, in the latter part of September, the British Foreign Secretary had been persuaded in New York by Mr. Dean Acheson of the U.S. State Department to alter his previous standpoint of refusing to consider the rearming of Germany. During this period the U.S.A. went ahead with successive steps for the rearming of both Germany and Japan. The standpoint of the Scottish miners was shown very clearly at their 1951 Annual Conference in a composite resolution, which was carried unanimously:

That Conference condemns the rearmament of Germany and Japan and demands fulfilment and conclusion of a peace treaty with Germany and Japan based on the will of the peace-loving people of these countries. (June 6, 1951.)

A further resolution was unanimously carried:

That Conference demands the conclusion of a peace pact between the five great powers—Britain, France, the United States of America, the Soviet Union and the People's Government of China. (June 6, 1951.)

Long after the June 1951 proposal of the Soviet representative J. Malik for a cease-fire in Korea had brought the belligerents into negotiations (eventually resulting in the armistice agreement of July 1953), the question of the rearming of Western Germany remained a burning issue of international politics. Throughout 1954 it had become the most disputed question within the labour movement. The Parliamentary Labour Party was almost equally divided in January 1954. The Co-operative Party Conference voted against rearming Germany at Easter, as did the Co-operative Congress (representing 11,000,000 members) at Whitsuntide. The standpoint of the Scottish miners was reaffirmed in an Executive resolution (confirmed by delegate conference) in March 1954:

That the Scottish Area of the N.U.M. protests against the Government's plan and support for German rearmament and the creation of the new German army which will again threaten world peace.

We call upon the Government to withdraw its support for such a disastrous policy that can lead to another world war. We demand that further negotiations should continue in place of force between the big powers, to establish a peaceful and united Germany in the interests of world peace.

We also call for the discussion of disarmament for all nations through the United Nations Organisation.

It seemed from all the indications that it would be a 'very close-run thing' when the question came up on the agenda of the Labour Party Conference at Scarborough at the end of September 1954. It was also clear that a great deal depended on how the miners' delegation to that conference[1] would cast their vote. Outside Britain, much depended on the attitude of

---

[1] At the Scottish Area Conference (148 delegates) on October 18 1954, the following resolution was 'accepted by an overwhelming majority, only four votes being registered against'. (Minute 11.)

That this Conference strongly protests against the procedure adopted at the meeting of the miners' delegation prior to the Labour Party Conference at Scarborough in dealing with the question of German rearmament.

Despite the fact that all discussion on this question was ruled out of order, the 700,000 votes of the British miners were cast in favour of German rearmament.

Following the Scarborough Conference a new situation has arisen as a result of the Nine Power Conference agreement which commits Britain to the maintenance of 120,000 troops in Germany for 44 years, with additional financial burdens for the people of Britain.

None of these questions was ever discussed at Scarborough or by the miners and we consider that the miners and all other sections of the trade union movement should be allowed to reconsider the whole position.

We protest against the implications of this agreement and welcome the unity of all workers and trade unionists in Western Germany who have voted solidly against this military agreement.

We call upon the National Executive Committee to convene a Special Coal-field Conference to deal with this new situation and to give the miners in the coal-field the right to discuss and decide policy on this important question facing the people of Britain. (Minute 11, October 18, 1954, pp. 249–50.)

the Assembly in France and of the trade union organisations
(in opposition to Dr. Adenauer) in Western Germany.

3. MINERS IN THE UNITED STATES AND IN FRANCE

The tradition, particularly strong in the Scottish coal-field,
of close connection and sympathy with the miners of other
countries was shown in the attitude both to French and
American strikes in the years 1948 and 1950. In each case
there were particular difficulties. The United States Congress
had passed an anti-trade union law known as the Taft-
Hartley Act, with the object of shackling the unions. This did
not prevent the American miners led by the redoubtable
John L. Lewis from going forward with their demands in the
early part of 1950. A press campaign of great virulence was
launched against them and every means was tried to break
their strikes. At the Scottish Executive it was unanimously
resolved:

We, the Scottish miners, send greetings of solidarity to the American miners in their magnificent fight to increase wages, to establish a
guaranteed five-day week and to secure improved safety precautions
in order to reduce the high death and accident rate in the American
mining industry. . . . We wish them final and speedy victory in their
struggle, realising that their fight for improved wages and conditions
is a splendid lead in the effort to improve wages and conditions of
mineworkers of all countries. (March 6, 1950.)

At the next meeting of the Scottish Executive the following
reply was received:

Greatly appreciate your cable of greetings and goodwill based upon
accomplishment of the United Mineworkers in their recent great
struggle. The mineworkers have not only won for themselves but up-
held the prestige of American labour. Greetings and good wishes in
every way to the Scottish Miners from all the members of our Union.
—Lewis.

The case of the French miners had a longer history which it
is necessary to give in some detail. It was in the autumn of
1948 that the French miners came out on strike, to be greeted
immediately by widespread condemnation not only in France
but in other countries, including Britain and the U.S.A. In

Scotland at the close of the Area Minute Conference on October 11, 1948, this resolution was carried unanimously:

That this Conference, representing 80,000 Scottish miners, expresses its solidarity with the French miners in the fight to defend their living standard. In the struggle we appreciate the action of the French miners in leading the fight to defend the living standards of the mineworkers of all lands.

LONG LIVE THE FIGHTING SPIRIT OF THE FRENCH MINERS! LONG LIVE THE SOLIDARITY OF THE INTERNATIONAL MINEWORKERS!

A fortnight later, October 25, 1948, the Scottish Executive received a letter of thanks from the French miners in the Nord and Pas-de-Calais coal-field in which they stated that they had been forced into strike action by the repeated attacks of their employer, the Government, on their purchasing power and conditions. The French miners were not, 'as you will have been told', continued the letter, 'on strike for causes foreign to our organisation. They said as much about you when, in 1921 and 1926, you were on strike like us in defence of your conditions.' But at this same meeting the Scottish Executive had to take note of severe criticism of their resolution from the National President. The minute describes this in Abe Moffat's report of the incident in which he

referred to the statement of the N.U.M. President, Mr. Lawther, that the resolution passed by the Scottish Area was nonsensical and that the strike of the French miners was a luxury. As President of the Scottish Area, when approached by newspapers on the question, he had avoided being drawn into controversy but had simply stated that he could not consider as nonsense any resolution passed by delegates representing the Scottish miners, nor could he consider a strike led by the Union for decent wages and living conditions a luxury.

The officials had that morning considered the letter received from the French miners and felt that the sincerity of the resolution passed by Conference should be demonstrated by material support. They therefore proposed that a contribution of £500 be sent to assist our fellow Trade Unionists.

Mr. Miller considered that this sum was inadequate and moved that at least double that amount should be sent if the Scottish funds would at all permit of it. . . .

Mr. Miller's amendment to the officials' proposal was carried.

It was further agreed that a copy of the letter from the French Miners' Federation should be sent out to all branches in order that any branch which wished to give financial assistance might have the opportunity to do so. (Minute 11, October 25, 1948, pp. 184-7.)

Meantime Mr. Arthur Horner, N.U.M. Secretary, having made a speech in France in support of the French miners, was on his return censured by a majority vote of the N.E.C. as having made statements 'contrary to union policy'. On the Scottish Executive the general view was expressed that the statement made by the General Secretary could not be contrary to Union policy, since there had been no declaration of Union policy on the question of the French strike or the strike of any other foreign workers. It was therefore decided to protest against 'such a decision being taken prior to the holding of a thorough investigation and a submission of a report to the Areas before any decision was reached against a national official of the N.U.M.' (Minute 12, November 8, 1948, pp. 208, 209.) On this the N.E.C. of the N.U.M., some three weeks later, having confirmed their previous minute, decided to take no action.

Two weeks later the Secretary reported to the Scottish Executive that £355 : 2 : 6 had been received from branches and other sources to be forwarded for the relief of the French miners on strike and their dependents. Over a score of branches had so far contributed, amongst them Devon Branch with over £60 and Ormiston with over £80 (of which £32 was a branch collection). But a letter from Stane and Southfield Branch contested 'the right of the Executive Committee to donate £1,000 towards the French miners without consulting the members or branch delegates. The ruling was endorsed that, as in many other donations which the Executive Committee had decided and had been entitled to decide between Conferences, and as in all decisions of the Executive Committee, the action of the Executive was subject to endorsement by the branches.' (Minute 13, November 22, 1948, pp. 240, 241.)

Within another couple of weeks further sums had been received, amounting to £205 : 9 : 6, of which over £185 was from Union branches. In the House of Commons Lieut.-Col. Baker White, M.P., stated that the £1000 sent by the Scottish miners for the relief of French miners and their dependents had not actually been used for that purpose. This was discussed at an Area Conference on December 13, 1948, and the following resolution was passed:

This Conference, representing 80,000 Scottish mineworkers, protests most emphatically against the false statement made by Lieut.-Col. Baker White, M.P., regarding the £1,000 granted by the Scottish miners to the French miners during their strike.

The statement made by this Member in the House of Commons last week that the £1,000 donated by the Scottish miners was being used by the C.G.T. (French T.U.C.) to reduce their bank overdraft instead of to relieve the distress of the dependents of the French miners, as was intended by the Scottish miners, is false and without foundation. We regard it as a slander not only against the French miners but against the Scottish miners, and demand a public withdrawal from Lieut.-Col. Baker White. (December 13, 1948.)

A Scottish Miners' delegation consisting of Abe Moffat, Magnus Fairnie, Executive Committee member, and Charles Burke of Coalsnaughton branch was sent to France. There in December they made a thorough investigation, got particulars from the Credit du Nord Bank, including photostats of important documents and attestations by a director of this bank. All of this was set forth in detail in their report (dated December 28) together with the conclusion:

Having made this thorough investigation, we have no hesitation in declaring that the money was used for the purpose for which it was intended by the Scottish miners—to relieve distress and suffering amongst the miners and their families, and that the statement of Lieut.-Colonel Baker White was false and without foundation. We recommend to the Executive Committee that he should be requested to withdraw his statement, in the interests of the Scottish and French miners. (Minute 19, December 29, 1938, p. 330.)

There was no escaping this conclusion and the honourable and gallant Member was forced to eat humble pie. In his letter of withdrawal of January 10, 1949, Lieut.-Col. Baker White, M.P., wrote:

When I spoke in the House of Commons I tried to make it perfectly clear that I did not in any way question the motives which impelled your Union to give this money. What I did question was what had happened to it in France. I should say that my statement in Parliament was founded upon a declaration by M. Moch, the French Minister of the Interior, which I had every reason to believe was accurate.

I am making the necessary arrangements to communicate the sense of this letter to the press.

The Scottish miners kept their eyes and ears open during their visit. As they wrote:

We took the opportunity of enquiring into the conditions of the French miners, in the course of which we made an inspection of No. 6 Colliery, Lens. The French miners suffered tremendously as a result of their strike for better wages and conditions. The Miners' officials informed us that over 6,000 miners had not been re-instated and over 2,000 were in prison, serving sentences ranging from one month to one year. One branch secretary was sentenced to one year's imprisonment and a fine of £5,000. The wages paid to the French miners are as follows:—Day wage workers' minimum—475.5 fr. or 9s. per day (£1 equals approximately 1,000 francs). A first grade hewer in the pit which we examined was paid only 10s. per day. The French miners were striking to establish a minimum wage of £17 : 15 : 8 per month for underground and £15 : 3 : 2 for surface workers. (Minute 19, December 29, 1948, pp. 330, 331.)

They dealt also with the rise in prices, safety, and housing (after visits to miners' homes), and concluded:

We have no hesitation in declaring that if the Scottish miners or any other section of the British miners were compelled to work under similar conditions there is no power in the country which would be strong enough to keep our men at work. . . . Low wages and bad conditions in France can be a real danger to the wages and conditions of miners in all other countries. In their fight the French miners have suffered as we did in 1926. Victimisation and imprisonment are the order of the day and naturally huge debts had been accumulated in the defence of their members. In addition, they still have a very heavy financial responsibility towards the dependents of those who are imprisoned and for this reason and in the interests of miners' solidarity we recommend to the Executive Committee that consideration should be given to the granting of a further donation to the French miners.

> (Sgd.) ABE MOFFAT, President.
> M. A. FAIRNIE, E.C. Member.
> CHARLES BURKE, Delegate.
> 28th December, 1948.

At the Scottish Executive of December 29:

It was unanimously agreed (1) that copies of the report should be circulated to all branches with a recommendation from the Executive Committee that a grant be made from the funds of the Scottish Area equivalent to 1s. per head of the membership; (2) that the branches be instructed to convene special meetings and to remit their decision on this question to Head Office not later than January 21,

1949; (3) that branches be invited to make special contributions to the fund over and above the grant; and (4) that a copy of the report be forwarded to the N.U.M. with a request that they should consider the possibility of sending a British delegation to enquire into conditions in France.

The N.U.M. rejected the proposal to send a delegation. The Scottish branches, however, by an overwhelming financial vote (£19,182 : 3 : 3 for, £4251 against), endorsed the recommendation to send 1s. per member to the French miners. By the end of February 1949, the last obstacle had been surmounted when the Bank of England Exchange Control granted permission to transfer the necessary funds to the French miners, on the evidence now provided that the previous £1000 had been duly used to relieve distress and suffering. It was nearly sixty years since miners in the British coalfields had readily given both sympathy and help to miners in other lands. The Scots had shown themselves to be steadfast in maintaining this noble tradition.

4. DELEGATIONS ABROAD

A notable feature of external or international relations of the Scottish miners was a series of delegations to other countries in the years after the war. These of course were reciprocal and the Scottish miners were pleased to extend their hospitality to visiting delegations of miners from some countries of Europe. In 1947 the President visited Czechoslovakia to witness the laying of the foundation stone of the new town to arise on the ruins of the martyred Lidice; the same year the Czechoslovak union had invited miners needing special treatment to visit a spa. The Scottish Area sent three members, William Thompson of Plean (Mid and East Lothian), Hugh Barr of Uddingston, and William Brown of Crosshouse.

The decision to organise official delegations had arisen at the Annual Conference of 1948, at which one of the fraternal delegates had been Signor Moretti, Technical Adviser of the Italian Miners' Federation. He was the first visitor to Conference from overseas since the war had ended. At this conference the Executive was instructed:

To organise delegations to visit the U.S.S.R. and other countries where the mines have been nationalised, in order to study working conditions and to consolidate the friendship of the Scottish miners with the miners of those other countries in Eastern Europe. (June, 1948.)

The first delegation of this kind visited the Pas de Calais coal-field on April 25, 1949, where they were received by the trade union officials at their head office in Lens. The delegation consisted of Vice-President John Wood, Executive member John McArthur and seven members from Branches: Peter O'Hara, John Boyd, Thomas Kerr, Robert Tennant, Alexander Sharp, William McLean, jnr., and James Gorman. Not unnaturally they were particularly interested in the aftermath of the strike, which had ended five months before. They found that the C.G.T. leaders who had been removed by the Government decrees, which had ordered new elections, had been re-elected by overwhelming majorities—sometimes as high as 84 per cent. But they also found that over 600 miners remained victimised, and sixty miners were still in prison. The union was caring for their dependents. The delegation went down the Fosse No. 5 and the Fosse No. 7 pits. After giving details of conditions, the report comments:

After seeing and experiencing these conditions, we are not surprised that the expectation of life (of a French miner) is 55 years. In fact we stated to the mine officials that they would not get Scottish miners to work under these conditions. . . . We are of opinion that anyone who states that it was wrong to take strike action simply because it is a nationalised industry should be prepared to go into the coalfields, not simply as a visitor, but to work in those mines under the wages and conditions operating. Alexander Sharp, Secretary of Comrie Branch, told the mine officials that if he was to apply the British Coal Mines Act the pit would not be allowed to carry on. We may state that we were informed before going underground that we were going down good pits.

On the morning that the Scots delegates left Lens they were informed that six more miners had been arrested during the night for participation in the 1948 strike.

At their Annual Conference that year, the Scottish miners welcomed two fraternal delegates: one was Mr. Seigel, formerly of the Scottish Miners' Union, but then of Australia; the second was Mr. Jean Seine of France.

SCOTTISH MINERS' GALA DAY, 1953

SCOTTISH MINERS' GALA DAY, 1953

Immediately following a Scottish Conference in 1950 a deputation went as fraternal delegates to the Annual Conference of the French Miners' Union, which took place in October 1950. The delegates on this occasion were Vice-President John Wood, Executive member John Sutherland, David Kelly of Dollar Colliery Branch and James Main of Larkhall Colliery Branch. Their report was received at the Executive Committee meeting of November 20, 1950. Much of their report was taken up with an examination of the French Miners' Charter which had been won in 1945 and which had largely been nullified by the 'Lacoste' Government Decrees of October/November 1948, particularly as to guaranteed wages, holidays with pay, family allowance, training schemes and safety in mines.

POLAND

The Polish Miners' Union invited Scotland to send a delegation of five, who would also have the opportunity of spending two weeks in a miners' holiday home in Poland. The delegation took place between July 12 and August 6, 1949; their report was considered at the Executive meeting of August 22, 1949, when it was decided that it should be circulated and later printed as a pamphlet.[1] The delegation consisted of President Moffat, Executive member Daniel Sim, Andrew Flynn of Valleyfield Branch, Thomas Stewart of Glencraig Branch and Thomas Wilson of Mauchline Branch. After describing experiences on housing schemes, and in tractor and chocolate factories which they visited, their report took note of the wide scheme organised by the Polish Government and the Trade Unions of workers' holiday homes. They stayed for several days, together with Polish miners on holiday, in the mountain health resort of Zakopane, where 'huge houses which were once the property of big landlords and German industrialists' were now put to this use. They noted that Polish miners 'receive eight days' holiday for the first year employed, 15 days after three years, and one month after ten years, all with full pay. . . . It should be noted also that a decision has

---

[1] *Scottish Miners' Delegation to Poland.* (1949.)

been taken to give all miners four weeks' holiday as soon as practicable.'

The report largely concentrates on the mining industry, noting that 'the pits suffered tremendous destruction at the hands of the Nazis. In the first year following liberation (1945), output was 27 million tons; in 1946, it was 47 million tons; and in 1948, it was 72 million tons'. They were struck by the speed at which new pits were sunk, being twice as fast as in Great Britain. They asked about the death and accident rate, and were informed by the Minister of Mines, previously chairman of the Polish Miners' Union, 'that the death rate was 1·9 persons per million tons of coal produced per year. This is indeed a very low death rate for the mining industry. A full-time doctor is employed at each colliery from 8 A.M. to 12 noon. Great attention is paid to Safety Committees, on which there are representatives of each grade of workmen at the Colliery'. They visited the Emma Colliery, sunk in 1870, employing 3200 workmen in all—producing 3500 tons per day. Their comment was:

We have no hesitation in saying that their geological conditions are more favourable than those in Scotland, but this is not the sole reason for the high output. As already explained, it is due to the effective organisation and particularly to the haulage system, which is the main problem facing the mining industry in any country.

Having examined the baths and lavatories on the surface at this colliery, we would say that they are not up to the standard at British mines, although it should be noted that one-third of our British miners are without any baths.

There were canteens at every colliery. Because of the currency exchange rates it was impossible to make an exact comparison of wages. But they note special emoluments, negligible house rents and 'a complete social insurance scheme covering illness, accident, pensions, etc. and for this they pay nothing, as it is maintained by the industry and the State'. Tools and working clothes were free; young miners had three years' training and continued education.

Four of the delegation attended chapel in Zakopane. It was overcrowded and 'many had to wait to get in until others came out'.

SOVIET UNION

The same year of 1949, in accordance with the 1948 conference decision, a deputation also went to the Soviet Union. By Executive Committee decision of September 20, 1949, their report, too, was circulated and printed as a pamphlet. The members of this delegation were: Secretary William Pearson, Executive Member Alex. Moffat, and Thomas Fowler, Hugh Geddes, John McLean, Robert McCutcheon of the Kingshill No. 1, Wellwood, Bannockburn and Broomfield Branches respectively. They were particularly impressed by the extraordinary level of mechanisation and technical skill; by the provision made for the ageing miner, who gets a pension of half wages at fifty in addition to his earnings; and by the four weeks' holiday with pay and remarkable welfare and cultural facilities. They did not regard the pithead baths as up to British standards.

The following year, 1950, Scotland received return visits from delegations from the Soviet Union, headed by Mr. S. I. Zaitzev, the President of the Central Council of the Mineworkers' Union; and from Poland. Thereafter at intervals of a year or two a more or less regular interchange of delegations followed. In 1953 the Scottish miners' delegation to the U.S.S.R. coal-fields was headed by the President, Abe Moffat. In the early summer of 1954 a return delegation of nine Soviet miners, headed by their President, Ivan Rossochinsky, were present at the Gala Day in Edinburgh, where their stalwart forms attracted attention as they marched with other guests at the head of the procession. They afterwards toured the coalfields, exchanged experiences with Scots miners and went home to write their official report.[1]

CZECHOSLOVAKIA

The year 1951 was to be Czechoslovakia's year, when there

[1] On this occasion one of the Soviet miners, by the name of Valigura, separately published a report of his own which was grossly misleading about wages and other conditions. This, when printed in *Izvestia* in mid-July, was immediately taken up by President Moffat: and in consequence on August 19 President Rossochinsky himself wrote to *Izvestia*: 'I wish to express regret concerning a series of irritating inaccuracies' (in the Valigura article) which he then detailed and corrected.

was an exchange of delegations between the miners of the two countries. The Secretary of the Czechoslovak Miners' Union, Joseph Kahout, addressed the Scottish Annual Conference. The British Government refused visas to other members of the Czechoslovak Miners' Union delegation. The delegation of Scots to visit Czechoslovakia from August 25 to September 10, 1951, consisted of President Abe Moffat, Executive Member John Sutherland, Thomas Gibb of Lochhead Branch, William Wood of Brucefield Branch and Robert Thomson of Cameron/Rosie Branch. The report describes their visits to many places of interest and in particular to the Barbora Colliery, Ostrava, where they noted two British machines, Jeffrey cutter loaders, in use.

For the 1953 Annual Conference representatives were invited from the U.S.A. and from Poland.

GERMANY

A representative of the East German Miners' Trade Union was invited to attend the 1952 Annual Conference as fraternal delegate, but at the last moment illness prevented him. But a few months later the Scottish miners were to be in touch with them nevertheless. An International Conference was called to consider the possibilities of the peaceful solution of the German problem, to be held in Stockholm, November 8–11, 1952. At the last moment, however, the venue had to be changed owing to certain difficulties with the Swedish Government over visas. It was transferred to Berlin.

The Scottish Miners were represented at the conference by Secretary William Pearson and Executive Committee member William Sneddon by an Executive Committee decision. (Minute 5, August 25, 1952.)

The delegates had an opportunity to make some brief enquiries into the position of miners in East Germany. But it was not until two years later that it was possible to accept an invitation from the Miners' Union of the German Democratic Republic for a two weeks' visit to that country, in October 1954. The decision to send Secretary William Pearson and Executive Committee member John Sutherland was minuted on September 2, 1954.[1] This was the first miners' delegation to East Germany.

Apart from exchange of delegations with miners' unions in various countries of Europe, the Scottish miners kept a close watch on happenings within the British Empire. Of this we need only give two examples. The first dealt with Nigeria, where coal-mines were Government-owned. On November 18, 1949, at the Enugu Colliery, twenty-one miners were shot dead and fifty-one were wounded in the course of a strike. The Scottish miners reacted strongly to this incident; and an Area Conference held on December 12, 1949, accepted an emergency resolution from Fordell Branch. Pursuant to this, a donation of £500 was allocated to the Nigerian miners, together with proceeds of pit collections. Other branches which passed resolutions of protest included Coylton/Rankinson, Kames, Fleets, Crosshouse/Dreghorn, Ormiston, Glencraig and Mary Branches.

A second example was the reaction of the Scottish miners to the suspension of the constitution granted to British Guiana, by Order-in-Council. Numerous branches protested, and the Scottish Executive passed a unanimous resolution on October 12, 1953. It was clear that the deposed Prime Minister of British Guiana, Dr. Cheddi Jagan, would get sympathetic hearing in Britain from many sections of the labour movement. Six weeks later a circular from the Scottish Trades Union Congress caused an animated discussion on the Scottish Area Executive, and a unanimous decision for 'a considered reply to the document'. The letter to the Secretary of the Scottish Trades Union Congress began with the announcement of the decision 'to lodge a strong protest against your scandalous statement on British Guiana': and went on to challenge 'your authority to publish such a declaration', which was described as being in complete opposition 'to all previous decisions and policy of Congress when dealing with colonial countries'. The letter then subjected the document to a destructive analysis (from which its contents may be gathered), as follows:

In the first paragraph of your statement you justify the suspension of the restricted constitution in British Guiana on the grounds that

[1] Their report was received and accepted on November 8, 1954.

there was incontrovertible evidence to prove that the People's Progressive Party was pursuing policies which were manifestly designed to subvert the development of democratic institutions. Where is this evidence? Why do you not quote the evidence? The only evidence submitted is that in the White Paper issued by the Tory Government, and you have the audacity to use this to confuse the Scottish trade union movement, and at the same time to ally yourself with the present Tory Government to destroy the people and the movement who are the victims of the most undemocratic action carried out by the present Government.

Why do you not come out and state the truth—that the action taken by the Tory Government is for the purpose of defending colonial exploitation? Why do you not come out and tell the workers who it is who controls British Guiana and extracts huge profits from British Guiana? Are you not aware that the *Daily Herald* correspondent wrote from Georgetown on October 9 as follows: 'This afternoon, eighteen hours after my arrival, I am still looking for the crisis'? This statement was backed up by many other correspondents.

What right have you or the Tory Government to decide that colonial constitutions, with all their restrictions, will only be allowed to exist providing the people vote as the Tories want them to? Where is all your talk about democracy and freedom for small nations when you support a policy of sending troops and warships to use brute force against a defenceless colonial people of not more than half a million? Who is the aggressor that we have heard so much about from the General Council on previous occasions?

We state quite emphatically that you do not speak for the Scottish trade union movement on this question. On the other hand, you ally yourselves with the Tory Government, the worst enemies of democracy, not only against the colonial people but against the British working class. What the Tory Government is prepared to do now against colonial people they would do to the British working class, and have done in the past when their power was being challenged.

The letter of rejoinder then went on to deal with the second paragraph of the offending circular:

The second paragraph of your statement is even more misleading. What are the improvements obtained by the Manpower Citizens' Association? Please be good enough to quote them and do not make general statements without evidence. On this you use the same statement as is contained in the Government White Paper. The Tory Government says the same thing about the British engineers today. Is this justification for your doing likewise?

Why do you not publish the starvation wages paid by British imperialists to the sugar-workers in British Guiana? Why do you not quote some facts regarding the workers' conditions from the report of the Commission of Inquiry set up by the Labour Government into the sugar industry in British Guiana? It described the appalling conditions, when it stated: 'Men and women up to their waists or even higher in water were pulling out weeds with their hands, or removing mud and debris in small baskets.'

It was against these appalling conditions that the sugar-workers came out on strike in August 1953, led by the Guiana Workers' Industrial Union. Where was the Manpower Citizens' Association, about which you are concerned in your circular? The White Paper indicates that the big employers and the Tory Government support the Manpower Citizens' Association.

We challenge you to quote any evidence to contradict these facts dealing with the situation in British Guiana.

The letter then ended, after dealing with these paragraphs, with a demand for 'complete withdrawal', as follows:

In connection with the association of the P.P.P. with other organisations and countries, we would have thought that members of the General Council would have been the last to use such a despicable argument, in view of their past associations. On this basis there is hardly a labour or trade union leader in the country who could not be placed in a similar category because of past associations.

The greatest crime of all, however, is to be associated with the present anti-working class policy of the Tory Government, which has demonstrated in the past and is demonstrating now more than ever that it has no regard whatever for the constitutional rights of colonial people, and is prepared to crush them with violence and bloodshed.

We demand the complete withdrawal of this circular in the interests of the constitutional rights of all colonial people, and in order to save the good name of the Scottish trade union movement, which has always been in the vanguard in the fight for colonial independence and progress.

Yours faithfully,

WILLIAM PEARSON
General Secretary,
on behalf of Executive Committee,
N.U.M. (Scottish Area).

To this broadside a reasoned reply from the General Council of the Scottish T.U.C. was awaited. It did not come for over two months. Then the minutes of February 23, 1954, record the receipt of a reply and add: 'The reply quoted merely the statements of a Miss Rita Hinden of the Fabian Society'. The matter was to be pursued further and raised at the forthcoming Scottish Trades Union Congress.

5. PEACE DELEGATIONS

In March 1949 the decision was taken to send a delegation to the First World Peace Congress in Paris, which was to take place at the end of April. Accordingly the delegation was composed of an official, Vice-President John Wood; a member of the Executive, John McArthur; and two members from branches, which, according to the vote on this occasion, were the Annbank and Thankerton Branches, Peter O'Hara and John Boyd. In addition to the Executive-appointed delegation, the following Branch delegates attended: Thomas Kerr, Robert Tennant, Alexander Sharp, William McLean, jnr., and James Gorman. A full and detailed report by the delegation was circulated, and accepted by the Executive Committee at their meeting of June 20, 1949 (Minute 1), and thence by the Minute Conference of August 29, 1949.

The report relates that John Wood was selected as one of the four British speakers.

The Congress decided to set up a permanent international co-ordinating committee to popularise and carry on its work, helping to make known campaigns for peace in all countries and to prepare a further World Congress. Its final policy resolution called for support of the U.N. Charter against military alliances; reduction of heavy military expenditure; banning of atomic weapons and other methods of mass destruction; limitation of the armed forces of the Great Powers and effective international control of atomic energy for peaceful means.

Following the First World Peace Congress, John Wood and William Rollo represented the miners at the British Peace Conference in London in October 1949, at which John Wood gave the main report to the assembled 1088 delegates.

The following year an invitation was received for representation at the Second World Peace Congress. This was to have been held at Sheffield, in November 1950; but owing to the Government's refusal to grant entry visas to foreign delegates, was transferred to Warsaw at the last moment. When the invitation was received and discussed at the Executive

Committee meeting of October 23, 1950, there was a differ-ence of opinion as to whether it should be accepted.

On a vote being taken it was agreed by 10 votes to 6 that the Union should be represented at the Conference by one Official, one Executive member and two Branch delegates. (Vol. 1950–1951, pp. 217, 218, October 23, 1950, Minute 15.)

The delegates who attended the Second World Peace Con-gress at Warsaw, November 18–22, 1950, were John Miller and William Rollo for the Executive Committee, and David McArthur and William Brown from the East Plean and Coylton/Rankinston Branches. Their report, dated December 11, 1950, was unanimously accepted at the meeting of Decem-ber 18, 1950 (Minute 23), and was circulated. John Miller was elected to the Presidium, says the report, and in a speech to the Congress expressed the indignation of the British dele-gates at the action of their Government, which did all in its power to prevent the Congress meeting in Sheffield.

'I want to say', he declared, 'that this is my first visit to Poland, and when I saw the devastation of Warsaw, having read of the heroic fight put up by the people of Warsaw, I think there is no better place in Europe to hold this Congress for peace. We hear a great many lies told about the Iron Curtain. In reality it exists on the other side of the English Channel, as shown by the attitude of the British Govern-ment. The miners of Scotland have sent delegations to both the U.S.S.R. and Poland, and we have received delegations in return. The report of our delegates to those two countries has been to the effect that there is no such curtain there. They were allowed to choose whatever place they wished to see. It is the intention of the miners of the Scottish Area to extend these delegations to other Eastern countries, as we feel by doing so we will strengthen the bond of friendship between ourselves and the people of the countries we visit, and thereby make a practicable contribution to peace.'

The Congress decided to put forward three main points for the consideration of the United Nations and all Parliaments: (1) unconditional prohibition of atomic, bacteriological and other weapons of mass destruction, enforced by rigorous inter-national control, (2) reduction of the five Great Powers' armed forces to one-half or one-third within a year, (3) an international body within the framework of the U.N. Security Council to supervise the carrying-out of these terms. Delegates to subsequent peace conferences were appointed: John Wood and Alex. Edgar to the British Peace Committee National Conference in October 1951; Alex. Edgar, John Rutherford and delegates from the East Whitburn and Balgonie Branches to the Scottish Peace Committee in March 1952; and John Wood and delegates from the Argyll and Newton Branches the same month to the British Peace Committee National Conference.

In 1952 Vice-President John Wood was given leave of absence to attend a Pacific Peace Congress held in Peking. (Minute 4, August 11, 1952.)

At the end of the year there took place the Congress of the Peoples for Peace held in Vienna from December 12 to 20. This was attended by Executive members James McKendrick and Alexander Edgar. The two delegates took the occasion to visit the mining community at Grunbach, where they were received by the miners' branch officials.

6. THE CHINESE PEOPLE'S REPUBLIC

The first miners' delegation from any country to China was sent by the Scottish miners (on the invitation of the Chinese Miners' Union) between April 25 and May 16, 1954: and, as their report stated:

The Scottish Miners can thus again be regarded as pioneers in strengthening the bond of friendship between miners throughout the world.

The delegates were: Abe Moffat, President, Scottish Miners; Magnus Fairnie, Executive member, Scottish Miners; Sam Copeland, President, Scottish Colliery Enginemen, Boiler-men and Tradesmen's Association; R. F. Young, B.Sc., Safety and Technical Officer, Scottish Miners (Secretary for the delegation); John Hanlon, Joe O'Neill, Andrew Mitchell, working miners, at Forthbank, Castlehill and Mary Collieries respectively.

Their unanimous report began with a reference to the bad housing, roads, transport, sanitation, etc., which they describe as legacies of the past system of feudal landlordism which the Chinese fought for thirty years to change, eventually succeeding in 1949.

The Chinese people, recognising that progress was impossible without industrialisation, were now engaged in a vast programme to this end, which would transform China. The purpose of the report, therefore, was

to bring out the achievements already made during the short period of five years and to show that once the power of capitalism and feudal landlordism is broken the people, led by the working class, can overcome all obstacles and build an economy which will provide security and happiness for the people.

The report, which in its draft form ran to over fifteen thousand words, describes what they saw and heard, under the main headings: the May Day Celebrations in Peking; the meeting with the National Committee of the Chinese Miners' Union (covering safety, wages and welfare); Peking reconstruction; sight-seeing in Peking; education; peasant farming; north-east coal-field; Shanghai. In their visit to the north-east coal-field they found that on the outskirts of Fushun 'a vast seam of coal, varying from 131 feet to 393 feet in thickness, outcrops'. The open-cast mine, here worked by modern excavating and transportation machinery, was 'so vast that the members of the delegation were completely awestruck at first sight'. The production was over 40,000 tons per day, which, they noted, was 'equivalent to about half the output of the whole Scottish coal-field. An extensive lighting arrangement is erected to allow work to continue during darkness.' They then saw Lung Fung Colliery, where nearly six thousand are employed underground: 'On our approach to the pit we saw the massive concrete structure of the tower Koepe winder and observed the orderly and planned layout of the whole surface plant without any redd bing[1] to mar the beauty of the countryside'. One seam now worked by long-wall faces was from nearly 100 to 131 feet thick: a drainage scheme extracts the methane from the coal in advance of the workings and the gas is being used for fuel and other purposes. Previous methods had been old-fashioned and dangerous,

[1] 'REDD BING—A debris heap.' A Glossary of Scotch Mining Terms by J. Barrowman. (1886.)

and there had been many explosions. Now conditions were different:

In the whole North China coal-field employing over 150,000 miners there were only five fatal accidents during 1953. In the British coal-field employing 711,000 miners 364 persons were killed last year and this is the lowest on record. It is significant that no effort and expense is considered too great for the provision of good safe working conditions. This is particularly creditable since the country is presently undergoing complete economic reconstruction.

A further comment (on Lung Fung Colliery) ran:

It should be appreciated that these expensive developments were undertaken at a time when the economy of the country was undergoing vital reconstruction. This indicates quite clearly the regard which the Chinese have for the safety of the workers and such an attitude will inevitably yield increased output and productivity.

The Soviet Union has greatly assisted the Chinese with these and other technical developments by sending experts and offering guidance. But the Chinese are ingenious and skilful and once having learned, their technicians can compare with those in any other country.

The report finally gave their press statement, in which they summed up their experience on the mining situation and then, after inviting a delegation to visit Scotland, ended with the words:

In saying good-bye to all our friends in China we pledge ourselves to carry on the good cause for trade, friendship and peace that will bring benefits to the people of both countries.

Long live the unity of the Chinese and Scottish miners. Long live peace and friendship all over the world.

This was followed later in the year by a series of delegations to China, including representatives from other trade unions; from cultural and business circles; and finally from the Executive Committee of the Labour Party, headed by Mr. Clement Attlee in August 1954.

PRESIDENTIAL ADDRESS BY WILLIAM PEARSON

(Scottish Trades Union Congress, Rothesay, 1950)

After recalling Bob Smillie and other miners' representatives who had been his predecessors and after a reference to the General Election of February 1950, the President of the S.T.U.C. said:

As a movement, we must do everything possible to ensure that the desires of the people for better living conditions are put into effect. This can only be done by the working class using their mass organisations to see that such a policy is put into operation. Let it be clearly understood that no progress can be made without a powerful, active and critical trade union movement. Any weakening of the trade unions must be fought with every weapon at our disposal. We must always be watchful for any attempts to split our movement on issues which have no relation to the purpose of the trade unions. The trade unions must reserve the right to determine their own domestic affairs and allow no outside person to dictate policy.

We should never forget that the pioneers of the trade unions built them in order to defend the interests of the workers irrespective of race, colour or creed. It will be a sorry day if we ever depart from this basic principle and allow discrimination to operate within the movement. I therefore appeal to all delegates at this Congress to take every possible step to ensure 100 per cent. organisation. I also appeal to the workers to realise that membership of the trade union movement is necessary if we are to make any progress towards improved conditions and to resist any attack on working conditions. Let us never forget that the capitalist class are always ready to attack.

WAGES AND WORKING CONDITIONS

One of the biggest issues facing the trade union movement is the questions of wages and working conditions, and there are many opinions on this subject. I want to make it clear where I stand in this matter. The economic condition of this country is not good and a crisis is rapidly developing. Despite all the talk about a 'mixed economy', this is still a capitalist country with 80 per cent. of the industry privately owned to produce profits for their capitalist owners.

In such a situation a policy of wage-restraint, while prices and profits continue to rise, can bring nothing but disaster to the workers and will never solve the economic difficulties which beset this country. On the contrary, such a policy will intensify the crisis.

Sir Stafford Cripps stated in the House of Commons on March 21, 1950, that the pound was only worth 16s. 2d. compared with 1945. It is clear that if a man was earning £5 per week in 1945 and is still earning that amount, the value of that £5 has been reduced by 19s. 2d. and is now worth only £4 0s. 10d. We should never forget that there are hundreds of thousands of persons in that position and many even worse. It is clear that this means a lowering of real wages, and that the working-class standard of living is lower today than in 1947 while the position of the capitalists has improved.

It is of no use for anyone to try and compare the present crisis with that of 1931. If we do we will arrive at a wrong conclusion because of two factors: (1) production generally has increased; (2) people naturally expect a higher standard of living than in 1931.

There is only one thing which stands between us and progress and that is monopoly capitalism, and the trade union movement must never agree to surrender its rights. In this situation we require a real anti-Tory and genuine working-class policy. That is the only fundamental answer to the crisis, and that should be the workers' demand. I therefore stand openly against a policy of wage-restraint and favour an immediate wage increase for all who are below a decent standard of living. Any other policy is against that which our trade union movement has stood for in the past.

Many important unions such as the N.U.M., A.E.U., E.T.U. and N.U.R. have all decided to reject the policy of wage-restraint and have put forward claims for increased wages on behalf of their members, particularly the lower-paid workers. There is a clear indication that millions of workers are entirely dissatisfied with the present position and will never be content until this problem has been solved to their satisfaction.

Do not let this Congress be complacent on the question of unemployment, for even in this period of full employment the economic survey for 1950 forecasts that the unemployed figures will rise to 400,000. Scotland's unemployed army, already 74,000, will be further increased this year. This Congress has always been watchful regarding this problem, and I hope they will continue to take a close interest in it and take every step possible to prevent a growth of unemployment in Scotland.

WAR AND PEACE

Linked with the fight for higher wages and improved conditions for the workers is the struggle for peace and fraternal relations between the common people of the world. This is a troubled world in which the people live in deadly fear of the weapons of mass destruction, the atomic and hydrogen bombs.

I have never, in all my experience, witnessed such a campaign as that which has been going on in the press and on the radio in this country. It is a campaign which can only lead to war, slaughter, chaos and disaster. Deliberate attempts are made to create and foster the idea that the Soviet Union endangers the peace of the world, and little attention is given to the positive proposals made by that country. Certain people want us to forget the important part played by the Soviet Union in the war against Fascism, when $7\frac{1}{2}$ million people were killed, 30 million casualties sustained, millions of homes destroyed, thousands of factories, pits and collective farms destroyed, and boundless acres of their earth scorched to frustrate and defeat the Fascist invaders. Does anyone, knowing these facts, really believe the Soviet people desire to experience such a disaster again?

Let us always remember that the Soviet Union is a land of Socialism, a country from which the exploiters have all disappeared, a land where all the industry and wealth are owned by the people. Such a country has no interest in another war. All they desire is to live in peace with the rest of the world.

During the recent visit of the Scottish Miners' delegation to the Soviet Union, of which I was leader, Mr. Kuznetsov, Chairman of the Russian T.U.C. and Deputy Chairman of the Supreme Soviet, said to us:

The Soviet Government has no desire for war. They will never be aggressors. They have no desire for any extra territory. The Soviet Government desire the utmost trade and friendly relations with all countries. The Soviet people resent such foul slanders appearing in the press and issued by the B.B.C.

The General Council of the Scottish Trades Union Congress, mindful of the desires of the Scottish trade unions, has placed on the agenda of this Congress a very important resolution dealing with the question of peace. I hope the delegates will give serious consideration to this resolution, and the three proposals which it makes: (1) ban the atomic and hydrogen bombs; (2) destroy all existing stocks of atomic weapons; (3) establish international control of the sources of atomic power as a guarantee of its use for peaceful purposes.

We live in a world where powerful imperialist forces still exist and are aggressively active. If nothing is done to curb them these imperialists will involve the world in a war in order to maintain their system of profit-making and their domination and exploitation of millions of men and women throughout the world. It is only madmen and criminals who talk about using the atomic bomb and they should be treated in an appropriate manner, and their power to incite war taken away from them. You cannot have progress and war at one and the same time. The people must choose either war and death or peace and progress. Speaking for myself, I would rather be a fighter for peace than an advocate and plotter for war. I am certain I express the heartfelt desires and aspirations of millions of people in Scotland and throughout the world.

In conclusion, may I remind delegates that we have still many problems to solve, such as housing, health centres, development of industry, and many others. I want to put in a plea here for the old-age pensioners whose allowances are also affected by the fact that the pound is only valued at 16s. 2d. They cannot afford to bear such a burden, and I appeal for immediate consideration being given to the people who have given of their best to this country. These problems can only be solved by Congress playing a more active part than it has ever done to meet the needs of the people.

Let this Congress give the people a message of hope, a guarantee that the power of our movement will be used to build in our country an economy which will banish for all time the prospect and possibility of hunger and war. Let us bend our every effort to the creation of Socialism here as the only real answer to our problems, a society in which all the latent talents and ability of the working class will find a fruitful outlet and human personality will grow in all its majestic splendour.

KNOCKSHINNOCH CASTLE COLLIERY DISASTER, AYRSHIRE, SEPTEMBER 1950
Two views of the cave-in

KNOCKSHINNOCH DISASTER, SEPTEMBER 1950
Rescue squad with breathing apparatus going into the pit

CHAPTER XV

KNOCKSHINNOCH

I. EARLIER MOSS DISASTERS

In the seven decades that followed the terrible Blantyre Calamity of 1877 there were not a few other disasters as well as the daily toll of accidents and, too often, fatal injuries. Here we deal with disasters of a special kind, of which Knockshinnoch in 1950 was the most terrible.

Scotland did not in this present century suffer from explosions of fire-damp or coal-dust which make up the tale of principal colliery disasters to anything like the extent found in some other British coal-fields. In one respect, however, the Scottish coal-field had an unenviable notoriety. This was by the abundance of moss or peat on the surface in the neighbourhood of coal-workings. No Act of Parliament and no General Rule under the Mines Acts made any provision whereby to avoid disaster arising from such a source. The terrible disaster at Knockshinnoch was not the first to be caused by an inflow of moss, rare though that is. The first of this kind during this century was that at the Donibristle Colliery on August 26, 1901, where men were smothered and suffocated underground by the inflow of moss, with the loss of eight lives.[1] It was situated in the parish of Aberdour, near Cowdenbeath, on the southern edge of the Fife coal-field. Most of the workings lay under Moss Morran, a mile square of moorland, 450 feet above sea level, which 240 years before had been a sheet of water. Underground some 270 men were employed. The Mynheer seam had been entered at seventy-seven fathoms and had then been worked up a long steep incline. Ten months before the disaster the heading had reached the outcrop, and operations were then stopped to see whether a connection could be made with the surface to get an easier access to the workings.

[1] Cd. 851, 1901; Cd. 1062, vii, 1902, p. 13.

It was known that an inrush forty years before had taken place only 300 yards away. Yet on August 22, 1901, operations were begun in the heading, probing upwards with a seventeen-foot rod. At 1.40 P.M. on August 26, as two men were continuing operations, the moss burst in. They were instantly smothered, and two men working at lower levels also lost their lives. Oversman Rattray at once led a rescue party of three others in from another level. None were ever seen again; and a stopping was put in. Six others were imprisoned.

Rescue work was hampered because the plans of the mine were not in the colliery offices. The only possibility of rescue was by going down from the surface, through the gaping chasm in the moss. This was at the bottom of an amphitheatre, hundreds of yards in circumference, round which large crowds stood watching. Twenty-four hours after the disaster, after wire ropes had been fixed across the hole and a carriage fitted, three volunteers went down to rescue five of those imprisoned. But while two of the rescuers were below searching for the sixth man, the moss flowed in upon them, 'the movement being helped by the weight of the large crowd, which eagerly pressed forward, and could not be kept back'. Many narrowly escaped being carried down with the moss. Wooden beams with iron hangers were improvised and 'about 2 A.M. on the 29th, Robert Law, miner, Cowdenbeath, having volunteered, was lowered down the heading at the end of a wire rope'. He succeeded. The last survivor and two entombed rescuers were safely drawn up. Later bodies of three of the eight victims were recovered.[1]

[1] A ballad is still sung of the rescue:

On the 26th of August our fatal moss gave way,
Although we did our level best its course we couldn't stay.
Ten precious lives there were at stake; who'll save them, was the cry.
We'll bring them to the surface, or along with them we'll die.
There were Rattray and McDonald, Hynd and Patterson,
Too well they knew the danger and the risk they had to run.
They never stopped to count the cost: We'll save them, was the cry
We'll bring them to the surface or along with them we'll die....
They lost their lives, God help them! Ah yes, it was a fact.
Someone put in a stopping and they never did get back.
Was that not another blunder? My God, it was a sin
To put in a stopping, for it closed our heroes in.
We never shall forget them now they have lost their lives,
So let us pay attention to their children and their wives.
It simply is our duty now, so let us all beware:
Their fathers died a noble death and left them to our care.

From *Come All Ye Bold Miners*, A. L. Lloyd.

An Enquiry was held in the Dunfermline Sheriff Court on September 25, 1901, with this finding:

The jury unanimously find that the deceased were killed in the Mynheer Seam of No. 12 Pit of Donibristle Colliery on August 26th, 1901, by a subsidence of the mossy surface, which flowed into the workings.

H.M. Inspector J. B. Atkinson in his Report comments: 'This colourless verdict satisfies all the requirements of the Fatal Accidents Inquiry (Scotland) Act so far as the jury is concerned'. He continued:

This accident shows plainly the danger of tapping moss from below, and that in making a connection between the surface and workings beneath through such material the work should be prosecuted downwards and not upwards.

Another passage has special significance:

It is an accident that might have been expected to have been more frequent in the early years of coal mining when shallow seams were more worked; but, *per contra*, it is only of late years that coal has been worked on a large scale under moorland, which usually lies at high elevations in sparsely-populated districts away from centres of industry, and this accident is a valuable object lesson to many mines now working under mosses. (P. 12.)

It should be noted that there was a war on: the Boer War had not yet concluded. Coal had leapt up in price. The increased demand for coal was highly profitable at that moment.

Again, during the first World War there occurred in 1918 an inflow of moss at Stanrigg which caused the loss of nineteen lives. It was after this that an Enquiry was held and the Moss Regulation of 1920 was issued. This Regulation prescribed the precautions to be taken when coal was being worked under moss and the thickness of strata above that must be maintained (sixty feet or ten times the thickness of the seam, whichever be the greater). Precautions were taken accordingly under this, and it was after Regulation 29 had been mining law for thirty years that there occurred the tragedy of Knockshinnoch.

2. KNOCKSHINNOCH

In the east of Ayrshire, in the parish of New Cumnock, lies Knockshinnoch Castle Colliery, with extensive workings underground and on the surface sixteen acres of peat as shown on the geological map. Late on Thursday evening, September 7, 1950, it was announced on the wireless that there had been a terrible disaster, and that 129 miners were entombed. A large volume of liquid peat or moss (60,000 tons according to one estimate) had rushed in where the workings had been driven to within much less than sixty feet of the surface. In the words of the official report:

> The inrush started at the point where the No. 5 Heading, which was rising at a gradient of 1 in 2, had effected a holing at the outcrop of the seam beneath superficial deposits and had made contact with the base of a relatively large natural basin containing glacial material and peat. The liquid matter, rushing down the steeply inclined heading, continued to flow for some time and soon filled up a large number of existing and abandoned roadways as well as several working places, until it eventually cut off the two means of egress to the surface from the underground workings of the colliery. (Cmd. 8180, p. 7.)

Thirteen men employed in or about the No. 5 Heading were missing; 116 men, finding themselves trapped, found their way inbye to a part of the mine then unaffected by the inrush. The peat continued to flow for some time and soon filled up miles of the underground roadways and blocked all means of exit from the underground workings to the surface.

The announcement of the disaster cast a gloom over the Scottish coal-field and throughout Britain. When it was learned that the underground telephone was intact and that through it the 116 could speak to the surface from their living tomb, there was a glimmering of hope. Was a rescue possible? The union representatives, as well as the higher officials of the N.C.B. Area and H.M. Inspector of Mines, were quickly on the scene. From the T.U.C. in session at Brighton, William Pearson, followed by Abe Moffat, sped northward to Knockshinnoch. Anxious hours followed, while on the surface miners and their families, wives who might for all they knew soon be widows, were waiting through the night.

It soon became clear that the only hope of rescue was through the neighbouring Bank No. 6 pit, where disused workings came near to the Knockshinnoch seams with a barrier of only 24 feet between. Rescue teams were soon present. At 11.30 on the Thursday night a first party of rescuers equipped with gas-masks (Proto apparatus) and headed by one of H.M. Inspectors of Mines set out to explore the rough sloping cavern that led down for two miles inbye towards the barrier at the 'Waterhead Dook'. A second party met them three hours later as they returned to report that accumulated gas from the disused workings made passage impossible. Thereupon on that Friday morning, September 8, powerful fans were installed to draw away the poisonous fire-damp. The 116 men underground were told through the still functioning telephone that they must wait patiently till the gas was sucked away. The fans worked on hour after hour: but more gas kept pouring from the seams, and by 4 P.M. on Friday it was clear that no real progress had been made. The gas remained, flooding the old channel of escape. But a new hazard arose. If the barrier were pierced (and the entombed men had already driven three-quarters way through it), the gas from the Bank pit might rush through the opening into Knockshinnoch workings and suffocate the miners entombed there. The entombed men were told of the new peril and were warned to pierce a hole in the barrier but to be ready to stop it up again if the fire-damp blew in upon them. Fortunately when this was done a current of air *from* the Knockshinnoch workings kept back the gas, and by the evening rescue teams (each equipped with an oxygen-breathing apparatus which had required several weeks' training to use) were able to pass food and drink through to the trapped men. As night fell on Knockshinnoch it was realised by the rescuers and by the thousands who were watching and waiting that, powerfully though the fans were running, the gas was not yet overcome. Meanwhile the 116 trapped men, for whom it had been night all the time, could only hope and hope, with no certainty that they would ever see the light again. Wm. Pearson, in the pamphlet[1] he wrote on the disaster, places on record 'the

---

[1] *The Tragedy of Knockshinnoch*, September 7, 1950, compiled by William Pearson, General Secretary, N.U.M. (Scottish Area).

splendid spirit shown by the men during their trying ordeal' which 'demonstrated the fine fighting nature of the miners'. But it was weary, weary waiting; and all the imprisoned men were cheered when the N.C.B. Deputy Labour Director, D. W. Park, wearing his breathing apparatus, arrived in their midst at 3.40 in the morning of Saturday. He had special knowledge of rescue technique, had previously worked in Knockshinnoch and was personally known to many of them. Having joined them, he would not leave them. He stayed on to the end.

By Saturday morning, September 9, on the surface it was realised that the plan of rescue was not likely to succeed: for there was no prospect of real progress in clearing the gas from the roadways of the Bank pit. Further, D. W. Park from below had sent a report that the ventilation in the Knockshinnoch workings was rapidly worsening: that the proportion of fire-damp in the atmosphere was steadily increasing: and that 'unless something was done very quickly, he was afraid it would be too late'.

Now there was another possibility which those in charge of the rescue work had been loth to apply. This was to employ the Salvus apparatus, whose use, though frequent in fire brigade work, they felt would not be in accordance with the Safety Regulations. William Pearson and others, worried that a strict compliance with the Regulations might hinder the saving of life, strongly urged its use. At length on Saturday those in charge of the rescue work agreed 'but with grave misgivings' to risk the wearing of the Salvus and that by men not previously trained to it. As described in the Government Report the new scheme for rescue was 'to form a "chain" of rescue brigade men along the whole length of the gas-filled roadway on the Bank side who would pass sets of Salvus apparatus through to the trapped men. A rescue team would enter the Knockshinnoch workings and instruct the men in the use of the apparatus, fit it on them, and pass them out along the "chain".' It may be imagined with what relief the trapped men heard of this scheme and then saw the first of their company guided out through the deadly gas. A sick man was brought out on a stretcher at 2.45 P.M. But this was succeeded by a dreadful period of over two hours when nobody came to their rescue. Five rescue teams had been exhausted, and there was two hours' delay before sufficient teams could be assembled. Shortly after 5 P.M. the rescue operation was resumed and went on steadily till the last of the trapped men was brought out just before midnight on Saturday, September 9, 1950. The risk taken had been justified.

Was there any possibility of rescuing the thirteen missing men who had been working near the inrush of peat? Early on the morning of Friday, September 8, with the aid of Messrs. Wimpey's organisation, work had begun to make safe the crater in the peat field, and by Sunday evening, September 10, two parties of brave men went down into the gulf and entered the workings. But nothing could make the crater safe. Heavy rain persisted. 'Masses of moss', says the Report, 'were slowly but continuously closing in on the opening into the No. 5 Heading': and by Monday, September 11, 'it was felt there was no hope of reaching or rescuing any of the thirteen missing men and that there was no justification for risking loss of life among the rescuers. Subsequent events have served to confirm that the decision was correct.'

On that same day, Monday, September 11, the Scottish Executive Committee meeting in Edinburgh, in a letter to the Knockshinnoch miners, expressed their deep sympathy for the hardship and suffering endured and their hope that the continuing rescue operations might yet be successful. If unsuccessful, the first consideration of the union would be to protect the women and children left. A special tribute was paid to the rescuers:

to all those who had been prepared to sacrifice their lives by participating in the rescue work at the colliery.

As always the response of the miners had been immediate: and indeed some neighbouring pits had been partially idle because of the number of men who had volunteered to assist. The spirit of the men was illustrated by an incident where one of the men who had been rescued on Saturday had explained to the President at midday on the following day that he had returned in order to volunteer to take part in the rescue work.[1]

---

[1] Pearson says in the Preface to his pamphlet:

I must place on record the splendid spirit shown by the men during their trying

The union had kept in constant touch with the position, the officials having been present throughout the week-end. 'Messrs. Sneddon, Young and Craig are at present at Knockshinnoch, and arrangements have been made for either the President or the Secretary to make a visit every day if possible. Conferences with the Board officials are also being held daily.' Finally it was agreed to call upon the Ministry of Fuel and Power to hold a public Inquiry into the cause of the disaster. The Minister agreed and appointed Sir Andrew Meikle Bryan, H.M. Chief Inspector of Mines, to be the Commissioner.

Meantime in the latter part of September investigations went forward. For the union they were carried out by the President, Abe Moffat, assisted by a member of the staff, Miss R. Barnes, by the Workmen's Electrical Inspector, Robert Young, by the Workmen's Inspectors, Andrew Craig and Robert Maxwell, by Daniel Sim, Ayrshire District Secretary, and by the local officials of the New Cumnock Branch. By this means very valuable evidence was made available for the Inquiry.

3. THE INQUIRY

The Inquiry, which opened at Ayr on November 7, 1950, and went on for eight days, was remarkable in several ways. Amongst the parties to the Inquiry, the N.C.B. was represented entirely by lawyers headed by R. P. Morison, K.C. The N.U.M. relied on the Scottish President Abe Moffat to conduct the case for the union on behalf of the dependents of the killed and injured miners. Three other Executive members, namely, Arthur Horner, General Secretary; J. A. Hall of Yorkshire; and William Pearson, General Secretary of the

ordeal. As usual, they demonstrated the fine fighting nature of the miners at this very difficult and trying period.

On behalf of the N.U.M. I wish to express to all rescue workers and volunteers our very best thanks for the grand work they did during the difficult period of rescue operations. No one flinched in the face of the grave danger which faced them at this stage. Each time an appeal was made for 25 volunteers there was a mighty rush of people all eager to do their part and render whatever assistance they could. I saw many men going down the mine dressed in their best clothes but no one gave a thought to the fact that their clothes would be ruined. All they were concerned with was the desperate plight of the entombed men.

I must also extend to all who gave valuable assistance in the rescue work, feeding and medical attention, the best thanks of the N.U.M. (Scottish Area).

Scottish Area, were appointed to attend the Inquiry. Witnesses, after their examination by H.M. Inspector of Mines for Scotland, were cross-examined by Abe Moffat and by R. P. Morison, K.C. It was unusual that an array of lawyers on one side should be confronted not by other lawyers but by elected trade union officials. William Pearson in his pamphlet says:

I think everyone will agree that the attitude of the N.U.M. was fully justified in every way, and that Mr. Abe Moffat was equal to the importance of the occasion. His manner of questioning, his patience with witnesses and his knowledge of mining left nothing to be desired. It will go down in history that he did a splendid job on behalf of the dependents of the thirteen men who lost their lives, and also a great deal in the interests of safety in the mines. While he showed the utmost patience with witnesses he also demonstrated his determination to receive answers to his questions.

The cross-examinations by Abe Moffat and by R. P. Morison, K.C., on the evidence led, especially that of responsible officials, often took on the appearance of a trial in which one was counsel for the prosecution and the other counsel for the defence. This was noted by the considerable audience of miners of whom Pearson writes:

The miners, old and young, followed the proceedings closely and made keen and critical comments. More than once the criticism was heard that the N.C.B.'s attitude appeared to be little different from that of the old colliery owners, who always sought to show that no blame could possibly attach to their officials and themselves. Others were heard to remark that the Coal Board was more concerned to avoid the risk of actions for Common Law damages. Whether these comments and questions were warranted or not, the fact that they were made shows the keen interest, and in some cases the bitter feeling, that was prevalent in the mining community.

The purpose of the Inquiry was to make formal investigation under the Acts 'into the causes of, and circumstances attending, the accident', which would also reveal who, if any, was responsible. On this the N.C.B., in so far as they did not impute blame to one of the men killed, tended to ascribe the cause to an Act of God and not to any human negligence. The union on the other hand maintained that the accident could have been prevented and would not have taken place but for breaches of the Coal Mines Act by those responsible for its enforcement.

What led up to the accident? First of all there was confusion in the organisation of the N.C.B.'s sub-area, in which lay the New Cumnock group of mines and Knockshinnoch Castle Colliery. The No. 5 Heading underground, shown on an April 1950 progress plan as being driven upward on a gradient of 1 in 4, had steepened by early July till the gradient of the seam was almost 1 in 2. 'This fact', says the Report, 'does not appear to have been treated by the management as a matter of concern, nor as something to which the attention of the planning department should have been drawn', and Sir Andrew Bryan concluded: 'Altogether, the evidence on this important matter of planning was unsatisfactory, conflicting and disappointing'. No. 5 Heading was driven rapidly upward till, on August 30, an explosive shot blew through the 'breast-coal' and exposed a bed of stones. Water started immediately to run out of this opening, in amount 'as from a 2-inch pipe'. The flow of water remained constant till the morning of the accident, when it doubled or trebled. This was reported about 9.30 A.M. to the responsible officials who, however, 'seem to have been more concerned as to whether the outbye pumps would be able to deal with the increased quantity of water than with any possible danger the increase might portend'. At 6.30 P.M. on September 7 the No. 5 Heading Section fireman reported a big fall of roof to the overman, who ascended to look at the surface, and found there in the field a hole some 400 feet square and 2 feet deep. The overman then went underground to investigate and at the entrance to No. 5 Heading, about 7.30 P.M., felt the sudden blast of air and then a 'terrific roar' as the peat rushed into the workings. One of the miners, sent to put a fence round the hole on the surface, found that the hole rapidly extended itself, 'the ground flowing in from all sides to the point where the first subsidence had appeared'. The Manager, questioned on what he saw of the movement at the crater, said 'The grass had gone down out of sight'.

Question: Was there a hole right down?
Answer: There was a hole—a deep hole.
Q.: Had it gone bodily or had it tapered in?

A.: It turned in like this (indicating). The grass broke when it turned in.

Q.: A sort of vortex?

A.: Yes, a sort of circular moving and tore the grass.

Q.: You have seen water running out of a bath or basin when the plug is pulled out; you get a vortex?

A.: It was something like that.

Those of us who listened to this evidence had an immediate vision of the disaster. Below this ten-thousand-year-old basin men had been tunnelling upwards for months through the coal until the plug was reached and pulled out, when the contents swirled down and whelmed miles of the workings in semi-liquid sludge.

How could such a thing have happened? Why, given the clear marking of surface peat on the geological map, had the precautions prescribed in the Moss Regulation not been taken? According to the sworn evidence of witnesses, none of those responsible had looked at the map, or, if they had looked at it, had not observed what was on it.

4. MOFFAT ON BEHALF OF THE N.U.M.

This and other disturbing facts about the accident, if not elicited by H.M. Divisional Inspector, were brought out mainly in the cross-examination from the side of the trade union. Indeed one of the remarkable features of the Inquiry was the part played by the miners' union. Not only had the whole energies of leading officials been given to the preliminary investigation, but a precedent was created when the union cited expert witnesses. In the past it had always been the employers who had made use of scientific and technical experts. But on this occasion the union cited a geologist (Mr. D. H. Gwinner), two analytical chemists (Mr. C. W. Herd and Mrs. L. M. Mundy), a former divisional Inspector of Mines (Mr. A. H. Steele): while the conclusive evidence of the farmer Andrew Wilson on the nature of the surface would not have been available but for the efforts of the union. The major responsibility in this union effort fell upon the Scottish President. He addressed himself more particularly to eliciting the sequence of events before the accident, the causes of the accident and the extent to which there appeared to have been contraventions of the Coal Mines Act, 1911. While always courteous, he was no respecter of persons: and one of 'the higher-ups', the Area General Manager, was at the insistence of the union put in the witness-box, where, under examination by Abe Moffat and afterwards by Sir Andrew Bryan, he gave useful evidence. Here is part of it:

ABE MOFFAT: Let me put to you just one or two other questions. What precautions, in your opinion, should be taken to prevent a repetition of this accident?
D. L. McCARDEL: A more thorough knowledge of the subject with regard to the surface.
Question: I think you will agree with me that you can't leave that entirely to the agents or managers?
Answer: No, I wouldn't agree there.
Q.: I say you can't leave it entirely?
A.: Not entirely, no. I might interpolate and say, again, that if peat had been known to exist here I am quite certain that the agent or manager would have brought it to the notice of others for consultation.
Q.: So you at least suggest a more thorough knowledge of the surface?
A.: Yes.
Q.: By all concerned?
A.: By all concerned.
Q. And all who have any responsibility whatever?
A.: Definitely.
Q.: Even although you had a more thorough knowledge of the surface what would be the good of the existing regulations if they were not put into practice?
A.: None.

In finding what led up to the disaster, which could have been prevented, much turned upon the Moss Regulation under the Act and in particular upon the geological map. Here are questions put by Abe Moffat to J. H. Cairns, Sub-Area Senior Planner:

Question: All planning in this area comes under your supervision?
Answer: Yes, it does.
Q.: And you accept responsibility for the planning?
A.: Yes, I do.
Q.: You said in reply to Mr. Houston this morning that you didn't know there was moss there until after the accident; is that correct?
A.: That is correct.

Q.: Is it your job, or is it not your job, to find out if there is moss?

A.: Well, you can't be running all round the country looking for moss.

Q.: I am not suggesting you should be running all round the country looking for moss. I am asking you a straight and simple question: Is it your job, or is it not, to find out if there is moss?

A.: Well, if it is necessary to know—like if you come within certain limits of the surface, it is then time to look for moss.

Q.: How would you find out, in any circumstances, to ascertain whether there was moss or not?

A.: By going over the surface to begin with.

Q.: You would go over the surface to find out if there was moss?

A.: Yes.

Q.: And if in your judgment you walked over the surface and you said within yourself: 'There is no moss', would that satisfy you?

A.: In most cases it would.

Q.: Do you agree with me, after this unfortunate experience, that it is not sufficient just to do that?

A.: No, I wouldn't; I would still use my judgment yet.

Q.: Did you see the geological map previous to this accident?

A.: Many a time.

Q.: As a very important surveyor did you see on this geological map any indication of moss in this area?

A.: Not in that actual area, I didn't.

Q.: Have you seen the geological map since the accident?

A.: Yes, I have.

Q.: Does the geological map indicate that there is moss in this area?

A.: Well, it is marked as 'peat'.

Q.: Peat or moss?

A.: It is marked 'peat' really on this geological sheet.

Q.: So that you are admitting that at least since the accident you have seen the geological map?

A.: Yes.

Q.: And it indicates peat or moss in this area; is that correct?

A.: Yes.

Q.: And still you are telling me that you have looked at that geological map on several occasions?

A.: Yes, many an occasion.

Q.: And still you never traced moss in this area?

A.: No, I never saw it.

Q.: You never saw it?

A.: No.

Q.: Would I be correct in saying that you never even looked for it?

A.: I didn't look for it. I didn't think there was any occasion to.

Q.: Do you consider now it would have been better if you had looked for it?

A.: It would now, yes, I would say, on the face of that.

Moffat tackled each responsible person (most of them had had to pass examinations in geology) on this matter of the peat as shown on the map and repeatedly got admissions from these witnesses. To give only one more example, here are the questions put by Abe Moffat to D. MacKinnon, Assistant Sub-Area Planning Engineer:

Question: And are you telling us in Court today that while you are responsible for planning you never at any time gave any consideration to the question of moss?
Answer: No.
Q.: Although you saw the geological map on several occasions?
A.: Yes.
Q.: So you would agree with me that a dirty map would not be a reasonable excuse for not seeing moss?
A.: But I am not making an excuse. I say that the colouring that is on the map, if it is dirty, a man short in the sight would have trouble finding the symbol.
Q.: Was your map dirty?
A.: No.
Q.: So on your map, the map I was concerned about, it was easily observed?
A.: Yes.
Q.: But you tell the Court today you did not see it?
A.: No.
Q.: Prior to the accident?
A.: No.
Q.: Have you seen that same geological map since the accident?
A.: Yes.
Q.: Did you see any indication showing moss?
A.: Showing peat.
Q.: Showing peat?
A.: Yes.
Q.: Or moss?
A.: Peat.
Q.: Does the geological map show any indication of moss?
A.: No.
Q.: Are you an expert on peat and moss?
A.: I have an average knowledge of it.[1]

What was elicited in the cross-examination was of material help to the Inquiry. The view of the union upon the facts, causes, circumstances and responsibility for the disaster was

[1] The attempt to draw a distinction between peat and moss, which was maintained by many witnesses (apparently on the advice of the Coal Board's solicitors), was later blown sky-high by the experts cited by the union: both the Geological Survey expert and H.M. Inspectorate of Mines concurred.

summed up on September 16 in Moffat's final statement[1] beginning with the words: 'Mr. Commissioner, at this Inquiry I speak to-day on behalf of the National Union of Mineworkers and the dependents whose relatives lie buried at Knockshinnoch Colliery. At the outset I want to express our thanks and appreciation to all those who played such a noble part in the rescue work which eventually saved 116 workmen out of the 129 men entombed.' In the course of the statement which went into full detail of points in the evidence Moffat said:

Never had we so many warnings of an impending disaster and so little attention given by those responsible at the colliery. As a matter of fact, I would go further and say that there was a complete disregard of those previous warnings by those responsible at the colliery. . . .

In all my mining experience I have never witnessed such a disregard for the elementary protection of men's lives. Such persons in my opinion should not be entrusted with the charge of mineworkers in conditions of this kind. . . .

We cannot under any circumstances allow those regulations to remain dead letters; we cannot allow them to be completely ignored, as they have been, in my opinion, at Knockshinnoch Colliery, otherwise the lives of miners can become cheaper than they were in the old days of slavery. I submit, therefore, that this accident could have been avoided and 13 miners' lives saved had this important and necessary regulation been carried out.

I would like to say a word or two, Mr. Commissioner, if you will bear with me, on the evidence led at this Inquiry. Never in all my experience have I listened to such contradictory and confusing evidence by those who had some responsibility for the surveying, planning and direction of this colliery. All the surveyors, including the chief sub-area surveyor, admit that they did not know No. 5 Heading was approaching the surface. They never knew it was coming out on the surface. There was never any mark on the plan to indicate where it was coming out, and there was no consultation with them in the planning of the colliery. . . .

I am sure that nobody realised until it was revealed at this Inquiry that there was such a state of disorganisation and complete lack of understanding and cohesion between one department and another. It is time, in my opinion, that those responsible should give this matter some very serious consideration. If we can't get proper planning, understanding and cohesion at pit level it is going to be very difficult to establish these vital principles in the industry as a whole.

[1] Given in full in Wm. Pearson's *The Tragedy of Knockshinnoch*, which also gives twenty-eight pages of passages from the evidence.

The main question, however, that I am concerned about here is the safety of our men, because we can't tolerate a position, when faced with such a disaster, that each department shirks its responsibilities and endeavours to place the responsibility on the shoulders of some other department. That is a very unsatisfactory position when dealing with human lives.

Unfortunately the only points they did reach agreement on were complete ignorance of moss in the area, their complete ignorance of the intervening strata and their complete ignorance of whereabouts this heading was to strike the surface. Unfortunately, I say, because it was due to this alleged complete ignorance that 13 of our miners have paid the supreme sacrifice. . . .

Some people may feel I have been hard in cross-examining witnesses and even in my final submission. Let me say this again. There is nothing harder, more heart-rending, than to know that 13 valuable lives, the bread-winners of 13 miners' families, have been lost, which in my opinion could have been avoided. In this Inquiry we have a duty to perform and sentiment cannot be allowed to stand in the way of exposing unsafe methods of mining and especially when it comes to questions of violations of regulations. On behalf of the National Union of Mineworkers and the relatives of the deceased I have endeavoured to bring out the facts and the causes of this terrible disaster and I hope that, whilst we cannot bring back our 13 miners, we can at least protect miners in the future by eliminating for all time such disasters as we have experienced at Knockshinnoch Colliery.

In his submission Abe Moffat argued that there had been a breach not only of the Moss Regulation No. 29 but also of two sections of the principal Act: he held that the men should have been withdrawn. On this there was a noteworthy passage in the evidence given by the Manager, William Halliday, when under cross-examination by Moffat. The Manager, when he heard of the first subsidence in the field, had given instructions to put up a fence:

MOFFAT: Why did you instruct him at that time to erect a fence?
HALLIDAY: Because I have had experience—in that field there was cattle kept generally, and I have had experience before in Dalmellington, at No. 5 Pennyvenie, where such a sit[1] took place in old places and we had always to get them filled in and fenced because if the cattle got injured then we were responsible.
Question: So your concern at that time was the safety of the cattle?
Answer: Yes.

---

[1] 'SIT—A subsidence of the surface caused by the removal of mineral under it.' *A Glossary of Scotch Mining Terms.*

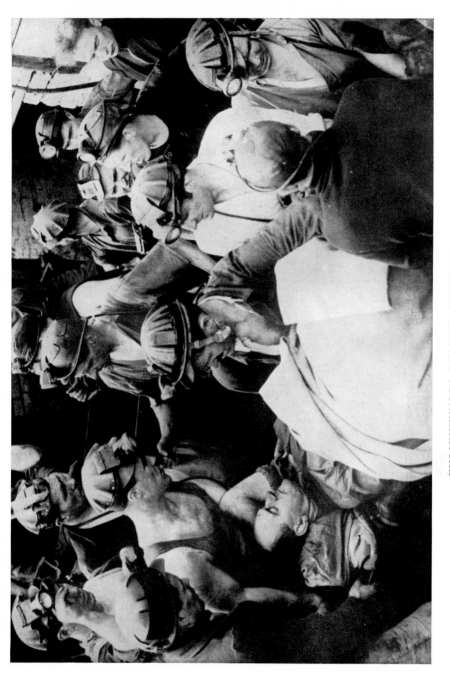

KNOCKSHINNOCH DISASTER, SEPTEMBER 1950
Rescuer overcome in attempt to reach entombed miners

VETERANS OF THE INDUSTRY
George McTurk, Ayrshire, 1953

Q.: Then, as you have already stated, you went over to Houston and had a talk with him, and even at that stage you didn't discuss with him the advisability of withdrawing the workmen?
A.: No.
Q.: Did you at any time at all during that unfortunate experience give any instructions that the workmen should be withdrawn?
A.: No.
Q.: I don't say when you could have given it. I say would it not have been better to have given the instruction prior to when you did give it?
A.: Can you tell me when I could have given that instruction with the information I had at my disposal?
THE COMMISSIONER: Don't ask questions. If you can't reply just say: 'I don't know the answer'. Mr. Moffat, will you put your question again?
By MOFFAT continued: Do you not consider, in the light of all that has been happening, that it would have been far better if you had given that instruction earlier?
A.: I consider that with the information I had at my disposal, I didn't require to give that instruction.

On this, however, Sir Andrew Bryan, as it turned out, took a different view from Moffat. On most of the other important points Moffat's statement correctly anticipated conclusions in the Report.

5. SIR ANDREW BRYAN'S REPORT

The Inquiry ended on November 16, but the great interest aroused amongst the miners and the public generally did not die away. At the next Scottish Executive Committee the Secretary, William Pearson, made appropriate comment on the attitude of the Divisional Coal Board and added:

Only the fact that the President had had the case so well prepared and had made such excellent presentation of every detail which would protect the interests of the miners and the dependents of the men killed, had enabled the Union to combat the Board's contention. By his skilful formulation of questions the President had been able to extract many important admissions from responsible officials of the Coal Board. (November 20, 1950.)

By this it had become clear that 'persons to whom the Board paid high salaries accepted no responsibility legally for the safe working of the mine'. This point, in Pearson's opinion, irrespective of the findings of the Inquiry, must receive consideration from the Executive. The union would also require to consider the position of the manager and agent, who had statutory authority, and to decide whether or not the members should again be allowed to work under them. (November 20, 1950.)

A week later William Pearson suffered a serious heart-attack (thrombosis) and was ordered a complete rest. After some nine weeks he was able to resume work and was present at the Area Delegate Conference of February 12, 1951, at which the President reported that, although confined to bed for so long, the Secretary had not been idle and one of the tasks he had undertaken was the compiling of a report, *The Tragedy of Knockshinnoch*: a copy would be issued free for every member of the union in Scotland. This pamphlet, published a few days later, had an immediate effect amongst the miners, particularly in Ayrshire. When, six months after the disaster, it was proposed to reopen Knockshinnoch Castle Colliery, a meeting of about 400 miners on March 4, 1951, unanimously passed a vote of no confidence in the management and asked the Scottish Executive 'to secure their dismissal'. The Executive, meeting next day, also heard a report from Mr. Sneddon that

The point had been brought out at the inquiry that an excessive amount of explosives was being used. The men were demanding a revision of rates and method of working in the places affected, since this dangerous practice could not continue and they would be unable to make decent wages if the excessive use of explosives were stopped.

These matters were taken up with the Coal Board: and the upshot of it, after some weeks, was that the agent retired and arrangements were made for another manager to be installed. Meantime the Report[1] of the Commissioner Sir Andrew Bryan, dated March 2, 1951, had been published. In this, after the necessary explanatory paragraphs of general information, a clear and succinct account was given of 'the accident and events leading up to it', followed at greater length by an

[1] Report on the causes of, and circumstances attending, the Accident which occurred at Knockshinnoch Castle Colliery, Ayrshire, on the 7th September 1950: by Sir Andrew Bryan, J.P., F.R.S.E., H.M. Chief Inspector of Mines. Presented by the Minister of Fuel and Power to Parliament by Command of His Majesty, March 1951. Cmd. 8180.

account of the rescue, including the outstanding part played by the overman Andrew Houston and by David Park, to whom high tribute was paid for his courage, calm demeanour and initiative.

Fully half the report is then taken up by a series of comments. The first four were:

(a) On the sequence of events at the face of No. 5 Heading before the inrush.
(b) On the relationship between the Planning Department and the Colliery Management and their responsibilities in respect of development plans.
(c) On the examination of the surface.
(d) On the condition of the peat or moss in the field before the moment of inrush.

The next three comments arose entirely from the submissions put forward by Abe Moffat. They were:

(e) On the application of Section 67 of the Coal Mines Act, 1911.
(f) On the application of Section 68 of the Coal Mines Act, 1911.
(g) On the interpretation of the word 'Agent' within the meaning of the Coal Mines Act, 1911.

The eighth comment 'On the application of the Moss Regulations' rebutted the case as argued on behalf of the Coal Board, while the ninth was 'On the rescue and the conduct of all concerned with it'.

In these comments, despite the mildness of their phrasing, there was material (as also in the account of the accident) for a formidable indictment of those responsible. Part of the comments were in rebuttal of the view that the Moss Regulation of 1920 had not been contravened as well as of other views put forward by Mr. Morison, K.C. For example, the Commissioner said that 'I cannot accept the statement' by Mr. Morison that 'there were no indications diagnostic of moss upon the surface at all', and continued:

As I have already said, moss was seen on the surface; the officers of the Geological Survey had observed it, mapped its extent and marked it on the geological map of the district; the farmer knew very well it was there; and, as previously indicated, I am convinced that had the examination of the surface which was made by the various responsible officials comprised even an elementary examination of the nature or character of the ground, they would also have found peat or moss.

His conclusion arising from these particular comments, namely, that the Moss Regulation had been contravened, was subject to questions of legal interpretation, as was also the Commissioner's opinion that there had been no contravention of Sections 67 or 68 of the Coal Mines Act, 1911 as Mr. Moffat had submitted.

The view taken in the Report on the legal inapplicability of these last two sections naturally brought some comment in contemporary journals. Mr. O. H. Parsons, a London solicitor, wrote:

First, Mr. Moffat (N.U.M.) submitted that there had been a failure to comply with S. 67 of the Coal Mines Act, 1911. This reads as follows:

> If at any time it is found by the person for the time being in charge of the mine, or any part thereof, that, by reason of the prevalence of inflammable or noxious gases, or of any cause whatever, the mine or any place in the mine is dangerous, every workman shall be withdrawn from the mine or place found dangerous.

The report says:

> Nevertheless, the fact remains, as the event proved, that danger of an inrush of moss existed, at least from the moment the shot blew through. But on the facts as known or ascertained by the colliery officials at that time, no one at the colliery was aware of the danger. Except as regards the presence of inflammable gas for which a definite withdrawal standard is laid down, withdrawal in other circumstances of danger is required only when the person or persons in charge *find* the mine or part of the mine to be dangerous. In this particular case, all the persons who may be regarded as being in charge, clearly did not know until the moment of final disaster of the presence of liquid moss, and, therefore, had no reason to consider the mine dangerous.

This finding raises a most serious question. With respect, Sir Andrew Bryan is quite clearly right in his view, but where does it lead us? Except in the case of inflammable gas, there can never be an offence under this Section—no matter how blatant the danger signals may be—unless the colliery officials are *of opinion* that there is danger. Their subjective opinion and no objective standard based on the facts: this is the test. The only time an offence under this Section could be established is if a colliery official says: 'I knew there was danger, but, despite this, did not withdraw the men', a fantastic possibility. The need for amendment of Section 67 by inserting a definite withdrawal standard for all classes of case is clear. It is appreciated that the drafting of such an amendment would not be easy but the Knockshinnoch tragedy shows the urgent need for a stringent tightening-up of this most vital Section. (*Labour Research*, May 1951, pp. 93–4.)

In the case of Section 68 the argument also turned on the precise meaning of the word 'place'. Sir Andrew Bryan, after quoting Mr. Morison's construction of the Section, comes to the view that the word 'place' has the same meaning as 'underground working'. Mr. Parsons argues that this question of legal applicability is one that, if the Commissioner is right in his view (Sir Andrew Bryan, it should be noted, said 'I cannot presume to give a legal interpretation'), would narrow the scope of the Section. To a layman it must certainly appear that each of these Sections would be all the better for being redrafted.

Apart from his conclusions (weakness in organisation, failure to observe the presence of peat, though shown on the geological survey map, failure to make proper examination of the ground in the field, and consequentially, a breach of the Moss Regulation) Sir Andrew Bryan made the following eleven recommendations, of which numbers 1–4 and 6, he was pleased to report, were being accepted and put into operation by the N.C.B.:

(1) A copy of any map and of any relevant memoir published by the Geological Survey and relating to the district in which a mine is situated should be kept in the office of the manager of the mine and also in the offices of the surveying and planning departments relating to that mine.
(2) Where the geological map or any boring, mining, geological or other record shows the presence of peat or any unconsolidated deposit within, or in proximity to, the boundaries of a mine, the limits and nature of such deposits should be shown on the working plan of the mine, and the General Regulations, 1920, No. 1423 (Workings under Moss, etc.—Precautions) should apply to all workings under areas so defined.
(3) Before any working approaches within 600 feet of the surface where the nature of the intervening ground between the surface and the expected horizon of the working has not been determined, the manager should obtain the advice of a competent field geologist as to the nature of the intervening ground, and should consider such advice in determining what precautions, if any, are necessary before further working is undertaken.

(4) No working should approach within 150 feet of the surface until the nature of the intervening ground between the surface and the expected horizon of the proposed working has been determined by boring or other approved means.

(5) Except with the permission of the inspector and subject to such conditions as he may think fit to impose, any working which is being driven towards the surface or a superficial deposit and has approached within fifty yards of the surface or the base of the deposit should not exceed ten feet in width.

(6) Research should be started to explore the possibilities of a rapid and accurate geophysical or other method of surveying to determine the thickness, nature and extent of all unconsolidated superficial deposits.

(7) The provision of some form of simple, light-weight, self-contained breathing apparatus which could be worn by any workman after the minimum instruction should be investigated without delay and, when such apparatus is available, arrangements should be made to maintain supplies at all Central Rescue Stations or other suitable centres in every mining district.

(8) Where practicable, the provision of an 'escape' roadway giving direct access to an adjacent mine should be considered.

(9) Consideration should be given to the provision of a type of telephone cable for underground use in mines which will be highly resistant to damage from inrush, inundation or fire.

(10) A suggestion I made in my Final Report on the Explosion at Whitehaven 'William' Colliery, Cumberland (Cmd. 7410), namely, that consideration should be given to the desirability of providing temporary erections such as tents or prefabricated structures, to cope with the accommodation necessary for the large number of persons employed in rescue and recovery operations at a time of disaster, should be acted upon.

(11) In the National Coal Board organisation the status and responsibility of all Planning Engineers, Planners and Surveyors at all levels should be clearly defined in relation to those of Colliery Agents and Managers.

This eleventh recommendation arose, it may be noted, almost entirely from his comment on the submission put forward by Abe Moffat, namely, *On the interpretation of the word 'Agent' within the meaning of the Coal Mines Act, 1911.*

6. JUSTICE FOR THE DEPENDENTS

An impartial observer might have expected that the Coal Board would be anxious to demonstrate that, in one respect at least, it was a model employer; in the attitude it would take towards the dependents of the thirteen dead miners, and to the claims for injuries and loss of wages of the 116 survivors. Indeed, since the Court of Inquiry had established that there was a major breach of the Moss Regulation, the general public must have taken it for granted that prompt payment on sympathetic lines would be a certainty.

In the event the union had to engage in a most determined and prolonged struggle, which had some unique features, before a satisfactory settlement could be wrung out of the body which conducted the mining industry in the name of the British people. It was eleven months after the thirteen tragic victims had gone below for the last time before those dependent upon them, including eight widows some with young families, knew what means they had on which to face their future.

The union had put forward claims for the widows and children ranging between £4000 and £10,000 and now sought an immediate meeting with officials of the Divisional Coal Board. They were met by the Deputy Chairman, Dr. Wm. Reid (formerly of the Fife Coal Company), supported by two of the Board's lawyers, who made it clear at once that the Board had already determined on a maximum payment to widows of £1750. No attempt, however, was made to disguise the calculations on which the Board reckoned: if a claim came before a Scottish court, it was said, there would not be an award of more than the Board was offering. Concerning a young widow with a family of four children, the Board's representatives argued that a Scottish judge would take into consideration: (1) that she could marry again; or alternatively, (2) that she could go and get work. The meeting then ended in deadlock, with the union protesting strongly 'against the cold-blooded attitude taken in relation to these claims', to quote the Scottish Executive's minute. The President commented 'that it was obvious that the Scottish Divisional Coal Board in their attitude to these claims were adopting the same policy as they did in regard to wages, and giving Scottish miners much worse treatment than was meted out to miners in other parts of the British coalfield'. The Executive determined on 'the strongest possible protest' to the Board, who 'appeared to be setting themselves up as representatives of Scottish law courts' instead of as model employers'.

Negotiations continued step by step without result until the end of April 1951 when, at yet another meeting with a Board official and attendant lawyers, the Scottish President dropped a bombshell. After the Board's representatives refused to reconsider their offers, Abe Moffat warned them of an unprecedented step which the union would adopt in this, and perhaps in all future cases. The Knockshinnoch men were in fact employees of the N.C.B., whose headquarters were in London. It was therefore perfectly open to the union to issue a writ against the N.C.B., and so bring the claim for damages before an English court. In England courts in general awarded substantially greater sums as damages in such cases. It followed that voluntary settlements out of court were also much higher in England than in Scotland.

It was a logical pursuance of the Board's own argument; and the miners' representatives might have added, in the words of Shakespeare's Portia:

> For, as thou arguest justice, be assur'd
> Thou shalt have justice, more than thou desir'st.

The Divisional Coal Board retired to consider their position. It took them some weeks: would they decide to stand pat? The Board was still considering its attitude to the dependents' claims when the Annual Conference took place on June 6, 1951, at which the President, after referring to the Inquiry, commented:

We know that there is much sentiment expressed when these things happen in the mining industry, but sentiment is not enough for us as miners. Sentiment is soon forgotten. What we demand, in the first place, is justice for the dependents of the men who have made the supreme sacrifice.

He could not yet report fruitful results of negotiations with the Board; but among the many expressions of sympathy[1] that continued to reach the Scottish miners there was one circu-

[1] In the middle of December the Scottish Executive meeting received a letter from the Secretary of the N.U.M. (Durham Area) together with a cheque for £25 from an anonymous donor for the dependents of miners killed in the Knockshinnoch Disaster. It was unanimously agreed that the branch should be asked to purchase gifts with this money to be distributed to the children of the victims of this disaster. (Minute 20, December 17, 1951, p. 314.)

lated in the minutes to branches which had a special aptness. It was a letter addressed to Secretary Pearson from Hungary:

DEAR MR. PEARSON,

We followed with great interest the investigation into the Knockshinnoch Mining Disaster, especially the part played in the investigation by your colleague Mr. Abe Moffat. The facts he brought to light were certainly not very pleasant ones. As you may know some months ago we experienced a similar mining disaster in our country in the Tatábányá area. After a thorough investigation it became clear that the tragic loss of life had been caused by flagrant violation of the existing Regulations and Safety Rules. The three men responsible were later tried and sentenced to fairly heavy terms of imprisonment. . . . The Government has of course made very widespread provisions to safeguard the future of the dependents of those killed in the Tatábányá disaster. For example they have undertaken to provide for the full education—up to the age of eighteen—of the children whose fathers lost their lives.

Yours fraternally,
For Peace and Friendship,
ANDRÁS SZABÓ,
International Relations Dept.

(Minute 38, June 4, 1951, p. 630.)

By the first week in July the Divisional Coal Board at last decided to adhere to their previous offers and make no advance upon them. Swiftly the Executive authorised the union officials 'to take appropriate action'.

Would it prove necessary, then, for the union to embark on expensive legal action before the English courts in their championship of the rights of the dependents and survivors? Last negotiations were made 'in an effort to avoid court action'. They were successful. On August 6, 1951, the President reported that final settlement had been reached on this matter without any legal expenses being incurred and that the following agreement had been made:

All widows would receive a minimum pension of £3,000 with additional allowances according to the number of children and their ages. The minimum would therefore be £3,000 and the maximum, according to children, would be £5,800, making a total of £31,500 amongst the eight widows. In another case a widowed mother and widowed sister would receive between them £1,000. In regard to the 104 non-fatal cases the Board would pay net loss of wages, i.e. the gross amount of wages, less one-half state benefit, statutory holiday pay and guaranteed wage equivalent, plus 50 per cent of gross wages lost, plus a

fixed addition of £40. This would mean approximately another
£10,000 for the non-fatal cases. With regard to the 12 non-fatal cases
who had not yet returned to work, further negotiation would take
place at a future date as it was not advisable to settle these cases until
the extent of their incapacity was understood.

Mr. Wood moved that special appreciation be placed on record to
the President for the personal interest he had taken in this case. This
was the highest sum negotiated in the history of the Scottish miners
and had been done without one penny of legal expenses being
charged against the union. This was seconded by Mr. Miller and
agreed to unanimously. (Minute 5, August 6, 1951, p. 55.)

The long battle in defence of the rights of the dependents
and survivors was over. Now an impartial observer could note
that if justice at first had not been done, yet justice had at last
been won.

7. THE PROSECUTION AND ITS SEQUEL

The Inquiry had found there was a contravention of Regulation 29 of the Coal Mines Act. It followed that there must be
a prosecution of those responsible. Which individual employees
of the Coal Board were to be held legally responsible within
the meaning of the Coal Mines Act? Under private ownership
there could be no doubt; the manager and agent of a colliery
where a breach of the regulations was found would be the men
liable to prosecution.

On May 15, 1951, two alternative charges were brought in
the Sheriff Court against A. M. Stewart, Sub-Area Produc-
tion Manager; A. Gardner, Sub-Area Planning Engineer; J.
Bone, who had been Agent of the New Cumnock group; and
W. C. Halliday, manager of Knockshinnoch Castle Colliery.
The first charge alleged that

They failed to ascertain as accurately as possible the nature and thickness both of the moss or other liquid matter and of the strata lying
between it and the said workings and roads by boring at a sufficient
number of points or otherwise, contrary to Regulation 29 (i).

The Sheriff Court dismissed this charge as being too vague to
be submitted to proof, and some weeks passed before this
decision was reversed by a higher court. Then the four men

were tried on this and on the second charge, which alleged that they,

having discovered the thickness of the intervening strata to be less than ten times the thickness of the coal seams being worked or proposed to be worked . . . allowed further work to be carried on below ground.

The adjourned trial was held on October 1–3, 1951; and each of the accused was found Not Guilty. The Procurator-Fiscal at once gave notice of appeal, but the appeal was dismissed on March 27, 1952, by the Lord-Justice General, Lord Cooper, with the concurrence of Lords Carmont and Keith.

Putting it in non-legal terms there were two basic reasons for the failure of the prosecution: first, there was a loophole in the wording of the Moss Regulation; second, with the new system of control under the Coal Board, the former clear-cut legal responsibilities of manager and agent are so distributed amongst a group of officials that what was everybody's business had become—in a legal sense—no one's business.

Amongst the miners there was bitter resentment. An Area Delegate Conference assembled on April 7, 1952, to discuss the next steps in the light of the legal decision. Two branches submitted resolutions, which demanded an immediate investigation into the Coal Mines Act.

Delegates listened to Mr. McGowan, of the stricken New Cumnock branch, recall the night when the disaster took place. Now, he said, we found we had a Coal Mines Act which covered up the negligence, and now a decision had been given that no one was responsible for the safety of these men working in the pit. Surely the time had come when the responsibility for every worker in the industry should be placed upon some individual. He therefore asked the Executive and Conference to give their wholehearted support to the resolution and demand that something more secure than the present Act should be devised to protect the miners, because otherwise the value of the exposures made by the President at the Inquiry would be lost. The miners were wholeheartedly behind the President in his efforts to secure greater safety precautions and he hoped that what had happened in Knockshinnoch would not be experienced again in the mining industry.

Mr. Stobbs, Coylton/Rankinston, said that his branch resented, and he felt sure that every branch in the Scottish coal-field resented, the final decision in relation to the Knock-shinnoch Inquiry which meant that the lives of the members were in the hands of people who had no responsibility. He maintained that those people who accepted jobs of responsi-bility with correspondingly high salaries must accept the responsibility of ensuring the safety of the workers. There ought to be a very serious investigation into the Coal Mines Act, and some very positive amendments to the Act should be made to place responsibility where it belonged, and have the effect of assuring the miners who worked day in and day out in the bowels of the earth that their safety was a responsibility on certain persons and that any failure in that responsibility would be dealt with.

The President replied that the acquittals 'did not mean that the Union's work at the Inquiry had been fruitless because, as a result of it, the Board had been compelled to pay the highest claim for damages ever known in the history of the Scottish miners. The Coal Mines Act, however, had become more obsolete now, because according to the verdict given no one—neither a manager, a colliery agent nor a higher Coal Board official—could be prosecuted under the Act where there had been a breach of the regulations.' He went on to examine in detail some of the implications of the legal decision:

He held that while no one above the status of agent had any obliga-tion to take precautions under the Regulations, the manager and agent at Knockshinnoch had fulfilled their duties by accepting instructions from other departments. The President maintained, however, that it was a terrible position for the mining industry to be in under Nationalisation. In the old days a manager and agent could at least have been prosecuted, but in 1952 a Sheriff Substitute had stated that not even an agent was responsible under the Coal Mines Act. Under the Coal Mines Act, as it now stood, therefore, the lives of the men could be destroyed and no one was held responsible.

In the High Court, Lord Cooper had stated that under the system of control which prevailed the hands of the manager and agent had been tied and their duties were so distributed amongst a group of officials that what was everybody's business was in fact no one's business. But what Lord Cooper had overlooked was the fact that it was the business of the Union that the lives of thirteen men had been lost.

It was obvious, he observed, that the interpretation of its terms showed that the Moss Regulation was not worth the paper it was written on; and after recalling the statements of Sir Andrew Bryan in his Report, he continued:

It was the only time in the history of the British mining industry where a court had gone against the viewpoint expressed by a Commissioner with regard to a breach of the Regulations. It was significant to note that Sir Andrew Bryan had stated, in regard to the set-up of the National Coal Board of which he was now a member, that the status and responsibility of all planning engineers, planners and surveyors at all levels should be clearly defined in relation to those of colliery agents and managers. There were, the President continued, officials beyond colliery agents who had more say in determining policy than any managerial staff but held no responsibility under the Coal Mines Act for the safety of the lives of the miners. In addition, however, something new had now developed, that if a manager or agent carried out the instructions of these people who decided policy, they could not be prosecuted even although men were killed.

On behalf of the Executive, he then moved this resolution:

That in view of the unsatisfactory results of the prosecution of Coal Board officials arising from the Knockshinnoch Disaster, this Conference calls upon the National Executive Committee to demand the following amendments to the Coal Mines Act and Regulations without delay:

(i) Amendments to Section 101, Sub-Section 2 and Section 122 of the Coal Mines Act 1911 to include the recommendation of the Royal Safety Commission when dealing with the responsibility of superior officials of colliery undertakings as also recommended by the Commissioner, Sir Andrew Bryan, at the inquiry into the Knockshinnoch Castle Colliery Disaster.

(ii) Amendments to the General Regulations 1920 No. 1423 (Precautions for working under moss, etc.) to include the recommendations Nos. 1, 2, 3, 4, 5 and 6 made by the Commissioner, Sir Andrew Bryan, at the Fatal Accident Inquiry into the Knockshinnoch Castle Colliery Disaster.

(Minute 31, April 7, 1952, pp. 541, 542, 543, 544.)

The resolution was unanimously accepted by Conference. Letters were received from all over the country in appreciation of the services rendered by the President for the union on behalf of the injured workmen and the dependents of those killed. It would be impossible to quote them all, but the following is an example:

KNOCKSHINNOCH INQUIRY

Concerning the above and the part played by our President, it gives me great pleasure and satisfaction to forward to your Executive on behalf of our members, our most sincere gratitude and highest respects for the unstinted and valiant service rendered to the unfortunate victims and their dependents, and in fact to all miners in the British coalfield.

May we be privileged to have the service of such a worthy leader for many years to come, and may he live to realise all that he has so unselfishly devoted his life to. We are proud to be led by such a man.

Yours faithfully,

Polkemmet Branch Secretary.

To the Scottish Executive, meeting on September 25, 1951, a proposal came from Bowhill Branch that a testimonial subscribed to by members should be given to the President for the work done in connection with the Knockshinnoch Colliery disaster, which they said had resulted in the Commissioner making strong recommendations for a change in the Coal Mines Act and a tightening-up of safety precautions which would prevent a repetition of such a disaster, and that already managers had been forced to exercise much greater care in approaching waste, old working and surface. The President made it clear that he could not agree to any membership levy for such a purpose, nor could he accept a monetary gift for work done on behalf of the miners. It was decided, however, to consider some form of testimonial, 'because never in history had a miners' leader conducted an enquiry of this character without legal assistance and never before had such substantial compensation payments been obtained for dependents of miners killed in a disaster in the Scottish Coalfield'. (Minute 10, September 25, 1951, p. 130.)

Following the decision to ask branches and Executive committee members for suggestions as to the form of the agreed upon testimonial to Abe Moffat for his work at Knockshinnoch, a great variety of suggestions came in letters from the branches. A series of these was printed in the minutes of August 11, 1952, and together with other suggestions by members of the Executive were remitted to a sub-committee. On

November 24 it was reported that some very good proposals had been submitted by branches and certain E.C. members. After careful consideration the officials were recommending the establishment of a permanent bed in the Edinburgh Royal Infirmary, the Glasgow Royal Infirmary and the infirmary to which the injured men had first been taken, where a plaque could be put up as a permanent record. The Committee agreed unanimously to this proposal.

By January 26, 1953, the Secretary was able to report that replies had been received from the Boards of Management of the Glasgow Royal Infirmary and Ballochmyle Hospital, each of whom indicated their willingness to accept a donation of £1000 (in the case of the Glasgow Royal Infirmary, £1250) for the establishment of a permanent bed in each. The Committee was unanimous in accepting this. Ballochmyle Hospital (where the victims of the disaster were first taken) and the other hospital intended to place on the wall in one of their wards a plaque bearing the following inscription:

ABE MOFFAT TESTIMONIAL

In recognition of the outstanding service given by Mr. Abe Moffat, President, Scottish Area, National Union of Mineworkers, to the miners and their families, arising out of the Knockshinnoch Colliery Disaster which occurred on 7th September, 1950.

The cause of miners' safety was greatly advanced by his actions.

The most important development arising from Knockshinnoch was the introduction of a new Coal Mines Act. Even the Conservative Minister of Fuel and Power, when introducing the new Bill in the House of Commons in 1954, had to refer to the Knockshinnoch disaster. New principles are contained in Parts I and II of the Bill, which deals with management and control, and the Minister said:

In this Bill, therefore, we place a firm obligation on the owners to see that the law is carried out and the duties of everyone acting between the owner and the colliery manager must be defined in writing and communicated to the Mines Inspector.

In addition, the new Bill makes the provision that a colliery manager shall not carry out instructions from higher authority which he considers prejudicial to safety, unless they are confirmed in writing by a person with special qualifications.

If he does carry them out, both he and the person giving the instructions shall be guilty if an offence is committed. The gap in the old 1911 Coal Mines Act exposed by the Scottish Miners' President in the Knockshinnoch disaster was thus removed by the new Coal Mines Act.

8. NEWCRAIGHALL COLLIERY

Three years after Knockshinnoch there occurred a case of neglect of safety on which the union took strong action. On Friday, August 14, 1953, five men involved in an accident at Newcraighall Colliery were entombed for twelve hours: no intimation was given to the union: and it appeared that an attempt had been made to cover the matter up. Inspection made by R. F. Young[1] showed several breaches of the law and safety regulations. Alexander Moffat, Lothians District Secretary, who had taken the matter up with the authorities immediately, said:

In all the three sections operating in the pit there was no second means of egress and some parts of the roadway were only 17″ in height and were referred to by Mr. Young as being simply holes. It was a breach of the Coal Mines Act, therefore, to have these roads in this condition.

The Executive Committee was unanimous in supporting the steps taken by the District Secretary and in addition agreed that a full report of the investigation should be given to the Executive. In addition it was also agreed that a protest should be made to the Divisional Board on their failure to report the accident to the head office. The manager had been suspended. But the union were not satisfied with this. They insisted on the removal of the manager, under-manager and other officials for neglect of safety. To this, after much argument, the Coal Board agreed. But this was not the end of it. Three months

[1] The Scottish Area of the N.U.M. broke new ground when it appointed two full-time safety inspectors, in addition to miners carrying out many inspections under Section 16 of the 1911 Coal Mines Act. The appointment of R. Young, Sr. as Electrical Safety Inspector assisted greatly in ensuring the safety of miners and brought about many exposures of unsafe conditions in the Scottish Coal-field. This was followed by the appointment of R. F. Young, Jr., B.Sc. (1st Class Honours), as Safety and Technical Officer for the union in Scotland. He is the main expert witness employed by the Union in all fatal accident court cases.

ARTHUR PIT, FIFE, 1953

SITE OF A NEW SINKING, GLEN OCHIL, CLACKMANNAN, 1952

afterwards, when the under-manager who had been dismissed was again given employment, this time as backshift oversman, at the nearby Woolmet Colliery, the miners' branch there sought to lodge seven days' notice for an official strike. The Executive could not sanction this but decided (on November 30, 1953) to raise the matter with the Ministry of Fuel and Power, and with Members of Parliament. They pressed for prosecution of the officials concerned in violation of the Coal Mines Act. Eventually a summons was issued and the offenders were prosecuted. The whole of this important fight by the union showed that beyond all other authorities the safety of the miners depended on the vigilance of their elected trade union representatives.

CHAPTER XVI

THE UNION TODAY

I. TRADE UNION DEMOCRACY

THE Scottish Area of the N.U.M. is one of the best examples
in Britain of a militant trade union organisation. Partly this is
due to the development of trade union democracy. This,
always a feature in the miners' associations as in the older
craft unions, has been recently developed to a quite remarkable
degree amongst the Scots. The branch or lodge sends its resolution or proposal to the Scottish Executive Committee, which
minutes the question raised together with any decision. This
of course is communicated to the branch. A conference of
delegates, elected from the branches, meets every eight weeks
and goes through the printed minutes of the Scottish Executive Committee whose decisions thus come up at short intervals for ratification—while Special Area Conferences are
called, whenever there is need, to make sure that the Executive standpoint on a policy issue has the backing of the
branches. If a question is controversial, as shown by majority
and minority vote at the conference, the matter may go to
a branch vote by which the Executive learns the opinion
of the whole of the membership. This was done, for example,
over the condemnation of British participation in the Korean
war, and over the banning of the atom bomb, as well as on
all important questions of wages policy.

Thus the machinery of democracy has come to be especially
well developed amongst the Scottish miners who are given
every opportunity to become an active, live body of trade
unionists, participating in decisions on policy and kept closely
in touch through their delegates or personally through branch
votes with all the affairs of the union. Besides this the leaders
are brought into personal contact with the membership in a
variety of ways. Wherever trouble arises leaders are soon on
the spot. In this there is a marked change in these last twelve

years from what was often the practice in the past amongst the
Scottish miners and in other coal-fields. For example, if an
unofficial strike began in the old days, it was nothing unusual
for the leaders to refuse to meet the men; or if it was some
other kind of trouble, the men would too often have occasion
to complain of a similar aloofness. In these last years in Scotland wherever difficulties have arisen the men in the pit have
been able to count on an early meeting with their leaders and
a full and frank discussion. Perhaps the most remarkable
example was when a group of Scottish miners, for infringe-
ment of the war-time regulations, had fines imposed upon
them, and in default of paying the fines had been sent to jail.
The fact that a number of their workmates were in Barlinnie
prison in Glasgow was anything but conducive to the smooth
working of the pits. Whether they agreed with them or not,
the miners in Lanarkshire were getting more and more angry
about the detention of their workmates in jail. The leaders
immediately came down to the pits affected by this spreading
feeling of resentment. What is more they visited the men in
jail, and demanded of the prison governor that they should be
allowed to address a meeting of the men inside Barlinnie
prison. This was unprecedented, but finally the governor
gave way. A formal meeting was held with one of the
prisoners as chairman. Abe Moffat was able to speak at this
meeting and to put a proposition on which a vote was taken.
An agreement was reached that brought about the release of
the men.

In the very difficult and awkward situations that arose
under the Coal Board, when pits were being closed down, it
was remarkable the extent to which meeting after meeting
was held, with the President of the union or others of the
Executive attending to put clearly before all the members,
e.g. in the Shotts district, the exact situation and the policy of
the union. In other places (the officials naturally could not be
everywhere at once) lodge mass meetings were held at all
times of difficulty. Thus the whole of the membership in this
way also could feel they were participating in union policy
and activity. Trade union democracy has been further
developed in Scotland in the last ten or twelve years by the
issue of information to members. This is in contrast to the past

when only meagre minutes circulated. Today the minutes of each Executive meeting are circulated to every branch. In addition, since the year 1950, the minute of each meeting of the Disputes Committee is circulated, which enables in the first place the pit delegates and lodge officials, and secondly the whole membership, to be fully acquainted with the cases that come up for decision. Beyond this the Scottish Area has taken the novel step of printing in pamphlet form matters of special interest. For example, by decision of Area Conference or of the Executive several of the President's speeches and lectures have been thus reprinted and circulated throughout the membership. Another example is the pamphlet written by Secretary William Pearson on the Knockshinnoch disaster. Again, the delegations made up of members of the Executive and members from the branches that have been sent to other countries, have made their reports in written form, and these, speedily printed and illustrated, have been distributed to the whole of the members. This applies to the delegations to Poland, the Soviet Union and other smaller delegations.

This steady development of a thorough-going democracy within the Scottish Area has naturally had its reflection in the attitude taken up by the Area within the national union. It is not too much to say that the Scots have carried on a fight for greater democracy within the N.U.M. Throughout the earlier history of the miners' associations, ever since conciliation machinery was established, there was continuous pressure from the employers to settle the question at issue within the four walls of the room in which they were meeting. The employers' pressure has always been to try and make the representatives of the miners into plenipotentiaries, that is, persons fully empowered to make an agreement without too much reference back to their constituents for ratification. Under State ownership this pressure has, if anything, increased. The result has been a tendency to regard the only necessary steps as first, agreement by the N.E.C., and second, agreement by a National Conference. As we have seen in an earlier chapter, the Scots fought persistently for a third stage of reference back to the Areas for their ratification, and where possible on matters of great importance, for a ballot vote of the members as final ratification. The importance of this was seen on the question of the wage-freeze, where, when the Scots had succeeded in obtaining the reference back to the men, it became clear that the findings of both the National Executive and the National Conference were not in accord with the wishes of the majority of the miners in the British coal-field. In contending for this greater degree of democracy the Scots were, of course, not putting forward something novel; they were preventing the loss of what had been the old custom within the M.F.G.B. where, though conference decisions were sometimes accepted, there were many occasions when they were reversed on ballot vote.

With a similar object the Scots have pressed that Special National Conferences should allow for any amendments to be brought forward to Executive resolutions, a course which was normal in the past but has in recent years been more than once disallowed. And similarly, in order that delegates may be fully informed, they have pressed for the issue of material before such Special Conferences are held. On the question of elections they have twice raised within the N.U.M. a proposal that officials should not hold office for life, but should be subject to five-yearly elections. Equally, with a view to keeping the whole life of the union at concert pitch, they have urged on big issues that there be demonstrations of members, and when the N.U.M. has sent out a call, there have been conducted in Scotland great campaigns of mass demonstrations of miners.

2. THE DISPUTES COMMITTEE

How does this trade union with its inner democracy operate when it is dealing on behalf of its members with the outside force of the employer? How are the immediate questions that arise in the daily working of a coal-pit negotiated with the owner or his representatives? The answer lies in the work of the local branch officials and the union agent in the first place: and secondly in the new conciliation machinery set up in 1947 to deal with pit disputes. In these two ways the members of the union can expect to find a remedy for grievances and a solution for their personal or group problems and difficulties. If a complaint on wages or conditions by a Scottish miner or group of miners is not satisfied by an under-official, the miner or miners can take the matter up with the manager of the colliery. If the complainants are not satisfied, they take it up with the trade union; and, if the trade union takes it up, it becomes a matter in dispute. This is handled by the pit delegate, who sees the manager, usually with the man or men concerned. The matter may also be discussed by the trade union branch committee (Chairman, Secretary and others including always the pit delegate) or even by the branch meeting. But the responsibility all the time rests with the pit delegate. If he still does not get satisfaction, he then may communicate, often by telephone, with the trade union official, the miners' agent, who will be responsible for anything from ten to twenty pits. But in any case the pit delegate *must* set out in writing the facts of the complaint and send this to the miners' agent.

On receipt of this letter or written statement the miners' agent arranges a discussion, called a *Pit Meeting*, with the employers' representatives. At the Pit Meeting there will be present the manager of the pit, the colliery agent and probably the agent for the sub-area on the one side; and on the other side the pit delegate and the miners' agent; the local Labour Relations Officer of the Coal Board may also be there. Often the matter in dispute is settled at the Pit Meeting. If, however, no satisfaction is obtained, the matter then goes to the Scottish Divisional Disputes Committee. A minute, more or less verbatim, is taken of the Pit Meeting, from which minute the miners' agent draws up his remit to the Disputes Committee. The colliery agent draws up his remit similarly. The Pit Meeting minutes are signed and countersigned and are available as evidence. But only the two remits (or joint remit), which are signed and countersigned, come before the Scottish Divisional Disputes Committee.

If this joint Disputes Committee (set up immediately after Vesting Day in January 1947) disagrees, the matter may be referred to two assessors. These two assessors are really a fact-finding commission; but their activities may result in a settlement. Where there is no settlement by any form of reference back to the locality, the dispute is referred to the Umpire, whose decision is final.

At the Scottish Divisional Disputes Committee, the work-men's side (who usually have met the previous day to discuss the remits from the miners' agent and from the colliery agent) has as spokesman the President of the union for the Scottish Area. He conducts the case. Before the Umpire, however, the case is conducted by the miners' agent. The Umpire sits with the two assessors, one from the Union and the other from the Board.

There are two exceptions to this procedure of appeal from the locality. The first is when the matter is or becomes an interpretation of the national agreement which affects the whole United Kingdom and is therefore transferred to the national conciliation machinery. The other exception is where a matter of principle affecting the whole Scottish Division and probably arising as a difference over interpretation of pre-viously existing agreements or customs has to be decided. This is referred to the Conciliation Board for Scotland, whose independent Chairman, usually a Court of Session judge, is called upon to give his award on the matter in dispute.

Little is now left for the Conciliation Board to do, as the above-described procedure for disputes (reduced to writing throughout) has *largely* taken over the functions of the Con-ciliation Board and has *entirely* taken over the functions of the County Disputes Committees, which now no longer exist. In-deed, it may be remarked that, except in times of a critical situation, the main function of a miners' agent in regard to wages and conditions is now carried out through this machin-ery, which keeps an agent busy several days in the week.

All the other matters on which the miners' agent is the responsible official of the trade union are now so many and so various that it is usually necessary to call upon a number of Executive Committee members to participate in the jobs to be done. These are working miners who, however, often have their time taken up mainly with trade union activity of this kind. In addition, for such matters as Social Insurance, Safety and Electricity, the union appoints special agents or working miners as assistant agents.

The way in which this procedure works may best be shown in the first instance by a practical example. We take first a case which, while it illustrates the usual procedure, is in some other ways not quite usual. For one thing it happens that this Ayrshire case went against the union, which as we shall see presently was by no means typical. Secondly, the wages claim was linked up with the question of safety: and thus the case illustrates the attitude of the employers' side in a county which within four months was to experience the most dreadful disaster since the end of the war.

Houldsworth Colliery in the South of Ayrshire lies in one of the few parts of the Scottish coal-field in which there occasionally takes place spontaneous combustion of the coal seam —a condition which elsewhere (in South Yorkshire, for example) is of more frequent occurrence. As is well known, when spontaneous combustion underground is threatened, the most effective measure is to shut off the coal seam from the supply of oxygen in the air which has reached it perhaps for the first time in scores of millions of years: and accordingly such places are sealed off. Before the coal actually bursts into flame it heats up and in the process evolves gases some of which have an unmistakeable smell. On this occasion in the Gilmour's Heading of the Drysdale Area of Houldsworth Colliery the men became aware of 'heating' of the coal, and realised that there was a 'paraffin' smell developing. Thereupon on May 3, 1950, in the interests of safety (on the need for which responsible Ministers had been making eloquent statements only a few days earlier) the men withdrew from the section and because of this danger returned home. The management would not pay them their wages for that day nor the bonus shift wage for that week. The men complained; and the pit delegate, after his local efforts had failed to settle, communicated with the agent (in this case Mr. Dan Sim), to whom all the circumstances not only of May 3 but of the days following were made known. Thereupon a Pit Meeting was arranged, and a prolonged and at times stormy discussion followed. The manager and the agent would not yield. The matter in dispute was then referred to the Scottish Divisional Disputes Committee, with a remit from the union agent. It showed that on May 4 the management stopped the section because of the conditions and proposed to withdraw the plant; that the Workmen's Inspector, Andrew Craig, had found there was no C.O. detector on the face on May 3; that the manager of the colliery had stated that they had been 'lucky to get the plant withdrawn in time'. It concluded:

We consider therefore that the men who withdrew from the section in the interests of safety should not be penalised by losing wages for the day in question and the bonus shift in the pay week concerned and claim that payment should be made to the men.

By May 26, 1950, the matter in dispute came before the Disputes Committee. There it was acknowledged by the union spokesman that the men had no claim for guaranteed wage or bonus shift under any agreement, but that the only alternative means by which justice could be secured for workmen where a question of safety was involved was by resorting to prosecution for alleged breach of the Coal Mines Act—a course which the union did not wish to adopt unless forced to it. In this case he contended that all safety measures had not been taken since there were no fire-damp detectors. He considered that an ex-gratia payment should be made.

The spokesman for the Coal Board proposed to have the whole question of the treatment of fires underground examined with a view to securing the confidence of the men. The question of payment was referred to the Divisional Board, which, a fortnight later, declined to make an ex-gratia payment. Thereupon it was intimated that the trade union side would have no alternative for the future in a case of this kind but to take legal action.

This example will show how the matter was argued where there was no agreement under which the union could make a claim. In many of the cases there would be an agreement but a difference as to its applicability. It was here that skill would tell, both in the preparation of the case for the claim and in its presentation. Normally the Chairman of the Divisional Coal Board or the Vice-Chairman or some other member, including sometimes the Labour Director, would argue for the Board. Normally the case for the workmen's side would be put by the union President. In his absence, which occurred very seldom and usually when negotiations in London compelled his presence there, the Vice-President would present the case: and in the absence of either Mr. Alex. Moffat would be called upon. But of course any one of the dozen to half-dozen present on the workmen's side could be chosen if need be. In practice, at something like 90 per cent of the meetings of the Scottish Divisional Disputes Committee the spokesman for the men's side was the union President. This of course made this part of the duties of a union President much more exacting and arduous than in the old days when only general wages advances were argued at a Conciliation Board, which sometimes would not meet from one year's end to another. It was very different after Vesting Day. Between mid-April 1947 and April 8, 1948, the Committee met twenty-two times: in the next twelvemonth, twenty-four times; in the next, twenty-three times. The minutes for these first three years, in three volumes running to 584 pages, make up the beginnings of a far-reaching series of precedents which are or should be binding, so far as the cases are similar, on all comparable matters in dispute.

There were brought before the Joint Disputes Committee (as it is usually called) matters in dispute which had not been settled at the colliery to a total number of 1870 in seven years. Reckoning from April to April of each year, these were as follows:

Year	No. of Cases
1947–1948	374
1948–1949	298
1949–1950	254
1950–1951	232
1951–1952	194
1952–1953	277
1953–1954	241

These figures were analysed in detail in the presidential address at each annual conference: this new machinery of conciliation was in the process of being tested in these seven years, and at the same time it was a test for nationalisation and for the Coal Board.

Some two-thirds of the cases were finally settled in favour of the men: never had so many cases been dealt with, or with such results. Moreover, there was a very large and impressive number of cases which could be settled by local branch officials and Agents at colliery level, on the basis of principles decided at the Disputes Committee.

From 1950 minutes of all Disputes Committee meetings and reports of all Umpire's Awards were circulated to the branches;

and this procedure had considerable influence in getting early settlement of cases arising day by day at the pits. It was not long before the men felt sufficient confidence in the value of the machinery and the way in which the union made full use of it for unnecessary unofficial local stoppages to be greatly reduced. This had an additional importance, for it had a bearing on the holiday pay of every miner; holiday pay was determined by the gross wages earned in the previous year, which unofficial stoppages reduced.

Cases covered the widest range of topics, including wrongful dismissal, the right to seven days' notice, payment to spare strippers, full increases to trainees, a proportionate bonus for redundant men who were re-employed in the middle of the week. Among the principles established was that the calculation of overtime payment to piece-rate workers should be based on gross earnings to include the cost of explosives, instead of deducting that item. Again, that all time actually worked underground beyond $7\frac{1}{2}$ hours would be paid at overtime rates, thus entitling continuous shift men and safety men to claim overtime which they were previously denied.

Another principle of considerable importance was that the full 4s. 11d. flat rate must be paid for any shift worked on piece-rates: the Board was obliged to issue a circular to this effect in the Fife coal-field and discontinue the practice of deducting a proportion of it where waiting-time payment was forfeited as a result of absenteeism.

But the most far-reaching gains were those won in connection with advancing the wages of piece-rate workers, reducing anomalies and reaching some degree of uniformity in this respect in different parts of the coal-field. No other single question is so pregnant with disputes; with no other problem is it so difficult to ensure that justice is done. The successes achieved here are illustrated by the fact that in his presidential address of 1952 Abe Moffat could report:

One of the positive aspects of these negotiations is the substantial increase in average piece-rate earnings in the Scottish coalfield. In 1947 the average piece-rate earnings in Scotland including payment for bonus shift and overtime was 32s. 8d. In 1952 the average is 46s. 8d., an increase of 14s. In July 1954 the average piece-rate in Scotland, including payment for bonus shift and overtime, was

£2 15s. 10d., which represented an increase of £1 3s. 4d. per shift compared with 1947.

The skilled use of the new conciliation machinery, during its first five years, had indeed shown—not least to the older men—what could be done.

It can be seen from these yearly summaries how important has become the work of the union in the joint Disputes Committee. This indeed was recognised from the beginning in April 1947, when besides the choice of the union president and the Coal Board chairman as main spokesmen for either side, the joint secretaries chosen were the Scottish Labour Relations Officer and the union general secretary. Since then there has been a division of labour in the work of the union headquarters and since the year 1949 the joint secretaryship effectively functions through Mr. J. Barrowman for the employers' side and Miss Renee Barnes for the workmen's side. The wording of the minute of each fortnightly meeting of the Disputes Committee is agreed jointly. Miss Barnes then has to arrange the multiplication of copies and their circulation to the branches. This entails also the keeping of the records, a detailed knowledge of which becomes of increasing importance as the number of decisions accumulates from year to year, with any one of them forming a possible precedent either for decision or for points in discussion. For the modern machinery of conciliation requires much greater exactitude in the preparation and a higher degree of skill in the presentation of each matter in dispute than in the old days. The employers' side is much better organised for dealing with these questions than in the era of private ownership: and so too must be the workmen's side. The result is that this activity of the union, both in the quantity of the work to be done and the way in which it is done, is now developed to a point far beyond the old somewhat haphazard methods of dealing with matters in dispute. The need for careful preparation through collective working on the union side, for sharp perception, through grasp of principle and native common sense on the part of the chief negotiator, are now more important than before.[1]

[1] Consideration of space precludes quoting in full several of the more important discussions of the Joint Disputes Committee. The same reason compels the omission of even the most important workmen's compensation cases.

3. EDUCATION

Along with the democracy of the union, by which every opportunity was given to the members to express their views and to determine policy, there has developed an increased opportunity for education in trade union matters, both in the general principles and in their detailed application. The two main forms of this education have been Summer Schools and Week-end Schools. Each year from 1947 there has been held in the month of May a week's school (extended to two weeks in 1954), attended by some sixty students under forty years of age, chosen for this by competitive examination. Miners coming from every part of the coal-field were given, at no expense to themselves and with payment of guaranteed wage for loss of work, an educational course not only on technical mining matters but on general social and political questions.

Each year the lecturers at the school have been drawn from a wide field. They usually included a Minister of the Crown or a prominent figure of the National Coal Board, as well as one or more of the three Scottish office-bearers and also a prominent member of the National Union of Mineworkers from some other coal-field. Fellows of the Royal Society, Members of Parliament, prominent publicists, authors of social, economic and historical studies—all have been ready to give their services. To the high standard of the lectures the Scottish Executive added features that were new in mining education. The students were divided into some half a dozen groups, each under a group leader, and each contained one of the youth contingent for whom, as well as for representatives of the Enginemen's Union, places in the school had been reserved. After each morning's lecture had been delivered and questions (between a dozen and a score) had been asked and answered, the students split up into their groups. There for a couple of hours they discussed the main topics, reached unanimous or majority and minority opinion upon each, once their differences had thus been hammered out. Then in the later afternoon one of each group (and a different one from day to day) expressed the collective opinion which on occasion might be critical of the lecturer's standpoint, and sometimes put forward new questions. Thus a thoroughly informed discussion would take place and give plenty of matter for the lecturer to deal with in his concluding remarks. The contents of each lecture were submitted to a very thorough discussion which could not fail to clarify and to enlighten. Discussion often continued informally in the evening, and the amount of lively cultural activity that was thus packed into one week was remarkably high. A full shift of $7\frac{1}{2}$ hours was the least given each day to these studies. In addition over half the students entered for the essay competition, upon a subject related to mining, the winner of which got as prize admission to a further school, often one of those international trade union schools where he would have the pleasure of foreign travel added to a somewhat less strenuous educational course. Printed reports with summaries of the lectures were issued each year to the branches. These reports by William Pearson re-create the friendly and informal atmosphere and indicate that in a brief history of half a dozen years a social and cultural tradition was growing up around the schools, alongside a tradition of hospitality on the part of the Provost and the folk of the town of Dunoon.

After three years a further step was taken. On February 20, 1950, the Scottish Executive decided 'as a continuation of developing the maximum amount of educational activity within the union' to hold Week-end Schools, one in each of the four districts of Scotland, to be attended by one official, one committee man and one member from each branch, and the subject to be Union Policy. These Week-end Schools like the Summer Schools were each to be held in a health resort where between 50 and 100 thus chosen could spend the week-end together making the acquaintance of one another, while at the same time they all made a special study of problems that they had in common. The Scottish Executive were anxious that the branches should understand the new problems, that there should be unity and confidence between the members and the leaders, and that their hard-won solidarity should not be impaired. President Abe Moffat took a deep and special interest in the development of these schools. He devised the syllabus, prepared and delivered a series of important lectures which covered comprehensively and thoroughly questions of vital significance to the miners,[1] for all of which he received 'our most sincere thanks for the fine job which he did'. These Week-end Schools were so successful that they were regularly continued from year to year, in addition to the Summer Schools. They represented a great educational advance. For one thing they comprised five times as many as could obtain admittance to the Summer Schools. Secondly, the participants were chosen not on the basis of a written examination, but by their fellow members who elected them as the most active trade unionists in the branch. Thirdly, the subjects handled were not general, but particular, being precisely the urgent problems for which the union had to find a solution. And fourthly, the discussions were initiated and guided by their President, who had the closest acquaintance with each problem, and whose 'clarity and patience in dealing with questions' was more than once minuted. The essence of these Week-end Schools was that they nurtured the men who would be responsible for the future of the union, and indeed of the trade union movement. The importance of these Week-end Schools was fully recognised by the branches, some of which expressed themselves in special resolutions or letters to the Scottish Executive.[2]

The Scottish Miner

A new venture, which has amongst all its other aims an educational purpose, was the publication in 1954 of a monthly paper called *The Scottish Miner*. For nearly three-quarters of a century the miners' trade unions had the aspiration to publish their own periodical press, but without any abiding results. The Scottish Area early set itself this aim: and this time it was successfully carried out. It began in February

[1] E.g. in 1950 the following questions were handled: (1) Wage claims for lower-paid workers; (2) developments in relation to the wages structure; (3) claim for holidays with pay; (4) welfare and programme for pithead baths; (5) 'Ladder Plan' for mining education; (6) Fatal Accidents Scheme.

[2] E.g. 'I have been instructed to write to you regarding the recent week-end school at Bridge of Allan. The delegates attending on behalf of this branch have reported that it was a great success and would like to congratulate the Executive for the able way in which everything was done, including lectures, catering, and transport to and from the school. We would like to see these schools continuing in the future.'

1954 as a monthly four-page newspaper but with all the usual features of a weekly. The main events of the trade union year, such as the annual conferences and the miners' Gala Day, were given full prominence and illustrated with many photographs. Personalities of the union or of its branches were featured, while articles dealing with union policy upon a variety of questions appeared in each issue. The intention of the paper is to build up a corps of colliery correspondents who will be in touch with every aspect of the life of the mining community.

4. YOUTH

One of the great problems of trade unions has been that of drawing into their ranks the youth, and once they have joined the union, of bringing forward these new members to take an active part. This problem existed already in the days of the old craft unions when the system of apprenticeship still retained much of its force. It was intensified in the present century. Lads entered industry at the age of fourteen, and while since the coming into effect of the Education Act of 1944 the age has been raised to fifteen, in the early years of this century there were many children at work who had only passed their thirteenth birthday. In the mining industry in the days of fifty years ago, wherever the pillar and stall method (or as it was called in Scotland stoup and room) was in operation, the task would often be performed by a family group; thus some at any rate of the youth would be working under the care and guidance of a father or an uncle from whom too they would learn something about the work of the union and be told that it was their duty to belong to it. But in the last generation these conditions have changed. In addition the increasing shortage of man-power in the last fifteen years has demanded that much more attention be paid to improvement of youth conditions than was previously thought necessary. In other industries unions that were alive to this problem have tried various means to reach a solution. In the mining industry Scotland was the first area to establish a real place for youth within the machinery of the union, and to provide full scope for discussion and consideration of youth problems.

VETERANS OF THE INDUSTRY
James Cook, Clackmannan, 1953

DEVON PIT, FROM TILLICOULTRY, CLACKMANNAN, 1953

The Youth Committee was set up in January 1946. It was an innovation, and was designed to educate young miners in the principles of trade unionism, and to train them for positions of responsibility in the future. The Youth Committee came under the fostering care of the three office-bearers and the Executive Committee, and was kept in being in a difficult period throughout 1946 to 1948 until the young miners responsible were able to organise their first annual Youth Conference in the autumn of 1949. The Scottish Executive on August 8, 1949, set up a constitution: there were to be two representatives annually elected by branch vote from each of the four districts of the Scottish area. The meetings were to be monthly and their policy was to be based on the recommendations of an annual Youth Conference, subject to the approval of the Executive. Furthermore, 'for the purpose of developing trade union work among young miners and to carry out the decisions of the S.M.Y.C.' each branch committee was to co-opt as members two young miners under the age of twenty-five. The development of the Scottish Youth Committee and the annual Youth Conference attended by the leaders of the area has had the beneficial effect that it has enabled much greater attention to be paid to the specific problems of young workers. This was carried further when from the beginning of 1951 the Scottish Executive invited the attendance at their meetings of a 'representative of the Youth Committee in a consultative capacity and without voting rights'. A further support to their activities was adding the Youth Committee minutes (as an appendix to the Executive printed minutes) which were thus brought each month to the attention of the members in their branch meetings. The Scottish Area also holds an annual Week-end School for young miners (as well as the day schools held in the various districts of Scotland). Such a carefully worked out and developing policy of directing attention to the young workers has had the further effect that it has brought forward a new generation of younger leaders who, instead of having to batter their way ahead against obstacles, have been helped ahead by the union itself.

The example thus set in Scotland has now been followed in other coal-fields, notably in South Wales, Nottingham and elsewhere.

The scope of the youth organisation was not limited to their own industry. The Scottish Miners' Youth Committee have been represented on the Scottish Trades Union Congress Youth Advisory Council; the British Youth Festival Committee; the World Federation of Democratic Youth, whose festivals they attended in Copenhagen and Berlin, Budapest and Bucharest; and they have also been represented at the Scottish Youth Peace Festival; and the Week-end or Summer Schools of the Scottish T.U.C., the Labour Party and the National Council of Labour Colleges. To record all its activities and to discuss all its problems the Youth Committee has a page made available to it each month in *The Scottish Miner*.

5. HEALTH AND WELFARE

After the war the union continued to be closely concerned with every aspect of miners' health. Apart from the main safety and compensation activities, the Scottish Executive co-operated readily with every health agency, and its members sat on hospital committees and the regional board. Fullest support was given to research into occupational diseases, such as nystagmus, Weil's disease and pneumoconiosis. Problems arose with the introduction of the National Health Service. For example, the Ministry of Health announced in July 1951 the taking over of the Uddingston Centre for rehabilitation, built up by the Miners' Welfare Commission with a management committee on which the union's first representatives were McKendrick, Pearson and Miller. This decision, ending any share in control by the union, would have endangered full co-operation from the miners themselves. The Scottish Executive made such an effective protest that by October 1951 the Ministry yielded: and a local board of management was set up with eleven members, five from the union, three from the Coal Board and three from the Regional Hospital Board. The union is also concerned with the upkeep of eight convalescent homes for miners or miners' wives and daughters. These were a heritage from the times of private ownership; and while after 1946 the Area Miners' Welfare Committee

took over a measure of responsibility for them, the management was still made up of representatives of employer and
employed, i.e. of the Coal Board and the Scottish Area. There
are eight such homes,[1] mostly old mansions standing in their
own policies and with modernised equipment for cooking and
all the other needs of convalescence. In addition to the continuance of this service to its ailing members and their families,
the Scottish Area initiated benefits for its older members. At
the 1952 annual conference, President Moffat told how
funeral benefit (historically the earliest of all trade union
benefits) had been provided as a gratuity since 1949, since
when, he said, 'we have paid out the sum of £3,896 in death
benefit, without any contributions whatever having been paid
by members'.

But the most remarkable decision of the Scottish Executive
was in connection with pensions. On this, as has been told
elsewhere, the Scots had put up a strong struggle for the
improvement of the national scheme which was to begin on
January 1, 1952. This scheme took no account of the position
of the old miners who had retired since Vesting Day. There
appeared no possibility of getting the Coal Board to grant
pensions to these men. The Scottish Executive therefore proposed that a small pension should be paid to miners in this
category. It would, said the President, be 'the biggest single
item of expenditure which the union had ever undertaken and
would involve an annual outlay, although one which would
diminish every year'. The proposal was accepted: the Area
had the funds to cover it: and it seemed the union's money
could be used for no better purpose. In the first year it meant
an expenditure of £26,000. No other trade union in the
country had ever paid out such a gratuity to old members
without any special contribution. The members of the union
were proud that they were able to do it.

The union took thought not only for the bodily health and
welfare of its members but also for their cultural needs. Other
unions have done something in this way, sometimes in the
same manner as the Scottish miners by encouraging the
development of music, art and the theatre: but apart from its

[1] For men at Culross, Gullane, Saltcoats, Maybole; for women at Leven, Gullane,
Skelmorlie, Troon.

support to the Edinburgh People's Festival (helped by MacColl's Theatre Workshop) and to the mobile Unity Theatre going round the Fife branches, there is no other trade union which arranged for the great singer Paul Robeson to give a special concert to all its members. On May 13, 1949, the Usher Hall in Edinburgh was crowded to the roof with miners and their wives or sweethearts who had come from every pit in the Scottish coal-field. It was a unique occasion.[1]

But all the cultural and other activities of the union are focussed upon the Scottish Miners' Gala Day instituted by the Executive Committee in 1947 to celebrate the winning of the five-day week and held annually on the first Monday of May in Holyrood Park in Edinburgh. After the first occasion Alexander Moffat was appointed convener. No finer choice could have been made. Alex. Moffat, steeled in the miners' struggles against the employers and the obstructors of unity, determined that the Annual Gala Day should express not only gaiety and the holiday spirit, but the miners' pride in their strength and unity and their hard-won victories.[2] He saw to it that Gala Day became the grandest day of the year for the Scottish mining community. His warm personal enthusiasm is shown in his 'Convener's Message' printed in successive Souvenir Programmes, for example:

Each year we have successfully introduced a new feature in our Programme. With our Fifth Annual Gala Day we bring you a Pageant, expressing the struggle of the pioneers of our union for improved conditions, higher wages, greater safety and for peace and prosperity.

Much water has flown under the bridge since their day of leadership, but the struggle is the same and our union by resolutions have fought, and are continuing the fight, for safety, higher wages and peace as definitely as the pioneers did.

[1] Two years later, in response to branch protests about the plight of Paul Robeson, then being persecuted by the U.S. Government for 'his contribution to the cause of peace and democracy and his fight against racial discrimination', the Scottish Executive raised the matter with the U.S. ambassador only to be told that nothing could be done until the U.S. courts decided whether he had been wrongfully refused his right to a passport. In December 1954, however, still supporting the campaign to secure the return of Paul Robeson's passport, the Scottish miners again held a concert in the Usher Hall, Edinburgh, attended by miners and their families from all over Scotland. Among the artistes participating was the well-known baritone Martin Lawrence, who sang many of the songs made famous by Robeson.

[2] Just twenty years earlier, in 1928, Alex. Moffat had organised the Fife Miners' Gala.

The artists have brought to life the work of the pioneers and I am sure that every miner will be proud of the traditional role of their leaders, past and present.

In the historic Holyrood Park year by year since 1947 has grown up a new tradition; sports competitions of all kinds are held; Pipe Band and Brass Band contests; Highland Dancing Championships; the ceremonial crowning of the Scottish Coal Queen (who must be the wife or daughter of a miner), and all kinds of amusements. Travelling and catering arrangements for such an enormous gathering are major operations requiring the most efficient organisation and attention to detail and involving the co-operation of the transport services of a wide area. Gala Day officials and representatives of the Edinburgh City Police consult over the procession arrangements—no light task, for the very first of these annually-growing processions with its bands and branch banners took three-quarters of an hour to pass a given point. How successful were Alex. Moffat and his committees emerges from tributes in successive minutes of the Executive Committee following the Annual Gala Day.

Attendance at the 1953 Gala was a record one, no newspaper in the country putting its estimate at less than 100,000. Posters and banners of old pioneers and present leaders of the movement brightened up the demonstration through the streets of Edinburgh. One outstanding feature of the Gala was the part played by the paraplegic miners, who gave an exhibition of work which they had produced. Thousands of miners and their wives queued up all day to see the handiwork of miners who in the past were forgotten men. A select team of Yorkshire footballers played Scotland, who scored a victory of 3 goals to 2 over their opponents from south of the Border.

With Abe Moffat in the Chair and Aneurin Bevan, M.P., and young Andrew Clark, Secretary of the Scottish Miners' Youth Committee, as speakers, vigorous statements were made on the national and international situation. These were summed up in the May Day resolution, passed unanimously by a record attendance of Scottish miners and ending with the traditional slogans:

'Long live the unity of the British working class!

'Long live the spirit of International May Day—workers of all lands unite!'

A new feature of the Miners' Gala was the sending of three runners and one boxer to represent the Scottish Miners at the International Sports Rally in Paris at Whitsun, convened by the French Sports Federation.

6. THE UNION IN THE LABOUR MOVEMENT AND IN POLITICS

The Scottish miners have taken a big part, of growing importance, in the post-war years within the N.U.M., while for a rather longer period their influence within Scotland, both in the Scottish Trades Union Congress and in scores of Trades Councils and constituency labour parties, has been increasingly exercised. What has been the main character of the stand they have taken in these bodies? First of all their stand has been for maintaining and improving the standard of living of the workers. Not only on the question of wages but on hours and all other conditions of life they have stood for a policy of struggle to attain the aims of the labour movement. Amid the economic difficulties of the war years and since the war the Scottish miners have consistently withstood all attempts to place burdens on the shoulders of the workers while capitalist profits were on the increase. Examples of this standpoint, already very clearly shown in conference decisions, are also to be found in their resolutions put forward to the annual meeting of the Scottish Trades Union Congress.

Their standpoint was maintained during the six years of the Labour Government from 1945–51, when there was very considerable pressure upon them to modify their outlook. Their standpoint was reinforced when the autumn General Election of 1951 resulted in a Conservative administration. When the General Council of the Trades Union Congress seemed to show a disposition of being willing to co-operate with the Tories, the Scottish miners took the strongest exception to any such attitude. Instead they urged from the beginning that any Conservative measures that bore hardly upon the people should be resisted with full vigour, and that a determined struggle should be waged to bring down the Government as soon as possible. Given working-class unity, they held that this aim could be achieved. Therefore from the end of 1951 they were unwearied in their support of every step that could unite the working class in struggle against the policy of the new Government. Some were against this standpoint on the ground that political questions were outside the scope of the union. The union, it was argued, should limit itself to what were described as industrial questions—an argument which was oddly reminiscent of the standpoint of a generation earlier, of old-fashioned lawyers in the House of Lords. To these arguments an answer was given by the President at the union's 1952 Week-end Schools:

When people like Keir Hardie first raised the necessity for the setting up of a political wing in the Trade Union movement to secure Parliamentary representation, they were opposed and regarded as dangerous by the orthodox leadership, to such an extent that the T.U.C. took a decision which precluded Keir Hardie from attending their Congresses. Yet he carried on the fight and his line of thought eventually won.

There are some people in the movement who advise us to wait until the next General Election, but if we do that we will probably be so weak by the next election from the attacks of the Tory Government that we will hardly be fit to go and mark our cross at the ballot box.

In 1926, the attack was launched to increase the hours and reduce the wages of miners, launched not merely by the coal-owners but by the Government. The miners did not sit back then and say that it was a political question which could only be dealt with at the next election, because they knew that every political issue is a bread and butter issue affecting their lives. They fought back, and despite all the weaknesses the fight was necessary because without it the Tories would simply have been encouraged to go ahead with more and more vicious attacks.

The same thing is taking place in 1952, and some of our own people even have been misled by the capitalist press who believe that the working of Saturday is a good thing for the miners. If our forefathers had not used the industrial machine against the die-hard Tory Government by accepting further sacrifices in refusing to work a ten-hour day at a time when they were on starvation wages for ten hours, the eight-hour day would not have been established. If our forefathers had decided that it was solely a political issue, they would not have achieved the abolition of the working of women and children in the darkness of the bowels of the earth. . . .

Bob Smillie in 1919, speaking at the Labour Party Conference, challenged anyone on the platform to tell him where industrial problems ended and political problems began. The platform could not answer the question then, and it could not be answered, because the fight for bread and butter was both an industrial and a political fight, and the two could not be separated. There may be disagreement on the form which industrial activity should take, but there can be no disagreement that the industrial movement should be used to influence the political movement, and when the workers take over the political machine in this country they will use it to influence the industrial machine in the interests of the working class.

(Report of Week-End Schools, 1952, pp. 4, 5, 7.)

In some ways the most remarkable activity of the union in politics has been its strong standpoint for world peace. This took a variety of forms as one or other issue became prominent in the post-war years. First came the standpoint for the banning of atomic energy from use in warfare: and, after the announcement of President Truman in February 1950 of preparations for the hydrogen bomb, for the banning also of this weapon. The course of the Scottish miners' fight for peace in Korea (already dealt with in an earlier chapter) was soon to be followed by a demand for peace talks between the Big Powers, and for the development of East-West trade. This standpoint on peace was not limited to a few of the leaders: it was general. At the Fourth Annual Conference of the Youth Committee its chairman, Michael McGahey, could say:

This vital fight on the question of peace is still before us. The Scottish miners were the first in the trade union movement to propose certain solutions to the international problems facing the world. In simple terms the Scottish miners advocated that the five great powers in the world—France, Britain, The Soviet Union, America and China—should meet to discuss and declare to the world that, irrespective of problems, irrespective of differences of opinion, they would not go to war but would sign a Five Power Peace Pact to make it clear that peace would be established in the world.

It would mean in this country the end to a terrific rearmament programme, which is dragging down the living conditions of every working-class man and woman. It would mean for the young people an end to the two years' conscription, which in my opinion is not for the defence of Britain but for the subjugation of Korean, Malayan and other colonial people fighting for the national independence of their countries. A cut in the conscription period to one year would mean that our young lads would be able to produce for the benefit of this country instead of squandering a year of their lives in uniform, breaking their hearts to get out of the Army as soon as possible. It would mean that the workers here could turn to the major problem of rebuilding Britain and establishing a happy and peaceful country.

On this and on other peace issues the Scottish miners carried on a consistent fight both at the Scottish Trades Union Congress and at the conferences of the National Union of Mineworkers. It should perhaps be considered, not only as a personal matter but also as a tribute to the forward-looking attitude of the Scottish miners, that when their president was candidate in the 1954 election for presidency of the N.U.M., well over 100,000 miners[1] outside Scotland voted in his favour. In addition to putting forward resolutions to these bodies, the Scottish miners exercised a considerable influence in the labour movement by the reports of delegations abroad to the various countries and to a series of international conferences. The Scottish delegates were thus equipped with facts of experience to back up their standpoint.

7. CONCLUSION

The story told in these pages has its background in the history of an ancient land for long an independent kingdom[2] with its own laws and institutions, and, as the Celtic tongue retreated into the Western nooks of the island, with a speech akin to that of the Yorkshire and the northern English counties and remote from the conquering dialects of the Midlands and the Thames. Lying on the Atlantic fringes, its acreage mostly mountain or high moorland, its soil yielding oats and a primitive barley, Scotland could never be called

---

[1] 'As one of the two nominees for that position the Scottish President had had to combat a campaign of misrepresentation by the capitalist press and the B.B.C. unprecedented in such an election. The fact that in such a situation Mr. Abe Moffat had obtained more than 162,000 votes was an indication of his standing, and of the fact that he had the confidence of thousands of miners, not only in Scotland, but in the British coal-field because of their recognition of his integrity, incorruptibility and qualities of fighting leadership. On behalf of the Scottish miners, therefore, he extended to the President congratulations on the magnificent vote which he had secured and assured him of the continued loyalty and support of the men and women of the Scottish coal-field whom he served.'—Vice-President John Wood at the Scottish Area Annual Conference in Rothesay on June 2, 1954.

[2] 'Scotland has a longer history as an independent unconquered country than any other nation in Europe.'—H. M. Chadwick, *Early Scotland* (1949), Intro., p. xiv.

one of the rich countries of feudal Europe—even before its medieval period ended in wars and frequent devastation. But beneath its soil there were riches awaiting exploitation. For the first four centuries of coal-mining from 1200 onwards, the conditions of the miners, for what little is known of them, appear to have been much the same as in other early coal-fields. The distinctive feature of the Scottish coal industry, affecting generations of miners, came only when their history had run half its course. For the statutory bondage (1606–1799) imposed on miners and salters in a country where capitalist production based on free labour was developing in its other industries was distinctive and indeed seems to have been unique in Europe. It was maintained throughout the eighteenth century, when England and Scotland had become one United Kingdom with the general name of Briton temporarily current. When the anthem 'Rule Britannia' was written, with its refrain 'Britons never will be slaves', the underground denizens of the Scottish pits were still fast in their bondage. The claim to be a philanthropist, 'one who loves his fellow men and exerts himself for their well-being', was not uncommon amongst persons of leisure in that eighteenth century, but none of those seem to have turned their solicitude to the condition of underground workers. The oracles were dumb. It was the resistance of the colliers themselves, in their secret combination or 'brotherings', that joined with other economic causes to bring about the emancipation.

Similarly, it was by concerted restriction of labour, the 'wee darg' in place of the masters' 'big darg', that a curb was put upon the unrestricted exploitation of the early nineteenth century, just as it was only in the turbulence of Chartist agitation that Parliament in 1842 passed the first measure of 'State interference' in the private business of the coal masters. The subsequent century of safety legislation, culminating in the Mines and Quarries Act, 1954, would not have been carried through but for the persistent pressure exercised by the miners themselves, of whose efforts in Scotland alone some picture has been given in this book. Mainly, and inevitably, it has been the story of an organised effort, of the mineworkers organised in their unions.

A hundred years ago the formation of the Scottish Coal and Iron Miners' Association set the aim of a single union for Scotland. But the way forward past such milestones as the winning of the eight-hour day in 1870 by the Fife miners, the first in Europe, proved to be through the building up of separate county associations, eight in all by the beginning of this century. By 1914 the title of National Union was adopted by the eight federated county associations; the reality to correspond with the title was not achieved until thirty years later. By that time the coal-mining industry which had already undergone far-reaching changes in technique through mechanisation was about to have its ownership transformed from the hundreds of colliery companies into the single monopoly of State ownership. For the mineworkers greater changes have been brought about in these last fifteen years than in any previous fifty: and not only for the mineworkers but by the mineworkers. Nor are these changes likely to come to a stop.

All these activities of the Scottish miners at the present day have been sustained and carried forward, not only as a response to material needs, but by the strength of an idea. The idea of a Socialist society has been part of the common outlook of thousands of Scottish miners. It has been part of all their history ever since Keir Hardie, William Small, Smillie and McAnulty began their propagandist and organising efforts three-quarters of a century ago. It is this idea of Socialism that nerves and sustains the most active and leading spirits among the Scottish miners today. Thus while the story of the past has been told in these chapters, the history is not finished. Whatever shifts there be in industry, whatever new sources of power may develop, the Scots miners will go on into the future, making their own history.

BIBLIOGRAPHY

SOURCES

As is said in the Preface, the main sources are the handwritten or printed proceedings of the miners' unions and their federation of unions (latterly the Scottish Area of the N.U.M.) together with Hansard and the H.M. Stationery Office publications. These, already dealt with in the Bibliographies to volumes one and two of the British miners' history (*The Miners* and *The Miners: Years of Struggle*) are supplemented by socialist and labour journals over the last seventy years. For the most part of the nineteenth century additional sources were found in Scottish newspapers, mainly from the 'fifties onwards; in labour periodicals of which *The Glasgow Sentinel* was the most useful; and in Chartist papers of which some half-dozen were circulating in Scotland in the 'forties. If not a harvest, at any rate gleanings are got from the reports of Commissions and House of Commons Select Committees, as referred to in the text or in footnotes. Among the sparse newspapers of the eighteenth century *The Caledonian Mercury* (1743, 1778), *Ruddiman's Weekly Mercury* (1778), *The Scots Magazine* (1799) yielded information on the colliers.

For book lists, see the references in volumes one and two of the British miners' history. I give below a short list of additional books consulted.

LIST OF BOOKS

ANDERSON, A. O., Early Sources of Scottish History, 1922.

ANDERSON, JOHN (ex-Miner), Coal: A History of the Coal Mining Industry in Scotland (n.d.).

ASHTON, T. S., The Coal-miners of the Eighteenth Century, *The Economic Journal*, Econ. Hist. Series, No. 3, January 1928.

BALD, ROBERT, A General View of the Coal Trade of Scotland, Edinburgh, 1808.

BARROWMAN, JAMES, Glossary of Scottish Mining Terms, 1886.
  Slavery in the Coal Mines of Scotland in *Transactions of the Fed. Instit. of Mining Engineers*, Vol. 14, 1897–8.

BOECE, HECTOR, The Chronicles of Scotland written in Latin and translated (into Scots) by John Bellenden in 1531: edition of 1821 (new edition ed. Chambers and Batho, 1941).

BROWN, P. HUME, History of Scotland to the Present Time, Cambridge, 1911.

BRYAN, Sir ANDREW, Address on the Centenary of H.M. Inspectorate of Mines.

BURTON, J. HILL, The History of Scotland, 1867.

Cambridge Economic History, Vols. I and II.

Cambridge Medieval History, Vol. VII.

CARVELL, J. L., One Hundred Years in Coal (History of the Alloa Coal Company). Privately printed, 1944.

CHADWICK, H. M., Early Scotland, 1949.

CHAMBERS, ROBERT, Domestic Annals of Scotland, 1861.

COCHRANE-PATRICK, R. G., Early Records relating to Mining in Scotland, Edinburgh, 1878.

COCKBURN, Lord HENRY, Memorials of his Time, 1856.

COUPLAND, R., The British Anti-Slavery Movement, 1933.

CORMACK, A. A., Poor Relief in Scotland, 1923.

CRAWFORD, O. G. S., Roman Scotland.

CUNNINGHAM, A. S., Mining in the Kingdom of Fife, 1913.
Mining in Mid and East Lothian, 1925.

DAVIDSON, MORRISON, Annals of Toil (n.d.).

DUTT, SALME A., When England Arose, 1938.

Edinburgh Review, The, Slavery in Modern Scotland. Anon., 1899.

ERSKINE, JOHN, An Institute of the Laws of Scotland, 1834 (1st ed., 1754).

Exchequer Rolls of Scotland, 1264–1600.

FARRINGTON, BENJAMIN, Head and Hand in Ancient Greece, 1947.

FERGUSON, JAMES, Alexander III, King of Scotland, 1937.
William Wallace, Guardian of Scotland, 1948.

FISCHER, T. A., The Scots in Germany, 1902.

FLETCHER OF SALTOUN, ANDREW, Two Discoveries concerning the Affairs of Scotland, Edinburgh, 1698.

GAMMAGE, R. G., The History of the Chartist Movement, London, 1854.

GILLESPIE, F. E., Labour and Politics in England, 1927.

GRAHAM, H. G., Social Life of Scotland in the Eighteenth Century, 1928.

GRANT, I. F., The Social and Economic Development of Scotland before 1603, 1930.

GRAY, J. L., The Law of Combination in Scotland. Economica, Dec. 1928.

HANNINGTON, WAL, The Problem of the Depressed Areas, 1937.

HEINEMANN, MARGOT, Britain's Coal, 1944.

HOVELL, MARK, The Chartist Movement, 1918.

INNES, COSMO, Sketches of Early Scottish History and Social Progress, 1861.
Lectures on Scotch Legal Antiquities, 1872.

JOHNSON, THOMAS, History of the Working Classes in Scotland, 1929.

KIDD, WILLIAM, Memorandum of the Chartist Agitation in Dundee, 1899.

MACKENZIE, AGNES M., Scotland in Modern Times, 1941.

MACKINNON, JAMES, The Social and Industrial History of Scotland, 1920.

MACPHERSON, DAVID, Annals of Commerce, 1805.

MARWICK, W. H., A Bibliography of Scottish Economic History, *Econ. Hist. Review*, 1931.

MILLAR, JOHN, Observations Concerning the Distinction of Ranks in Society, London, 1771.

New Statistical Account of Scotland, The, 1845.

PENNANT, THOMAS, A Tour in Scotland, 1769.

PINCHBECK, IVY, Women Workers and the Industrial Revolution, 1930.

PRINCE, HOARE, Memoirs of Granville Sharp, London, 1820.

RAIT, R. S., The Parliaments of Scotland, 1924.
    Scotland, 1934.

Register of the Privy Council of Scotland, 1545–1684.

ROTHSTEIN, THEODORE, From Chartism to Labourism, 1929.

SAVILLE, JOHN, Ernest Jones: Chartist, 1952.

Scottish Historical Review.

SHARP, GRANVILLE, A Representation of the Injustice and Dangerous Tendency of Tolerating Slavery, London, 1769.

SIMPSON, J. B., Presidential Address 1910. North of England Institute of Mining Engineers, *Transactions*, Vol. 39.

SINCLAIR, Sir JOHN, The Statistical Account of Scotland. 21 vols. Edinburgh, 1791–9.

SMITH, ADAM, An Enquiry into the Nature and Causes of the Wealth of Nations, 1776. Ed. Cannan, 1925.
    Lectures 1763. Ed. Cannan, 1896.

The Acts of the Parliaments of Scotland, 1134–1707.

TUFNELL, E. C., The Character, Object and Effects of Trade Unions, London, 1834. (A pamphlet at British Museum.)

WILLIAMS, W. H. (Ed.), The Miners' Two Bob, 1936.

WILSON, HAROLD, New Deal for Coal, 1945.

WRIGHT, LESLIE C., Scottish Chartism, 1953.

WYNTOUN, ANDREW of, The Orygynale Cronykil of Scotland. Ed. Laing. Edinburgh, 1872.

INDEX OF NAMES

Abercorn, Earl of: 8
Abraham, William: 107
Acheson, Dean: 344
Adamson, William: 167–8, 182–3 (n), 190–193, 195, 197, 219, 222, 232, 245
Adenauer, Dr. K.: 346
Aitken, Hugh: 165
Alison, Dr. S. S.: 31
Allan, William: 168, 183 (n), 184, 185 (n), 189, 191 (n), 194–5, 214 (n)
Anstruther-Gray, Maj.: 181
Ardevall, Lord: 105
Armstrong, John: 245, 251
Ashfield, Lord: 274
Ashton, Thomas: 77, 81, 86, 106–7
Ashton and Sykes, *Coal Industry of the Eighteenth Century*: 3 (n)
Askwith, Lord: 107 (n), 108
Asquith, H. H.: 113, 122, 126–7, 129, 131
Atkinson, J. B.: 371
Attlee, Clement: 225, 246, 326, 364

Baird, Charles: 17
Bald, Robert: 12
Baldwin, Stanley: 161, 163–4, 197, 201, 224, 228, 232
Balfour, Earl of: 299
Balfour of Burleigh, Lord: 110
Balfour, A. J.: 104
Barbour, James, 137, 236, 244–5, 251, 259, 261
Barnes, G. N.: 113
Barnes, Renée: 376, 412
Barr, Hugh: 351
Barrowman, J.: 412
Barrowman, James, *Slavery in the Coal-Mines of Scotland*: 12 (n)
    Glossary of Scotch Mining Terms: 363 (n), 384 (n)
Baxter, Maj. Noel: 181
Beresford, Rev. J. J.: 26
Bevan, Aneurin: 240, 421
Bevin, Ernest: 246, 253, 301
Bird, John: 183 (n), 184 (n)
Blair, J. R.: 286–7
Bonar Law, A.: 148
Bone, J.: 394
Boyd, Ernest: 195
Boyd, John: 352, 360
Boyd, R., *Coal Pits and Pitmen*: 10 (n)
Brailsford, H. N.: 199
Brannan, Hugh: 264 (n), 313
Brown, A. J. Youngson, Article in *Economic History Review*: 64
Brown, James: 209, 236
Brown, Robert: 76, 85, 104, 124–5
Brown, William: 351
Bryan, Sir Andrew M.: 244 (n), 376, 378, 380, 385–6, 388–9, 397
Buckmaster, Lord, 162

Burke, Charles, 349–50
Burns, Robert: 14, 55
Burnside, Robert: 251 (n)
Burt, Thomas: 39, 62, 67
Buxton, Sydney: 123
Byron, Lord: 14

Cairns, J. H.: 380
Cameron, Alexander: 137, 236, 301 (n)
Cameron, John, Q.C.: 281, 300
Campbell, Alex.: 191
Campbell-Bannerman, Sir H.: 104, 113
Carlow, Charles Augustus: 135
Carmont, Lord: 395
Carson, Sir Edward: 127
Castlereagh, Lord: 63
Cation, James: 195
Chamberlain, Neville: 224, 229, 238, 246
Chambers, Thomas: 78
Chiang Kai-shek: 341
Churchill, Winston: 107–8, 113, 163–4, 170, 176, 246, 254, 262, 327–8
Citrine, Sir Walter: 303
Clark, Andrew: 421
Clarke, Andrew B.: 144, 158 (n), 210–12, 216, 221, 226–8, 236, 244
Clerk, Sir George, Bt., M.P.: 23
Cloughan, W.: 36
Cobbett, William: 14, 127
Cochrane, Archibald, *Description of the Estate and Abbey of Culross*: 10 (n)
Cockburn, Lord Henry: 6
Colthart, John: 251, 257, 264 (n), 268
Comerford, George: 313, 343
Connelly, James: 264 (n)
Connolly, Patrick: 183 (n)
Cook, A.: 257
Cook, A. J.: 162–4, 173, 183, 188–9, 190 (n), 207–8
    Is it Peace?: 201
Cook, James: 94, 170, 183, 231, 244–5, 251, 257, 263, 264 (n)
    career: 268
Cooke, Henry: 51–2, 55, 58, 66
Cooper, Lord: 395–6
Copeland, Sam: 362
Cowan, William: 303–4
Cowey, Ned: 85, 94–5
Craig, Andrew: 376, 408
Cripps, Sir Stafford: 302, 307, 309, 313, 366
Culbert, T.: 153
Cumming, Janet: 23
Cumming, Superintendent: 154

Davidson, A. K.: 226, 247, 301 (n)
Davies, S. O.: 189, 189 (n), 190 (n)
Deakin, Arthur: 320
Dingwall, W.J.: 51

Disraeli, B.: 299
Donaldson, J.: 184 (n)
Doonan, James: 170, 185 (n), 205–10
Drinnan, John: 55, 58
Drylie, William: 248
Duncan, Thomas: 29

Easton, William: 155–6, 165
Edgar, A.: 260
Edgar, Alex.: 362
Edwards, Ebby: 207 (n), 221, 226, 230, 231 (n), 236
Edwards, Enoch: 102–4, 116, 124
Elcho, Lord: 54
Elliott, James: 341
Erskine, Sir Thomas: 181
Evers, John: 165

Fairnie, Magnus: 349–50, 362
Flynn, Andrew: 243–4, 353
Ford, Henry: 199
Fowler, Thomas: 355
Franks, R. H.: 20, 22, 24, 28, 31, 34
Fullerton, Joseph: 313
Fynes, R., History of The Durham and North-umberland Miners: 34, 35

Gaitskell, Hugh: 307, 324
Gallacher, William: 141, 202 (n), 221–2, 232–3, 243
Gardner, A.: 394
Geddes, Hugh: 355
Gibb, Thomas: 356
Gillespie, John: 55, 58
Gilmour, Sir Alexander: 8
Gilmour, David: 135
Gladstone, W. E.: 63, 122, 129
Gorman, James: 352, 360
Graham, Duncan: 186, 201, 227, 247
Greenall, Tom: 75, 95
Greene, Lord: 250, 251, 253
Grey, Sir Edward: 123, 129
Grieg, John: 191
Gwinner, D. H.: 379

Hall, J. A.: 376
Halliday, William C.: 384, 394
Hamilton, Andrew: 264 (n), 331, 343
Hancock, F. J.: 190
Hanlon, John: 362
Hardie, Keir: 66–71, 78, 91–2, 95, 113, 166, 427
  early history: 66–7
  and Labour Party: 69, 88, 97, 423
  M.F.G.B. Executive: 71
  M.P.: 71 (n), 74
  on police in strikes: 81–2, 87
  and Scottish Labour Party: 61 (n)
  on troops in strikes: 128–9
  wage policy: 69, 87
  and war: 140–1
Hart, Finlay: 231
Harvey, W. E., M.P.: 78, 107, 109, 115
Hawke, Edward: 183 (n), 185 (n), 236, 235, 250

Hay, Matthew: 29
Henderson, Arthur: 113, 140, 200
Henderson, Peter: 137, 227, 251 (n), 264 (n)
Herd, C. W.: 379
Hicken, Harry: 190
Hinden, Rita: 359
Hitler, Adolf: 223–5, 228, 230, 238, 247, 265
Hodge, Philip: 167, 182–3 (n), 191 (n), 194–5
Hodges, Frank: 162
Hogg, Isabel: 27
Hood, James: 169, 210
Hope, Sir John: 23
Horner, Arthur: 171, 190, 268, 273, 348, 376
Houston, Andrew: 385, 387
Hughes, Sam: 55
Hunter, Alex.: 251 (n), 188 (n)
Hunter, John: 185 (n)
Hunter, Lord: 132
Hyndley, Lord: 290, 306–8
Hyndman, H. M.: 141

Innes, William: 343
Isaacs, Sir Rufus: 128

Jack, Alison: 24
Jagan, Dr. Cheddi: 357
Jameson, Sheriff: 101
Johnson, Dr. Samuel: 8
Johnstone, William: 343
Jude, Martin: 34, 36

Kahout, Joseph: 356
Keith, Lord: 395
Kellachan, Daniel: 343
Kelly, David: 353
Kennedy, Tom: 159
Kenny, Alexander: 25
Kent, John: 165
Kerr, Jane: 25
Kerr, Thomas: 303, 352, 360
Keynes, J. M.: 163
Kuznetsov, V.: 367

Lansbury, George: 127, 200
Law, Robert: 370
Lawrence, Martin: 420 (n)
Lawther, William: 190, 236, 308–16, 322, 347
Lenin, V. I.: 144
Leveston, Margaret: 26
Lewis, John L.: 346
Lincoln, Abraham: 5
Lindsay, Earl: 181
Lloyd, A. L., Come All Ye Bold Miners, 370 (n)
Lloyd, Geoffrey: 285
Lloyd George, David: 113–14, 123, 129, 134, 143, 145, 148–9, 151, 159, 201, 238
Lloyd George, Maj. Gwilym: 255
Londonderry, Marquis of: 32, 33
Loreburn, Lord: 110
Lothian, Marquis of: 28

McAnulty, Andrew: 61 (n), 65, 91, 92, 172 (n), 177, 184, 427
MacArthur, Gen. Douglas: 342
McArthur, John: 183–4, 186, 195, 286–7, 305, 325, 352, 360
Macbeth, James: 130
McCann, Patrick: 304, 313, 343
McCardel, D. L.: 380
McCarthy, Joseph: 187
MacColl, Ewan: 420
McCosh, A. K.: 98, 107, 110, 118, 120, 132
McCutcheon, Robert: 355
McDonagh, James: 314
McDonald, Alexander: 37–9, 41–58, 60–7, 91, 252
    chairman T.U.C. Parliamentary Committee: 51, 56
    M.P.: 56
MacDonald, J. Ramsay: 88, 113, 161–2, 197, 200–1, 205, 209, 224, 274
McEwan, James: 169
McGahey, Michael: 424
McGhee, E.: 301 (n)
McGilvray, D.: 343
McGowan, Joseph: 395
McGowan, Lord: 273
Machen, J. R. A.: 244 (n)
McInnes, Archibald: 165
McInulty, Joseph: 61
McKendrick, J.: 189, 226, 236, 245, 251 (n), 257, 259, 264 (n), 281, 362, 418
McKenna, Paul: 250
McKibbon, William: 264 (n)
MacKinnon, D.: 382
McLaren, Angus: 188 (n)
McLaughlan, Hugh: 264 (n)
MacLean, John: 141, 144, 184
McLean, John (of Bannockburn): 355
McLean, W.: 245
McLean, William, jun.: 352, 360
McLean, John (of Broomfield): 343
McLean, William (of Harthill): 343
McQuade, Peter: 343
Main, James: 353
Malik, J.: 344
Mann, Tom: 95, 127, 171, 201–2
Marx, Karl: 64, 200
Maxwell, Colin: 48
Maxwell, Robert: 376
May, Sir George, 199
Middleton, James: 141
Milgrew, John: 264 (n)
Millar, Prof. John, Observations Concerning the Distinction of Ranks: 7 (n)
Miller, John: 205, 347, 361, 394, 418
Mitchell, Andrew: 362
Moffat, Abe: 253–4, 258, 263–4, 287–8, 298 (n), 300, 315, 339, 347, 349–51, 353, 355–6, 362, 411, 414–15, 421, 425
    checkweigher: 93, 190, 197, 216
    and closing of pits: 291–2
    and disputes: 281, 409–11
    early history: 252
    and Knockshinnoch disaster: 372, 376–7, 379–88, 392–8

Moffat, Abe—continued
    and nationalisation: 278 (n), 279, 283
    on need for wage increases: 303, 305, 317–19, 323, 327
    N.U.S.M.W. Executive: 236–7, 245
    on political issues: 265, 423–4
    President: 251, 257
    and U.M.S.: 214–15, 218, 222
    and Valleyfield disaster: 242–4
    and wage structure: 312, 332–3
Moffat, Agnes: 23
Moffat, Alex.: 190, 195–6, 216, 236–7, 252, 312, 325, 355, 400, 409, 420–1
Moffat, David: 55, 66, 252
Moncrieff, Lord: 192 (n)
Mond, Sir Alfred: 183 (n)
Mooney, Tom: 144
Moore, Frank: 214 (n), 222
Morison, R. P., K.C.: 242, 376–7, 387, 389
Morris, William: 88, 275
Morrison, Herbert: 258 (n), 273–4, 301, 324
Muir, John: 40
Muir, P.: 78
Mundy, Mrs. L. M.: 379
Munro, Robert: 165
Murnin, Hugh: 159, 166, 183 (n), 185 (n), 210
Murray, Harry: 312
Mussolini, B.: 224–5, 265

Napier, John: 3
Nef, J. U., Rise of the British Coal Industry: 3 (n), 6 (n), 8 (n)
Nehru, Jawaharlal: 342
Nimmo, Adam: 130, 132, 234
Normansell, John: 53

O'Connor, Feargus: 21, 64
O'Hara, Peter: 352, 360
O'Neill, Joe: 362
Owen, Robert: 14

Palmerston, Lord: 32
Park, D. W.: 374, 387
Parrott, W.: 75, 84
Parsons, O. H.: 388–9
Pearson, William: 235, 255, 266–7, 297, 359, 414, 418
    and claim for lower-paid workers: 307–8, 313–14
    committee on Scottish coalfield: 137
    foreign delegations: 355–6
    illness: 386
    and Knockshinnoch disaster: 372, 373 (n), 374, 375 (n), 376–7, 385–6
    and Spain: 227
    at S.T.U.C.: 341, 365–8
    T.U. positions: 236, 250–1, 257, 264 (n), 268
    and war situation, 1940: 246–7
Peaston, Stephen: 312
Pender, William: 264 (n)
Penman, A.: 341
Penman, Richard: 51–2
Pickard, Ben: 93–4, 102, 114

Potter, J.: 183 (*n*)
Proudfoot, David: 183, 186, 195, 214 (*n*)

Rattray, Thomas: 370
Reid, Alexander: 28
Reid, Carlow: 152, 261
Reid, Charles C.: 196, 242
Reid, Dr. William: 391
Roberts, W. P.: 35
Robertson, D.: 245
Robertson, John: 141, 143, 146–8
Robertson, R. Chisholm: 68, 71, 77, 80–1, 83, 85–7, 90
Robeson, Paul: 420
Rollo, William: 360–1
Ross, Major: 181
Rossochinsky, Ivan: 355
Rutherford, John: 250, 264 (*n*), 362

Salisbury, Lord: 110
Sankey, Lord Justice: 146–7
Saville, J., *Ernest Jones, Chartist*: 36 (*n*)
Scambler, Richard: 264 (*n*)
Scobie, William: 55
Seigel: 352
Seine, Jean: 352
Shackleton, D. J.: 113
Shaftesbury, Lord: 18, 19, 32, 34
Sharp, Alexander: 352, 360
Shearer, J.: 299
Shelley, P. B.: 15
Shinwell, Emanuel: 162, 207, 307 (*n*)
Sim, Daniel: 183 (*n*), 185 (*n*), 245, 252, 268, 301 (*n*), 305, 353, 376, 408
Simpson, James: 47–8, 50
Sloan, Alexander: 236, 244, 247, 268
Small, William B.: 91–2, 184, 189 (*n*), 260, 427
Smillie, Robert: 98, 141, 168–9, 182, 184 (*n*), 187, 189 (*n*), 365, 424, 427
  and 1894 strike: 74–6, 78, 83, 85
  and 1921 lock-out: 160
  death: 244–5
  debate with Chisholm Robertson: 90 (*n*)
  on industrial action for political purposes: 148
  in Lanarkshire: 73, 91–2
  M.P.: 166
  and negotiations: 103–6, 108–10, 118–19, 130, 132
  on private ownership: 117
  and Sankey Commission: 145, 148
  and Socialism: 92, 94–5, 97
  and Triple Alliance: 142–3
  T.U. positions: 73–4, 116, 131 (*n*), 144–5, 166, 183, 183 (*n*), 185, 185 (*n*), 205
Smillie, R. (jun.): 299
Smith, Adam, *Wealth of Nations*: 7
Smith, Alex.: 183, 251 (*n*)
Smith, Robert: 183 (*n*), 185 (*n*)
Sneddon, William: 236, 356, 376, 386
Snowden, Philip: 199–201
Spalding, William: 154–5, 158
Spencer, George: 204
Stalin, J. V.: 173 (*n*)

Steele, A. H.: 379
Steele, Graham: 314, 341
Stephenson, T.: 244 (*n*)
Stevens, W. C.: 306 (*n*)
Stewart, A. M.: 394
Stewart, James: 178–81, 183 (*n*), 190, 195
Stewart, Thomas: 303, 353
Stobbs, Gavin: 315, 396
Sutherland, John: 353, 356
Szabó, András: 393

Tancred, Thomas: 20, 21, 22
Tennant, Robert: 352, 360
Tewson, V.: 307
Thomas, J. H.: 158, 199–201
Thompson, William: 351
Thomson, Alexander: 183 (*n*), 185 (*n*)
Thomson, Robert: 356
Thyssen, F.: 223
Toal, George: 242
Tonner, C.: 183 (*n*)
Tonner, James: 145, 166
Traprain, Lord (*see also* Balfour): 261
Tremenheere, Seymour: 17, 34, 36
Truman, H.: 424
Turner, Malcolm: 170

Valigura: 355 (*n*)

Watson, Margaret: 26
Waugh, James: 29
Waugh, M.: 260
Webb, Beatrice: 163 (*n*)
Webb, Sidney: 201
Webb, S. and B., *History of Trade Unionism*: 57, 58 (*n*)
Wedgwood, Josiah: 127–8
Weir, John: 66, 74, 76, 78, 86, 94, 97, 103
White, John Baker: 348–9
White, Walter: 195
Whitelaw, Thomas: 279–80
Whyte, John: 165
Williams, D. J.: 183 (*n*)
Williams, Francis, *Fifty Years' March*: 197–198
Williams, W. H., *The Miners' Two Bob*: 230 (*n*)
Williamson, Tom: 320
Wilson, Andrew: 379
Wilson, John: 83, 94
Wilson, Thomas: 353
Wood, John: 252, 260, 301, 341, 352–3, 360, 362, 394, 409, 425 (*n*)
Wood, William: 356
Woods, G.: 190
Woods, Sam: 78
Wright, O.: 190

Young, Sir Eric: 306
Young, Joseph: 144
Young, Robert: 376, 400 (*n*)
Young, R. F.: 362, 400 (*n*)

Zaitzev, S. I.: 355

GENERAL INDEX

Aberdeen: 231
Aberdeenshire: 156
Aberdour: 369
Abnormal Places: 115–18, 120
Absenteeism: 261, 307, 314
Abyssinia: 224
Accidents: 19, 20, 71, 146, 159, 216, 218, 314, 346, 364, 369, 415 (n)
  Newcraighall Colliery: 400
  in other counties: 364
  See also Disasters; Safety
Acts of the Parliament of Scotland:
  1579 Scots Poor Law: 3
  1597 Scots Poor Law: 3
  1606 Anent Colliers and Coalbearers: 3, 4
  1641 Act of 1606 extended: 4
  1701 Act against Wrongous Imprisonment (not to apply to colliers): 7, 9
Acts of the Parliament of the United Kingdom of Great Britain:
  1774 Emancipation (partial): 8–9
  1797 Incitement to Mutiny, 128
  1799 Emancipation (full): 10, 12
  1832 Reform Act: 14, 19
  1834 Poor Law: 15
  1842 Women and Children in Mines: 33
  1855 Coal Mines Inspection: 41
  1860 Coal Mines Regulation, 45–6
  1872 Mines: 51, 53, 60, 62
  1881 Protection of Persons and Property (Ireland): 63
  1906 Trade Disputes: 105, 112
  1908 Coal Mines (Eight Hours): 105, 112, 142, 206
  1911 Coal Mines: 132, 272 (n), 378, 380, 384, 387–8, 394–8, 400–1, 409
  1911 National Insurance: 132
  1912 Coal Mines (Minimum Wage): 129–31
  1919 Coal Mines (Seven Hours): 149
  1920 Emergency Powers: 172, 181
  1926 Coal Mines (Eight Hours): 198, 208
  1927 Trade Union and Disputes: 197, 277
  1930 Coal Mines (7½ Hours): 198, 206, 208
  1931 Coal Mines: 208
  1940 Emergency Powers: 246–7
  1944 Education: 416
  1946 Coal Industry Nationalisation: 271–2, 274
  1949 Coal Industry: 272 (n)
  1954 Mines and Quarries: 399–400
Agents (Colliery): 380, 386–7, 390, 394–7, 406–7
Agents (Miners'): 67, 81, 92, 97, 141, 145 (n), 182–4, 186, 195, 247, 405–8, 410

Agreements: 204, 217–19, 230, 246, 287, 409
  1909: 109–10, 119, 122, 132–3
  1921: 162
  1924: 162–3
  1931: 208
  1932: 210–12
  1934: 234
  1940, war additions: 245–6, 307, 311, 316, 319, 321–2
  1942: 253
  1944: 256, 297
  1944, holidays: 256–7
  1947: 298
  1947, five-day week: 296–7, 301
  1948, weekly paid industrial staff: 298–9
  1950: 323
  1951: 326–8, 334
  1953: 334
  See also Extended Hours; Minimum Wage; Wage Advances
Airdrie: 39, 41, 289
Amalgamated Engineering Union: 277, 366
Amalgamated Section of Scottish Miners and Oilworkers: 70
Amalgamated Society of Engineers: 113
Anglo-German Fellowship: 238
Arbitration: 42, 54, 57, 123, 280, 315
  Compulsory: 335–6
  Order 1305: 335
  See also National Reference Tribunal; Wage Awards
Argyll: 203
Argyll and Sutherland Highlanders: 158
Arles: 6, 9–11
Armed Forces: 34, 35, 42, 128–9, 152, 154, 158, 168, 172, 358
  miners in: 10, 142, 240, 249
  Yeomanry: 42–3
Ascertainment System: 234, 239, 247, 256, 262, 282
Associated Blacksmiths' and Ironworkers' Society: 150
Asturias: 226–7
Atomic Weapons: 339, 341, 360–1, 366–7, 402, 424
Australia: 352
Austria: 228, 362
Avondale: 176
Ayr: 376
Ayrshire: 48, 73, 137, 210 (n), 213, 236, 252, 268, 372, 376, 386, 408
  Coal and Iron Miners' Association in: 41, 44
  early trade unions in: 15, 21
  Keir Hardie and: 68, 70, 88, 91
  man-power: 203
  Miners' Association in: 36
  strikes in: 42, 67, 75

Ayrshire Miners' Federal Union: 67, 70, 78, 150, 169, 227, 248, 251 (*n*), 264

Baillieston: 41, 55
Ballochmyle Hospital: 399
Bellshill: 91
Black Friday: 158
Blacklegs: 35, 42, 83–4, 87, 168, 173
Blairadam: 152
Blairhall: 252
Blantyre: 60, 70, 137, 177, 369
  Miners' Association: 91
Bo'ness: 48–9, 220
Bowhill: 185
Boys' Wages: 118–20, 234, 246. *See also* Young Miners
British Association of Colliery Management: 280–1
British Guiana: 357–9
British Miners' Reform Movement: 157
British Socialist Party: 141, 144
British Youth Festival Committee: 418
Brotherings: 11, 12, 47
Buckhaven: 159, 331

Capital Levy: 314
Chartism: 14–16, 18–19, 21–2, 30, 33, 35–6, 39, 63–4, 181, 299
Checkweighers: 46, 93, 185, 190, 196, 250. *See also* Weighing
Child Labour: 3, 6, 16, 18–33, 38, 423
Children's Employment Commission, 1840–2: 6, 7, 18–19, 21 (*n*), 30 (*n*), 31 (*n*), 32
China: 229, 340–4, 362–4, 424
  Chinese labour: 54, 143
Clackmannan: 22, 34, 73, 91, 203, 237
  1877 lockout: 59
Clackmannanshire Miners' Association: 70, 244, 263, 269
Clarion: 95
Cleland: 41
Clerical and Administrative Workers' Union: 331
Closing of Pits: 287–91, 403
Coal (White Paper, 1942): 249, 261
Coal and Iron Miners' Association, 1855: 41, 44–5, 64–5, 427
Coal Charges Fund: 255
Coal, Concessionary: 59, 295, 315
Coal Distillation: 289, 291
Coal Distribution: 282, 284
Coal Exports: 96, 202, 209, 211, 240, 324
Coal Imports: 326
Coal Output: 151, 245, 324
  16th century: 1
  1681–90: 2
  1924–38: 239–40
  first World War: 142
  highest: 115, 202–3
  per man-shift, Scotland and Britain: 212
  Poland: 354
  See also Production, Restriction of Output

Coal Price: 54, 56–7, 73, 97, 99–100, 105, 110–11, 132–3, 143, 148, 151, 206, 273, 371
  under nationalisation: 282–4
Coalburn: 82, 250
Coal-owners: 31–2, 34, 40, 47–8, 52, 87–8, 98–104, 203, 205, 234, 241, 246, 277, 299, 332
  attempts to hinder organisation: 16–17, 93, 204, 216, 235
  demands for wage-cuts: 79, 101–13, 163–4, 208, 214–15
  meetings with miners' leaders: 99, 104, 107–9, 116–19, 122, 127, 130–2, 142, 159, 208, 233, 287
  and minimum wage: 123–5
  and national negotiations: 54, 143, 193, 230–3
  refusal of meetings: 75, 80, 98, 239
  and Sankey Commission: 146–8, 272
  and second World War: 260–2
  in strikes and lockouts: 34, 81, 151, 170–172, 175, 182, 184
  and U.M.S.: 213
  See also Colliery Companies
Coatbridge: 41, 81
Colliery Companies:
  profits: 143, 146, 213, 239
  share prices: 131
  See also Fife Coal Co.
Colliery Officials and Staffs' Association: 299
Combination Acts, 1799–1800: 14–15
Communism: 157
Communist Party: 61 (*n*), 252, 265, 331
  Communists: 178, 182, 188 (*n*), 189 (*n*), 216, 228, 232
Compensation:
  for injury: 71, 217, 266, 269, 412 (*n*), 418
  Knockshinnoch: 393–4, 398
  for mine-owners: 275–7, 283, 310, 313–314, 316
  for redundant miners: 269, 284
Compensation Secretaries: 195
Competition: 35, 196, 209, 239
Conciliation: 57
  machinery (1943): 254, 286, 323, 330, 335–7, 405–12
  See also Conciliation Boards, Joint Negotiating Committee
Conciliation Boards:
  English Federated Area: 73, 79, 101, 103–4, 111
  Scottish: 82–3, 87, 99–100, 104–6, 110–111, 115, 117, 119–20, 122, 132–3, 234, 246, 262, 277 (*n*), 282, 299–300, 407, 410
    formed: 99
    renewed: 110
  Welsh: 103
Conferences:
  1844 Miners' Association of Great Britain and Ireland: 35
  1856 Coal and Iron Miners of Scotland: 43–4

Conferences—*continued*
1863 National Association of Coal, Lime and Ironstone Miners of Great Britain: 47
1887 Scottish Miners' National Federation: 68
1894 Miners' Federation of Great Britain Annual: 71
1894 M.F.G.B. Special: 75, 78, 82–6
1894 Scottish Miners' Federation Special: 80–1, 83
1897 M.F.G.B. Annual: 93–6, 268
1904 M.F.G.B. Special: 102–3
1909 M.F.G.B. Special: 106–9
1910 M.F.G.B. Annual: 115–16
1911 M.F.G.B. Annual: 117
1911 M.F.G.B. Special: 116–17, 119–20
1912 M.F.G.B. Special: 120–1, 123–4, 127, 129, 131
1913 M.F.G.B. Annual: 142
1918 Scottish Annual: 143
1919 Scottish Annual: 148
1921 Scottish Annual: 159–60
1922 Scottish Annual: 165–6
1924 Scottish Annual: 163
1925 Scottish Annual: 168
1925 Scottish Special: 169
1926 Scottish Special: 184
1927 Scottish Annual: 182, 185–7
1928 M.F.G.B. Annual: 189
1928 Scottish Annual: 191–2
1928 Scottish Special: 193–4
1929 Scottish Annual: 205
1929 Scottish Special: 206
1930 Scottish Annual: 206
1931 M.F.G.B. Special: 207
1931 Scottish Annual: 208–9
1931 Scottish Special: 209
1932 Scottish Annual: 210
1933 Scottish Annual: 211
1934 Scottish Annual: 212
1935 M.F.G.B. Annual: 230
1935 M.F.G.B. Special: 231, 233
1935 Scottish Half-Yearly: 220
1935 Scottish Special: 232
1936 M.F.G.B. Special: 231 (n), 234
1937 Scottish Annual: 226
1938 Scottish Annual: 227
1939 Scottish Annual: 228
1940 Scottish Annual: 245, 257
1940 Scottish Special: 244
1941 M.F.G.B. Annual: 258
1941 Scottish Annual: 248, 257–8
1942 Scottish Annual: 259, 263
1942 Scottish Special: 251
1943 M.F.G.B. Annual: 253
1943 M.F.G.B. Special: 254
1943 Scottish Annual: 253–4, 257, 260, 263
1943 Scottish Special: 255, 263
1944 M.F.G.B. Special: 255
1944 Scottish Annual: 264
1945 Scottish Annual: 265–6
1945 Scottish Special: 267
1946 Scottish Annual: 270, 277 (n)

Conferences—*continued*
1946 Scottish Area: 278
1947 National Union of Mineworkers Annual: 297
1947 N.U.M. Special: 301
1947 Scottish Area: 296, 301–2
1948 N.U.M. Special: 324
1948 Scottish Annual: 339–40, 351, 355
1948 Scottish Area: 302–3, 324, 348–9
1949 N.U.M. Annual: 307–8, 311, 316, 319, 321, 323
1949 N.U.M. Special: 320
1949 Scottish Annual: 291, 340, 352
1949 Scottish Area: 290, 310–19, 357
1949 Scottish Youth: 417
1950 N.U.M. Annual: 321
1950 N.U.M. Special: 320, 323
1950 Scottish Annual: 321, 341
1950 Scottish Area: 281, 321–2, 324, 342–3, 353
1950 Scottish Youth: 323
1951 N.U.M. Annual: 327, 336
1951 N.U.M. Special: 325, 328
1951 Scottish Annual: 327, 344, 356, 392
1951 Scottish Area: 327–8, 386
1952 N.U.M. Annual: 329
1952 N.U.M. Special: 329, 331–2
1952 Scottish Annual: 329, 356, 419
1952 Scottish Area: 328–32, 395–7
1953 N.U.M. Annual: 337
1953 Scottish Annual: 283, 356
1954 Scottish Annual: 337–8, 425 (n)
1954 Scottish Area: 337, 345 (n)
Conscription: 241, 301, 424
for mines: 253, 270
Conservative Party: 161, 163, 172, 197, 200–1, 246, 258, 262, 286, 327, 422
Moffat on: 265
Consultation: 274, 289
Contracting System: 211, 299–300
Control of Engagement Order: 302
Co-operative Congress: 345
Co-operative Party: 345
Co-operative Production: 70
Co-operative Societies: 14, 223, 289
Cost of Living: 110, 112, 114–15, 142, 151, 245–6, 248, 250, 307, 310–12, 318–19, 321, 325, 327, 332, 337
index: 303, 307, 327
sliding scales: 317, 320
Covenanters: 181
Cowdenbeath: 154–5, 157–8, 369–70
Crises, Economic: 33, 161, 302
1837: 16, 17
1847: 36
1877: 59, 66
1920: 151, 159
1930: 203, 205, 209, 213, 223, 230, 288, 366
Culross: 10 (n), 242, 419
Cumberland: 174
Czechoslovakia: 228–9, 238, 340, 351, 355–356

Daily Herald: 358
Daily Mail: 172 (*n*)
Daily Worker: 258
Dalkeith Advertiser: 157 (*n*)
Dalry: 55
Dawes Plan: 203
Den: 55
Denny: 29
Derbyshire: 78, 121, 190, 253
Devaluation: 306, 309, 311–12, 314
Disarmament: 360–1
Disasters: 35
    1877: Blantyre: 60–2, 369
    1901: Donibristle: 369–71
    1918: Stanrigg: 371
    1939: Valleyfield: 242–4
    1947: William pit, Whitehaven: 244 (*n*),
      390
    1950: Knockshinnoch: 369, 371–6,
      392 (*n*), 393, 395, 397, 399–400
Disputes Committee: 406–12
Dockers: 126, 248
Donibristle: 369, 371
Dumbarton: 73, 91–2, 169
Dumfries: 203
Dunbartonshire: 184 (*n*), 203
Dundee: 231
Dunfermline: 35, 55, 154, 156, 158, 181 (*n*)
Dunfermline Press: 152–5, 158, 179, 181
Dunoon: 174, 414
Durham: 35, 119, 121, 146, 169, 174, 190,
    258, 315, 392 (*n*)
Dysart: 231

East Houses: 28–9
East Scotland: 20, 69, 92
Eastern Europe: 339–40, 352
Edinburgh: 158, 310, 399
    People's Festival: 420
Education: 19, 21, 23–5, 30, 36, 38–9, 146
    'Ladder Plan': 415 (*n*)
    trade union: 413–15, 417
Eight-Hour Day: 51, 53, 64 (*n*), 69, 71,
    142, 198, 207, 214, 301, 423
Elections, General: 104, 114, 161, 163, 197,
    200–1, 232, 262, 265–7, 275, 327, 365
Electrical Trades Union: 277, 306 (*n*), 337,
    366
Emergency Powers Act:
    1920: 172, 181
    1940: 246–7
Engineers: 337. *See also* Amalgamated
    Engineering Union; Amalgamated
    Society of Engineers
Engine-Keepers' Association: *See* Scottish
    Colliery Enginemen, etc.
England: 30, 135
    coal-fields in: 31, 35, 73, 75, 111, 203,
      256
    law courts in: 392
    miners' unions in: 37, 47, 67–9, 78, 83–5,
      116, 219
    See also English counties under own
      names
Essential Work Order: 241, 247, 249

Evening Times (Glasgow): 186–7
Evictions: 216
Extended Hours Agreement: 301–2, 315,
    324–6, 328–30, 332

Fabian Society: 97, 275, 359
Factory Acts: 16
Falkirk: 47–9, 50, 55, 193
Fascism: 169, 223–30, 241, 247, 258–60,
    265, 267, 339–40, 367
Federated Area, English: 71, 73, 75, 119
Fife: 6–7, 12 (*n*), 21–2, 31, 42, 73, 91, 97,
    133, 137, 203, 205, 210 (*n*), 213, 220,
    231–2, 242, 245, 252, 287, 331, 369,
    411, 420
    1877 lockout in: 59
    1926 lockout in: 178, 183–4
    Coal and Iron Miners' Association in: 41
    coal-owners in: 98, 237
    eight hours in: 51, 53, 64 (*n*)
    Free Colliers in: 48–50
    split in union: 167–8, 182, 236
    strikes in: 78, 86, 152, 157, 220
    T.U. membership: 76
    wages in: 74, 89
Fife and Clackmannan Miners' Associa-
    tion: 51–3, 55, 58–9
Fife, Clackmannan and Kinross Miners'
    Association, 1928: 137, 192, 221–2,
    227, 243–4, 248, 251 (*n*), 260, 264
Fife Coal Co.: 93, 131, 154, 158, 179 (*n*),
    196, 221, 231, 237, 242–4, 261, 391
Fife and Kinross Miners' Association: 66,
    70, 74
Fife, Kinross and Clackmannan Miners'
    Association: 156, 166, 169–70, 237,
    263, 268
    differences with N.U.S.M.W.: 186–7,
    188 (*n*), 189 (*n*), 190–5
Fife Reform Union: 167–8, 178, 182
Fines: 12, 21
Firemen and Shotfirers: 234–5, 253
    See also Scottish Colliery Deputies and
    Shotfirers' Association; Scottish Colli-
    ery Enginemen, etc.
First International: 64
Five-Day Week: 69, 270, 296, 325, 329,
    420
    Agreement: 296–7, 301
Forth and Clyde Valley Miners' Associa-
    tion: 70, 90–1
Forty-Hour Week: 270, 325 (*n*)
France: 224, 228, 238, 240, 246, 247, 260,
    314, 344, 346, 422, 424
    miners in: 346–50, 352–3
    Revolution: 10, 14
Free Colliers: 47–50
Friendly Benefit Societies: 18, 31
Fuel and Power, Ministry of: 256, 262, 269,
    273, 279, 285, 289, 295–6, 299, 307–8,
    324, 333 (*n*), 335, 376, 399, 401

Gala Day: 51–2, 420–2
Germany: 203, 223, 225, 228, 257 (*n*), 258,
    266, 346

Germany—*continued*
  East: 356–7
  rearming: 344–5
Gladsmuir: 26
Glasgow: 2, 18, 35, 40–1, 43, 44, 58, 66, 91,
    153–4, 194, 208, 399, 403
  Trades Council: 90 (*n*)
Glasgow Herald: 57
Glasgow Sentinel: 40, 43, 59
Glencraig: 178, 180, 303
Governments:
  1918 Coalition: 148, 152, 159, 161, 275
  1924 Labour: 161–3, 267
  1924 Conservative: 170–2, 184, 198, 277
  1929 Labour: 197–9, 209, 267, 274
  1931 National: 200–2, 204, 211, 219–20,
    223–4
  1935 Conservative: 224–5, 227–32, 240–
    242, 245, 247, 257
  1940 Coalition: 246, 248, 254–6, 258,
    262
  1945 Labour: 262, 267–8, 271, 286,
    302–4, 306, 313, 327, 340, 422
  1950 Labour: 327, 343–4, 360
  1951 Conservative: 329–32, 338, 343,
    358–9, 422–3
Greece: 340
Greene Award: 250, 253, 256, 261–2
Greenock: 232
Guaranteed Week: 241, 248. *See also*
    Minimum Wage
Gullane: 419

Hamilton: 66–7, 91, 176, 201, 280, 289
Hamilton Advertiser: 176–7
Health: 270, 418–19
Holidays: 4, 5, 9, 19
  in other countries: 353–5
  paid: 157, 256–7, 270, 295, 319, 327,
    411, 415 (*n*)
Holytown: 40–1, 66, 91, 168
Home Rule, Scottish: 150
Hours of Work: 39, 43, 45, 51, 163, 206,
    209, 214, 219–20, 234, 239, 248, 285,
    301–2, 324
  of children: 19, 23
  Sankey Commission on: 147, 209
  See also Eight-Hour Day; Five-Day
    Week; Forty-Hour Week; Six-Hour
    Day; Seven-Hour Day; Seven-and-a-
    Half-hour Day
Housing: 270, 295
  colliery houses: 16, 43, 59, 135–8
  in Scotland: 134–5, 146–8
Hungary: 393

Independent Labour Party: 94, 97, 140–1,
    189
India: 128, 150, 266
Industrial Revolution: 7, 14, 135
Inflation: 302–3, 306 (*n*)
Inspection of Mines: 16, 32–3, 36
  Scottish Area N.U.M. appointments:
    400 (*n*)
  See also Inspectors

Inspectors of Mines: 46, 61–2, 215–16,
    371–3, 376–7, 379, 382 (*n*), 390, 399
  Workmen's: 196, 214–18, 236, 242–4,
    376, 408
International Brigade: 225, 228
Inveresk: 26
Ireland: 17, 33, 63–5, 139
Italy: 224–5, 240, 246, 271, 351
Izvestia: 355 (*n*)

Japan: 223, 229, 344
Joint District Wages Board: 130, 132
Joint Negotiating Committee: 287, 309
Justices of the Peace: 12

Kent: 305
Kilmarnock: 15, 46, 48
Kinross: 203
Kirkcaldy: 52, 159
Kirkcaldy Times: 157
Kirkintilloch and Twechar Miners' Asso-
    ciation: 92, 184 (*n*)
Knockshinnoch:
  Coal Board and: 372, 374, 376–8,
    382 (*n*), 385–7, 389–97
  Coal Mines Act and: 380, 384, 387–8,
    394–8
  compensation: 393–4, 398
  disaster: 369, 371–6, 392 (*n*), 393, 395,
    397, 399–400
  Inquiry: 376–85
  Moffat Testimonial: 398–9
  Report: 385–90, 397
Korea: 342–4, 424

Labour, Ministry of: 253
Labour Leader: 81, 87, 92
Labour Monthly: 214 (*n*), 218 (*n*), 273
Labour Party: 112–13, 139–41, 161, 163,
    172, 197, 200–1, 225, 246, 258, 262,
    267, 273, 275, 316, 331, 364, 418, 424
  1918 Programme: 198
  formation: 97, 104
  Keir Hardie on need for: 69, 88
  local Parties: 156, 422
  Parliamentary: 345
  Scarborough Conference: 345
  See also Government; Labour Represen-
    tation Committee; Members of Parlia-
    ment
Labour Relations Officers: 280, 406, 412
Labour Representation Committee: 97,
    104, 112, 275
Labour Research Department: 162, 230 (*n*),
    250 (*n*), 284, 389
'Ladder Plan': 415 (*n*)
Lanark: 176
Lanarkshire: 39–40, 51, 54, 70, 88, 97,
    137, 203, 205, 210 (*n*), 213, 232, 403
  closing of pits in: 287–91
  Coal and Iron Miners' Association in:
    41, 44, 65, 91
  county union: 61 (*n*), 67, 90–2, 98
  district unions: 73, 91, 93
  early trade unions in: 15–17

Lanarkshire—*continued*
  Miners' Association in: 36
  strikes in: 17, 36, 38, 42, 56–7, 75, 98, 321
  wages in: 58, 73, 89
Lanarkshire (Miners' Union): 135, 141, 144, 147, 165–6, 168–9, 172 (*n*), 184–186, 188, 226–7, 234, 248, 250–1, 257 (*n*), 260, 264
  differences with N.U.S.M.W.: 187, 190, 195
Lanarkshire Miners' County Federation, 1893: 73, 90, 92–3, 98
Lancashire: 75, 116, 119, 121, 169, 190, 248, 253
Landowners: 114
Larkhall Miners' Association: 55, 70, 73, 91
Lasswade: 23
Law Courts: 178–81, 214, 231, 300, 391–5, 400 (*n*), 409
League of Nations: 227
Leaving Certificate: 4
Leicester: 78
Leven: 419
Liberal Party: 63–4, 67, 97, 113–14, 129, 141, 161, 163, 167, 197, 200–1, 246, 258, 267
  Lib-Labs: 74, 78, 97, 268
Linlithgow: 203
Lochgelly: 152, 155–8, 181
Lochore: 178, 180
Lockouts: 46, 59
  1893, England: 71, 73, 79, 84, 88, 122, 126
  1921: 151–61, 165–6, 172, 252
  1926: 172, 178, 182–3, 198, 204, 235
  notices: 107–8, 164
Lothians: 21–2, 31, 51, 66, 73, 133, 143, 213, 215, 250, 400
  county unions: 52, 91
  Free Colliers in: 49
  Miners' Association in: 34
  wages in: 89
Lothians—East: 26–7, 203, 210 (*n*)
Lothians—Mid: 41, 137, 203, 210 (*n*), 236
Lothians—West: 41–2, 75, 169, 210 (*n*), 220, 245
Lumphinnans: 154, 158, 190, 195, 217, 237, 252

Magistrates: 178
Managers, Colliery: 39, 62, 243–4, 260–1, 280–1, 380, 386–7, 390, 394–7, 399–400, 406, 409
Man-power: 249, 253, 272, 297–8, 324, 326. *See also* Miners, Number of
Marshall Aid: 301, 339
Maryhill: 42, 44, 55
May Day: 421–2
Means Test: 201, 204, 210, 220
Mechanisation: 286, 355
Members of Parliament: 180, 231, 289, 401, 413
  Conservative: 127
  Labour: 39, 104, 112–13, 129, 158–9, 161, 172

Members of Parliament—*continued*
  Lib-Lab: 74, 78
  lobbying: 42, 45, 68
  miners': 62–3, 68, 78, 104, 112, 129, 161, 201, 211, 217, 268
Methil: 331
Mid and East Lothian Miners' Association: 55, 58, 70, 76, 85, 137, 157 (*n*), 169, 227, 248, 251, 264, 351
Midlands: 331
Miner, The (M.F.G.B.): 188
Miner, The (S.M.N.F.): 67
Miners, The: 3 (*n*), 36 (*n*), 151 (*n*), 171 (*n*), 173 (*n*), 313
Miners, Number of: 78, 121, 133, 175, 203, 240. *See also* Man-power
Miners' Association of Great Britain and Ireland (1841): 33–7
Miners' Charter (1946): 269–71, 274, 278, 284, 296, 302, 307 (*n*), 324
Miners' Federation of Great Britain: 70–1, 73–86, 90, 93, 96, 102, 104–7, 114, 143, 162, 204, 207, 239–40, 242, 248, 250 (*n*), 265, 335, 405
  and 1921 lockout: 157, 158 (*n*)
  and 1926 lockout: 174, 184
  and arbitration: 93, 123
  changes in organisation: 144
  and Czechoslovakia: 229–30
  and differences in Scotland: 187–92, 195, 213
  and hours: 207
  meetings with coal-owners: 107–9, 122, 127, 233, 255–6
  meetings with Government: 107–9, 151, 163, 202, 211
  and Miners' Two Bob: 230–1, 233–4
  and nationalisation: 262, 273–5
  and Parliament: 201, 232
  policy on wages: 75, 78, 93, 99, 102
  rules: 93, 102, 107, 117–18, 296
  and Sankey Commission: 146–7
  and sliding scales: 93, 101
  and Spain: 227–8
  and State control of mines: 254–5
  and U.M.S.: 219, 221
  and young miners: 252–3
  and war: 141, 257
Miners' International Federation: 230, 311, 313, 315
Miners' National Union: 58–9, 70. *See also* National Association of Coal, Lime and Ironstone Miners
'Miners' Two Bob': 220, 230, 232–4
Minimum Wage:
  Bill: 127, 129
  district: 99–110
  individual: 117–24, 131, 132, 164
  national: 248–50, 255–6, 298, 323, 326, 327 (*n*), 328, 332, 337
  See also Strikes, 1912 Minimum Wage
Mining Association: 233, 240, 256
Minority Movement: 162–3, 168, 171, 187, 189
Modernisation: 269, 284–7

Mondism: 183, 189, 198, 201–2, 212–13
Motherwell: 82, 289
Munich: 229

National Association of Coal, Lime and Ironstone Miners: 47, 49. *See also* Miners' National Union
National Coal Board (1942): 249
National Coal Board (1946): 272–3, 278–9, 284, 286, 290, 295–6, 304, 306–8, 311, 316, 321–2, 326–32, 334–8, 376–8, 382 (*n*), 390, 392, 394–6, 410, 413, 419
price policy: 282–3, 287
Sir A. Bryan on organisation: 397
National Coal Board, Scottish Division: 280–1, 287–91, 299–300, 372, 374, 385–7, 389, 391–3, 396, 400, 403, 409, 418–19
National Conciliation Board (1934): 254
National Consultative Council: 311
National Council of Labour: 226, 257 (*n*)
National Council of Labour Colleges: 418
National Health Service: 418
National Reference Tribunal: 255, 286, 311, 322, 330–1, 335
suggestion of altering: 323, 336–7
National Union of Mineworkers: 252, 265, 284, 286, 298, 304–5, 307, 309–11, 315–18, 320, 325–7, 329–32, 337, 347–348, 351, 366, 376–7, 383, 392 (*n*), 397, 413, 422, 425
and closing of pits: 288
and compensation to coal-owners: 316
democracy in: 404–5
and five-day week: 296
See also Scottish Area N.U.M.
National Union of Railwaymen: 366
National Union of Scottish Mineworkers: 134, 137, 150, 165, 202, 205, 235
changes in officers and E.C.: 183–5, 236, 244–5, 250–2, 268
and Czechoslovakia: 229
Fife and: 167–8, 182–4, 221–2, 236–7
and M.F.G.B.: 213, 236
one union, 1943: 263–4, 266
rules: 150, 169–70, 193–4
and Soviet Union: 257–9
and Spain: 226–8
and spread-over: 207, 214
strife on E.C.: 184–95
and strikes: 152, 215, 220
and U.M.S.: 217–18, 220
and wages: 209–12, 234, 246, 253–6
and war: 150, 257–60, 265
Nationalisation: 96, 143–9, 197–8, 219, 239, 262, 268–76, 279, 282, 295, 297, 334–5, 396, 404, 410
1919 Bill: 145
1946 Act: 271–2, 274
in other countries: 352
personnel of Boards: 278–9
Nationalisation of Mines and Minerals Bill: 145
Nazis: 223, 229, 240
New Cumnock: 372

New Leader, The: 199
New Statesman and Nation: 173 (*n*)
Newbattle: 1, 28–9
Newport Rising: 18
Nigeria: 357
North Atlantic Treaty Pact: 339
Northumberland: 35, 119, 121, 123, 174
Nottinghamshire: 121, 253, 331, 417

Oncost Men: 118–20, 122, 313–14. *See also* Wages: lower-paid workers
Organisation for the Maintenance of Supplies: 168, 173
Overtime: 206, 211–12, 214, 217–20, 331
payment for: 254, 296, 301, 325, 411
piece-workers and: 411
See also Extended Hours Agreement; Week-end Work

Paisley: 231
Parliament: 45, 159, 232–3, 311
Mid-Lanark by-election, 1888: 74
Morpeth by-election: 167
See also Members of Parliament; Elections, General
Peace: 420, 424–5
British conference: 360, 362
Pacific conference: 362
Scottish conference: 362
World congresses: 360–2
Peeblesshire: 26, 203
Pensions: 270, 319, 327, 419
in other countries: 354–5
Picketing: 126, 154, 180
Piecework: 157, 208, 328
overtime payments: 411
rates: 34–5, 255–6, 278, 329, 333–4, 411–12
Pit Delegates: 406, 408
Pit Meetings: 406, 408
Pit Production Committees: 242, 261, 268
Pithead Baths: 148, 295, 354–5, 415 (*n*)
Pits and Branches:
Aitken: 153, 196, 218 (*n*)
Annbank: 360
Argyll: 362
Auchinbeg: 250
Balgonie: 362
Bannockburn: 355
Barbauchlaw: 250
Bardykes: 313
Bedlay: 343
Blairhall: 154, 220
Bowhill: 154, 218 (*n*), 398
Broomfield: 343, 355
Brucefield: 237, 245, 356
Bryants: 28
Butress: 250
Cameron/Rosie: 356
Carron: 29
Castlehill: 362
Coaly Burn: 26
Colsnaughton: 349
Comrie: 313, 343, 352
Coylton/Rankinson: 357, 361, 396

Pits and Branches—*continued*
  Crosshouse/Dreghorn: 342, 351, 357
  Dalbeath: 155
  Devon: 348
  Dewshill: 314
  Dollar: 353
  Donibristle: 369
  Dryden: 25
  Elphinstone: 303–4
  Fordell: 357
  Forthbank: 362
  Fortissat: 289
  Francis: 218 (*n*)
  Gartshore: 304, 313, 343
  Glencraig: 303, 353, 357
  Harlaw Muir: 26
  Harthill: 314, 343
  Hartwoodhill: 289
  Hill of Beath: 155
  Hillhouserigg: 289–90
  Houldsworth: 408
  Jenny Gray: 181
  Kames: 312, 357
  Kelty: 252, 303
  Kilmaurs: 252
  Kinedar: 154
  Kinglassie: 154
  Kingshill: 313, 355
  Kinniel: 220
  Kirkford: 155
  Klondyke: 215, 218 (*n*)
  Knockshinnoch Castle: 372, 378, 383–
    384, 386, 394
  Larkhall: 353
  Leven: 159
  Lingerwood: 343
  Loanhead: 23
  Lockhead: 218 (*n*), 356
  Lumphinnans: 218 (*n*)
  Manor Powis: 310
  Mary: 196, 357, 362
  Mauchline: 353
  Michael: 218 (*n*)
  Minto: 218 (*n*)
  Nellie: 153
  New Cumnock: 376, 378, 395
  Newcraighall: 23
  Newton: 343, 362
  Oakley: 154
  Ormiston: 312, 348, 357
  Peeweep: 196, 217
  Penston: 26–7
  Plean: 351, 361
  Polkemmet: 398
  Ponfeigh: 16, 343
  Priory: 218 (*n*), 343
  Raith: 218 (*n*)
  Rigside: 16
  Stane and Southfield: 348
  Still: 29
  Thankerton: 360
  Uddingston: 351
  Valleyfield: 242, 353
  Wellesley: 331, 343
  Wellwood: 355

Pits and Branches—*continued*
  Whitburn: 362
  Whitrig: 220
  Woolmet: 401
Plan for Coal (1950): 284–6
'Playing the Pits': 69
Pneumoconiosis: 266
Poland: 238, 257 (*n*), 271, 353, 355–6, 361,
    404
Police: 17, 35, 42, 81–2, 87, 127, 152–9,
    172, 177–81, 216, 218
Poor Relief: 30, 31, 175–6, 204, 209, 215
Porter Award: 255
Power Loading: 286–7, 291
Press: 83, 87, 126–8, 158–9, 186, 199, 272,
    347, 366–7, 423, 425 (*n*)
  Chartist: 21, 36 (*n*)
Production: 259–61, 268, 271–2, 296–7,
    307–8, 313–15, 366. *See also* Coal Out-
    put
Profit Sharing: 148
Profits: 303–5, 310, 314, 317–18, 321, 365
Prussia: 3 (*n*)

Railwaymen: 62, 126, 142, 158, 164, 170,
    313, 337, 366
Rationalisation: 188, 193, 199, 212–13
Red Friday: 164–5, 168, 170–1
Regulations, Coal Mine: 243–4, 280–1,
    374, 396–7, 400
  Moss: 371, 379–80, 383–4, 387–90,
    394–5, 397
Reid Report: 262, 269, 284
Religion: 23–5, 42
Renfrew: 73, 91, 203
Restriction of Output: 17, 36, 426
Ridley Report: 282
Rope Workers: 150
Rothesay: 174, 341, 425
Royal Commission on the Coal Industry,
    1919. *See* Sankey Commission
Royal Commission on Housing in Scot-
    land: 134–8, 147
Royal Commission on Trade Unions, 1867–
    1868: 15
Ruhr: 97, 162, 223
Rules:
  Coal and Iron Miners' Association: 41,
    44
  Fife county union: 167
  M.F.G.B.: 75, 78, 93, 102, 107, 117–18,
    191, 296
  N.U.S.M.W.: 150, 169–70, 193–4, 236,
    263
  Special, under Coal Mines Act, 1855:
    41–2
Rutherglen: 289

Safety: 35–6, 62, 214–16, 219–20, 269, 274,
    280, 377, 384, 395–6, 398, 400–1,
    407–9, 418, 420
  agents: 407
  inspectors: 400 (*n*)
  in other countries: 346, 353–4, 363–4, 393
  See also Accidents; Disasters; Regulations

Safety Men: 158–9
Saltcoats: 419
Samuel Commission: 170–1
Sankey Commission: 145–9, 153, 198, 271
Saturday Working. *See* Week-end Working
Save-the-Union Council: 193–5
Scottish Area N.U.M.: 265, 278, 295–7, 300, 341–64
  and closing of pits: 289–91
  and coal prices: 282–4
  cultural activities: 419–22
  democracy in: 402–5
  and disasters: 375, 385–6, 391, 393, 395–400
  and disputes: 280–1, 336, 405–12
  donations: 347–51, 357
  and education: 413–15, 417
  and health and welfare: 418–19
  and nationalisation: 277, 279
  and *Plan for Coal*: 285
  and wage freeze: 302–6
  and wages: 291, 298–9, 307–10, 315, 319–25, 328, 332, 334
  and young miners: 416–18
  See also Conferences
Scottish Board of Health: 175–6, 178
Scottish Coalfields (Report, 1942): 137
Scottish Colliery Deputies' and Shot-firers' Association: 277. *See also* Firemen and Shotfirers
Scottish Colliery Enginemen, Boiler-Firemen and Tradesmen's Association: 153, 165, 235, 277–8, 299, 362, 413
Scottish Labour College: 184
Scottish Labour Party: 61 (*n*)
Scottish Miner, The: 415, 418
Scottish Miners' Federation, 1894–1914: 71–2, 74–5, 80–1, 85–6, 94, 98, 102, 133–4, 141
Scottish Miners in Battle (1933): 213–14
Scottish Miners' National Federation, 1886–7: 67–70
Scottish Mineworker, The: 195, 197
Scottish Oil Workers' Association: 150, 159, 165
Scottish Shale Miners: 159
Scottish T.U.C.: 247, 289, 341, 357, 359, 418, 422, 425
  Presidential address by Wm. Pearson: 365–8
Scottish Youth Peace Festival: 418
Seaforth Highlanders: 158
Seamen: 62, 126
Seven Days' Notice Agreement: 300, 411
Seven-Hour Day: 149, 168, 197, 218, 248, 270
Seven-and-a-half-Hour Day: 198, 206–209, 214, 248, 285, 325
Short Time: 43, 75, 84–5, 211, 220, 295
Shotts: 55, 91, 287, 290–1, 403
Six-Hour Day: 145, 157
Slavery: 3–13, 23, 137, 383
Sliding Scales: 57, 59 (*n*), 73, 93, 100–1, 108 (*n*), 110–11, 282
  alterations: 104, 110–11

Social Democratic Federation: 97, 141
Socialism: 88, 91–7, 113, 141, 167, 247, 267–8, 273–5, 331, 367–8, 427
Socialist International (Second): 112–13, 139–40, 144
Society for Prevention of Cruelty to Animals: 159
Somerset: 78
South Africa: 54 (*n*), 97
Soviet Union: 150, 174, 198, 203, 224, 238, 257–60, 265, 339–40, 342–4, 352, 364, 367, 404, 424
  Delegation to: 355, 361
Spain: 224–8, 267
Spread-over: 198, 207–8, 214
Stanrigg: 371
State Control of Mines: 143, 151–2, 249, 254–5, 262
  dual control: 255, 261
Steel Industry: 282, 284
Stirling and Linlithgow (Miners' Association): 55
Stirlingshire: 22, 29, 41–2, 73, 90 (*n*), 91, 137, 203, 210 (*n*), 213, 220
  strikes in: 75, 220
Stirlingshire, Forth and Clyde Miners' Association: 74, 169–70, 184 (*n*), 191, 234, 251, 264
Stonehouse: 250
Strikes: 9, 12, 15–17, 34–6, 40, 44, 48, 53, 56, 65, 143, 214–16, 248, 256, 335
  1856: 42–3
  1894: 75–89, 213
  1912 Minimum Wage: 125–6, 129, 132–134, 239, 296
  1920 Datum Line: 151, 172
  1926 General: 173
  1930 Spread-over: 214
  ballots: 108, 120–1, 129, 145, 151, 231–233, 296
  collections: 43, 174
  funds: 43, 84, 86, 125
  general: 128, 169, 172 (*n*), 173
  levies: 56, 59, 72, 76–9, 83–6
  non-unionists in: 77–9, 84, 213
  Scottish Miners' Federation rules on: 72
  threats: 102–4, 147, 149, 164, 309–10, 312
  unofficial: 297, 309, 321, 336, 403, 411
  See also Lockouts
Subsidies: 170, 248
  food: 329
Sunday Worker: 188
Sutherland: 203
Sweden: 356
Syndicalism: 157, 274 (*n*)
Syndicalist, The: 127–8

Taff Vale Judgment: 103, 112
Taft-Hartley Act: 346
Teheran Conference: 259
Ten-Hour Day: 19, 423
Theatre Workshop: 420
Thinacres: 280–1
'Tory Gold': 74

Trade Unions: 14–16, 31, 33, 39, 223–4,
    247, 338, 365–6
  benefits: 58
  colliers' early: 15–17, 20
  county: 51–6, 58, 66, 69, 204–5, 213,
    216–17, 226
  demarcation lines: 150
  district: 37, 41, 44, 69
  duties: 311
  funds: 46, 52–3, 55, 84, 89, 143, 166, 266
  membership: 46, 53, 55, 67–8, 70–1,
    75–6, 78, 235
    1894–7: 89
    1900–14: 133
    1919–20: 150
    1922: 165
  non-political: 204
  subscriptions: 44
  See also under counties
Trades Councils: 90 (n), 175, 178, 289, 422
Trades Union Congress: 51, 149, 173,
    183 (n), 257, 259, 316–17, 321, 324,
    335, 340–1, 372
  Conference of Executives: 171, 302,
    305–7, 317, 320
  General Council: 164, 170–3, 225, 422
  and nationalisation: 273–4, 276
  Parliamentary Committee: 39, 51, 56
  and wage restraint: 302–6, 317–22
Triple Alliance: 142–3, 152, 158
Troon: 419
Truck: 10, 11, 36, 39, 45
Truman Doctrine: 339

Uddingston Centre: 418
Unemployment: 30, 31, 126, 151, 157,
    160–1, 165, 193, 199, 201, 203–4, 206,
    210–12, 217, 220, 239–40, 264, 366
  Benefit: 160, 197, 199–201, 204, 210,
    221–2
United Mineworkers of Scotland, 1929–
    1936: 195, 205–6, 213–18, 231, 236
  approaches for unity: 217–22
  and M.F.G.B.: 219
United Nations Organisation: 341–3, 345,
    360–1
United Trades of Scotland: 43–4
Unity Theatre: 420
U.S.A.: 3 (n), 5, 56, 64, 198–200, 260, 301,
    326, 339–44, 356, 420 (n), 424
  miners in: 346

Valleyfield: 153, 220–1, 242–4, 252
Ventilation: 23, 25–6, 45, 244, 374
Victimisation: 215–16, 217 (n), 352

Wage Advances: 40, 51, 73, 97, 99, 100–1,
    105, 132–3, 142, 147, 149, 152, 234,
    246, 249, 298, 304, 323, 326–8, 332,
    337. See also Wage Awards
Wage Awards: 110, 131–3, 253, 255, 286–
    287, 323, 327, 334
  Greene: 250, 253
  Porter: 255
  See also Arbitration

Wage Claims: 40, 51, 98, 101, 105, 132,
    142, 145, 151, 162, 217–18, 230–3,
    248, 253, 255, 297–9, 316–23, 327,
    329–32, 337–8, 408
  campaign for: 330–1
Wage-cuts: 40, 42, 44–5, 53, 56–9, 75–6,
    79–80, 82–3, 85, 87, 89, 100–3, 105,
    208–10, 213
Wage Freeze: 302–6, 309–10, 312, 314–17,
    320–1, 323–4, 330, 344, 365–6, 405
  coal-field ballot on: 320
Wage Rates:
    1679: 6
    1771: 7 (n)
    1812–41: 30
    1836: 34
    1856: 40, 43
    1858: 44
    1859: 45
    1861–2: 46
    1872: 52
    1874: 57
    1876: 59
    1887: 69
    1888: 72–3, 99
    1894: 87, 89
    1899: 99
    1901: 100
    1902: 101
    1903–5: 104
    1907–9: 105
    1912: 121
    1931: 210
    1936: 234
    1940: 246
    1947: 298
  stabilisation: 334
  See also Minimum Wage, national
Wage Restraint. See Wage Freeze; also
    Trades Union Congress
Wage Structure: 278, 304, 309, 311–13,
    319, 327, 332–4, 415 (n)
  Memorandum on: 333 (n)
Wages:
  attendance bonus: 245 (n), 254
  cost-of-living advances: 245 (n), 256
  day-wage system: 269
  earnings: 87, 211–12, 333, 411–12
  firemen and shotfirers: 253–4
  in France: 350
  of lower paid: 210–11, 307–13, 316–24,
    415 (n)
  M.F.G.B. and 'living wage': 93, 99, 102
  on power loaders: 286–7, 291
  and Public Assistance: 210
  S.M.F. and 'set wage': 69
  weekly payment of: 131
  women: 253–4
  See also Boys' Wages; Minimum Wage;
    Young Miners
Wales: 36, 78, 101, 116, 119, 121, 123, 126,
    169, 190, 203–4, 219, 248, 256, 417
War: 112, 139, 223–4, 229–30, 339–40,
    367
  Boer: 371

War—*continued*
  first World: 138–43, 263, 276, 288, 335, 339, 371
  Korean: 342–4, 402
  second World: 238–42, 244–7, 253, 255, 257–62, 265, 296, 335
Weavers: 16–18
Week-end Work: 296, 325, 329–31, 423. *See also* Extended Hours Agreement; Overtime
Weekly Paid Industrial Staff: 299
Weighing: 36, 39, 45. *See also* Check-weighers
Welfare: 311, 415 (*n*), 418–19
  Commission: 148, 418
  levy: 147, 295
West Linton: 26
West Lothian (Union): 234, 251 (*n*), 260, 264

West Scotland: 20, 69, 73–5, 86, 92, 186
Wimpey, George, & Co.: 375
Wishaw: 41, 50, 55
Women:
  around mines: 253–4, 298
  in mines: 6, 11, 20–2, 27–8, 32–3, 423
Workers' Control: 274, 278, 283
World Federation of Democratic Youth: 418
World Federation of Trade Unions: 340–1

Yalta Conference: 266
Yorkshire: 75, 84–5, 121, 169, 174, 253, 408, 421
Young Miners: 413, 416–18, 421, 424
  training: 269
  wages: 252–3, 255 (*n*), 297–8, 333
  See also Boys' Wages

GEORGE ALLEN & UNWIN LTD
London: 40 Museum Street, W.C.1

Auckland: Haddon Hall, City Road
Sydney, N.S.W.: Bradbury House, 55 York Street
Cape Town: 58–60 Long Street
Bombay: 15 Graham Road, Ballard Estate, Bombay 1
Calcutta: 17 Chittaranjan Avenue, Calcutta 13
New Delhi: 13–14 Ajmere Gate Extension, New Delhi 1
Karachi: Haroon Chambers, South Napier Road, Karachi 2
Toronto: 91 Wellington Street West
Sao Paulo: Avenida 9 de Julho 11388–Ap. 51

By R. PAGE ARNOT

THE MINERS

A HISTORY OF THE MINERS' FEDERATION
OF GREAT BRITAIN, 1889–1910

Small Royal 8vo   *Illustrated*   25s. net

Second Impression

"This is more than a mere trade union history—though it is probably quite the best yet to be written. It is a contribution to an understanding of the social pattern of Britain today. Authoritative, scholarly, and very readable. . . . The book is especially noteworthy for its balance and sense of history. There are fascinating pen pictures of the miners' leaders."—*Yorkshire Observer*.

"Mr. Page Arnot has written a very good book, and the Mineworkers' Federation is to be congratulated on its choice of him to do its official history."—*Manchester Guardian*.

"Four hundred pages of unemotional, detached documentation. . . . It is solid history."—*Daily Mail*.

"The nation needs more recent facts to help it understand its own miners—facts presented in Mr. Arnot's lively narrative style."—*Daily Herald*.

"Here is something finer than the bare chronicles of a trade union. It is a piece of history that lives as the men lived who wrought the deeds and endured the hardships, who shared the hopes, and shaped the events that compose the story of the coalfields."—*Times Literary Supplement*.

"A thorough scholarly job. Part of its worth is the skill with which he assembles the best that others have said and written on this subject. He has compiled a reference book with much in it to interest the general student of social history, but above all a book for the miners themselves."—*Tribune*.

"Though necessarily a partisan interpretation of the history of industrial relations in the mining industry, this story of the growth of the miners' national trade union organization is a most valuable document."—*Cardiff Western Mail*.

"As a contribution to social history the work has been exceedingly well executed, and may well become the standard reference."—*Iron & Coal Trades Review*.

"Undeniably this book must be regarded as a valuable contribution to the industrial history of this country."—*Colliery Guardian*.

By R. PAGE ARNOT

THE MINERS

YEARS OF STRUGGLE,
1910 ONWARDS

Small Royal 8vo   *Illustrated*   35s. *net*

"This is a book of outstanding importance. In nothing is it more impressive than its study of miners' strategy and tactics in particular and trade union strategy and tactics in general. . . . The greatness of Robert Smillie, the solid sterling qualities of Herbert Smith, the brilliant, wayward personality of A. J. Cook—these are imprinted on the reader's mind by a book which, in its class, has not many superiors."—*Birmingham Post*.

"For Mr. Arnot there can be only commendation for a masterly achievement. Another might have written a different history from the same facts, but none could have written one more absorbingly interesting."—*Sheffield Telegraph*.

"A graphic, lucidly arranged, and admirably documented record of a phase in the class struggle in which the miners were the spearhead."—*New Statesman and Nation*.

"And for the Socialist and trade union worker it has in store, not only lessons, but the inspiration of a mighty and still unfinished epic."—*The Tribune*.

"An interesting and important book. . . . The most important contribution published for a long time towards the record of British industry and social politics in the nineteen-twenties."—*The Listener*.

LONDON: GEORGE ALLEN & UNWIN LIMITED

£ 1.15,